United States History Regents Vocabulary Workbook

By Lewis Morris

Copyright © Network4Learning, Inc. 2019.

www.insiderswords.com/usregents/

ISBN-13: 978-1694096432

Copyright © 2019, Network4Learning, inc.

All rights reserved. No part of this publication may be reproduced, distributed, or transmitted in any form or by any means, including photocopying, recording, or other electronic or mechanical methods, without the prior written permission of the publisher, except in the case of brief quotations embodied in critical reviews and certain other noncommercial uses permitted by copyright law. For permission requests, write to the publisher, addressed

"Attention: Permissions Coordinator," at the address below.

Network4Learning, inc.
109 E 17th St STE 63
Cheyenne, WY 82001-4584

www.InsidersWords.com

We hope you find this vocabulary workbook helpful with your studies. If you do, please consider leaving a brief review at this link:

http://www.amazon.com/review/create-review?&asin=1694096432

Table of Contents

Introduction	5
Crossword Puzzles	24
Multiple Choice	84
Matching	124
Word Search	180

What is "Insider Language"?

Recent research has confirmed what we have known for decades: The strongest students and leaders in industry have a mastered an Insider Language in their subject and field. This Insider language is made up of the technical terms and vocabulary necessary to communicate effectively in classes or the workplace. For those who master it, learning is easier, faster, and much more enjoyable.

Most students who are surveyed report that the greatest challenge to any course of study is learning the vocabulary. When we examine typical college courses, we discover that there is, on average, 250 Insider Terms a student must learn over the course of a semester. Further, most exams rely heavily on this set of words for assessment purposes. The structure of multiple choice exams lends itself perfectly to the testing of this Insider Language. Students who can differentiate between Insider Language terms can handle challenging exam questions with ease and confidence.

From recent research on learning and vocabulary we have learned:

- Your knowledge of any subject is contained in the content-specific words you know. The more of these terms that you know, the easier it is to understand and recall important information; the easier it will be to communicate your ideas to peers, professors, supervisors, and co-workers. The stronger your content-area vocabulary is, the higher your scores will be on your exams and written assignments.

- Students who develop a strong Insider Language perform better on tests, learn faster, retain more information, and express greater satisfaction in learning.

- Familiarizing yourself with subject-area vocabulary before formal study (pre-learning) is the most effective way to learn this language and reap the most benefit.

- The vocabulary on standardized exams come directly from the stated objectives of the test-makers. This means that the vocabulary found on standardized exams is predictable. Our books focus on this vocabulary.

- Most multiple-choice exams are glorified vocabulary quizzes. Think about the format of a multiple-choice question. The question stem is a definition of a term and the choices (known as distractors) are 4 or 5 similar words. Your task is to differentiate between the meanings of those terms and choose the correct word.

- It takes a person several exposures to a new word to be able to use it with confidence in conversation or in writing. You need to process these words several different ways to make them part of your long-term memory.

The goals of this book are:
- To give you an "Insider Language" for your subject.
- Pre-teach the most important words before you set out on a traditional course of review or study.
- Teach you the most important words in your subject area.
- Teach you strategies for learning subject-area words on your own.
- Boost your confidence in your ability to master this language and support you in your study.
- Reduce the stress of studying and provide you with fun activities that work.

How it works:

The secret to mastering Insider Language is through repetition and exposure. We have eleven steps for you to follow:

1. Read the word and definition in the glossary out loud. "See it, Say it"
2. Identify the part of speech the word belongs to such as noun, verb, adverb, or adjective. This will help you group the word and identify similar words.
3. Place the word in context by using it in a sentence. Write this sentence down and read it aloud.
4. Use "Chunking" to group the words. Make a diagram or word cloud using these groups.
5. Make connections to the words by creating analogies.
6. Create mnemonics that help you recognize patterns and orders of words by substituting the words for more memorable items or actions.
7. Examine the morphology of the word, that is, identify the root, prefix, and suffix that make up the word. Identify similar and related words.
8. Complete word games and puzzles such as crosswords and word searches.
9. Complete matching questions that require you to differentiate between related words.
10. Complete Multiple-choice questions containing the words.
11. Create a visual metaphor or "memory cartoon" to make a mental picture of the word and related processes.

By completing this word study process, you will be exposed to the terminology in various ways that will activate your memory and create a lasting understanding of this language.

The strategies in this book are designed to make you an independent expert at learning insider language. These strategies include:

- Verbalizing the word by reading it and its definition aloud ("See It, Say It"). This allows you to make visual, auditory, and speech connections with its meaning.

- Identifying the type of word (Noun, verb, adverb, and adjective). Making this distinction helps you understand how to visualize the word. It helps you "chunk" the words into groups, and gives you clues on how to use the word.

- Place the word in context by using it in a sentence. Write this sentence down and read it aloud. This will give you an example of how the word is used.

- "Chunking". By breaking down the word list into groups of closely related words, you will learn them better and be able to remember them faster. Once you have group the terms, you can then make word clouds using a free online service. These word clouds provide visual cues to remembering the words and their meanings.

- Analogies. By creating analogies for essential words, you will be making connections that you can see on paper. These connections can trigger your memory and activate your ability to use the word in your writing as you begin to use them. Many of these analogies also use visual cues. In a sense, you can make a mental picture from the analogy.

- Mnemonics. A device such as a pattern of letters, ideas, or associations that assists in remembering something. A mnemonic is especially useful for remembering the order of a set of words or the order of a process.

- Morphology. The study of word roots, prefixes, and suffixes. By examining the structure of the words, you will gain insight into other words that are closely related, and learn how to best use the word.

- Visual metaphors. This is the most sophisticated and entertaining strategy for learning vocabulary. Create a "memory cartoon" using one or more of the vocabulary terms. This activity triggers the visual part of your memory and makes fast, permanent, imprints of the word on your memory. By combining the terms in your visual metaphor, you can "chunk" the entire set of vocabulary terms into several visual metaphors and benefit from the brain's tendency to group these terms.

The activities in this book are designed to imprint the words and their meanings in your memory in different ways. By completing each activity, you will gain the necessary exposures to the word to make it a permanent part of your vocabulary. Each activity uses a different part of your memory. The result is that you will be comfortable using these words and be able to tell the difference between closely related words. The activities include:

A. Crossword Puzzles and Word Searches- These are proven to increase test scores and improve comprehension. Students frequently report that they are fun and engaging, while requiring them to analyze the structure and meaning of the words.

B. Matching- This activity is effective because it forces you to differentiate between many closely related terms.

C. Multiple Choice- This classic question format lends itself to vocabulary study perfectly. Most exams are in this format because they are simple to make, easy to score, and are a reliable type of assessment. (Perfect for the Vocabulary Master!) One strategy to use with multiple choice questions that enhance their effectiveness is to cover the answer choices while you read the question. After reading the question, see if you can answer it before looking at the choices. Then look at the choices to see if you match one of them.

Conducting a thorough "word study" of your insider language will take time and effort, but the rewards will be well worth it. By following this guide and completing the exercises thoughtfully, you will become a stronger, more effective, and satisfied student. Best of luck on your mastery of this Insider Language!

Insider Language Strategies

"See It, Say It!" Reading your Insider Language set aloud

"IT IS BETTER TO FAIL IN ORIGINALITY THAN TO SUCCEED IN IMITATION."
–HERMAN MELVILLE

Reading aloud is the foundation for the development of an Insider Language. It is the single most important thing you can do for vocabulary acquisition. Done correctly, it engages the visual, auditory, and speech centers of the brain and hastens its storage in your long-term memory.

Reading aloud demonstrates the relationship between the printed word and its meaning.

You can read aloud on a higher level than you can initially understand, so reading aloud makes complex ideas more accessible and exposes you to vocabulary and patterns that are not part of your typical speech. Reading aloud helps you understand the complicated text better and makes more challenging text easier to grasp and understand. Reading aloud helps you to develop the "habits of mind" the strongest students use.

Reading aloud will make connections to concepts in the reading that requires you to relate the new vocabulary to things you already know. Go to the glossary at the end of this book and for each word complete the five steps outlined below:

1. Read the word and its definition aloud. Focus on the sound of the word and how it looks on the paper.
2. Read the word aloud again try to say three or four similar words; this will help you build connections to closely related words.
3. Read the word aloud a third time. Try to make a connection to something you have read or heard.
4. Visualize the concept described in the term. Paint a mental picture of the word in use.
5. Try to think of the opposite of the word. Discovering a close antonym will help you place this word in context.

Create a sentence using the word in its proper context

"OPPORTUNITIES DON'T HAPPEN. YOU CREATE THEM." –CHRIS GROSSER

Context means the circumstances that form the setting for an event, statement, or idea, and which it can be fully understood and assessed. Synonyms for context include conditions, factors, situation, background, and setting.
Place the word in context by using it in a sentence. Write this sentence down and read it aloud. By creating sentences, you are practicing using the word correctly. If you strive to make these sentences interesting and creative, they will become more memorable and effective in activating your long-term memory.

Identify the Parts of Speech
"SUCCESS IS NOT FINAL; FAILURE IS NOT FATAL: IT IS THE COURAGE TO CONTINUE THAT COUNTS." –WINSTON S. CHURCHILL

Read through each term in the glossary and make a note of what part of speech each term is. Studying and identifying parts of speech shows us how the words relate to each other. It also helps you create a visualization of each term. Below are brief descriptions of the parts of speech for you to use as a guide.

VERB: A word denoting action, occurrence, or existence. Examples: walk, hop, whisper, sweat, dribbles, feels, sleeps, drink, smile, are, is, was, has.

NOUN: A word that names a person, place, thing, idea, animal, quality, or action. Nouns are the subject of the sentence. Examples: dog, Tom, Florida, CD, pasta, hate, tiger.

ADJECTIVE: A word that modifies, qualifies, or describes nouns and pronouns. Generally, adjectives appear immediately before the words they modify. Examples: smart girl, gifted teacher, old car, red door.

ADVERB: A word that modifies verbs, adjectives and other adverbs. An "ly" ending almost always changes an adjective to an adverb. Examples: ran swiftly, worked slowly, and drifted aimlessly. Many adverbs do not end in "ly." However, all adverbs identify when, where, how, how far, how much, etc. Examples: run hot, lived hard, moved right, study smart.

Chunking

"YOUR POSITIVE ACTION COMBINED WITH POSITIVE THINKING RESULTS IN SUCCESS." SHIV KHERA

Chunking is when you take a set of words and break it down into groups based on a common relationship. Research has shown that our brains learn by chunking information. By grouping your terms, you will be able to recall large sets of these words easily. To help make your chunking go easily use an online word cloud generator to make a set of word clouds representing your chunks.

1. Study the glossary and decide how you want to chunk the set of words. You can group by part of speech, topic, letter of the alphabet, word length, etc. Try to find an easy way to group each term.
2. Once you have your different groups, visit www.wordclouds.com to create a custom word cloud for each group. Print each one of these clouds and post it in a prominent place to serve as constant visual aids for your learning.

Analogies

"CHOOSE THE POSITIVE. YOU HAVE CHOICE, YOU ARE MASTER OF YOUR ATTITUDE, CHOOSE THE POSITIVE, THE CONSTRUCTIVE. OPTIMISM IS A FAITH THAT LEADS TO SUCCESS."– BRUCE LEE

An analogy is a comparison in which an idea or a thing is compared to another thing that is quite different from it. Analogies aim at explaining an idea by comparing it to something that is familiar. Metaphors and similes are tools used to create analogies.

Analogies are useful for learning vocabulary because they require you to analyze a word (or words), and then transfer that analysis to another word. This transfer reinforces the understanding of all the words.

As you analyze the relationships between the analogies you are creating, you will begin to understand the complex relationships between the seemingly unrelated words.

 A is to B as C is to D

This can be written using colons in place of the terms "is to" and "as."

 A:B::C:D

The two items on the left (items A & B) describe a relationship and are separated by a single colon. The two items on the right (items C & D) are shown on the right and are also separated by a colon. Together, both sides are then separated by two colons in the middle, as shown here: Tall: Short :: Skinny: Fat. The relationship used in this analogy is the antonym.

How to create an analogy

Start with the basic formula for an analogy:

____ : ____ :: ____ : ____

Next, we will examine a simple synonym analogy:

automobile : car :: box : crate

The key to figuring out a set of word analogies is determining the relationship between the paired set of words.

Here is a list of the most common types of Analogies and examples

Synonym	Scream : Yell :: Push : Shove
Antonym	Rich : Poor :: Empty : Full
Cause is to Effect	Prosperity : Happiness :: Success : Joy
A Part is to its Whole	Toe : Foot :: Piece : Set
An Object to its Function	Car : Travel :: Read : Learn
A Item is to its Category	Tabby : House Cat :: Doberman : Dog
Word is a symptom of the other	Pain : Fracture :: Wheezing : Allergy
An object and it's description	Glass : Brittle :: Lead : Dense
The word is lacking the second word	Amputee : Limb :: Deaf : Hearing
The first word Hinders the second word	Shackles : Movement :: Stagger : Walk
The first word helps the action of the second	Knife : Bread :: Screwdriver : Screw
This word is made up of the second word	Sweater : Wool :: Jeans : Denim
A word and it's definition	Cede: Break Away :: Abolish : To get rid of

Using words from the glossary, make a set of analogies using each one. As a bonus, use more than one glossary term in a single analogy.

_____ : _____ :: _____ : _____

Name the relationship between the words in your analogy:_____

_____ : _____ :: _____ : _____

Name the relationship between the words in your analogy:_____

_____ : _____ :: _____ : _____

Name the relationship between the words in your analogy:_____

Mnemonics

"IT ISN'T THE MOUNTAINS AHEAD TO CLIMB THAT WEAR YOU OUT; IT'S THE PEBBLE IN YOUR SHOE."   –MUHAMMAD ALI

A mnemonic is a learning technique that helps you retain and remember information. Mnemonics are one of the best learning methods for remembering lists or processes in order. Mnemonics make the material more meaningful by adding associations and creating patterns. Interestingly, mnemonics may work better when they utilize absurd, startling, or shocking examples and references. Mnemonics help organize the information so that you can easily retrieve it later. By giving you associations and cues, mnemonics allow you to form a mental structure ordering a list or process to help you remember it better. This mental structure allows you to create a structure of association between items that may not appear to have any relationship. Mnemonics typically use references that are easy to visualize and thus easier to remember. Through visualization of vivid images and references, the information is much easier to imprint into long-term memory. The power of making mnemonics lies in converting dull, inert and uninspiring information into something vibrant and memorable.

How to make simple and effective mnemonics
Some of the best mnemonics help us remember simple rules or lists in order.

Step 1. Take a list of terms you are trying to remember in order. For example, we will use the scientific method:

> observation, question, hypothesis, methods, results, and conclusion.

Next, we will replace each word on the list with a new word that starts with the same letter. These new words will together form a vivid sentence that is easy to remember:

> Objectionable Queens Haunted Macho Rednecks Creatively.

As silly as the above sentence seems, it is easy to remember, and now we can call on this sentence to remind us of the order of the scientific method.

Visit http://www.mnemonicgenerator.com/ and try typing in a list of words. It is fun to see the mnemonics that it makes and shows how easy it is to make great mnemonics to help your studying.

Using vivid words in your mnemonics allows you to see the sentence you are making. Words that are gross, scary, or name interesting animals are helpful. Profanity is also useful because the shock value can trigger memory. The following are lists of vivid words to use in your mnemonics:

Gross words
Moist, Gurgle, Phlegm, Fetus, Curd, Smear, Squirt, Chunky, Orifice, Maggots, Viscous, Queasy, Bulbous, Pustule, Putrid, Fester, Secrete, Munch, Vomit, Ooze, Dripping, Roaches, Mucus, Stink, Stank, Stunk, Slurp, Pus, Lick, Salty, Tongue, Fart, Flatulence, Hemorrhoid.

Interesting Animals
Aardvark, Baboon, Chicken, Chinchilla, Duck, Dragonfly, Emu, Electric Eel, Frog, Flamingo, Gecko, Hedgehog, Hyena, Iguana, Jackal, Jaguar, Leopard, Lynx, Minnow, Manatee, Mongoose, Neanderthal, Newt, Octopus, Oyster, Pelican, Penguin, Platypus, Quail, Racoon, Rattlesnake, Rhinoceros, Scorpion, Seahorse, Toucan, Turkey, Vulture, Weasel, Woodpecker, Yak, Zebra.

Superhero Words
Diabolical, Activate, Boom, Clutch, Dastardly, Dynamic, Dynamite, Shazam, Kaboom, Zip, Zap, Zoom, Zany, Crushing, Smashing, Exploding, Ripping, Tearing.

Scary Words
Apparition, Bat, Chill, Demon, Eerie, Fangs, Genie, Hell, Lantern, Macabre, Nightmare, Owl, Ogre, Phantasm, Repulsive, Scarecrow, Tarantula, Undead, Vampire, Wraith, Zombie.

There are several types of mnemonics that can help your memory.

1. Images
Visual mnemonics are a type of mnemonic that works by associating an image with characters or objects whose name sounds like the item that must be memorized. This is one of the easiest ways to create effective mnemonics. An example would be to use the shape of numbers to help memorize a long list of them. Numbers can be memorized by their shapes, so that: 0 -looks like an egg; 1 -a pencil, or a candle; 2 -a snake; 3 -an ear; 4 -a sailboat; 5 -a key; 6 -a comet; 7 -a knee; 8 -a snowman; 9 -a comma.

Another type of visual mnemonic is the word-length mnemonic in which the number of letters in each word corresponds to a digit. This simple mnemonic gives pi to seven decimal places:

3.141582 becomes "How I wish I could calculate pi."

Of course, you could use this type of mnemonic to create a longer sentence showing the digits of an important number. Some people have used this type of mnemonic to memorize thousands of digits.

Using the hands is also an important tool for creating visual objects. Making the hands into specific shapes can help us remember the pattern of things or the order of a list of things.

2. Rhyming
Rhyming mnemonics are quick ways to make things memorable. A classic example is a mnemonic for the number of days in each month:
"30 days hath September, April, June, and November.
All the rest have 31
Except February, my dear son.
It has 28, and that is fine
But in Leap Year it has 29."

Another example of a rhyming mnemonic is a common spelling rule:
"I before e except after c
or when sounding like a
in neighbor and weigh."

Use **rhymer.com** to get large lists of rhyming words.

3. Homonym
A homonym is one of a group of words that share the same pronunciation but have different meanings, whether spelled the same or not.

Try saying what you're attempting to remember out loud or very quickly, and see if anything leaps out. If you know other languages, using similar-sounding words from those can be effective.

You could also browse this list of homonyms
at http://www.cooper.com/alan/homonym_list.html.

4. Onomatopoeia
An Onomatopeia is a word that phonetically imitates, resembles or suggests the source of the sound that it describes. Are there any noises made by the thing you're trying to memorize? Is it often associated with some other sound? Failing that, just make up a noise that seems to fit.

Achoo, ahem, baa, bam, bark, beep, beep beep, belch, bleat, boo, boo hoo, boom, burp, buzz, chirp, click clack, crash, croak, crunch, cuckoo, dash, drip, ding dong, eek, fizz, flit, flutter, gasp, grrr, ha ha, hee hee, hiccup, hiss, hissing, honk, icky, itchy, jiggly, jangle, knock knock, lush, la la la, mash, meow, moan, murmur, neigh, oink, ouch, plop, pow, quack, quick, rapping, rattle, ribbit, roar, rumble, rustle, scratch, sizzle, skittering, snap crackle pop, splash, splish splash, spurt, swish, swoosh, tap, tapping, tick tock, tinkle, tweet, ugh, vroom, wham, whinny, whip, whooping, woof.

5. Acronyms
An acronym is a word or name formed as an abbreviation from the initial components of a word, such as NATO, which stands for North Atlantic Treaty Organization. If you're trying to memorize something involving letters, this is often a good bet. A lot of famous mnemonics are acronyms, such as ROYGBIV which stands for the order of colors in the light spectrum (Red, Orange, Yellow, Green, Blue, Indigo, and Violet).
A great acronym generator to try is: www.all-acronyms.com.

A different spin on an acronym is a backronym. A **backronym** is a specially constructed phrase that is supposed to be the source of a word that is an acronym. A backronym is constructed by creating a new phrase to fit an already existing word, name, or acronym.

The word is a combination of *backward* and *acronym*, and has been defined as a "reverse acronym." For example, the United States Department of Justice assigns to their Amber Alert program the meaning "**A**merica's **M**issing: **B**roadcast **E**mergency **R**esponse." The process can go either way to make good mnemonics.

Visit: https://arthurdick.com/projects/backronym/ to try out a simple backronym generator.

6. Anagrams
An anagram is a direct word switch or word play, the result of rearranging the letters of a word or phrase to produce a new word or phrase, using all the original letters exactly once; for example, the word anagram can be rearranged into nag-a-ram.

Try re-arranging letters or components and see if anything memorable emerges. Visit http://www.nameacronym.net/ to use a simple anagram generator.

One particularly memorable form of anagram is the spoonerism, where you swap the initial syllables or letters of words to make new phrases. These are usually humorous, and this makes them easier to remember. Here are some examples:

"Is it kisstomary to cuss the bride?" (as opposed to "customary to kiss")
"The Lord is a shoving leopard." (instead of "a loving shepherd")
"A blushing crow." ("crushing blow")
"A well-boiled icicle" ("well-oiled bicycle")
"You were fighting a liar in the quadrangle." ("lighting a fire")
"Is the bean dizzy?" (as opposed to "is the dean busy?")

7. Stories
Make up quick stories or incidents involving the material you want to memorize. For larger chunks of information, the stories can get more elaborate. Structured stories are particularly good for remembering lists or other sequenced information. Have a look at https://en.wikipedia.org/wiki/Method_of_loci for a more advanced memory sequencing technique.

Visual Metaphors

"Limits, like fear, is often an illusion." –Michael Jordan

What is a Metaphor?

A metaphor is a figure of speech that refers to one thing by mentioning another thing. Metaphors provide clarity and identify hidden similarities between two seemingly unrelated ideas. A visual metaphor is an image that creates a link between different ideas.

Visual metaphors help us use our understanding of the world to learn new concepts, skills, and ideas. Visual metaphors help us relate new material to what we already know. Visual metaphors must be clear and simple enough to spark a connection and understanding. Visual metaphors should use familiar things to help you be less fearful of new, complex, or challenging topics. Metaphors trigger a sense of familiarity so that you are more accepting of the new idea. Metaphors work best when you associate a familiar, easy to understand idea with a challenging, obscure, or abstract concept.

How to make a visual metaphor

1. Brainstorm using the words of the concept. Use different fonts, colors, or shapes to represent parts of the concept.

2. Merge these images together

3. Show the process using arrows, accents, etc.

4. Think about the story line your metaphor projects.

Examples of visual metaphors:

A skeleton used to show a framework of something.

A cloud showing an outline.

A bodybuilder whose muscles represent supporting ideas and details.

A sandwich where the meat, tomato, and lettuce represent supporting ideas.

A recipe card to show a process.

Your metaphor should be accurate. It should be complex enough to convey meaning, but simple and clear enough to be easily understood.

Morphology
"SCIENCE IS THE CAPTAIN, AND PRACTICE THE SOLDIERS." LEONARDO DA VINCI

Morphology is the study of the origin, roots, suffixes, and prefixes of the words. Understanding the meaning of prefixes, suffixes, and roots make it easier to decode the meaning of new vocabulary. Having the ability to decode using morphology increases text comprehension when initially reading as well.

The capability of identifying meaningful parts of words (morphemes), including prefixes, suffixes, and roots can be helpful. Identifying morphemes improves decoding accuracy and fluency. Reading speed improves when you can decode larger chunks of text quickly. When you can recognize morphemes in words, you will be better able to make sense of new words in context. Below are charts containing the most common prefixes, suffixes, and root words. Use them to help you decode your vocabulary terms.

Prefixes

Prefix	Meaning	Example words	and meanings
a, ab, abs	away from	absent abdicate	not to be present, to give up an office or throne.
ad, a, ac, af, ag, an, ar, at, as	to, toward	Advance advantage	To move forward To have the upper hand
anti	against	Antidote antisocial antibiotic	To repair poisoning refers to someone who's not social
bi, bis	two	bicycle binary biweekly	two-wheeled cycle two number system every two weeks
circum, cir	around	circumnavigate circle	Travel around the world a figure that goes all around
com, con, co, col	with, together	Complete Complement	To finish To go along with
de	away from, down, the opposite of	depart detour	to go away from to go out of your way
dis, dif, di	apart	dislike dishonest distant	not to like not honest away
En-, em-	Cause to	Entrance	the way in.
epi	upon, on top of	epitaph epilogue epidemic	writing upon a tombstone speech at the end, on top of the rest
equ, equi	equal	equalize equitable	to make equal fair, equal
ex, e, ef	out, from	exit eject exhale	to go out to throw out to breathe out
Fore-	Before	Forewarned	To have prior warning

Prefix	Meaning	Example Words and Meanings	
in, il, ir, im, en	in, into	Infield Imbibe	The inner playing field to take part in
in, il, ig, ir, im	not	inactive ignorant irreversible irritate	not active not knowing not reversible to put into discomfort
inter	between, among	international interact	among nations to mix with
mal, male	bad, ill, wrong	malpractice malfunction	bad practice fail to function, bad function
Mid	Middle	Amidships	In the middle of a ship
mis	wrong, badly	misnomer	The wrong name
mono	one, alone, single	monocle	one lensed glasses
non	not, the reverse of	nonprofit	not making a profit
ob	in front, against, in front of, in the way of	Obsolete	No longer needed
omni	everywhere, all	omnipresent omnipotent	always present, everywhere all powerful
Over	On top	Overdose	Take too much medication
Pre	Before	Preview	Happens before a show.
per	through	Permeable pervasive	to pass through, all encompassing
poly	many	Polygamy polygon	many spouses figure with many sides
post	after	postpone postmortem	to do after after death
pre	before, earlier than	Predict Preview	To know before To view before release
pro	forward, going ahead of, supporting	proceed pro-war promote	to go forward supporting the war to raise or move forward
re	again, back	retell recall reverse	to tell again to call back to go back
se	apart	secede seclude	to withdraw, become apart to stay apart from others
Semi	Half	Semipermeable	Half-permeable

Prefix	Meaning	Example Words and Meanings	
Sub	under, less than	Submarine	under water
super	over, above, greater	superstar superimpose	a start greater than her stars to put over something else
trans	across	transcontinental transverse	across the continent to lie or go across
un, uni	one	unidirectional unanimous unilateral	having one direction sharing one view having one side
un	not	uninterested unhelpful unethical	not interested not helpful not ethical

Roots

Root	Meaning	Example words & meanings	
act, ag	to do, to act	Agent Activity	One who acts as a representative Action
Aqua	Water	Aquamarine	The color of water
Aud	To hear	Auditorium	A place to hear music
apert	open	Aperture	An opening
bas	low	Basement Basement	Something that is low, at the bottom A room that is low
Bio	Living thing	Biological	Living matter
cap, capt, cip, cept, ceive	to take, to hold, to seize	Captive Receive Capable Recipient	One who is held To take Able to take hold of things One who takes hold or receives
ced, cede, ceed, cess	to go, to give in	Precede Access Proceed	To go before Means of going to To go forward
Cogn	Know	Cognitive	Ability to think
cred, credit	to believe	Credible Incredible Credit	Believable Not believable Belief, trust
curr, curs, cours	to run	Current Precursory Recourse	Now in progress, running Running (going) before To run for aid
Cycle	Circle	Lifecycle	The circle of life
dic, dict	to say	Dictionary Indict	A book explaining words (sayings)

21

Root	Meaning	Examples and meanings	
duc, duct	to lead	Induce Conduct Aqueduct	To lead to action To lead or guide Pipe that leads water somewhere
equ	equal, even	Equality Equanimity	Equal in social, political rights Evenness of mind, tranquility
fac, fact, fic, fect, fy	to make, to do	Facile Fiction Factory Affect	Easy to do Something that is made up Place that makes things To make a change in
fer, ferr	to carry, bring	Defer Referral	To carry away Bring a source for help/information
Gen	Birth	Generate	To create something
graph	write	Monograph Graphite	A writing on a particular subject A form of carbon used for writing
Loc	Place	Location	A place
Mater	Mother	Maternity	Expecting birth
Mem	Recall	Memory	The recall experiences
mit, mis	to send	Admit Missile	To send in Something sent through the air
Nat	Born	Native	Born in a place
par	equal	Parity Disparate	Equality No equal, not alike
Ped	Foot	Podiatrist	Foot doctor
Photo	Light	Photograph	A picture
plic	to fold, to bend, to turn	Complicate Implicate	To fold (mix) together To fold in, to involve
pon, pos, posit, pose	to place	Component Transpose Compose Deposit	A part placed together with others A place across To put many parts into place To place for safekeeping
scrib, script	to write	Describe Transcript Subscription	To write about or tell about A written copy A written signature or document
sequ, secu	to follow	Sequence	In following order

Root	Meaning	Examples and Meanings	
Sign	Mark	Signal	to alert somebody
spec, spect, spic	to appear, to look, to see	Specimen Aspect	An example to look at One way to see something
sta, stat, sist, stit, sisto	to stand, or make stand Stable, steady	Constant Status Stable Desist	Standing with Social standing Steady (standing) To stand away from
Struct	To build	Construction	To build a thing
tact	to touch	Contact Tactile	To touch together To be able to be touched
ten, tent, tain	to hold	Tenable Retentive Maintain	Able to be held, holding Holding To keep or hold up
tend, tens, tent	to stretch	Extend Tension	To stretch or draw out Stretched
Therm	Temperature	Thermometer	Detects temperature
tract	to draw	Attract Contract	To draw together An agreement drawn up
ven, vent	to come	Convene Advent	To come together A coming
Vis	See	Invisible	Cannot be seen
ver, vert, vers	to turn	Avert Revert Reverse	To turn away To turn back To turn around

Crossword Puzzles

1. Using the Across and Down clues, write the correct words in the numbered grid below.

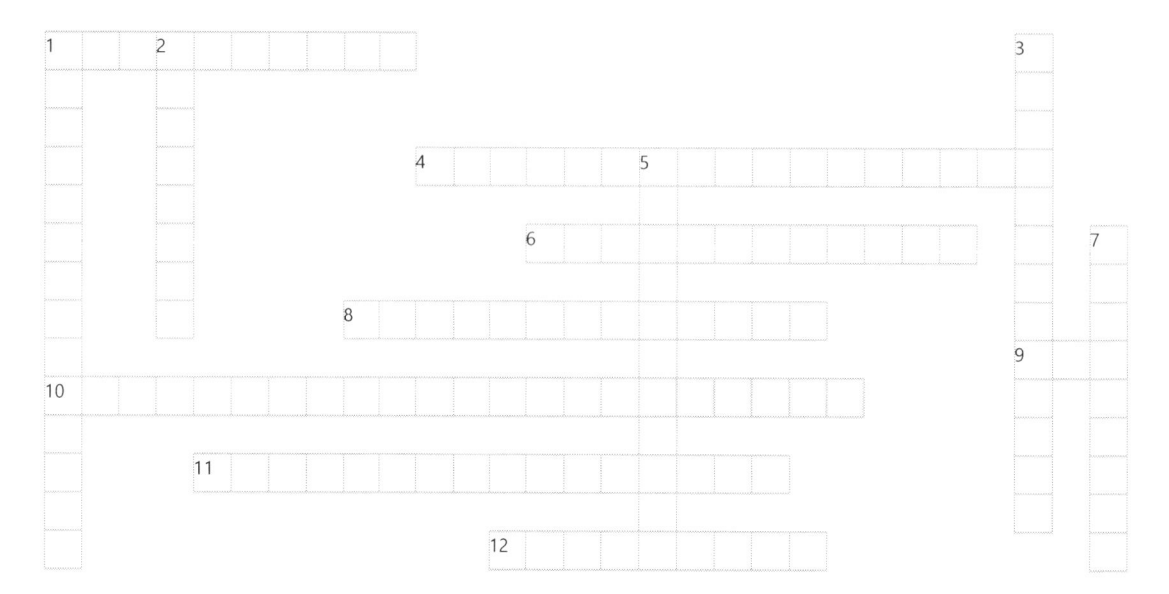

ACROSS

1. A rallying cry for more militant blacks advocated by younger leaders beginning in the mid-1960s.
4. The proclaimed foreign policy of Theodore Roosevelt, it was based on the proverb, "Speak softly and carry a big stick,".
6. The first ten amendments to the U.S. Constitution, which protect the rights of individuals from the powers of the national government.
8. In World War I, Germany and Austria-Hungary and their allies.
9. A confederation of labor unions founded in 1886, it was composed mainly of skilled craft unions.
10. Notion that America houses biologically superior people and can spread democracy to the rest of the world.
11. An historic 1979 peace agreement negotiated between Egypt and Israel at the U.S. presidential retreat at Camp David, Maryland.
12. Thomas Jefferson's first vice president, who killed Alexander Hamilton in a duel in 1804.

DOWN

1. A cultural style and artistic movement of the 1950s that rejected traditional American family life and material values and celebrated African-American culture.
2. America's leading exponent of religious liberalism, Channing was one of the founders of American Unitarianism.
3. Phrase from John Winthrop's sermon, "A Model of Christian Charity," in which he challenged his fellow Puritans to build a model, ideal community in America.
5. As vice president, Calhoun anonymously expounded the doctrine of nullification, which held that states could prevent the enforcement of a federal law within their boundaries.
7. This appellation was used to refer to common soldiers serving in Union armies during the Civil War.

A. City Upon a Hill
B. AFL
C. Billy Yank
D. Central Powers
E. American Exceptionalism
F. Big Stick Diplomacy
G. Channing
H. Camp David Accords
I. Calhoun, John
J. Aaron Burr
K. Beat Generation
L. Black Power
M. Bill of Rights

2. Using the Across and Down clues, write the correct words in the numbered grid below.

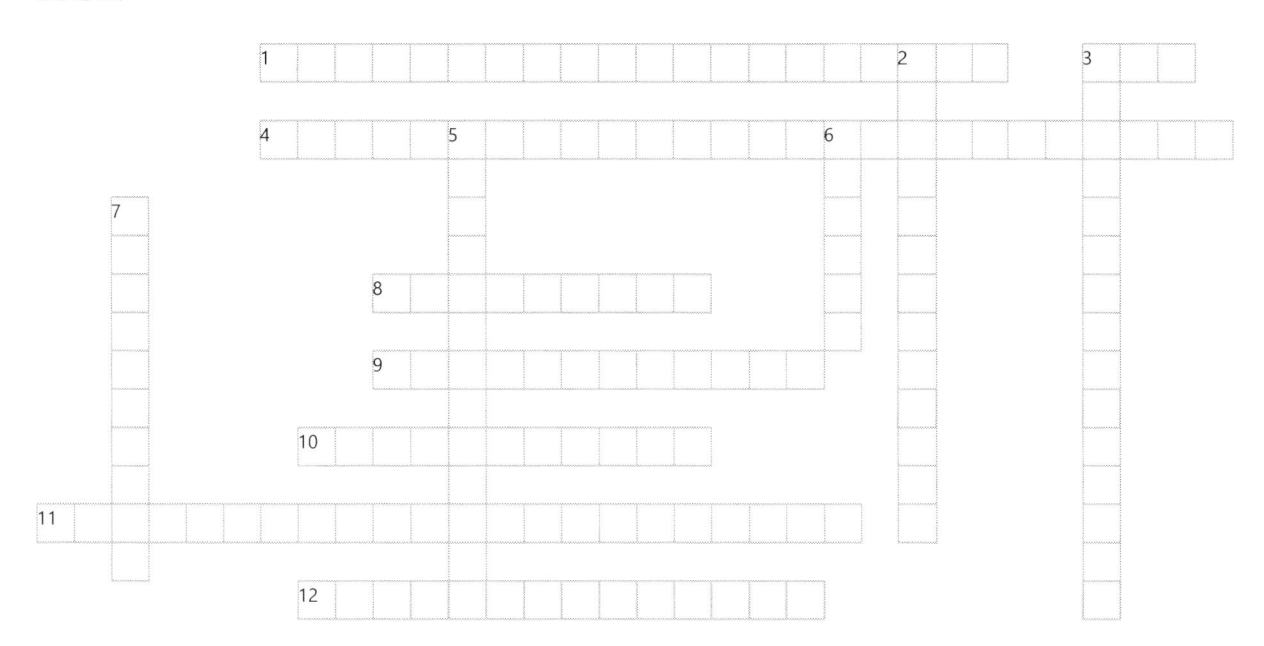

ACROSS

1. Passed in 1798 designed to curb criticism of the federal government.
3. A confederation of labor unions founded in 1886, it was composed mainly of skilled craft unions.
4. The high cost of labor led to the establishment of a system of mass production through the manufacture of interchangeable parts.
8. Thomas Jefferson's first vice president, who killed Alexander Hamilton in a duel in 1804.
9. The first ten amendments to the U.S. Constitution, which protect the rights of individuals from the powers of the national government.
10. As vice president, Calhoun anonymously expounded the doctrine of nullification, which held that states could prevent the enforcement of a federal law within their boundaries.
11. Notion that America houses biologically superior people and can spread democracy to the rest of the world.
12. Immigrants who never intended to make the United States their home.

DOWN

2. People who moved to the South following the Civil War and helped to bring Republican control of southern state governments during Reconstruction.
3. These were opponents of the Constitution of 1787 who sought to continue the confederation of sovereign states and to keep power as close as possible to the people.
5. In World War I, Germany and Austria-Hungary and their allies.
6. The "father of modern revivalism," Finney devised many techniques adopted by later revival preachers. He encouraged many women to participate actively in revival.
7. A rallying cry for more militant blacks advocated by younger leaders beginning in the mid-1960s.

A. Calhoun, John
C. Black Power
E. Bill of Rights
G. Carpetbaggers
I. Birds of Passage
K. AFL
M. American Exceptionalism

B. American System of Production
D. Antifederalists
F. Alien and Sedition Acts
H. Central Powers
J. Finney
L. Aaron Burr

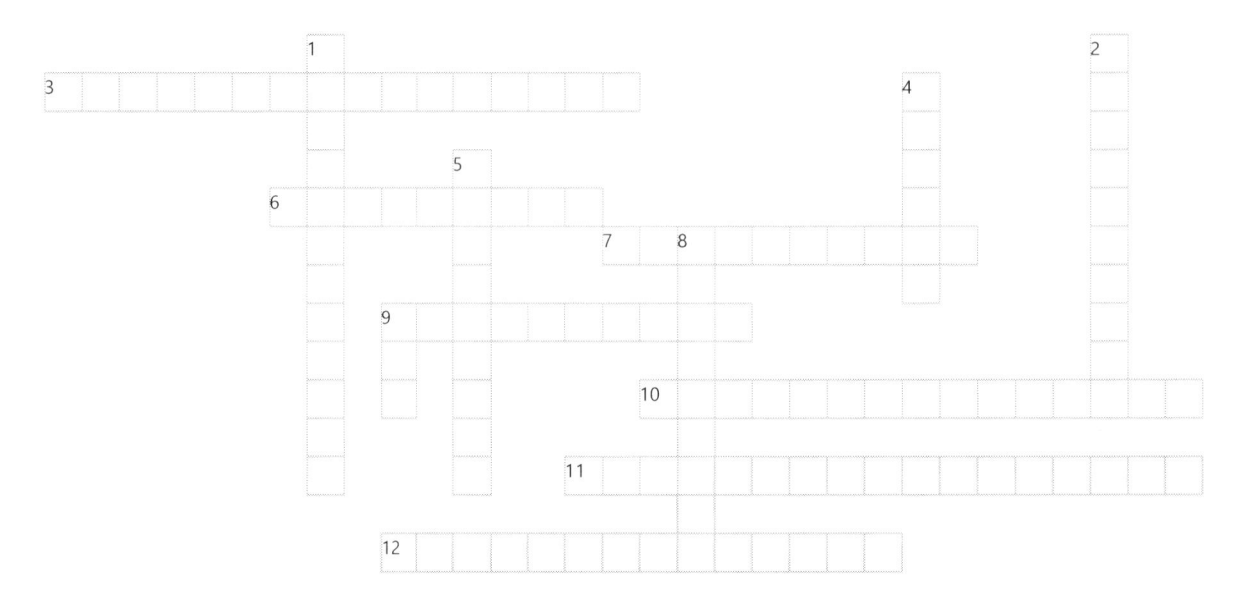

3. Using the Across and Down clues, write the correct words in the numbered grid below.

ACROSS

3. An historic 1979 peace agreement negotiated between Egypt and Israel at the U.S. presidential retreat at Camp David, Maryland.
6. Group of unemployed World War I veterans who marched on Washington, D.C., in June 1932 to ask for immediate payment of their war pensions.
7. A rallying cry for more militant blacks advocated by younger leaders beginning in the mid-1960s.
9. In World War II, the alliance of German and Italy, and later Japan.
10. These were opponents of the Constitution of 1787 who sought to continue the confederation of sovereign states and to keep power as close as possible to the people.
11. The process of transferring plants, animals, foods, diseases, wealth, and culture between Europe and the Americas.
12. A cultural style and artistic movement of the 1950s that rejected traditional American family life and material values and celebrated African-American culture.

DOWN

1. The first ten amendments to the U.S. Constitution, which protect the rights of individuals from the powers of the national government.
2. Laws passed by Southern state legislatures during Reconstruction, while Congress was out of session.
4. President, 1976. His progressive racial views reflected an emergent South less concerned with racial distinctions and more concerned with economic development and political power.
5. Emphasized the power and omnipotence of God and the importance of seeking to earn saving grace and salvation.
8. Thomas Jefferson's first vice president, who killed Alexander Hamilton in a duel in 1804.
9. A confederation of labor unions founded in 1886, it was composed mainly of skilled craft unions.

A. Carter
B. Camp David Accords
C. Bonus Army
D. Antifederalists
E. Aaron Burr
F. Black Power
G. Columbian Exchange
H. Calvinism
I. Beat Generation
J. Bill of Rights
K. Black Codes
L. Axis Powers
M. AFL

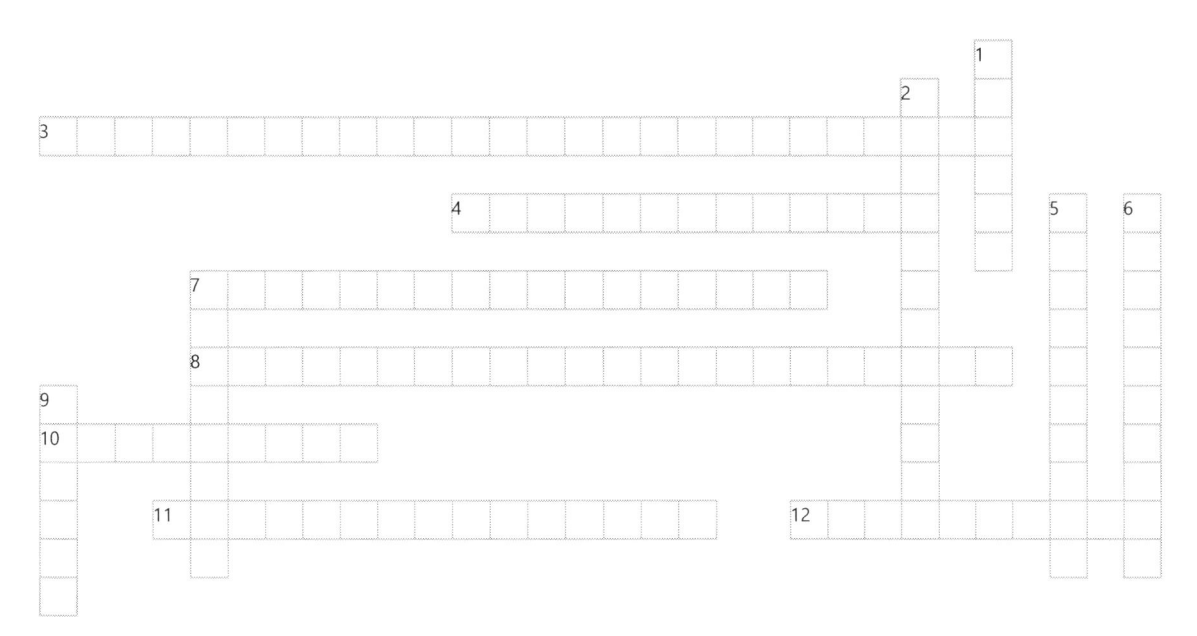

4. Using the Across and Down clues, write the correct words in the numbered grid below.

ACROSS

3. The high cost of labor led to the establishment of a system of mass production through the manufacture of interchangeable parts.
4. Phrase from John Winthrop's sermon, "A Model of Christian Charity," in which he challenged his fellow Puritans to build a model, ideal community in America.
7. During the early nineteenth century, a movement arose to end the death penalty.
8. Notion that America houses biologically superior people and can spread democracy to the rest of the world.
10. Thomas Jefferson's first vice president, who killed Alexander Hamilton in a duel in 1804.
11. These were opponents of the Constitution of 1787 who sought to continue the confederation of sovereign states and to keep power as close as possible to the people.
12. In World War II, the alliance of German and Italy, and later Japan.

A. Finney
C. American Exceptionalism
E. Channing
G. Aaron Burr
I. Capital Punishment
K. Bill of Rights
M. Axis Powers

DOWN

1. The "father of modern revivalism," Finney devised many techniques adopted by later revival preachers. He encouraged many women to participate actively in revival.
2. The first ten amendments to the U.S. Constitution, which protect the rights of individuals from the powers of the national government.
5. Laws passed by Southern state legislatures during Reconstruction, while Congress was out of session.
6. Close advisors to President Franklin Delano Roosevelt during the early days of his first term whose policy suggestions influenced much New Deal legislation.
7. America's leading exponent of religious liberalism, Channing was one of the founders of American Unitarianism.
9. President, 1976. His progressive racial views reflected an emergent South less concerned with racial distinctions and more concerned with economic development and political power.

B. Black Codes
D. Antifederalists
F. Carter
H. City Upon a Hill
J. Brain Trust
L. American System of Production

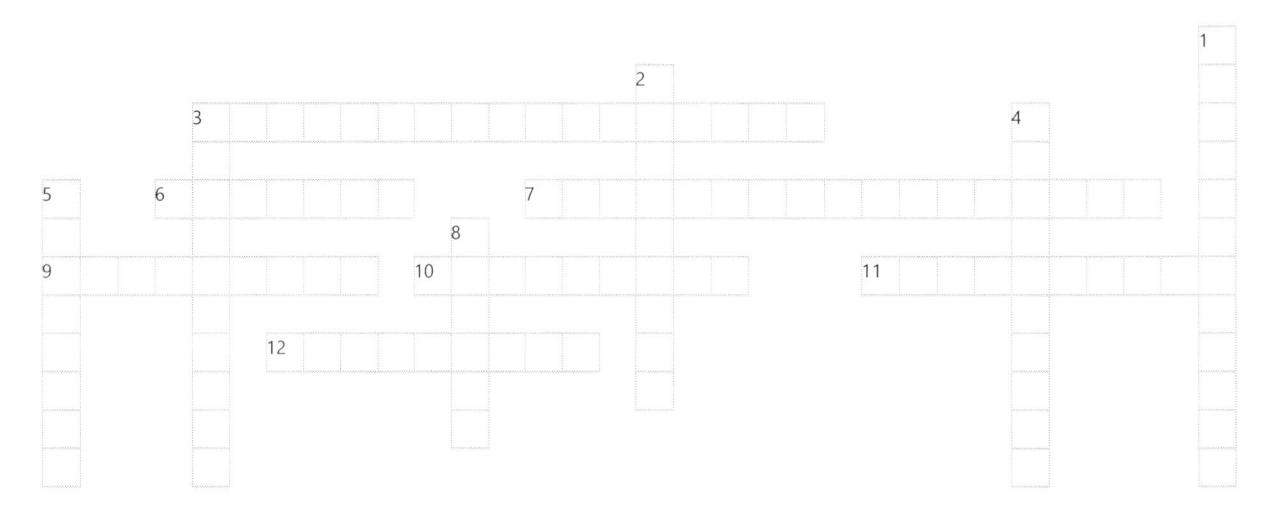

5. Using the Across and Down clues, write the correct words in the numbered grid below.

ACROSS

3. The proclaimed foreign policy of Theodore Roosevelt, it was based on the proverb, "Speak softly and carry a big stick,".
6. This term refers to the heads of the executive departments.
7. The process of transferring plants, animals, foods, diseases, wealth, and culture between Europe and the Americas.
9. Thomas Jefferson's first vice president, who killed Alexander Hamilton in a duel in 1804.
10. This appellation was used to refer to common soldiers serving in Union armies during the Civil War.
11. A rallying cry for more militant blacks advocated by younger leaders beginning in the mid-1960s.
12. Emphasized the power and omnipotence of God and the importance of seeking to earn saving grace and salvation.

DOWN

1. The first ten amendments to the U.S. Constitution, which protect the rights of individuals from the powers of the national government.
2. Group of unemployed World War I veterans who marched on Washington, D.C., in June 1932 to ask for immediate payment of their war pensions.
3. Close advisors to President Franklin Delano Roosevelt during the early days of his first term whose policy suggestions influenced much New Deal legislation.
4. Laws passed by Southern state legislatures during Reconstruction, while Congress was out of session.
5. America's leading exponent of religious liberalism, Channing was one of the founders of American Unitarianism.
8. The "father of modern revivalism," Finney devised many techniques adopted by later revival preachers. He encouraged many women to participate actively in revival.

A. Calvinism
B. Billy Yank
C. Channing
D. Finney
E. Columbian Exchange
F. Big Stick Diplomacy
G. Cabinet
H. Brain Trust
I. Aaron Burr
J. Black Codes
K. Bill of Rights
L. Bonus Army
M. Black Power

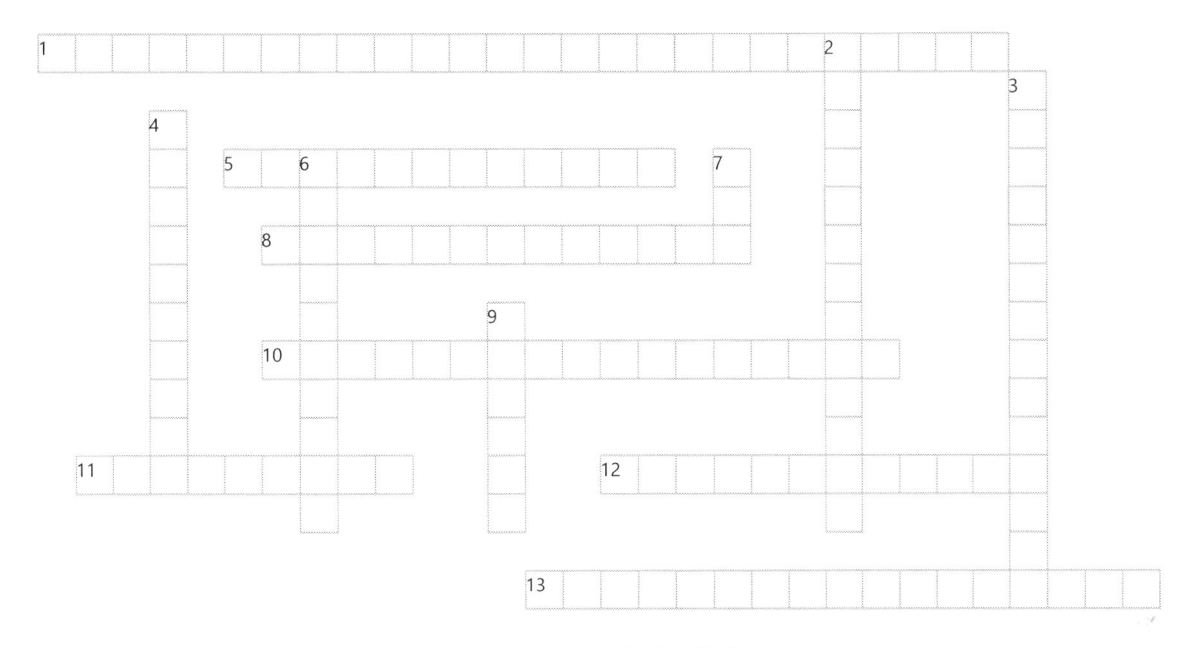

6. Using the Across and Down clues, write the correct words in the numbered grid below.

ACROSS

1. The high cost of labor led to the establishment of a system of mass production through the manufacture of interchangeable parts.
5. October 29, 1929, the day of the stock market crash that initiated the Great Depression.
8. Phrase from John Winthrop's sermon, "A Model of Christian Charity," in which he challenged his fellow Puritans to build a model, ideal community in America.
10. The process of transferring plants, animals, foods, diseases, wealth, and culture between Europe and the Americas.
11. Group of unemployed World War I veterans who marched on Washington, D.C., in June 1932 to ask for immediate payment of their war pensions.
12. The first ten amendments to the U.S. Constitution, which protect the rights of individuals from the powers of the national government.
13. The proclaimed foreign policy of Theodore Roosevelt, it was based on the proverb, "Speak softly and carry a big stick,".

DOWN

2. People who moved to the South following the Civil War and helped to bring Republican control of southern state governments during Reconstruction.
3. Henry Clay's program for the national economy, which included a protective tariff to stimulate industry and a national bank to provide credit.
4. Literally meaning against the laws of human governance.
6. In World War II, the alliance of German and Italy, and later Japan.
7. A confederation of labor unions founded in 1886, it was composed mainly of skilled craft unions.
9. The "father of modern revivalism," Finney devised many techniques adopted by later revival preachers. He encouraged many women to participate actively in revival.

A. Black Tuesday
C. Finney
E. Axis Powers
G. AFL
I. Big Stick Diplomacy
K. City Upon a Hill
M. Bill of Rights

B. Bonus Army
D. Carpetbaggers
F. Columbian Exchange
H. American System of Production
J. American System
L. Antinomian

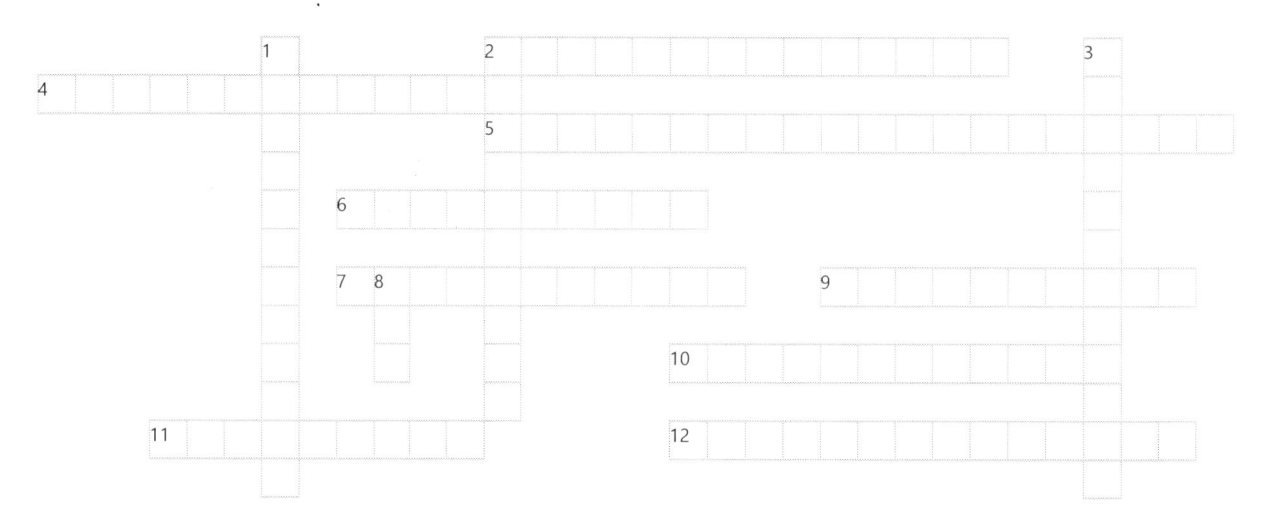

7. Using the Across and Down clues, write the correct words in the numbered grid below.

ACROSS

2. A cultural style and artistic movement of the 1950s that rejected traditional American family life and material values and celebrated African-American culture.
4. Phrase from John Winthrop's sermon, "A Model of Christian Charity," in which he challenged his fellow Puritans to build a model, ideal community in America.
5. Passed in 1798 designed to curb criticism of the federal government.
6. Laws passed by Southern state legislatures during Reconstruction, while Congress was out of session.
7. As vice president, Calhoun anonymously expounded the doctrine of nullification, which held that states could prevent the enforcement of a federal law within their boundaries.
9. Close advisors to President Franklin Delano Roosevelt during the early days of his first term whose policy suggestions influenced much New Deal legislation.
10. The first ten amendments to the U.S. Constitution, which protect the rights of individuals from the powers of the national government.
11. A failed plan to assassinate Cuban leader Fidel Castro and liberate Cuba with a trained military force of political exiles.
12. Immigrants who never intended to make the United States their home.

DOWN

1. The effort to encourage masters to voluntarily emancipate their slaves and to resettle free blacks in Africa.
2. A rallying cry for more militant blacks advocated by younger leaders beginning in the mid-1960s.
3. October 29, 1929, the day of the stock market crash that initiated the Great Depression.
8. A confederation of labor unions founded in 1886, it was composed mainly of skilled craft unions.

A. Birds of Passage
B. Beat Generation
C. Calhoun, John
D. City Upon a Hill
E. Alien and Sedition Acts
F. Black Codes
G. Brain Trust
H. Bay of Pigs
I. Colonization
J. Bill of Rights
K. AFL
L. Black Power
M. Black Tuesday

30

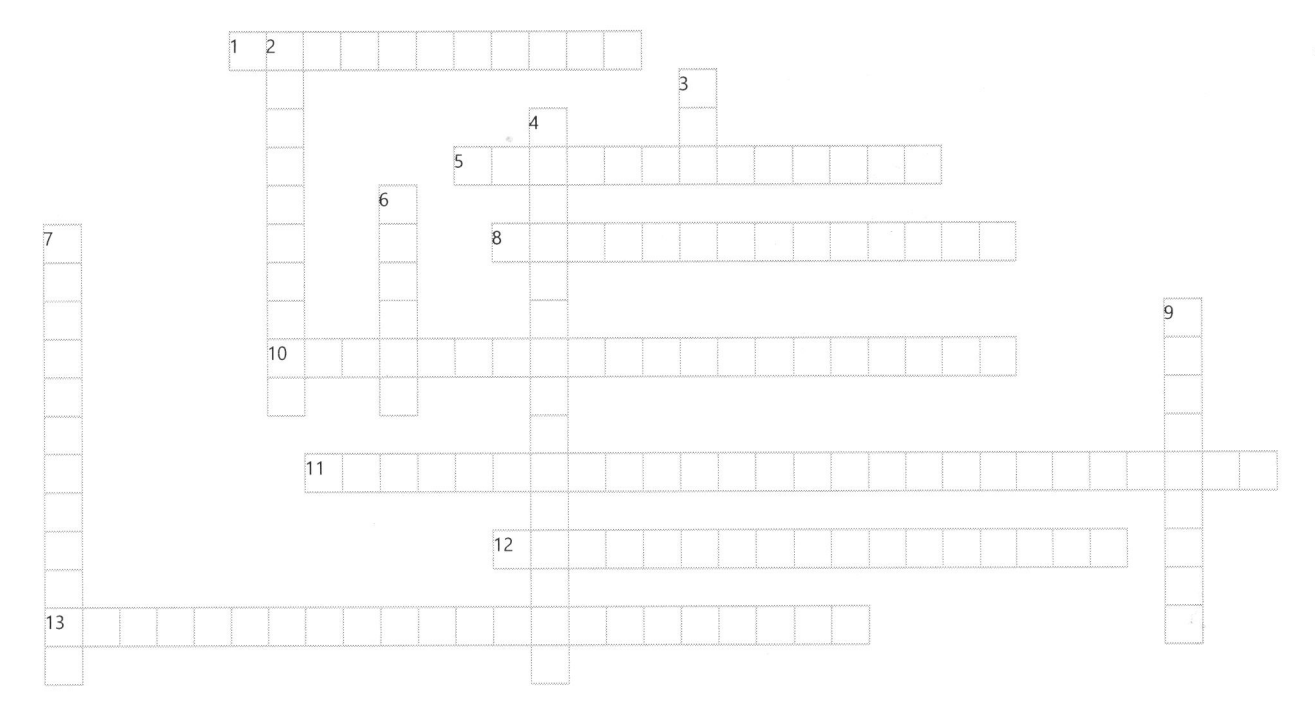

8. Using the Across and Down clues, write the correct words in the numbered grid below.

ACROSS

1. As vice president, Calhoun anonymously expounded the doctrine of nullification, which held that states could prevent the enforcement of a federal law within their boundaries.
5. In World War I, Germany and Austria-Hungary and their allies.
8. Immigrants who never intended to make the United States their home.
10. Passed in 1798 designed to curb criticism of the federal government.
11. The high cost of labor led to the establishment of a system of mass production through the manufacture of interchangeable parts.
12. The proclaimed foreign policy of Theodore Roosevelt, it was based on the proverb, "Speak softly and carry a big stick,".
13. Notion that America houses biologically superior people and can spread democracy to the rest of the world.

DOWN

2. Literally meaning against the laws of human governance.
3. A confederation of labor unions founded in 1886, it was composed mainly of skilled craft unions.
4. These were opponents of the Constitution of 1787 who sought to continue the confederation of sovereign states and to keep power as close as possible to the people.
6. President, 1976. His progressive racial views reflected an emergent South less concerned with racial distinctions and more concerned with economic development and political power.
7. October 29,1929, the day of the stock market crash that initiated the Great Depression.
9. Emphasized the power and omnipotence of God and the importance of seeking to earn saving grace and salvation.

A. AFL
C. Birds of Passage
E. Carter
G. Calhoun, John
I. American Exceptionalism
K. Antinomian
M. Calvinism

B. Big Stick Diplomacy
D. Antifederalists
F. Alien and Sedition Acts
H. American System of Production
J. Central Powers
L. Black Tuesday

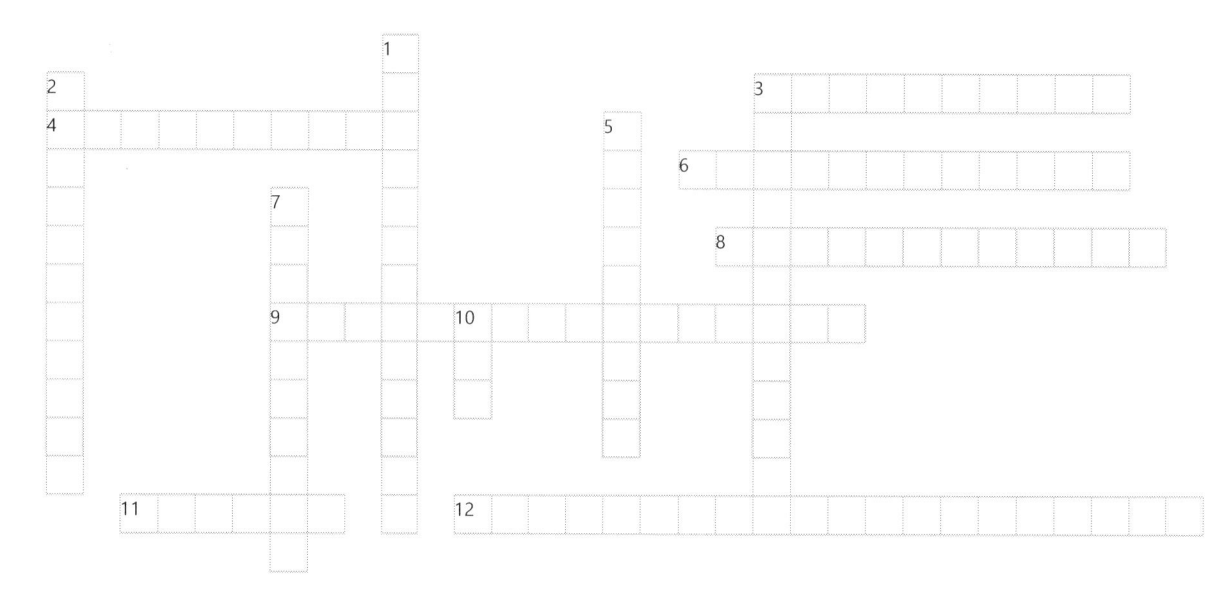

9. Using the Across and Down clues, write the correct words in the numbered grid below.

ACROSS

3. Laws passed by Southern state legislatures during Reconstruction, while Congress was out of session.
4. Literally meaning against the laws of human governance.
6. The effort to encourage masters to voluntarily emancipate their slaves and to resettle free blacks in Africa.
8. President Franklin Delano Roosevelt's controversial plan to appoint Supreme Court justices who were sympathetic to his views, by offering retirement benefits to the sitting justices.
9. An historic 1979 peace agreement negotiated between Egypt and Israel at the U.S. presidential retreat at Camp David, Maryland.
11. The "father of modern revivalism," Finney devised many techniques adopted by later revival preachers. He encouraged many women to participate actively in revival.
12. Passed in 1798 designed to curb criticism of the federal government.

DOWN

1. In World War I, Germany and Austria-Hungary and their allies.
2. As vice president, Calhoun anonymously expounded the doctrine of nullification, which held that states could prevent the enforcement of a federal law within their boundaries.
3. The first ten amendments to the U.S. Constitution, which protect the rights of individuals from the powers of the national government.
5. Group of unemployed World War I veterans who marched on Washington, D.C., in June 1932 to ask for immediate payment of their war pensions.
7. A rallying cry for more militant blacks advocated by younger leaders beginning in the mid-1960s.
10. A confederation of labor unions founded in 1886, it was composed mainly of skilled craft unions.

A. AFL
B. Bill of Rights
C. Black Power
D. Camp David Accords
E. Colonization
F. Calhoun, John
G. Alien and Sedition Acts
H. Central Powers
I. Court Packing
J. Antinomian
K. Finney
L. Black Codes
M. Bonus Army

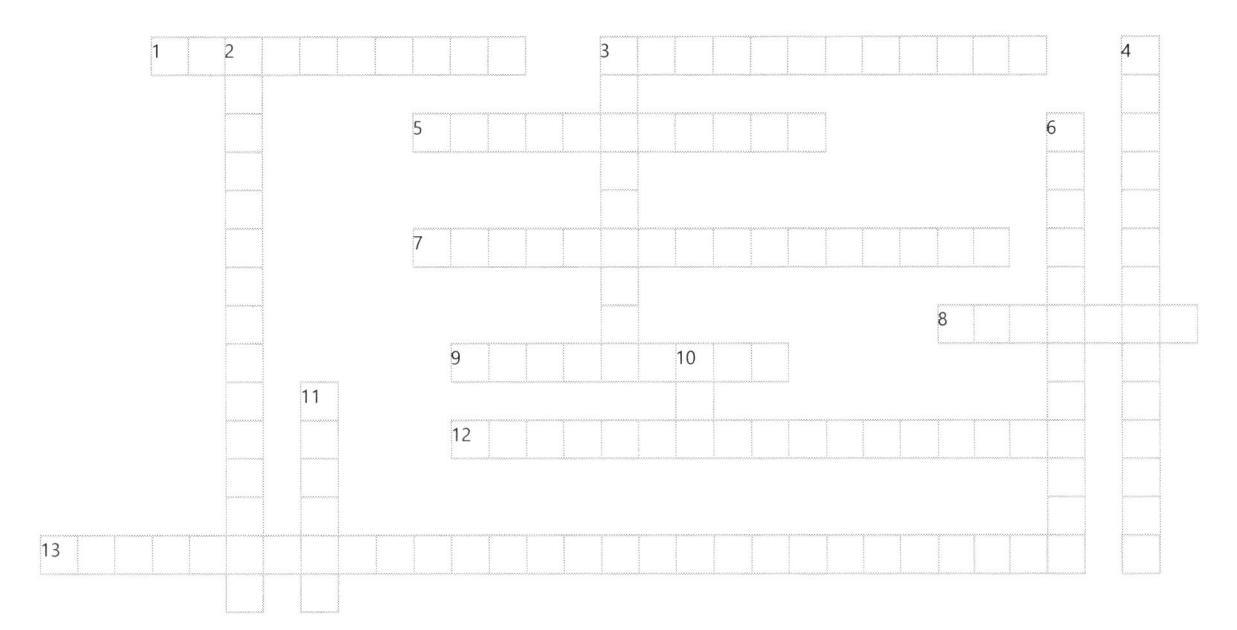

10. Using the Across and Down clues, write the correct words in the numbered grid below.

ACROSS

1. Laws passed by Southern state legislatures during Reconstruction, while Congress was out of session.
3. The first ten amendments to the U.S. Constitution, which protect the rights of individuals from the powers of the national government.
5. This best-selling pamphlet by Thomas Paine, first published in 1776, denounced the British monarchy, called for American independence.
7. An historic 1979 peace agreement negotiated between Egypt and Israel at the U.S. presidential retreat at Camp David, Maryland.
8. This term refers to the heads of the executive departments.
9. This appellation was used to refer to common soldiers serving in Union armies during the Civil War.
12. During the early nineteenth century, a movement arose to end the death penalty.
13. U.S. propaganda agency of World War I.

DOWN

2. These were opponents of the Constitution of 1787 who sought to continue the confederation of sovereign states and to keep power as close as possible to the people.
3. Group of unemployed World War I veterans who marched on Washington, D.C., in June 1932 to ask for immediate payment of their war pensions.
4. A cultural style and artistic movement of the 1950s that rejected traditional American family life and material values and celebrated African-American culture.
6. The effort to encourage masters to voluntarily emancipate their slaves and to resettle free blacks in Africa.
10. A confederation of labor unions founded in 1886, it was composed mainly of skilled craft unions.
11. President, 1976. His progressive racial views reflected an emergent South less concerned with racial distinctions and more concerned with economic development and political power.

A. Bill of Rights
C. Colonization
E. Antifederalists
G. Capital Punishment
I. Billy Yank
K. Common Sense
M. Bonus Army

B. Black Codes
D. Beat Generation
F. Cabinet
H. Carter
J. Committee on Public Information
L. Camp David Accords
N. AFL

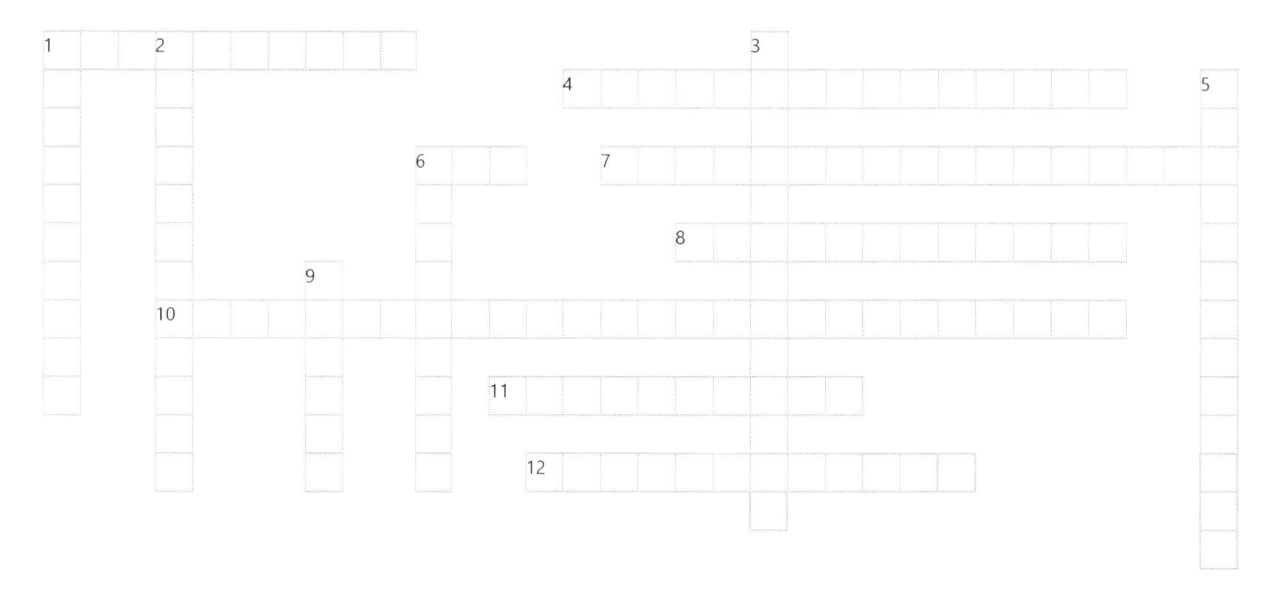

11. Using the Across and Down clues, write the correct words in the numbered grid below.

ACROSS

1. Laws passed by Southern state legislatures during Reconstruction, while Congress was out of session.
4. These were opponents of the Constitution of 1787 who sought to continue the confederation of sovereign states and to keep power as close as possible to the people.
6. A confederation of labor unions founded in 1886, it was composed mainly of skilled craft unions.
7. During the early nineteenth century, a movement arose to end the death penalty.
8. October 29, 1929, the day of the stock market crash that initiated the Great Depression.
10. The high cost of labor led to the establishment of a system of mass production through the manufacture of interchangeable parts.
11. A rallying cry for more militant blacks advocated by younger leaders beginning in the mid-1960s.
12. The first ten amendments to the U.S. Constitution, which protect the rights of individuals from the powers of the national government.

DOWN

1. Close advisors to President Franklin Delano Roosevelt during the early days of his first term whose policy suggestions influenced much New Deal legislation.
2. The effort to encourage masters to voluntarily emancipate their slaves and to resettle free blacks in Africa.
3. In World War I, Germany and Austria-Hungary and their allies.
5. Phrase from John Winthrop's sermon, "A Model of Christian Charity," in which he challenged his fellow Puritans to build a model, ideal community in America.
6. Thomas Jefferson's first vice president, who killed Alexander Hamilton in a duel in 1804.
9. The "father of modern revivalism," Finney devised many techniques adopted by later revival preachers. He encouraged many women to participate actively in revival.

A. Bill of Rights
C. Brain Trust
E. Aaron Burr
G. American System of Production
I. Antifederalists
K. Colonization
M. City Upon a Hill

B. Finney
D. AFL
F. Capital Punishment
H. Black Codes
J. Central Powers
L. Black Tuesday
N. Black Power

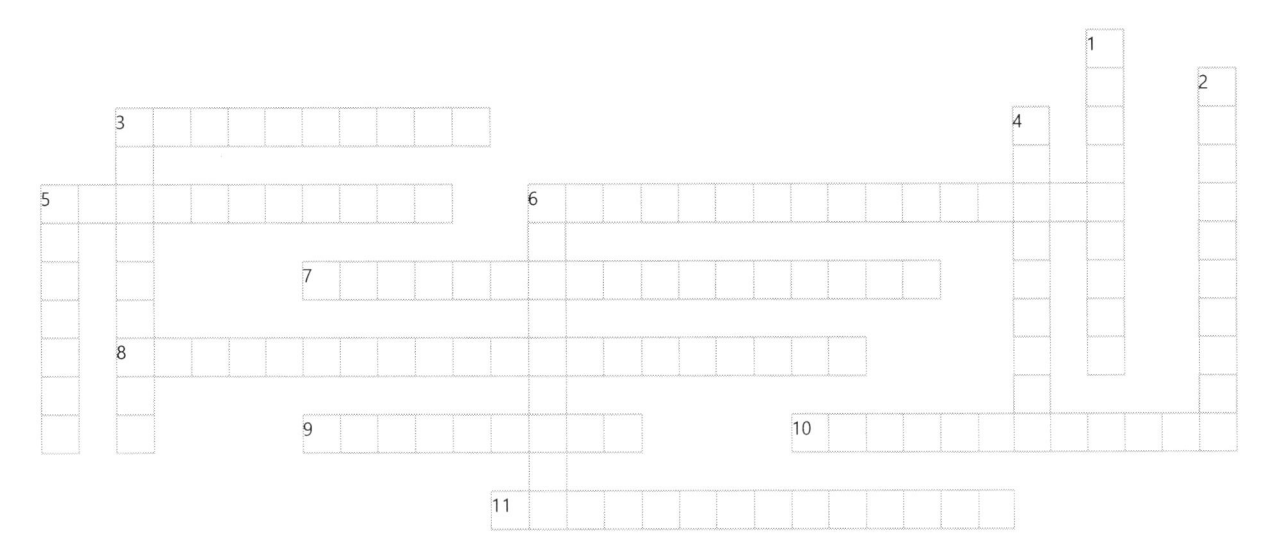

12. Using the Across and Down clues, write the correct words in the numbered grid below.

ACROSS

3. Laws passed by Southern state legislatures during Reconstruction, while Congress was out of session.
5. As vice president, Calhoun anonymously expounded the doctrine of nullification, which held that states could prevent the enforcement of a federal law within their boundaries.
6. An historic 1979 peace agreement negotiated between Egypt and Israel at the U.S. presidential retreat at Camp David, Maryland.
7. During the early nineteenth century, a movement arose to end the death penalty.
8. Passed in 1798 designed to curb criticism of the federal government.
9. A failed plan to assassinate Cuban leader Fidel Castro and liberate Cuba with a trained military force of political exiles.
10. The first ten amendments to the U.S. Constitution, which protect the rights of individuals from the powers of the national government.
11. Henry Clay's program for the national economy, which included a protective tariff to stimulate industry and a national bank to provide credit.

DOWN

1. Group of unemployed World War I veterans who marched on Washington, D.C., in June 1932 to ask for immediate payment of their war pensions.
2. In World War II, the alliance of German and Italy, and later Japan.
3. This appellation was used to refer to common soldiers serving in Union armies during the Civil War.
4. Thomas Jefferson's first vice president, who killed Alexander Hamilton in a duel in 1804.
5. This term refers to the heads of the executive departments.
6. Emphasized the power and omnipotence of God and the importance of seeking to earn saving grace and salvation.

A. Bonus Army
D. Black Codes
G. Billy Yank
J. Cabinet
M. Aaron Burr

B. American System
E. Calhoun, John
H. Bill of Rights
K. Capital Punishment
N. Bay of Pigs

C. Camp David Accords
F. Alien and Sedition Acts
I. Calvinism
L. Axis Powers

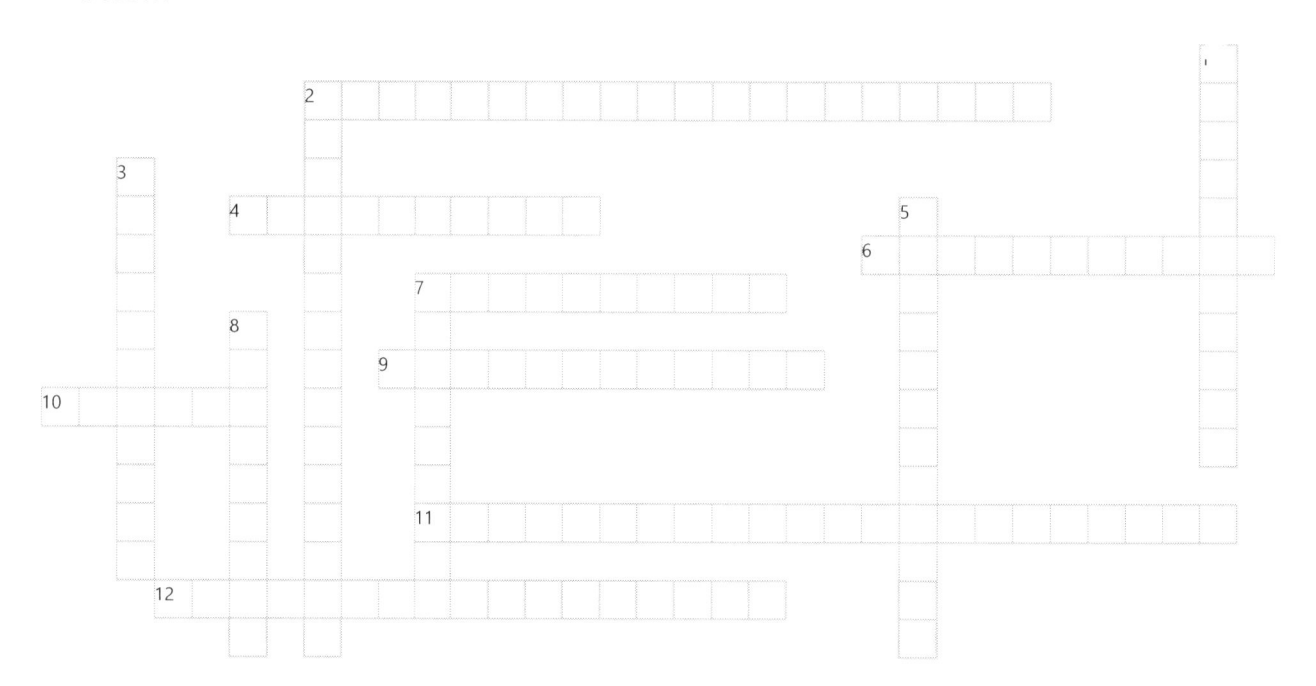

13. Using the Across and Down clues, write the correct words in the numbered grid below.

ACROSS

2. Passed in 1798 designed to curb criticism of the federal government.
4. In World War II, the alliance of German and Italy, and later Japan.
6. Popular site of New York amusement parks opening in 1890s, attracting working class Americans with rides and games celebrating abandon and instant gratification.
7. Laws passed by Southern state legislatures during Reconstruction, while Congress was out of session.
9. October 29,1929, the day of the stock market crash that initiated the Great Depression.
10. The "father of modern revivalism," Finney devised many techniques adopted by later revival preachers. He encouraged many women to participate actively in revival.
11. Notion that America houses biologically superior people and can spread democracy to the rest of the world.
12. The proclaimed foreign policy of Theodore Roosevelt, it was based on the proverb, "Speak softly and carry a big stick,".

DOWN

1. This best-selling pamphlet by Thomas Paine, first published in 1776, denounced the British monarchy, called for American independence.
2. These were opponents of the Constitution of 1787 who sought to continue the confederation of sovereign states and to keep power as close as possible to the people.
3. As vice president, Calhoun anonymously expounded the doctrine of nullification, which held that states could prevent the enforcement of a federal law within their boundaries.
5. The effort to encourage masters to voluntarily emancipate their slaves and to resettle free blacks in Africa.
7. This appellation was used to refer to common soldiers serving in Union armies during the Civil War.
8. A failed plan to assassinate Cuban leader Fidel Castro and liberate Cuba with a trained military force of political exiles.

- A. Coney Island
- B. Alien and Sedition Acts
- C. Bay of Pigs
- D. Axis Powers
- E. Antifederalists
- F. Big Stick Diplomacy
- G. Finney
- H. Black Codes
- I. Colonization
- J. American Exceptionalism
- K. Black Tuesday
- L. Calhoun, John
- M. Common Sense
- N. Billy Yank

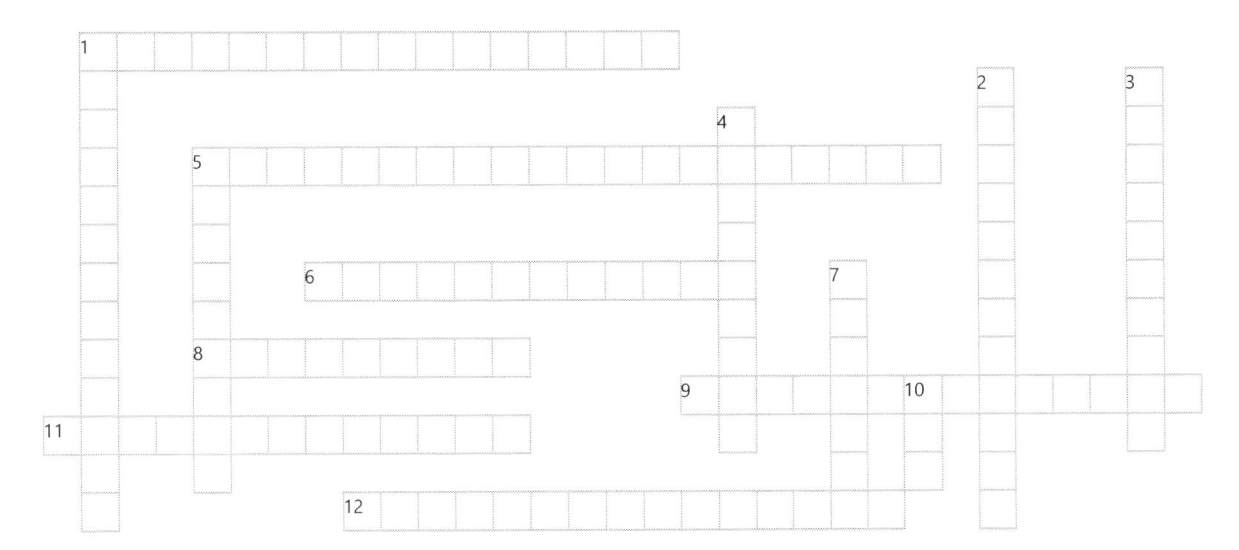

14. Using the Across and Down clues, write the correct words in the numbered grid below.

ACROSS

1. An historic 1979 peace agreement negotiated between Egypt and Israel at the U.S. presidential retreat at Camp David, Maryland.
5. Passed in 1798 designed to curb criticism of the federal government.
6. The first ten amendments to the U.S. Constitution, which protect the rights of individuals from the powers of the national government.
8. This appellation was used to refer to common soldiers serving in Union armies during the Civil War.
9. Henry Clay's program for the national economy, which included a protective tariff to stimulate industry and a national bank to provide credit.
11. In World War I, Germany and Austria-Hungary and their allies.
12. These were opponents of the Constitution of 1787 who sought to continue the confederation of sovereign states and to keep power as close as possible to the people.

DOWN

1. People who moved to the South following the Civil War and helped to bring Republican control of southern state governments during Reconstruction.
2. October 29, 1929, the day of the stock market crash that initiated the Great Depression.
3. A rallying cry for more militant blacks advocated by younger leaders beginning in the mid-1960s.
4. Group of unemployed World War I veterans who marched on Washington, D.C., in June 1932 to ask for immediate payment of their war pensions.
5. Thomas Jefferson's first vice president, who killed Alexander Hamilton in a duel in 1804.
7. This term refers to the heads of the executive departments.
10. A confederation of labor unions founded in 1886, it was composed mainly of skilled craft unions.

A. Camp David Accords
B. Aaron Burr
C. Bonus Army
D. Carpetbaggers
E. American System
F. Cabinet
G. Black Tuesday
H. Bill of Rights
I. Central Powers
J. Alien and Sedition Acts
K. Antifederalists
L. AFL
M. Black Power
N. Billy Yank

15. Using the Across and Down clues, write the correct words in the numbered grid below.

ACROSS

3. Notion that America houses biologically superior people and can spread democracy to the rest of the world.
7. A rallying cry for more militant blacks advocated by younger leaders beginning in the mid-1960s.
8. Close advisors to President Franklin Delano Roosevelt during the early days of his first term whose policy suggestions influenced much New Deal legislation.
9. The first ten amendments to the U.S. Constitution, which protect the rights of individuals from the powers of the national government.
10. The "father of modern revivalism," Finney devised many techniques adopted by later revival preachers. He encouraged many women to participate actively in revival.
11. Passed in 1798 designed to curb criticism of the federal government.
12. The process of transferring plants, animals, foods, diseases, wealth, and culture between Europe and the Americas.
13. President, 1976. His progressive racial views reflected an emergent South less concerned with racial distinctions and more concerned with economic development and political power.
14. Laws passed by Southern state legislatures during Reconstruction, while Congress was out of session.

DOWN

1. Group of unemployed World War I veterans who marched on Washington, D.C., in June 1932 to ask for immediate payment of their war pensions.
2. Immigrants who never intended to make the United States their home.
4. As vice president, Calhoun anonymously expounded the doctrine of nullification, which held that states could prevent the enforcement of a federal law within their boundaries.
5. In World War II, the alliance of German and Italy, and later Japan.
6. Literally meaning against the laws of human governance.

A. Brain Trust
B. Antinomian
C. American Exceptionalism
D. Finney
E. Black Power
F. Axis Powers
G. Alien and Sedition Acts
H. Bill of Rights
I. Carter
J. Birds of Passage
K. Columbian Exchange
L. Bonus Army
M. Black Codes
N. Calhoun, John

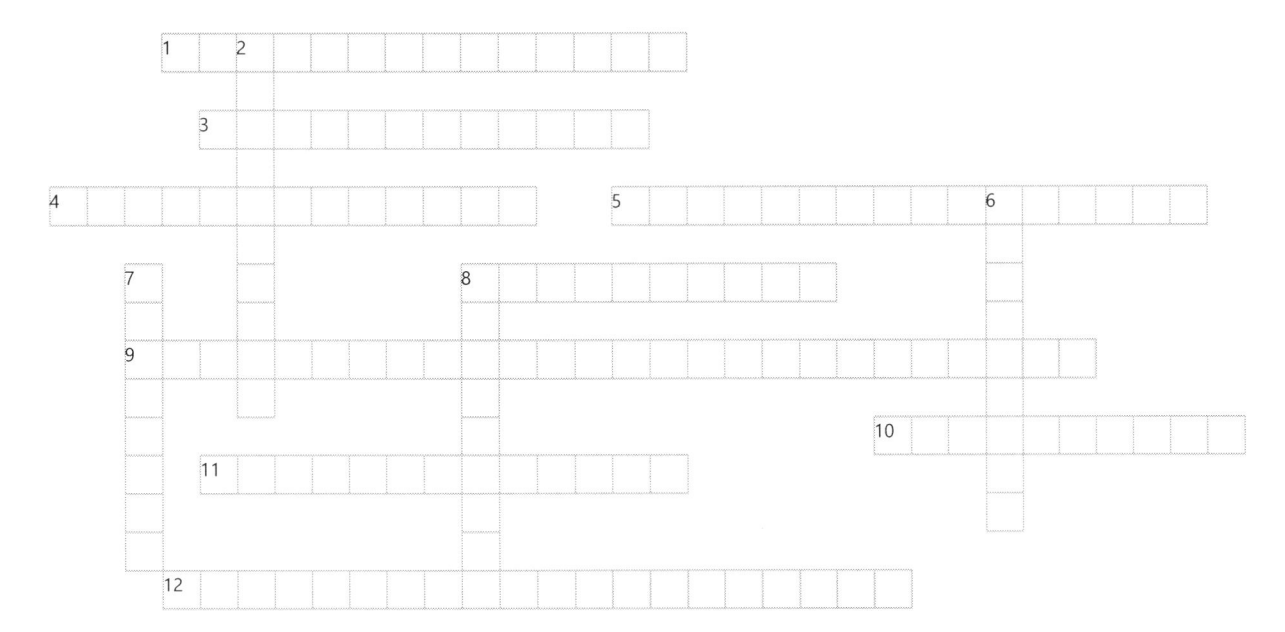

16. Using the Across and Down clues, write the correct words in the numbered grid below.

ACROSS

1. A cultural style and artistic movement of the 1950s that rejected traditional American family life and material values and celebrated African-American culture.
3. The first ten amendments to the U.S. Constitution, which protect the rights of individuals from the powers of the national government.
4. Phrase from John Winthrop's sermon, "A Model of Christian Charity," in which he challenged his fellow Puritans to build a model, ideal community in America.
5. An historic 1979 peace agreement negotiated between Egypt and Israel at the U.S. presidential retreat at Camp David, Maryland.
8. Laws passed by Southern state legislatures during Reconstruction, while Congress was out of session.
9. The high cost of labor led to the establishment of a system of mass production through the manufacture of interchangeable parts.
10. Close advisors to President Franklin Delano Roosevelt during the early days of his first term whose policy suggestions influenced much New Deal legislation.
11. In World War I, Germany and Austria-Hungary and their allies.
12. Passed in 1798 designed to curb criticism of the federal government.

DOWN

2. In World War II, the alliance of German and Italy, and later Japan.
6. Emphasized the power and omnipotence of God and the importance of seeking to earn saving grace and salvation.
7. America's leading exponent of religious liberalism, Channing was one of the founders of American Unitarianism.
8. A failed plan to assassinate Cuban leader Fidel Castro and liberate Cuba with a trained military force of political exiles.

A. Calvinism
B. Brain Trust
C. Bill of Rights
D. Alien and Sedition Acts
E. City Upon a Hill
F. Camp David Accords
G. Channing
H. Black Codes
I. American System of Production
J. Axis Powers
K. Beat Generation
L. Central Powers
M. Bay of Pigs

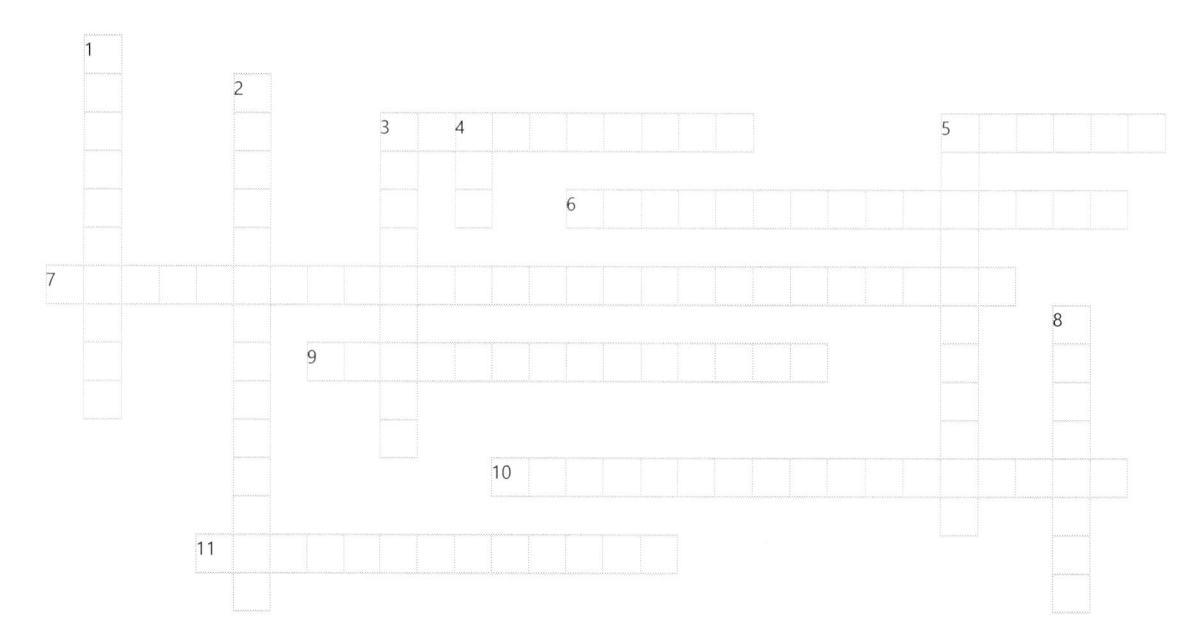

17. Using the Across and Down clues, write the correct words in the numbered grid below.

ACROSS

3. Laws passed by Southern state legislatures during Reconstruction, while Congress was out of session.
5. President, 1976. His progressive racial views reflected an emergent South less concerned with racial distinctions and more concerned with economic development and political power.
6. These were opponents of the Constitution of 1787 who sought to continue the confederation of sovereign states and to keep power as close as possible to the people.
7. The high cost of labor led to the establishment of a system of mass production through the manufacture of interchangeable parts.
9. A cultural style and artistic movement of the 1950s that rejected traditional American family life and material values and celebrated African-American culture.
10. During the early nineteenth century, a movement arose to end the death penalty.
11. In World War I, Germany and Austria-Hungary and their allies.

DOWN

1. Literally meaning against the laws of human governance.
2. Henry Clay's program for the national economy, which included a protective tariff to stimulate industry and a national bank to provide credit.
3. This appellation was used to refer to common soldiers serving in Union armies during the Civil War.
4. A confederation of labor unions founded in 1886, it was composed mainly of skilled craft unions.
5. As vice president, Calhoun anonymously expounded the doctrine of nullification, which held that states could prevent the enforcement of a federal law within their boundaries.
8. America's leading exponent of religious liberalism, Channing was one of the founders of American Unitarianism.

A. American System of Production
B. Carter
C. Central Powers
D. Antifederalists
E. Channing
F. AFL
G. Black Codes
H. American System
I. Calhoun, John
J. Billy Yank
K. Capital Punishment
L. Beat Generation
M. Antinomian

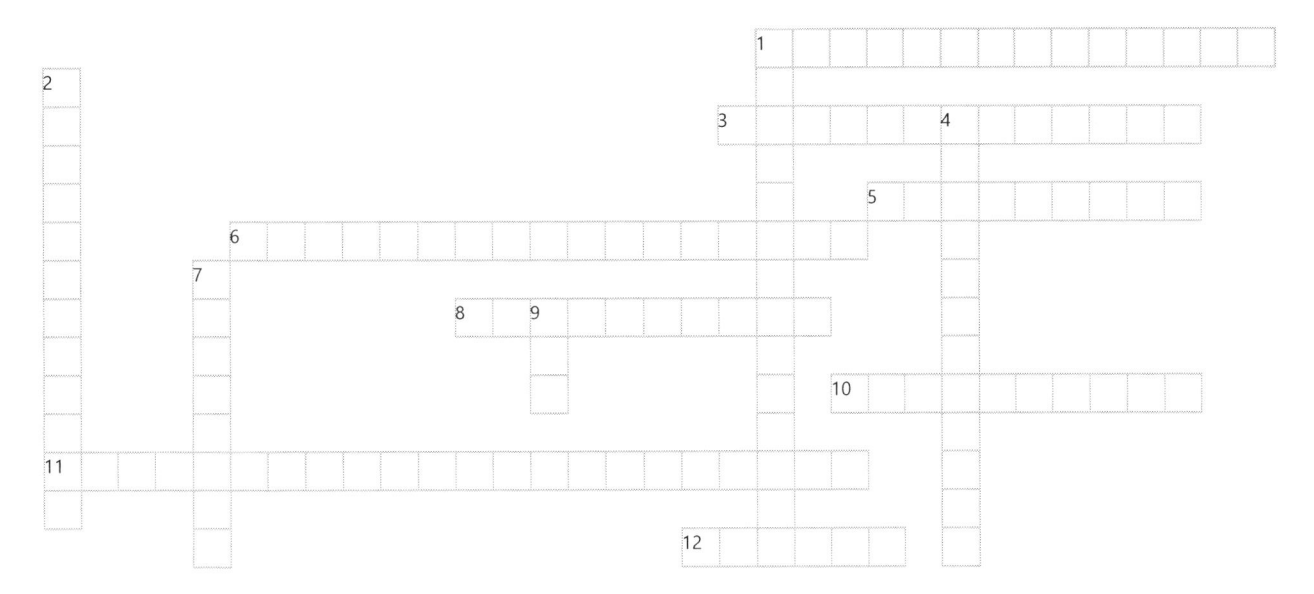

18. Using the Across and Down clues, write the correct words in the numbered grid below.

ACROSS

1. Immigrants who never intended to make the United States their home.
3. People who moved to the South following the Civil War and helped to bring Republican control of southern state governments during Reconstruction.
5. Emphasized the power and omnipotence of God and the importance of seeking to earn saving grace and salvation.
6. During the early nineteenth century, a movement arose to end the death penalty.
8. Laws passed by Southern state legislatures during Reconstruction, while Congress was out of session.
10. Literally meaning against the laws of human governance.
11. Notion that America houses biologically superior people and can spread democracy to the rest of the world.
12. The "father of modern revivalism," Finney devised many techniques adopted by later revival preachers. He encouraged many women to participate actively in revival.

DOWN

1. A cultural style and artistic movement of the 1950s that rejected traditional American family life and material values and celebrated African-American culture.
2. October 29, 1929, the day of the stock market crash that initiated the Great Depression.
4. The first ten amendments to the U.S. Constitution, which protect the rights of individuals from the powers of the national government.
7. America's leading exponent of religious liberalism, Channing was one of the founders of American Unitarianism.
9. A confederation of labor unions founded in 1886, it was composed mainly of skilled craft unions.

A. Carpetbaggers
B. Channing
C. Capital Punishment
D. Black Codes
E. Beat Generation
F. Finney
G. Birds of Passage
H. AFL
I. Bill of Rights
J. American Exceptionalism
K. Black Tuesday
L. Calvinism
M. Antinomian

19. Using the Across and Down clues, write the correct words in the numbered grid below.

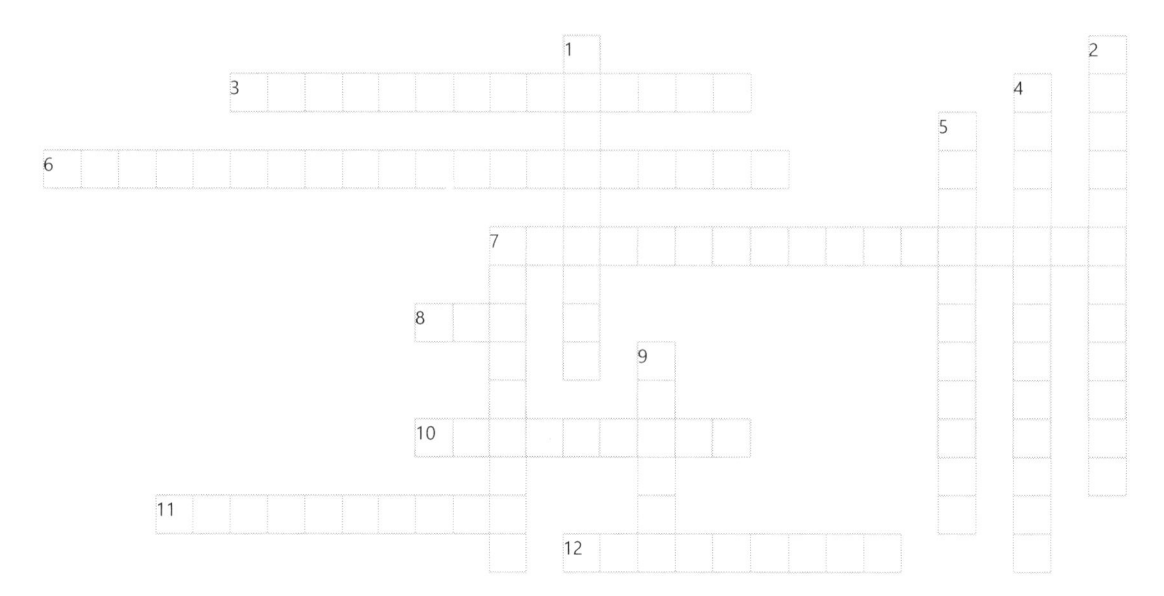

ACROSS

3. A cultural style and artistic movement of the 1950s that rejected traditional American family life and material values and celebrated African-American culture.
6. Passed in 1798 designed to curb criticism of the federal government.
7. During the early nineteenth century, a movement arose to end the death penalty.
8. A confederation of labor unions founded in 1886, it was composed mainly of skilled craft unions.
10. Group of unemployed World War I veterans who marched on Washington, D.C., in June 1932 to ask for immediate payment of their war pensions.
11. Laws passed by Southern state legislatures during Reconstruction, while Congress was out of session.
12. Thomas Jefferson's first vice president, who killed Alexander Hamilton in a duel in 1804.

DOWN

1. A failed plan to assassinate Cuban leader Fidel Castro and liberate Cuba with a trained military force of political exiles.
2. October 29, 1929, the day of the stock market crash that initiated the Great Depression.
4. People who moved to the South following the Civil War and helped to bring Republican control of southern state governments during Reconstruction.
5. As vice president, Calhoun anonymously expounded the doctrine of nullification, which held that states could prevent the enforcement of a federal law within their boundaries.
7. Emphasized the power and omnipotence of God and the importance of seeking to earn saving grace and salvation.
9. President, 1976. His progressive racial views reflected an emergent South less concerned with racial distinctions and more concerned with economic development and political power.

A. Beat Generation
B. AFL
C. Calvinism
D. Aaron Burr
E. Calhoun, John
F. Carter
G. Alien and Sedition Acts
H. Black Tuesday
I. Black Codes
J. Bay of Pigs
K. Capital Punishment
L. Carpetbaggers
M. Bonus Army

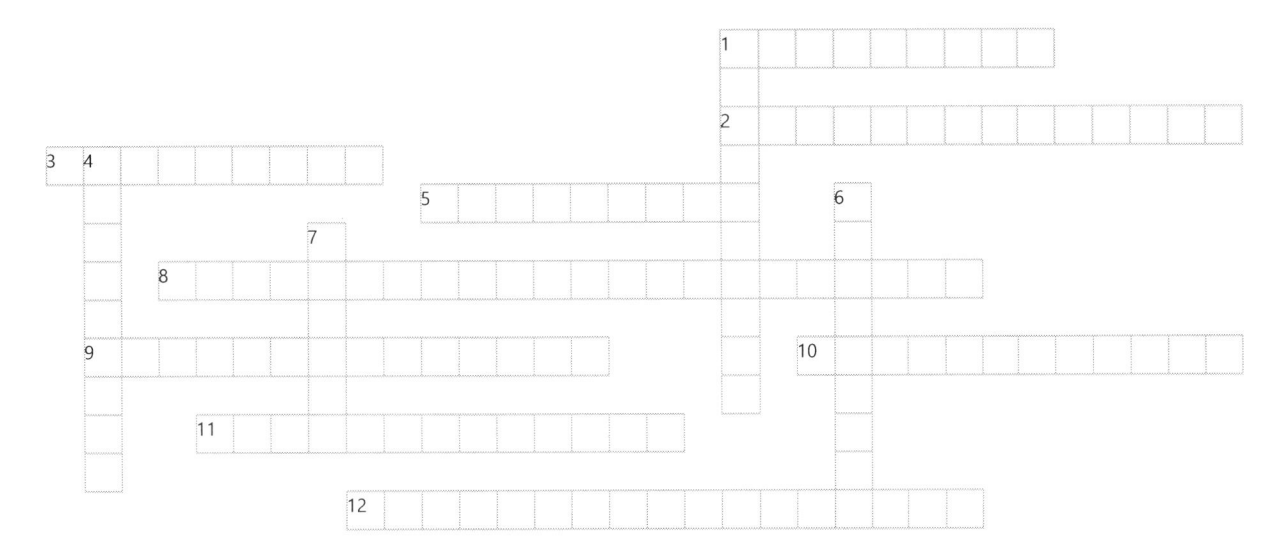

20. Using the Across and Down clues, write the correct words in the numbered grid below.

ACROSS

1. Group of unemployed World War I veterans who marched on Washington, D.C., in June 1932 to ask for immediate payment of their war pensions.
2. Henry Clay's program for the national economy, which included a protective tariff to stimulate industry and a national bank to provide credit.
3. A failed plan to assassinate Cuban leader Fidel Castro and liberate Cuba with a trained military force of political exiles.
5. This appellation was used to refer to common soldiers serving in Union armies during the Civil War.
8. Notion that America houses biologically superior people and can spread democracy to the rest of the world.
9. A cultural style and artistic movement of the 1950s that rejected traditional American family life and material values and celebrated African-American culture.
10. The first ten amendments to the U.S. Constitution, which protect the rights of individuals from the powers of the national government.
11. Phrase from John Winthrop's sermon, "A Model of Christian Charity," in which he challenged his fellow Puritans to build a model, ideal community in America.
12. The proclaimed foreign policy of Theodore Roosevelt, it was based on the proverb, "Speak softly and carry a big stick,".

DOWN

1. Laws passed by Southern state legislatures during Reconstruction, while Congress was out of session.
4. Thomas Jefferson's first vice president, who killed Alexander Hamilton in a duel in 1804.
6. Emphasized the power and omnipotence of God and the importance of seeking to earn saving grace and salvation.
7. The "father of modern revivalism," Finney devised many techniques adopted by later revival preachers. He encouraged many women to participate actively in revival.

A. Beat Generation
B. American Exceptionalism
C. Bonus Army
D. City Upon a Hill
E. Billy Yank
F. American System
G. Black Codes
H. Calvinism
I. Finney
J. Big Stick Diplomacy
K. Bay of Pigs
L. Aaron Burr
M. Bill of Rights

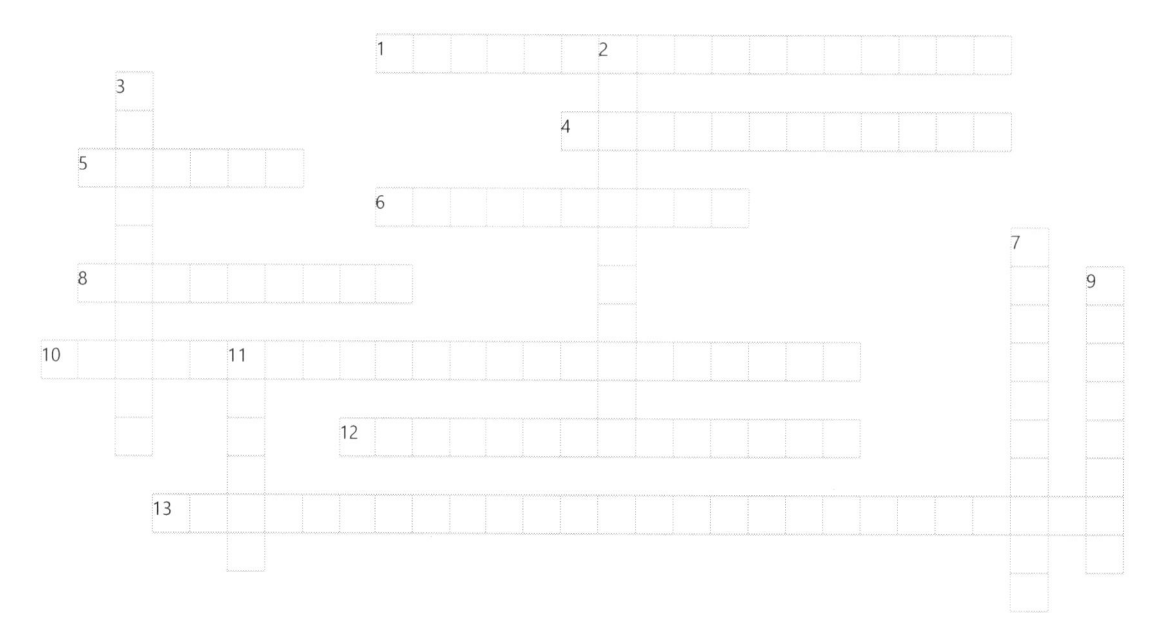

21. Using the Across and Down clues, write the correct words in the numbered grid below.

ACROSS

1. The proclaimed foreign policy of Theodore Roosevelt, it was based on the proverb, "Speak softly and carry a big stick,".
4. October 29,1929, the day of the stock market crash that initiated the Great Depression.
5. The "father of modern revivalism," Finney devised many techniques adopted by later revival preachers. He encouraged many women to participate actively in revival.
6. Laws passed by Southern state legislatures during Reconstruction, while Congress was out of session.
8. Group of unemployed World War I veterans who marched on Washington, D.C., in June 1932 to ask for immediate payment of their war pensions.
10. Notion that America houses biologically superior people and can spread democracy to the rest of the world.
12. Henry Clay's program for the national economy, which included a protective tariff to stimulate industry and a national bank to provide credit.
13. The high cost of labor led to the establishment of a system of mass production through the manufacture of interchangeable parts.

DOWN

2. As vice president, Calhoun anonymously expounded the doctrine of nullification, which held that states could prevent the enforcement of a federal law within their boundaries.
3. In World War II, the alliance of German and Italy, and later Japan.
7. Literally meaning against the laws of human governance.
9. America's leading exponent of religious liberalism, Channing was one of the founders of American Unitarianism.
11. President, 1976. His progressive racial views reflected an emergent South less concerned with racial distinctions and more concerned with economic development and political power.

- A. American System of Production
- C. Channing
- E. Finney
- G. American Exceptionalism
- I. Carter
- K. Antinomian
- M. Black Codes
- B. American System
- D. Calhoun, John
- F. Bonus Army
- H. Axis Powers
- J. Big Stick Diplomacy
- L. Black Tuesday

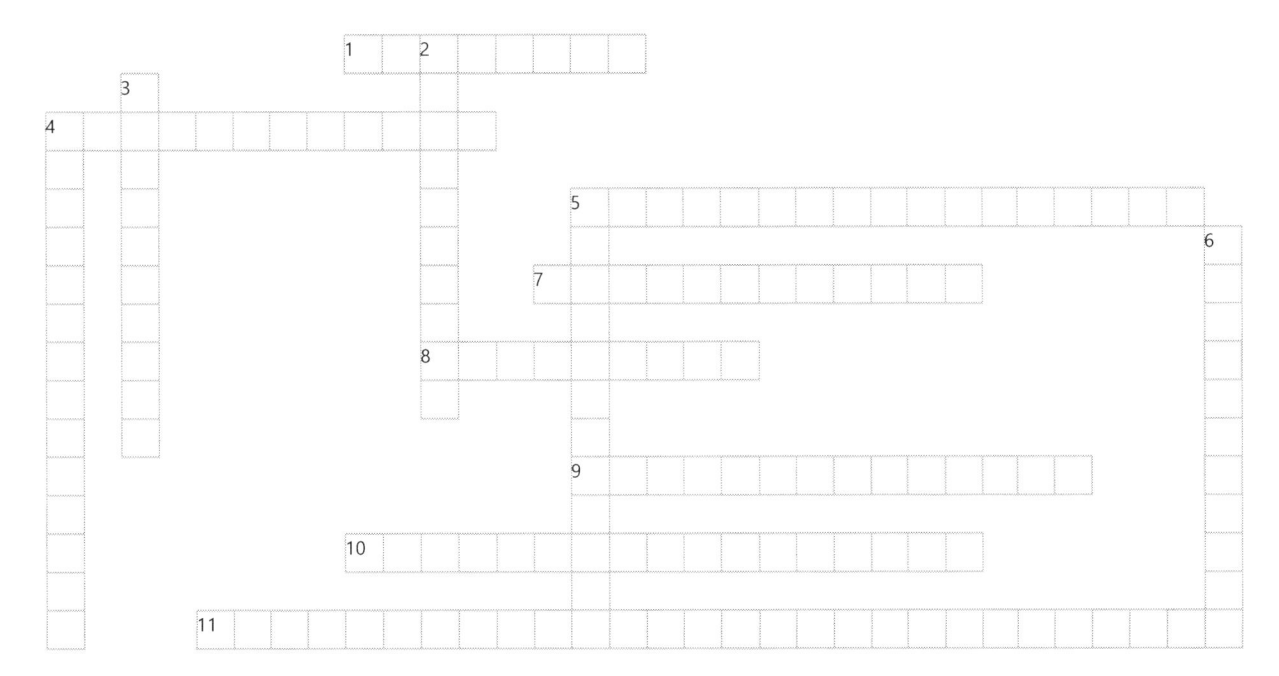

22. Using the Across and Down clues, write the correct words in the numbered grid below.

ACROSS

1. America's leading exponent of religious liberalism, Channing was one of the founders of American Unitarianism.
4. The first ten amendments to the U.S. Constitution, which protect the rights of individuals from the powers of the national government.
5. During the early nineteenth century, a movement arose to end the death penalty.
7. October 29, 1929, the day of the stock market crash that initiated the Great Depression.
8. Thomas Jefferson's first vice president, who killed Alexander Hamilton in a duel in 1804.
9. Henry Clay's program for the national economy, which included a protective tariff to stimulate industry and a national bank to provide credit.
10. The process of transferring plants, animals, foods, diseases, wealth, and culture between Europe and the Americas.
11. U.S. propaganda agency of World War I.

DOWN

2. Literally meaning against the laws of human governance.
3. A rallying cry for more militant blacks advocated by younger leaders beginning in the mid-1960s.
4. Immigrants who never intended to make the United States their home.
5. The effort to encourage masters to voluntarily emancipate their slaves and to resettle free blacks in Africa.
6. As vice president, Calhoun anonymously expounded the doctrine of nullification, which held that states could prevent the enforcement of a federal law within their boundaries.

A. Aaron Burr
B. Black Tuesday
C. American System
D. Black Power
E. Colonization
F. Antinomian
G. Bill of Rights
H. Columbian Exchange
I. Committee on Public Information
J. Channing
K. Birds of Passage
L. Capital Punishment
M. Calhoun, John

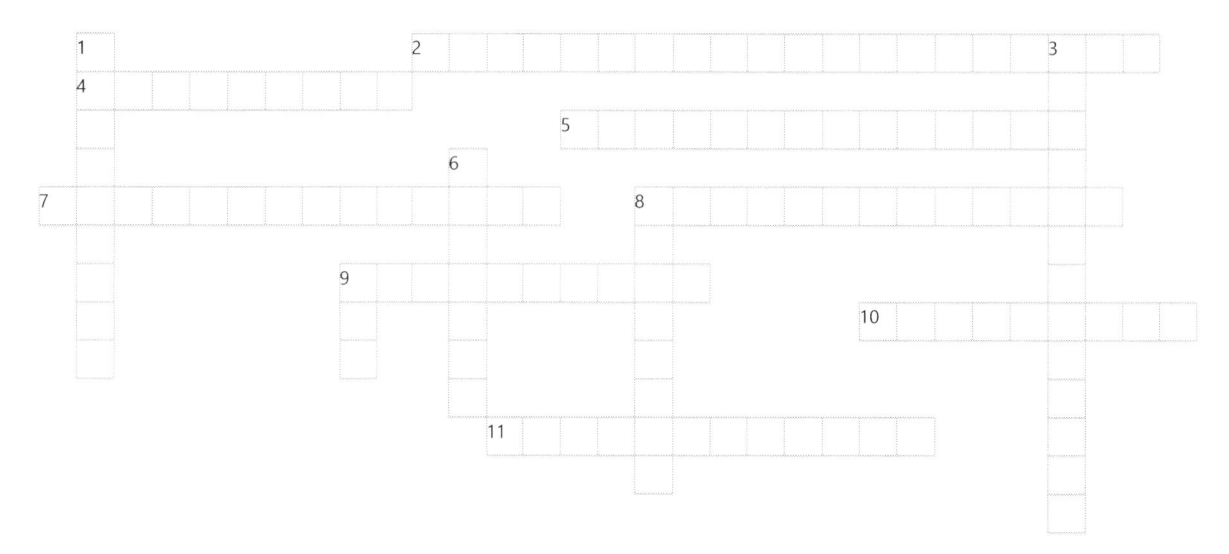

23. Using the Across and Down clues, write the correct words in the numbered grid below.

ACROSS

2. Passed in 1798 designed to curb criticism of the federal government.
4. Thomas Jefferson's first vice president, who killed Alexander Hamilton in a duel in 1804.
5. A cultural style and artistic movement of the 1950s that rejected traditional American family life and material values and celebrated African-American culture.
7. Immigrants who never intended to make the United States their home.
8. People who moved to the South following the Civil War and helped to bring Republican control of southern state governments during Reconstruction.
9. Literally meaning against the laws of human governance.
10. A failed plan to assassinate Cuban leader Fidel Castro and liberate Cuba with a trained military force of political exiles.
11. The effort to encourage masters to voluntarily emancipate their slaves and to resettle free blacks in Africa.

DOWN

1. Emphasized the power and omnipotence of God and the importance of seeking to earn saving grace and salvation.
3. In World War I, Germany and Austria-Hungary and their allies.
6. This term refers to the heads of the executive departments.
8. America's leading exponent of religious liberalism, Channing was one of the founders of American Unitarianism.
9. A confederation of labor unions founded in 1886, it was composed mainly of skilled craft unions.

A. Aaron Burr
B. Cabinet
C. Antinomian
D. Colonization
E. Beat Generation
F. Central Powers
G. Birds of Passage
H. Alien and Sedition Acts
I. Bay of Pigs
J. Calvinism
K. AFL
L. Channing
M. Carpetbaggers

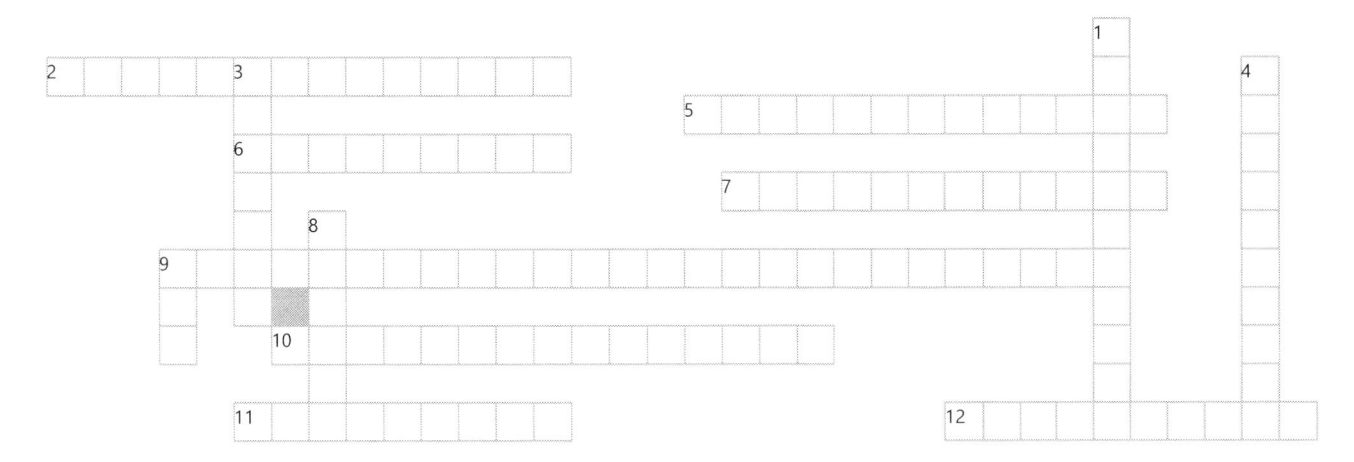

24. Using the Across and Down clues, write the correct words in the numbered grid below.

ACROSS

2. Henry Clay's program for the national economy, which included a protective tariff to stimulate industry and a national bank to provide credit.
5. Phrase from John Winthrop's sermon, "A Model of Christian Charity," in which he challenged his fellow Puritans to build a model, ideal community in America.
6. Group of unemployed World War I veterans who marched on Washington, D.C., in June 1932 to ask for immediate payment of their war pensions.
7. The effort to encourage masters to voluntarily emancipate their slaves and to resettle free blacks in Africa.
9. The high cost of labor led to the establishment of a system of mass production through the manufacture of interchangeable parts.
10. These were opponents of the Constitution of 1787 who sought to continue the confederation of sovereign states and to keep power as close as possible to the people.
11. A failed plan to assassinate Cuban leader Fidel Castro and liberate Cuba with a trained military force of political exiles.
12. Close advisors to President Franklin Delano Roosevelt during the early days of his first term whose policy suggestions influenced much New Deal legislation.

DOWN

1. As vice president, Calhoun anonymously expounded the doctrine of nullification, which held that states could prevent the enforcement of a federal law within their boundaries.
3. This term refers to the heads of the executive departments.
4. Laws passed by Southern state legislatures during Reconstruction, while Congress was out of session.
8. The "father of modern revivalism," Finney devised many techniques adopted by later revival preachers. He encouraged many women to participate actively in revival.
9. A confederation of labor unions founded in 1886, it was composed mainly of skilled craft unions.

A. Brain Trust
C. Bonus Army
E. Cabinet
G. Colonization
I. Bay of Pigs
K. Finney
M. Calhoun, John

B. Antifederalists
D. AFL
F. City Upon a Hill
H. American System
J. American System of Production
L. Black Codes

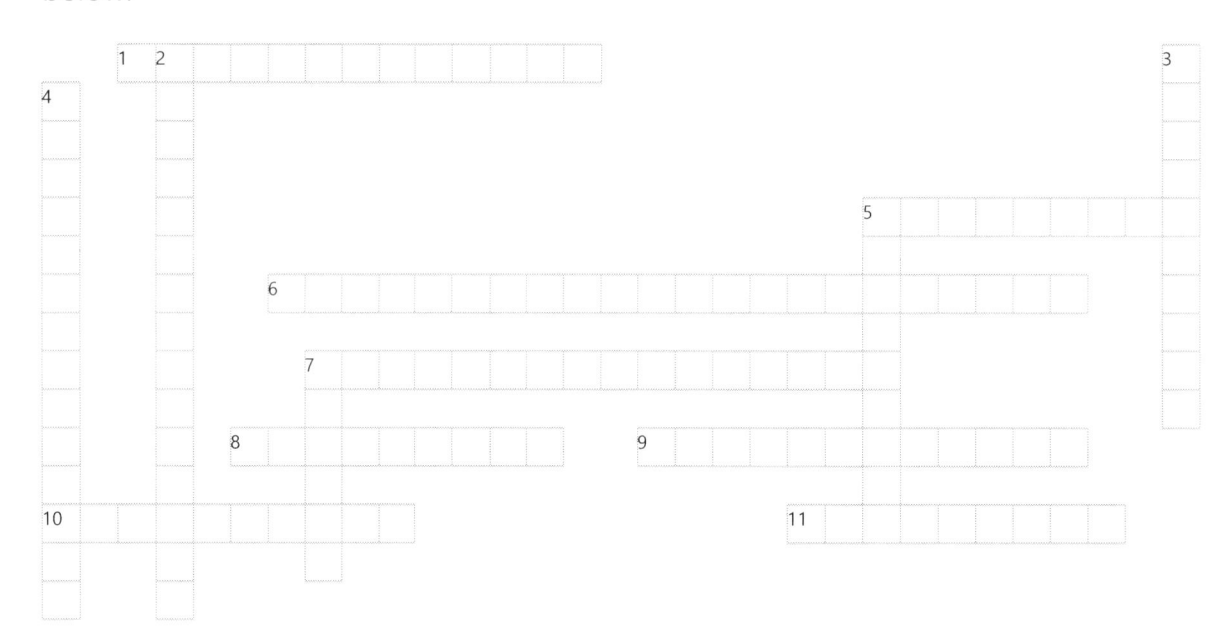

25. Using the Across and Down clues, write the correct words in the numbered grid below.

ACROSS

1. People who moved to the South following the Civil War and helped to bring Republican control of southern state governments during Reconstruction.
5. This appellation was used to refer to common soldiers serving in Union armies during the Civil War.
6. Notion that America houses biologically superior people and can spread democracy to the rest of the world.
7. An historic 1979 peace agreement negotiated between Egypt and Israel at the U.S. presidential retreat at Camp David, Maryland.
8. Thomas Jefferson's first vice president, who killed Alexander Hamilton in a duel in 1804.
9. The first ten amendments to the U.S. Constitution, which protect the rights of individuals from the powers of the national government.
10. In World War II, the alliance of German and Italy, and later Japan.
11. A failed plan to assassinate Cuban leader Fidel Castro and liberate Cuba with a trained military force of political exiles.

DOWN

2. These were opponents of the Constitution of 1787 who sought to continue the confederation of sovereign states and to keep power as close as possible to the people.
3. Laws passed by Southern state legislatures during Reconstruction, while Congress was out of session.
4. Immigrants who never intended to make the United States their home.
5. Group of unemployed World War I veterans who marched on Washington, D.C., in June 1932 to ask for immediate payment of their war pensions.
7. President, 1976. His progressive racial views reflected an emergent South less concerned with racial distinctions and more concerned with economic development and political power.

A. Camp David Accords
B. Birds of Passage
C. Black Codes
D. Aaron Burr
E. American Exceptionalism
F. Antifederalists
G. Bonus Army
H. Billy Yank
I. Bay of Pigs
J. Bill of Rights
K. Carpetbaggers
L. Axis Powers
M. Carter

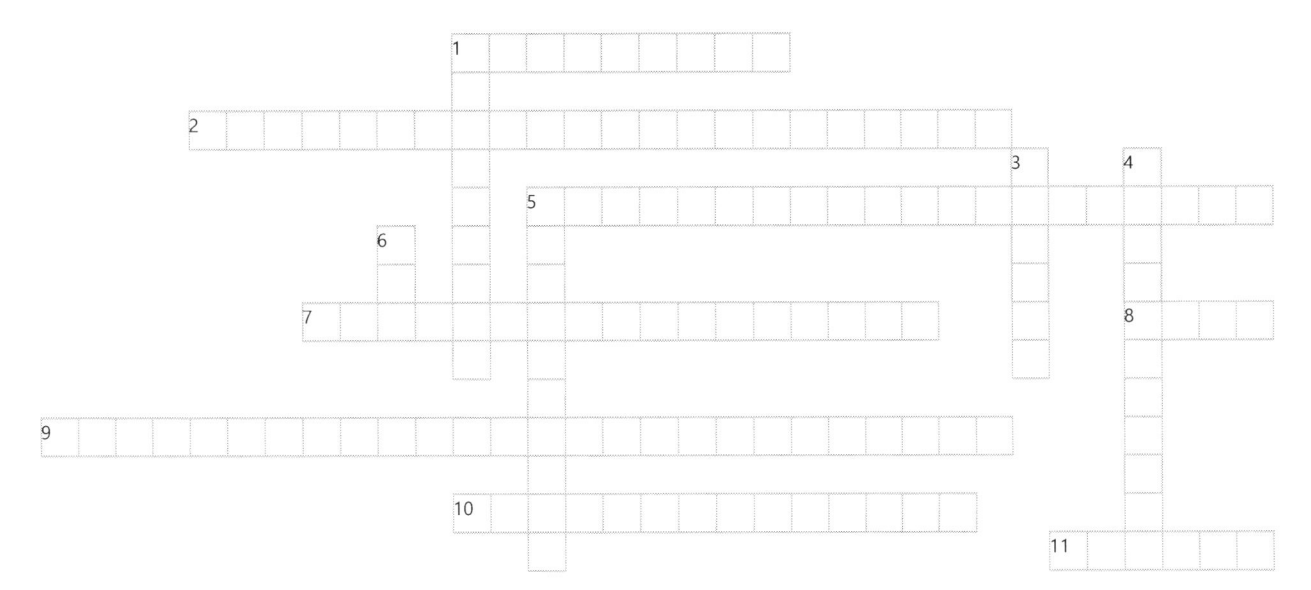

26. Using the Across and Down clues, write the correct words in the numbered grid below.

ACROSS

1. A failed plan to assassinate Cuban leader Fidel Castro and liberate Cuba with a trained military force of political exiles.
2. Notion that America houses biologically superior people and can spread democracy to the rest of the world.
5. Passed in 1798 designed to curb criticism of the federal government.
7. The process of transferring plants, animals, foods, diseases, wealth, and culture between Europe and the Americas.
8. June 6, 1944, the day Allied forces landed on the beaches of Normandy, in France, leading to the defeat of Germany.
9. The high cost of labor led to the establishment of a system of mass production through the manufacture of interchangeable parts.
10. A cultural style and artistic movement of the 1950s that rejected traditional American family life and material values and celebrated African-American culture.
11. President, 1976. His progressive racial views reflected an emergent South less concerned with racial distinctions and more concerned with economic development and political power.

DOWN

1. Group of unemployed World War I veterans who marched on Washington, D.C., in June 1932 to ask for immediate payment of their war pensions.
3. The "father of modern revivalism," Finney devised many techniques adopted by later revival preachers. He encouraged many women to participate actively in revival.
4. The free black author of An Appeal to the Colored Citizens of the World, which threatened violence if slavery was not abolished.
5. Literally meaning against the laws of human governance.
6. A confederation of labor unions founded in 1886, it was composed mainly of skilled craft unions.

A. Antinomian
B. Carter
C. Finney
D. David Walker
E. American System of Production
F. Alien and Sedition Acts
G. Bay of Pigs
H. AFL
I. D Day
J. Columbian Exchange
K. American Exceptionalism
L. Beat Generation
M. Bonus Army

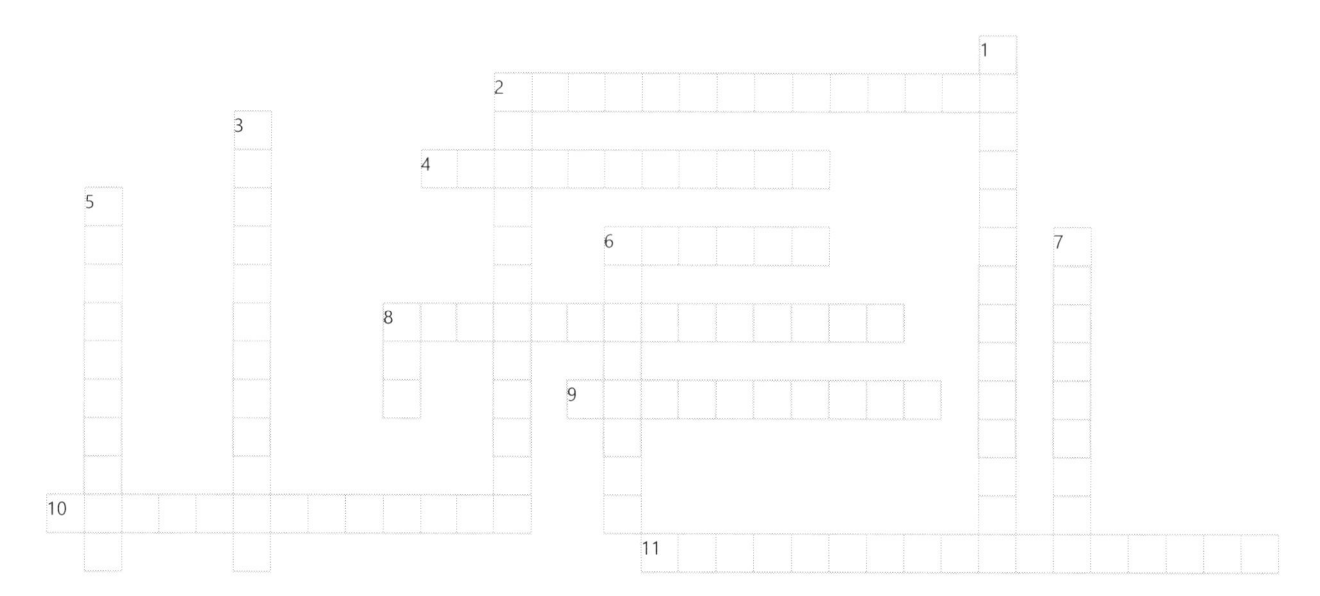

27. Using the Across and Down clues, write the correct words in the numbered grid below.

ACROSS

2. Immigrants who never intended to make the United States their home.
4. As vice president, Calhoun anonymously expounded the doctrine of nullification, which held that states could prevent the enforcement of a federal law within their boundaries.
6. President, 1976. His progressive racial views reflected an emergent South less concerned with racial distinctions and more concerned with economic development and political power.
8. Henry Clay's program for the national economy, which included a protective tariff to stimulate industry and a national bank to provide credit.
9. Literally meaning against the laws of human governance.
10. In World War I, Germany and Austria-Hungary and their allies.
11. During the early nineteenth century, a movement arose to end the death penalty.

DOWN

1. A cultural style and artistic movement of the 1950s that rejected traditional American family life and material values and celebrated African-American culture.
2. The first ten amendments to the U.S. Constitution, which protect the rights of individuals from the powers of the national government.
3. October 29, 1929, the day of the stock market crash that initiated the Great Depression.
5. A rallying cry for more militant blacks advocated by younger leaders beginning in the mid-1960s.
6. America's leading exponent of religious liberalism, Channing was one of the founders of American Unitarianism.
7. A failed plan to assassinate Cuban leader Fidel Castro and liberate Cuba with a trained military force of political exiles.
8. A confederation of labor unions founded in 1886, it was composed mainly of skilled craft unions.

A. Beat Generation
B. Calhoun, John
C. Bay of Pigs
D. Black Power
E. Capital Punishment
F. Birds of Passage
G. Bill of Rights
H. Channing
I. Antinomian
J. Carter
K. AFL
L. American System
M. Black Tuesday
N. Central Powers

28. Using the Across and Down clues, write the correct words in the numbered grid below.

ACROSS

4. An historic 1979 peace agreement negotiated between Egypt and Israel at the U.S. presidential retreat at Camp David, Maryland.
6. During the early nineteenth century, a movement arose to end the death penalty.
7. October 29,1929, the day of the stock market crash that initiated the Great Depression.
8. A confederation of labor unions founded in 1886, it was composed mainly of skilled craft unions.
10. Notion that America houses biologically superior people and can spread democracy to the rest of the world.
11. As vice president, Calhoun anonymously expounded the doctrine of nullification, which held that states could prevent the enforcement of a federal law within their boundaries.
12. Literally meaning against the laws of human governance.
13. This term refers to the heads of the executive departments.

DOWN

1. Close advisors to President Franklin Delano Roosevelt during the early days of his first term whose policy suggestions influenced much New Deal legislation.
2. Immigrants who never intended to make the United States their home.
3. Laws passed by Southern state legislatures during Reconstruction, while Congress was out of session.
5. This appellation was used to refer to common soldiers serving in Union armies during the Civil War.
7. A rallying cry for more militant blacks advocated by younger leaders beginning in the mid-1960s.
9. Emphasized the power and omnipotence of God and the importance of seeking to earn saving grace and salvation.

A. Camp David Accords
B. Billy Yank
C. AFL
D. Cabinet
E. Black Tuesday
F. Calhoun, John
G. Birds of Passage
H. Capital Punishment
I. Brain Trust
J. American Exceptionalism
K. Black Power
L. Antinomian
M. Calvinism
N. Black Codes

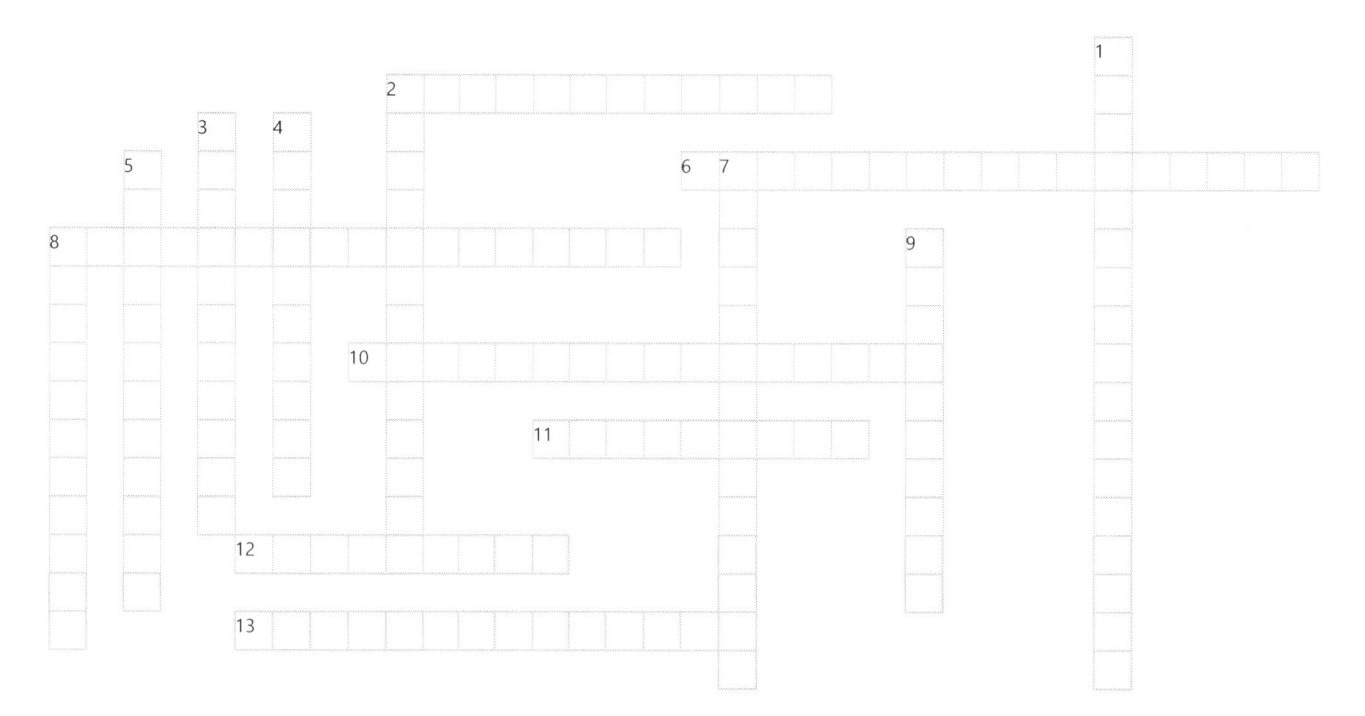

29. Using the Across and Down clues, write the correct words in the numbered grid below.

ACROSS

2. The effort to encourage masters to voluntarily emancipate their slaves and to resettle free blacks in Africa.
6. During the early nineteenth century, a movement arose to end the death penalty.
8. The process of transferring plants, animals, foods, diseases, wealth, and culture between Europe and the Americas.
10. An historic 1979 peace agreement negotiated between Egypt and Israel at the U.S. presidential retreat at Camp David, Maryland.
11. Emphasized the power and omnipotence of God and the importance of seeking to earn saving grace and salvation.
12. Group of unemployed World War I veterans who marched on Washington, D.C., in June 1932 to ask for immediate payment of their war pensions.
13. Immigrants who never intended to make the United States their home.

DOWN

1. The proclaimed foreign policy of Theodore Roosevelt, it was based on the proverb, "Speak softly and carry a big stick,".
2. People who moved to the South following the Civil War and helped to bring Republican control of southern state governments during Reconstruction.
3. This best-selling pamphlet by Thomas Paine, first published in 1776, denounced the British monarchy, called for American independence.
4. Close advisors to President Franklin Delano Roosevelt during the early days of his first term whose policy suggestions influenced much New Deal legislation.
5. The first ten amendments to the U.S. Constitution, which protect the rights of individuals from the powers of the national government.
7. Henry Clay's program for the national economy, which included a protective tariff to stimulate industry and a national bank to provide credit.
8. As vice president, Calhoun anonymously expounded the doctrine of nullification, which held that states could prevent the enforcement of a federal law within their boundaries.
9. In World War II, the alliance of German and Italy, and later Japan.

A. Calvinism
B. Bonus Army
C. Bill of Rights
D. Axis Powers
E. Capital Punishment
F. Birds of Passage
G. American System
H. Camp David Accords
I. Carpetbaggers
J. Common Sense
K. Columbian Exchange
L. Brain Trust
M. Colonization
N. Big Stick Diplomacy
O. Calhoun, John

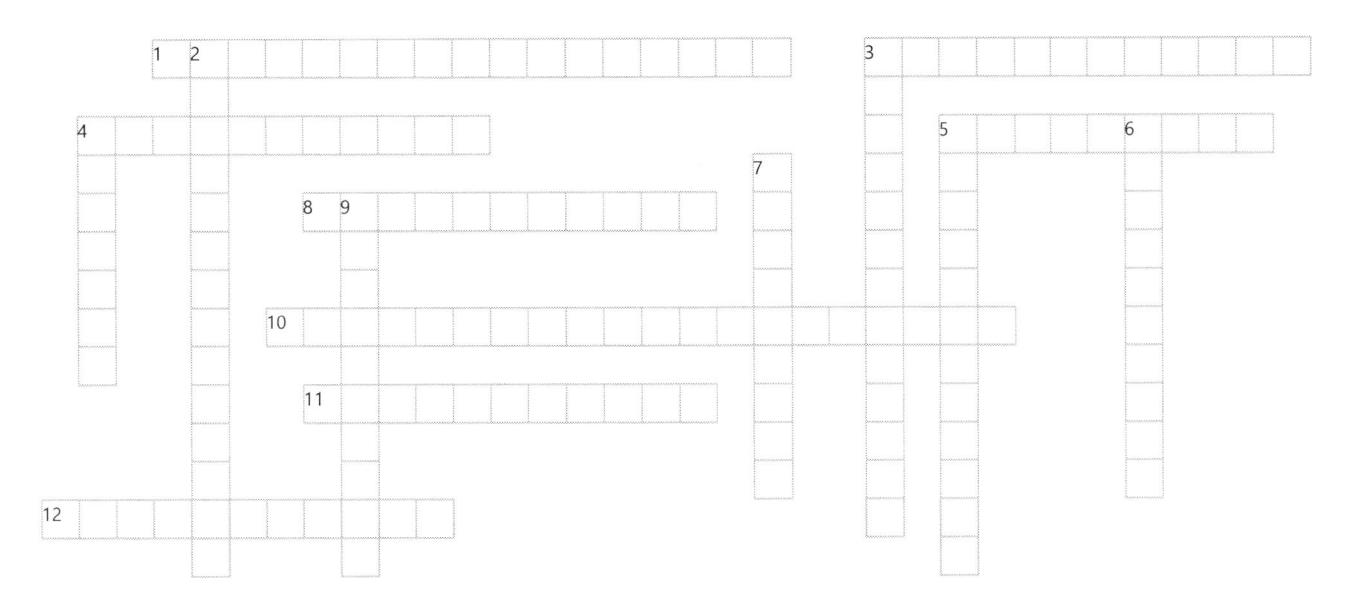

30. Using the Across and Down clues, write the correct words in the numbered grid below.

ACROSS

1. During the early nineteenth century, a movement arose to end the death penalty.
3. The effort to encourage masters to voluntarily emancipate their slaves and to resettle free blacks in Africa.
4. A movement founded to help the unemployed during the depression of the 1890s, it demanded that the federal government provide jobs and inflate the currency.
5. Group of unemployed World War I veterans who marched on Washington, D.C., in June 1932 to ask for immediate payment of their war pensions.
8. As vice president, Calhoun anonymously expounded the doctrine of nullification, which held that states could prevent the enforcement of a federal law within their boundaries.
10. Passed in 1798 designed to curb criticism of the federal government.
11. This best-selling pamphlet by Thomas Paine, first published in 1776, denounced the British monarchy, called for American independence.
12. Not every person living in the North during the Civil War favored making war against the Confederacy. Such persons came to be identified as Copperheads.

DOWN

2. Henry Clay's program for the national economy, which included a protective tariff to stimulate industry and a national bank to provide credit.
3. People who moved to the South following the Civil War and helped to bring Republican control of southern state governments during Reconstruction.
4. This term refers to the heads of the executive departments.
5. October 29,1929, the day of the stock market crash that initiated the Great Depression.
6. In World War II, the alliance of German and Italy, and later Japan.
7. Emphasized the power and omnipotence of God and the importance of seeking to earn saving grace and salvation.
9. Literally meaning against the laws of human governance.

A. Antinomian
B. Carpetbaggers
C. Calhoun, John
D. Alien and Sedition Acts
E. Axis Powers
F. Capital Punishment
G. Calvinism
H. Common Sense
I. Copperheads
J. Black Tuesday
K. Bonus Army
L. Coxey's Army
M. American System
N. Cabinet
O. Colonization

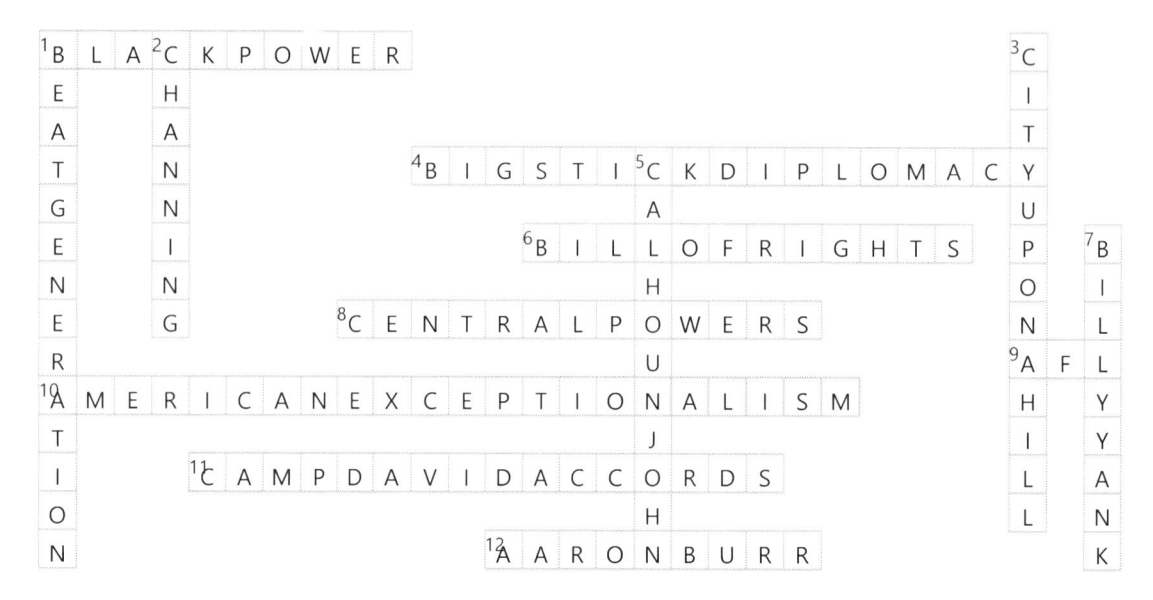

1. Using the Across and Down clues, write the correct words in the numbered grid below.

¹B	L	A	²C	K	P	O	W	E	R							³C	
E			H													I	
A			A													T	
T			N				⁴B	I	G	S	T	I	⁵C	K	D	I	P	L	O	M	A	C	Y
G			N									A				U	
E			I				⁶B	I	L	L	O	F	R	I	G	H	T	S	P	⁷B
N			N								H					O	I
E			G		⁸C	E	N	T	R	A	L	P	O	W	E	R	S	N	L
R									U						⁹A	F	L
¹⁰A	M	E	R	I	C	A	N	E	X	C	E	P	T	I	O	N	A	L	I	S	M	H	Y
T									J						I	Y
I			¹¹C	A	M	P	D	A	V	I	D	A	C	C	O	R	D	S	L	A
O									H						L	N
N				¹²A	A	R	O	N	B	U	R	R				K	

ACROSS

1. A rallying cry for more militant blacks advocated by younger leaders beginning in the mid-1960s.
4. The proclaimed foreign policy of Theodore Roosevelt, it was based on the proverb, "Speak softly and carry a big stick,".
6. The first ten amendments to the U.S. Constitution, which protect the rights of individuals from the powers of the national government.
8. In World War I, Germany and Austria-Hungary and their allies.
9. A confederation of labor unions founded in 1886, it was composed mainly of skilled craft unions.
10. Notion that America houses biologically superior people and can spread democracy to the rest of the world.
11. An historic 1979 peace agreement negotiated between Egypt and Israel at the U.S. presidential retreat at Camp David, Maryland.
12. Thomas Jefferson's first vice president, who killed Alexander Hamilton in a duel in 1804.

DOWN

1. A cultural style and artistic movement of the 1950s that rejected traditional American family life and material values and celebrated African-American culture.
2. America's leading exponent of religious liberalism, Channing was one of the founders of American Unitarianism.
3. Phrase from John Winthrop's sermon, "A Model of Christian Charity," in which he challenged his fellow Puritans to build a model, ideal community in America.
5. As vice president, Calhoun anonymously expounded the doctrine of nullification, which held that states could prevent the enforcement of a federal law within their boundaries.
7. This appellation was used to refer to common soldiers serving in Union armies during the Civil War.

A. City Upon a Hill
D. Central Powers
G. Channing
J. Aaron Burr
M. Bill of Rights

B. AFL
E. American Exceptionalism
H. Camp David Accords
K. Beat Generation

C. Billy Yank
F. Big Stick Diplomacy
I. Calhoun, John
L. Black Power

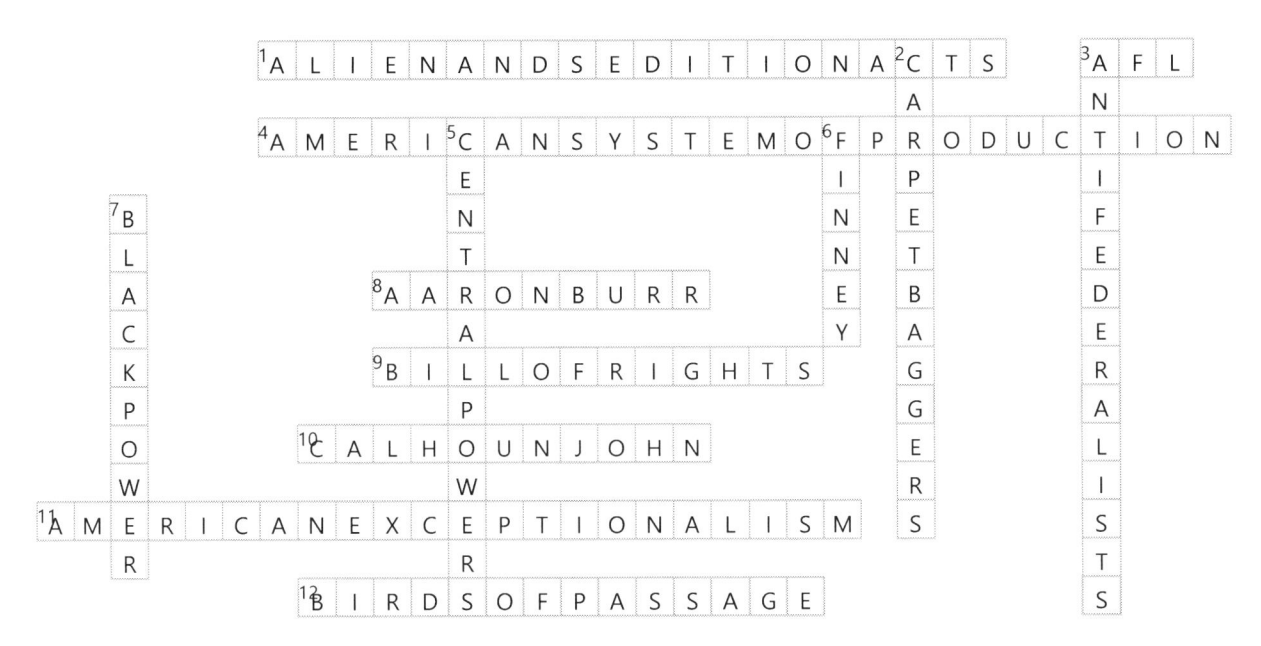

2. Using the Across and Down clues, write the correct words in the numbered grid below.

ACROSS

1. Passed in 1798 designed to curb criticism of the federal government.
3. A confederation of labor unions founded in 1886, it was composed mainly of skilled craft unions.
4. The high cost of labor led to the establishment of a system of mass production through the manufacture of interchangeable parts.
8. Thomas Jefferson's first vice president, who killed Alexander Hamilton in a duel in 1804.
9. The first ten amendments to the U.S. Constitution, which protect the rights of individuals from the powers of the national government.
10. As vice president, Calhoun anonymously expounded the doctrine of nullification, which held that states could prevent the enforcement of a federal law within their boundaries.
11. Notion that America houses biologically superior people and can spread democracy to the rest of the world.
12. Immigrants who never intended to make the United States their home.

DOWN

2. People who moved to the South following the Civil War and helped to bring Republican control of southern state governments during Reconstruction.
3. These were opponents of the Constitution of 1787 who sought to continue the confederation of sovereign states and to keep power as close as possible to the people.
5. In World War I, Germany and Austria-Hungary and their allies.
6. The "father of modern revivalism," Finney devised many techniques adopted by later revival preachers. He encouraged many women to participate actively in revival.
7. A rallying cry for more militant blacks advocated by younger leaders beginning in the mid-1960s.

A. Calhoun, John
C. Black Power
E. Bill of Rights
G. Carpetbaggers
I. Birds of Passage
K. AFL
M. American Exceptionalism

B. American System of Production
D. Antifederalists
F. Alien and Sedition Acts
H. Central Powers
J. Finney
L. Aaron Burr

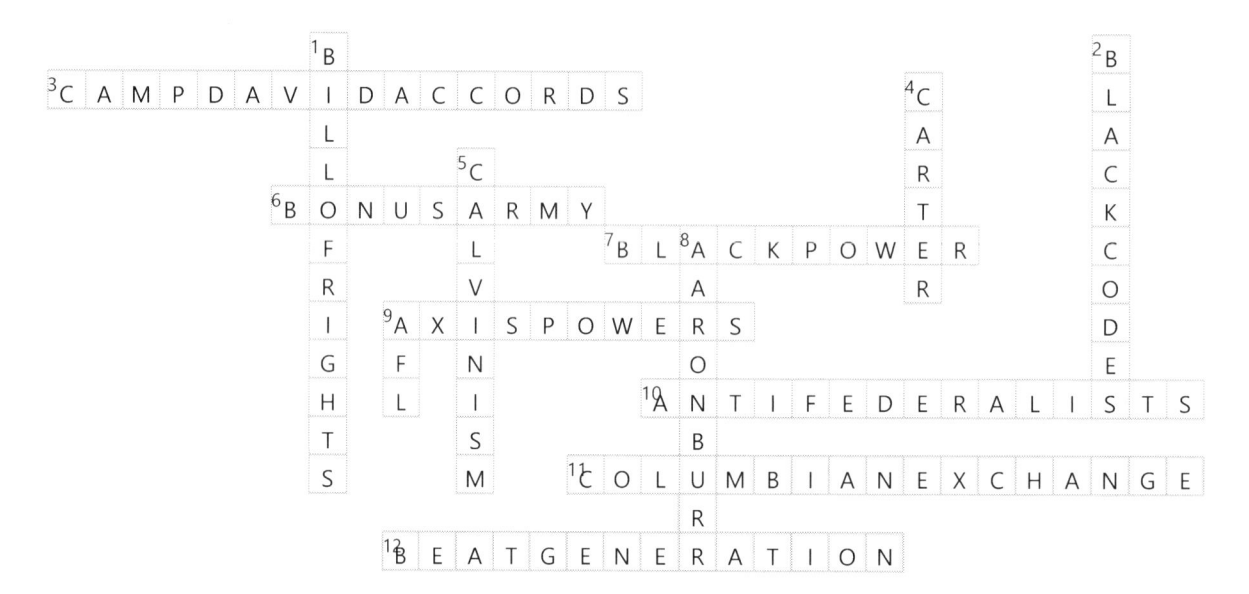

3. Using the Across and Down clues, write the correct words in the numbered grid below.

```
                    ¹B                                          ²B
³C A M P D A V I D A C C O R D S              ⁴C               L
                    L                          A               A
                    L         ⁵C               R               C
             ⁶B O N U S A R M Y                T               K
                    F         L      ⁷B L ⁸A C K P O W E R     C
                    R         V               A       R        O
                    I        ⁹A X I S P O W E R S              D
                    G         F     N          O               E
                    H         L     I     ¹⁰A N T I F E D E R A L I S T S
                    T         S     B
                    S         M    ¹¹C O L U M B I A N E X C H A N G E
                                    R
                              ¹²B E A T G E N E R A T I O N
```

ACROSS

3. An historic 1979 peace agreement negotiated between Egypt and Israel at the U.S. presidential retreat at Camp David, Maryland.
6. Group of unemployed World War I veterans who marched on Washington, D.C., in June 1932 to ask for immediate payment of their war pensions.
7. A rallying cry for more militant blacks advocated by younger leaders beginning in the mid-1960s.
9. In World War II, the alliance of German and Italy, and later Japan.
10. These were opponents of the Constitution of 1787 who sought to continue the confederation of sovereign states and to keep power as close as possible to the people.
11. The process of transferring plants, animals, foods, diseases, wealth, and culture between Europe and the Americas.
12. A cultural style and artistic movement of the 1950s that rejected traditional American family life and material values and celebrated African-American culture.

DOWN

1. The first ten amendments to the U.S. Constitution, which protect the rights of individuals from the powers of the national government.
2. Laws passed by Southern state legislatures during Reconstruction, while Congress was out of session.
4. President, 1976. His progressive racial views reflected an emergent South less concerned with racial distinctions and more concerned with economic development and political power.
5. Emphasized the power and omnipotence of God and the importance of seeking to earn saving grace and salvation.
8. Thomas Jefferson's first vice president, who killed Alexander Hamilton in a duel in 1804.
9. A confederation of labor unions founded in 1886, it was composed mainly of skilled craft unions.

A. Carter
D. Antifederalists
G. Columbian Exchange
J. Bill of Rights
M. AFL

B. Camp David Accords
E. Aaron Burr
H. Calvinism
K. Black Codes

C. Bonus Army
F. Black Power
I. Beat Generation
L. Axis Powers

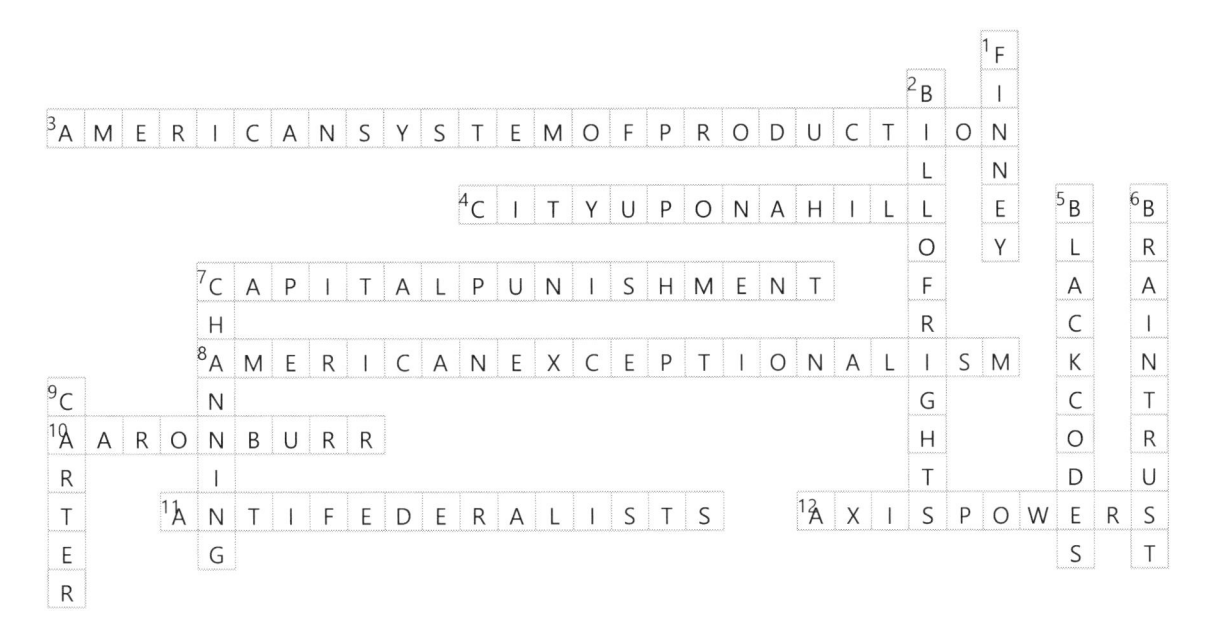

4. Using the Across and Down clues, write the correct words in the numbered grid below.

ACROSS

3. The high cost of labor led to the establishment of a system of mass production through the manufacture of interchangeable parts.
4. Phrase from John Winthrop's sermon, "A Model of Christian Charity," in which he challenged his fellow Puritans to build a model, ideal community in America.
7. During the early nineteenth century, a movement arose to end the death penalty.
8. Notion that America houses biologically superior people and can spread democracy to the rest of the world.
10. Thomas Jefferson's first vice president, who killed Alexander Hamilton in a duel in 1804.
11. These were opponents of the Constitution of 1787 who sought to continue the confederation of sovereign states and to keep power as close as possible to the people.
12. In World War II, the alliance of German and Italy, and later Japan.

A. Finney
C. American Exceptionalism
E. Channing
G. Aaron Burr
I. Capital Punishment
K. Bill of Rights
M. Axis Powers

DOWN

1. The "father of modern revivalism," Finney devised many techniques adopted by later revival preachers. He encouraged many women to participate actively in revival.
2. The first ten amendments to the U.S. Constitution, which protect the rights of individuals from the powers of the national government.
5. Laws passed by Southern state legislatures during Reconstruction, while Congress was out of session.
6. Close advisors to President Franklin Delano Roosevelt during the early days of his first term whose policy suggestions influenced much New Deal legislation.
7. America's leading exponent of religious liberalism, Channing was one of the founders of American Unitarianism.
9. President, 1976. His progressive racial views reflected an emergent South less concerned with racial distinctions and more concerned with economic development and political power.

B. Black Codes
D. Antifederalists
F. Carter
H. City Upon a Hill
J. Brain Trust
L. American System of Production

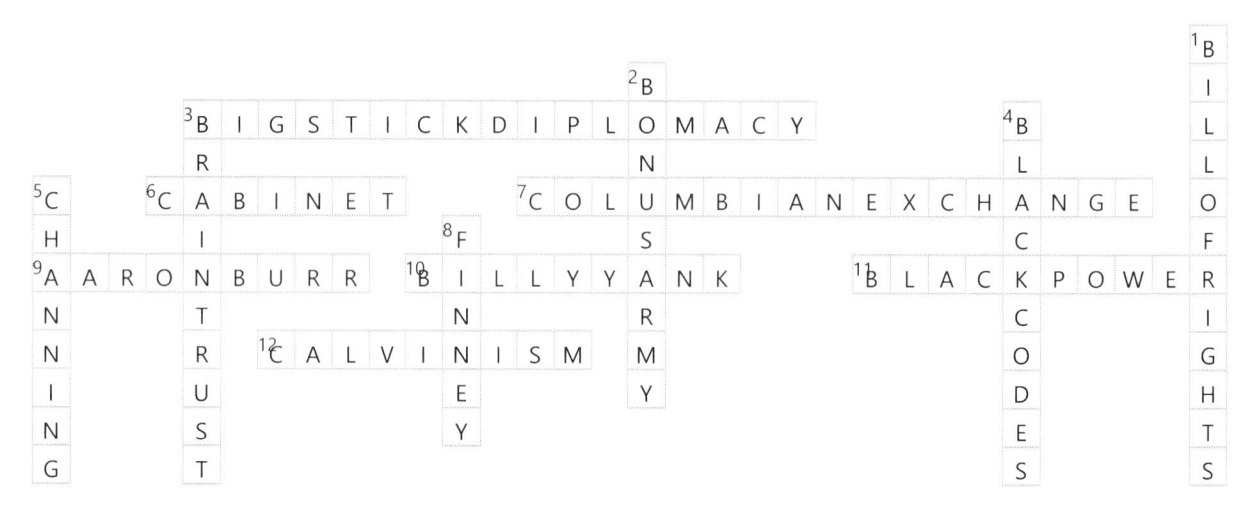

5. Using the Across and Down clues, write the correct words in the numbered grid below.

```
                        ²B                         ¹B
         ³B I G S T I C K D I P L O M A C Y    ⁴B    I
          R                 N                   L    L
⁵C   ⁶C A B I N E T      ⁷C O L U M B I A N E X C H A N G E
 H    I           ⁸F      S                     C    O
 ⁹A A R O N B U R R  ¹⁰B I L L Y Y A N K    ¹¹B L A C K P O W E R
  N   T           N       R                     C    I
  N   R     ¹²C A L V I N I S M                 O    G
  I   U           E       Y                     D    H
  N   S           Y                             E    T
  G   T                                         S    S
```

ACROSS

3. The proclaimed foreign policy of Theodore Roosevelt, it was based on the proverb, "Speak softly and carry a big stick,".
6. This term refers to the heads of the executive departments.
7. The process of transferring plants, animals, foods, diseases, wealth, and culture between Europe and the Americas.
9. Thomas Jefferson's first vice president, who killed Alexander Hamilton in a duel in 1804.
10. This appellation was used to refer to common soldiers serving in Union armies during the Civil War.
11. A rallying cry for more militant blacks advocated by younger leaders beginning in the mid-1960s.
12. Emphasized the power and omnipotence of God and the importance of seeking to earn saving grace and salvation.

DOWN

1. The first ten amendments to the U.S. Constitution, which protect the rights of individuals from the powers of the national government.
2. Group of unemployed World War I veterans who marched on Washington, D.C., in June 1932 to ask for immediate payment of their war pensions.
3. Close advisors to President Franklin Delano Roosevelt during the early days of his first term whose policy suggestions influenced much New Deal legislation.
4. Laws passed by Southern state legislatures during Reconstruction, while Congress was out of session.
5. America's leading exponent of religious liberalism, Channing was one of the founders of American Unitarianism.
8. The "father of modern revivalism," Finney devised many techniques adopted by later revival preachers. He encouraged many women to participate actively in revival.

A. Calvinism
D. Finney
G. Cabinet
J. Black Codes
M. Black Power

B. Billy Yank
E. Columbian Exchange
H. Brain Trust
K. Bill of Rights

C. Channing
F. Big Stick Diplomacy
I. Aaron Burr
L. Bonus Army

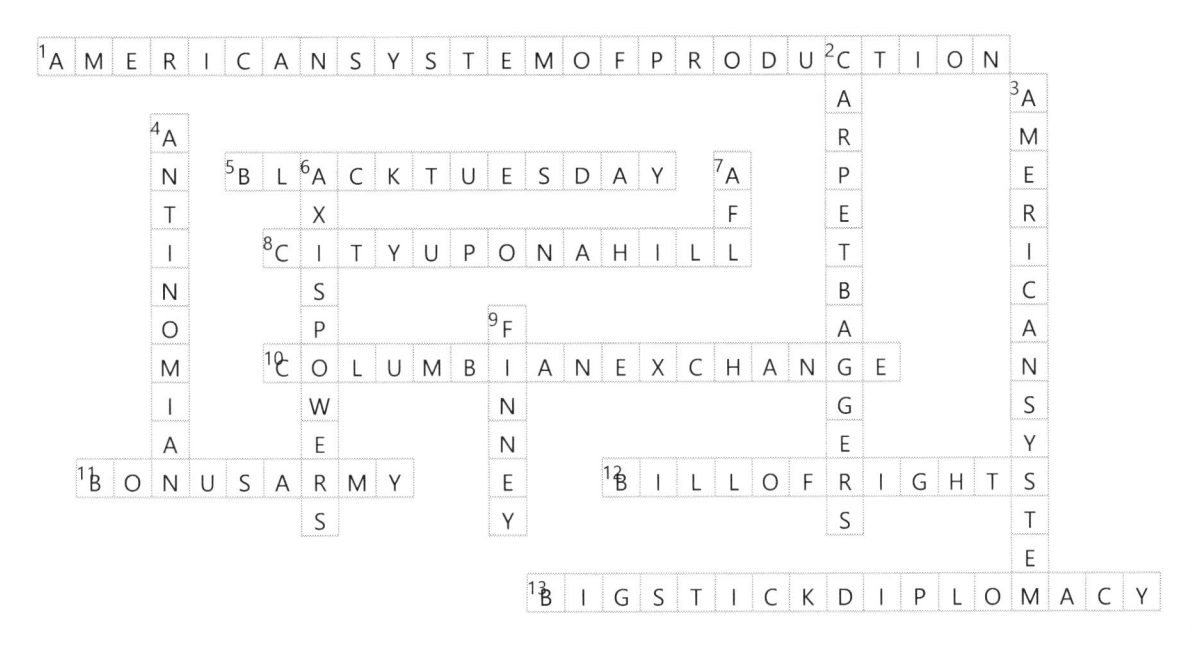

6. Using the Across and Down clues, write the correct words in the numbered grid below.

```
 1                                         2       3
 A M E R I C A N S Y S T E M O F P R O D U C T I O N
                                           A       A
       4                                   R       M
       A      5   6                        P       E
       N      B L A C K T U E S D A Y   7  E       R
       T          X                     A  T       I
       I        8 C I T Y U P O N A H I L L        C
       N          S                     L  B       A
       O          P              9         A       N
       M        10C O L U M B I A N E X C H A N G E
       I          W              N         G       S
       A          E              N         E       Y
     11B O N U S  A R M Y        E      12 B I L L O F R I G H T S
                  S              Y         S       T
                                                   E
                              13 B I G S T I C K D I P L O M A C Y
```

ACROSS

1. The high cost of labor led to the establishment of a system of mass production through the manufacture of interchangeable parts.
5. October 29,1929, the day of the stock market crash that initiated the Great Depression.
8. Phrase from John Winthrop's sermon, "A Model of Christian Charity," in which he challenged his fellow Puritans to build a model, ideal community in America.
10. The process of transferring plants, animals, foods, diseases, wealth, and culture between Europe and the Americas.
11. Group of unemployed World War I veterans who marched on Washington, D.C., in June 1932 to ask for immediate payment of their war pensions.
12. The first ten amendments to the U.S. Constitution, which protect the rights of individuals from the powers of the national government.
13. The proclaimed foreign policy of Theodore Roosevelt, it was based on the proverb, "Speak softly and carry a big stick,".

DOWN

2. People who moved to the South following the Civil War and helped to bring Republican control of southern state governments during Reconstruction.
3. Henry Clay's program for the national economy, which included a protective tariff to stimulate industry and a national bank to provide credit.
4. Literally meaning against the laws of human governance.
6. In World War II, the alliance of German and Italy, and later Japan.
7. A confederation of labor unions founded in 1886, it was composed mainly of skilled craft unions.
9. The "father of modern revivalism," Finney devised many techniques adopted by later revival preachers. He encouraged many women to participate actively in revival.

A. Black Tuesday
C. Finney
E. Axis Powers
G. AFL
I. Big Stick Diplomacy
K. City Upon a Hill
M. Bill of Rights

B. Bonus Army
D. Carpetbaggers
F. Columbian Exchange
H. American System of Production
J. American System
L. Antinomian

7. Using the Across and Down clues, write the correct words in the numbered grid below.

```
              ¹C            ²B E A T G E N E R A T I O N              ³B
⁴C I T Y U P O N A H I L L                                             L
              O                     ⁵A L I E N A N D S E D I T I O N A C T S
              O                         C                              C
              N       ⁶B L A C K C O D E S                             K
              I                         P                              T
              Z       ⁷C ⁸A L H O U N J O H N        ⁹B R A I N T R U S T
              A          F           W                                 E
              T          L           E              ¹⁰B I L L O F R I G H T S
              I                      R                                 D
           ¹¹B A Y O F P I G S                  ¹²B I R D S O F P A S S A G E
              N                                                        Y
```

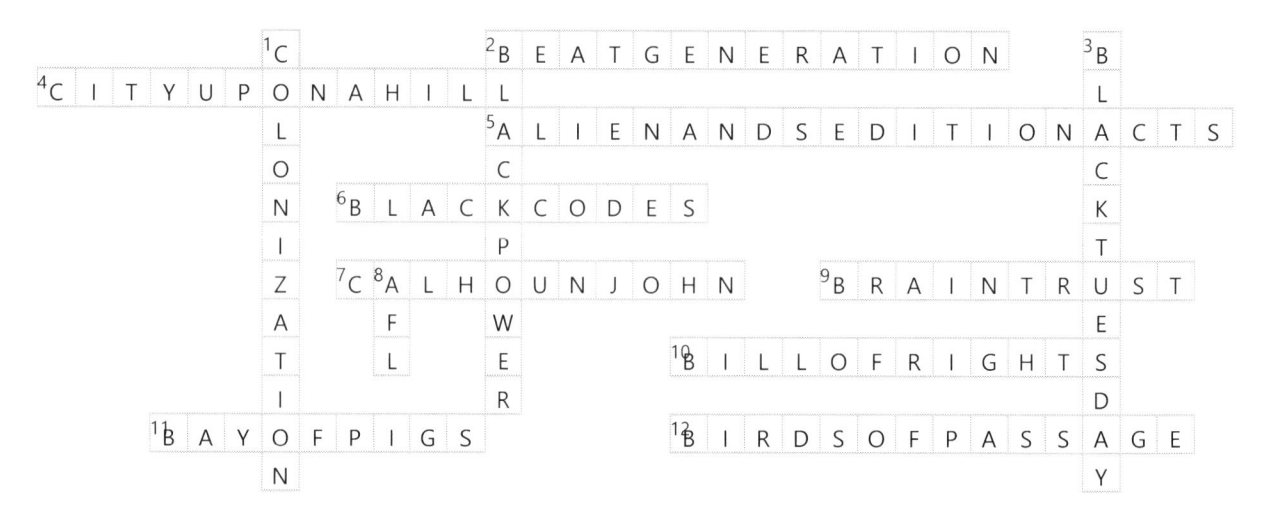

ACROSS

2. A cultural style and artistic movement of the 1950s that rejected traditional American family life and material values and celebrated African-American culture.
4. Phrase from John Winthrop's sermon, "A Model of Christian Charity," in which he challenged his fellow Puritans to build a model, ideal community in America.
5. Passed in 1798 designed to curb criticism of the federal government.
6. Laws passed by Southern state legislatures during Reconstruction, while Congress was out of session.
7. As vice president, Calhoun anonymously expounded the doctrine of nullification, which held that states could prevent the enforcement of a federal law within their boundaries.
9. Close advisors to President Franklin Delano Roosevelt during the early days of his first term whose policy suggestions influenced much New Deal legislation.
10. The first ten amendments to the U.S. Constitution, which protect the rights of individuals from the powers of the national government.
11. A failed plan to assassinate Cuban leader Fidel Castro and liberate Cuba with a trained military force of political exiles.
12. Immigrants who never intended to make the United States their home.

DOWN

1. The effort to encourage masters to voluntarily emancipate their slaves and to resettle free blacks in Africa.
2. A rallying cry for more militant blacks advocated by younger leaders beginning in the mid-1960s.
3. October 29, 1929, the day of the stock market crash that initiated the Great Depression.
8. A confederation of labor unions founded in 1886, it was composed mainly of skilled craft unions.

A. Birds of Passage
D. City Upon a Hill
G. Brain Trust
J. Bill of Rights
M. Black Tuesday

B. Beat Generation
E. Alien and Sedition Acts
H. Bay of Pigs
K. AFL

C. Calhoun, John
F. Black Codes
I. Colonization
L. Black Power

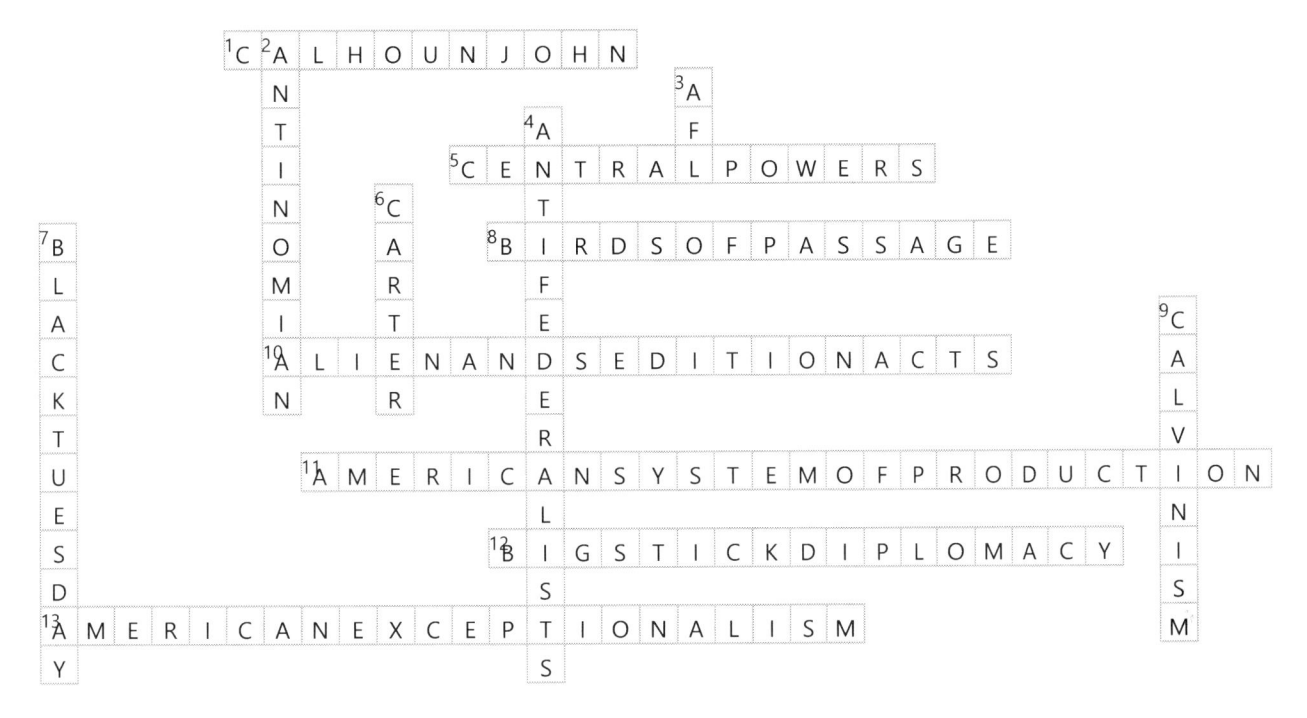

8. Using the Across and Down clues, write the correct words in the numbered grid below.

ACROSS

1. As vice president, Calhoun anonymously expounded the doctrine of nullification, which held that states could prevent the enforcement of a federal law within their boundaries.
5. In World War I, Germany and Austria-Hungary and their allies.
8. Immigrants who never intended to make the United States their home.
10. Passed in 1798 designed to curb criticism of the federal government.
11. The high cost of labor led to the establishment of a system of mass production through the manufacture of interchangeable parts.
12. The proclaimed foreign policy of Theodore Roosevelt, it was based on the proverb, "Speak softly and carry a big stick,".
13. Notion that America houses biologically superior people and can spread democracy to the rest of the world.

A. AFL
C. Birds of Passage
E. Carter
G. Calhoun, John
I. American Exceptionalism
K. Antinomian
M. Calvinism

DOWN

2. Literally meaning against the laws of human governance.
3. A confederation of labor unions founded in 1886, it was composed mainly of skilled craft unions.
4. These were opponents of the Constitution of 1787 who sought to continue the confederation of sovereign states and to keep power as close as possible to the people.
6. President, 1976. His progressive racial views reflected an emergent South less concerned with racial distinctions and more concerned with economic development and political power.
7. October 29,1929, the day of the stock market crash that initiated the Great Depression.
9. Emphasized the power and omnipotence of God and the importance of seeking to earn saving grace and salvation.

B. Big Stick Diplomacy
D. Antifederalists
F. Alien and Sedition Acts
H. American System of Production
J. Central Powers
L. Black Tuesday

9. Using the Across and Down clues, write the correct words in the numbered grid below.

```
         ¹C
²C       E           ³B L A C K C O D E S
⁴A N T I N O M I A N   ⁵B   I
 L       T             O   ⁶C O L O N I Z A T I O N
 H     ⁷B R            N   L
 O     L A             U   ⁸C O U R T P A C K I N G
 U     A L             S   F
 N     ⁹C A M P D ¹⁰A V I D A C C O R D S
 J     K   O   F       R   I
 O     P   W   L       M   G
 H     O   E           Y   H
 N     W   R               T
   ¹¹F I N N E Y   ¹²A L I E N A N D S E D I T I O N A C T S
       R
```

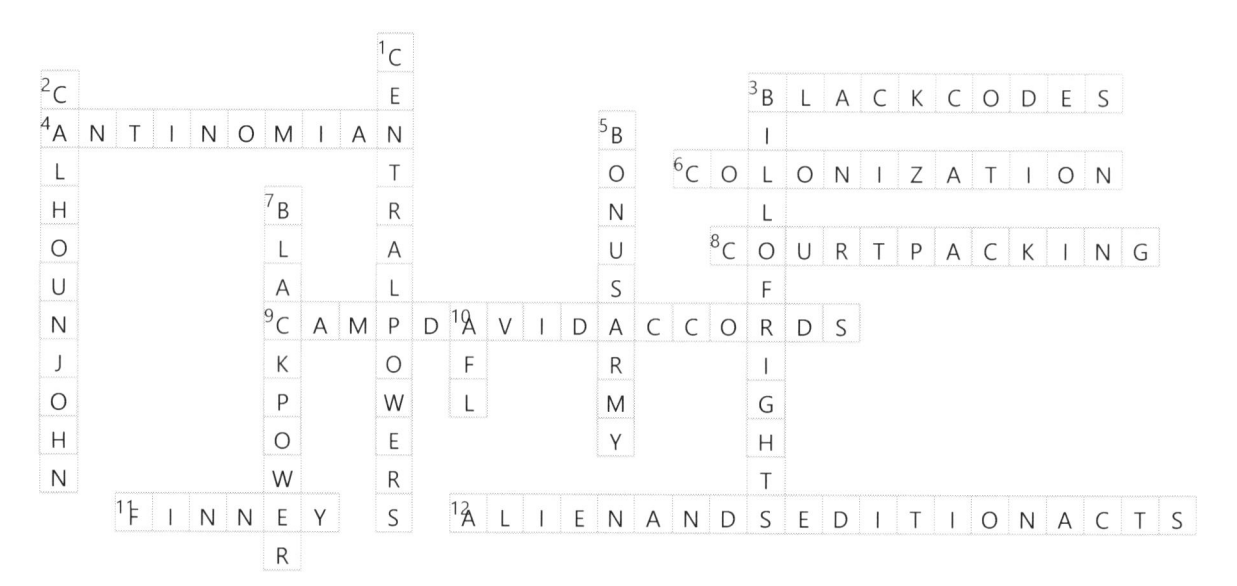

ACROSS

3. Laws passed by Southern state legislatures during Reconstruction, while Congress was out of session.
4. Literally meaning against the laws of human governance.
6. The effort to encourage masters to voluntarily emancipate their slaves and to resettle free blacks in Africa.
8. President Franklin Delano Roosevelt's controversial plan to appoint Supreme Court justices who were sympathetic to his views, by offering retirement benefits to the sitting justices.
9. An historic 1979 peace agreement negotiated between Egypt and Israel at the U.S. presidential retreat at Camp David, Maryland.
11. The "father of modern revivalism," Finney devised many techniques adopted by later revival preachers. He encouraged many women to participate actively in revival.
12. Passed in 1798 designed to curb criticism of the federal government.

DOWN

1. In World War I, Germany and Austria-Hungary and their allies.
2. As vice president, Calhoun anonymously expounded the doctrine of nullification, which held that states could prevent the enforcement of a federal law within their boundaries.
3. The first ten amendments to the U.S. Constitution, which protect the rights of individuals from the powers of the national government.
5. Group of unemployed World War I veterans who marched on Washington, D.C., in June 1932 to ask for immediate payment of their war pensions.
7. A rallying cry for more militant blacks advocated by younger leaders beginning in the mid-1960s.
10. A confederation of labor unions founded in 1886, it was composed mainly of skilled craft unions.

A. AFL
B. Bill of Rights
C. Black Power
D. Camp David Accords
E. Colonization
F. Calhoun, John
G. Alien and Sedition Acts
H. Central Powers
I. Court Packing
J. Antinomian
K. Finney
L. Black Codes
M. Bonus Army

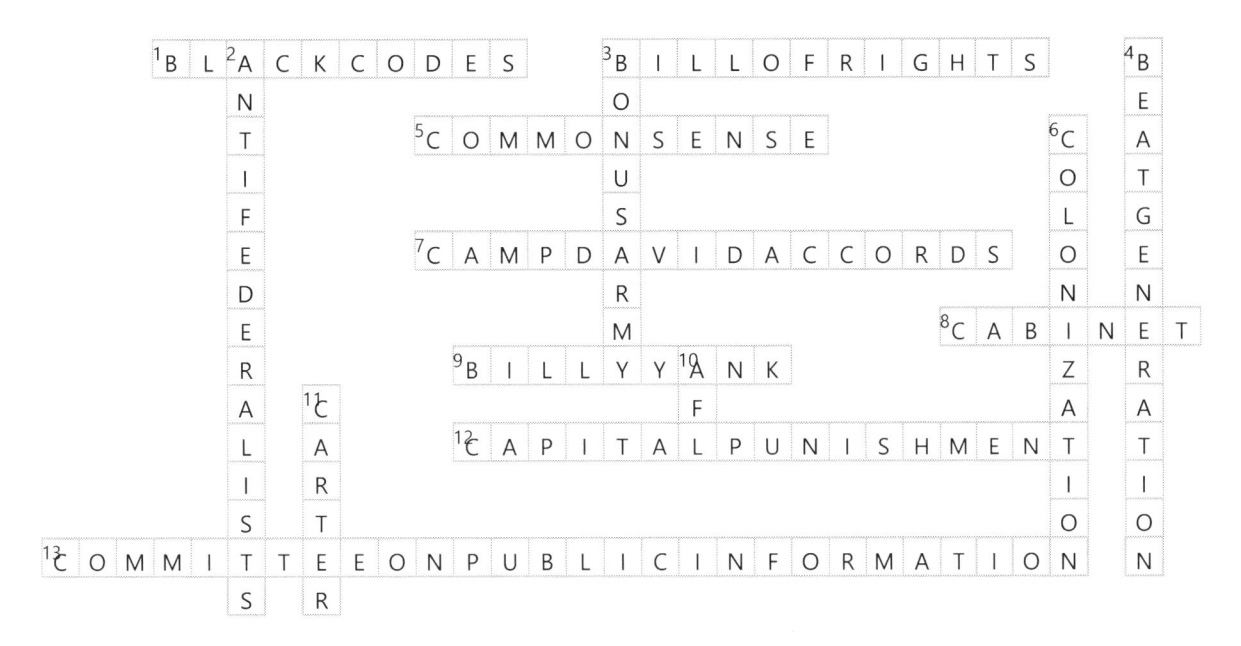

10. Using the Across and Down clues, write the correct words in the numbered grid below.

```
¹B L ²A C K C O D E S      ³B I L L O F R I G H T S       ⁴B
    N                       O                              E
    T          ⁵C O M M O N S E N S E          ⁶C          A
    I                       U                   O          T
    F                       S                   L          G
    E          ⁷C A M P D A V I D A C C O R D S O          E
    D                       R                   N          N
    E                       M                  ⁸C A B I N E T
    R          ⁹B I L L Y Y ¹⁰A N K             Z          R
    A    ¹¹C                F                   A          A
    L     A    ¹²C A P I T A L P U N I S H M E N T         T
    I     R                                     I          I
    S     T                                     O          O
¹³C O M M I T T E E O N P U B L I C I N F O R M A T I O N
    S     R
```

ACROSS

1. Laws passed by Southern state legislatures during Reconstruction, while Congress was out of session.
3. The first ten amendments to the U.S. Constitution, which protect the rights of individuals from the powers of the national government.
5. This best-selling pamphlet by Thomas Paine, first published in 1776, denounced the British monarchy, called for American independence.
7. An historic 1979 peace agreement negotiated between Egypt and Israel at the U.S. presidential retreat at Camp David, Maryland.
8. This term refers to the heads of the executive departments.
9. This appellation was used to refer to common soldiers serving in Union armies during the Civil War.
12. During the early nineteenth century, a movement arose to end the death penalty.
13. U.S. propaganda agency of World War I.

DOWN

2. These were opponents of the Constitution of 1787 who sought to continue the confederation of sovereign states and to keep power as close as possible to the people.
3. Group of unemployed World War I veterans who marched on Washington, D.C., in June 1932 to ask for immediate payment of their war pensions.
4. A cultural style and artistic movement of the 1950s that rejected traditional American family life and material values and celebrated African-American culture.
6. The effort to encourage masters to voluntarily emancipate their slaves and to resettle free blacks in Africa.
10. A confederation of labor unions founded in 1886, it was composed mainly of skilled craft unions.
11. President, 1976. His progressive racial views reflected an emergent South less concerned with racial distinctions and more concerned with economic development and political power.

A. Bill of Rights
C. Colonization
E. Antifederalists
G. Capital Punishment
I. Billy Yank
K. Common Sense
M. Bonus Army

B. Black Codes
D. Beat Generation
F. Cabinet
H. Carter
J. Committee on Public Information
L. Camp David Accords
N. AFL

11. Using the Across and Down clues, write the correct words in the numbered grid below.

```
¹B  L  A  ²C  K  C  O  D  E  S                    ³C
R         O                              ⁴A  N  T  I  F  E  D  E  R  A  L  I  S  T  S        ⁵C
A         L                                       N                                            I
I         O              ⁶A  F  L        ⁷C  A  P  I  T  A  L  P  U  N  I  S  H  M  E  N  T
N         N              A               R                                                    Y
T         I              R               ⁸B  L  A  C  K  T  U  E  S  D  A  Y                  U
R         Z        ⁹F    O               L                                                    P
U        ¹⁰A  M  E  R  I  C  A  N  S  Y  S  T  E  M  O  F  P  R  O  D  U  C  T  I  O  N        O
S         T        N     B               O                                                    N
T         I        N     U   ¹¹B  L  A  C  K  P  O  W  E  R                                    A
          O        E     R               E                                                    H
          N        Y     R   ¹²B  I  L  L  O  F  R  I  G  H  T  S                              I
                         S                                                                    L
                                                                                              L
```

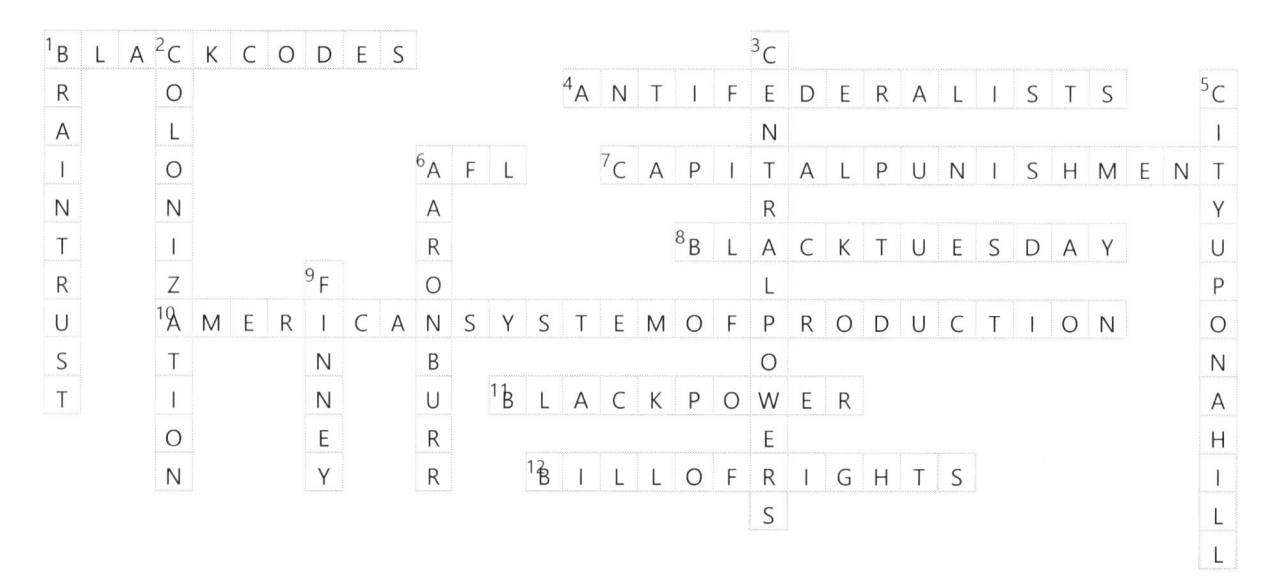

ACROSS

1. Laws passed by Southern state legislatures during Reconstruction, while Congress was out of session.
4. These were opponents of the Constitution of 1787 who sought to continue the confederation of sovereign states and to keep power as close as possible to the people.
6. A confederation of labor unions founded in 1886, it was composed mainly of skilled craft unions.
7. During the early nineteenth century, a movement arose to end the death penalty.
8. October 29,1929, the day of the stock market crash that initiated the Great Depression.
10. The high cost of labor led to the establishment of a system of mass production through the manufacture of interchangeable parts.
11. A rallying cry for more militant blacks advocated by younger leaders beginning in the mid-1960s.
12. The first ten amendments to the U.S. Constitution, which protect the rights of individuals from the powers of the national government.

DOWN

1. Close advisors to President Franklin Delano Roosevelt during the early days of his first term whose policy suggestions influenced much New Deal legislation.
2. The effort to encourage masters to voluntarily emancipate their slaves and to resettle free blacks in Africa.
3. In World War I, Germany and Austria-Hungary and their allies.
5. Phrase from John Winthrop's sermon, "A Model of Christian Charity," in which he challenged his fellow Puritans to build a model, ideal community in America.
6. Thomas Jefferson's first vice president, who killed Alexander Hamilton in a duel in 1804.
9. The "father of modern revivalism," Finney devised many techniques adopted by later revival preachers. He encouraged many women to participate actively in revival.

A. Bill of Rights
C. Brain Trust
E. Aaron Burr
G. American System of Production
I. Antifederalists
K. Colonization
M. City Upon a Hill

B. Finney
D. AFL
F. Capital Punishment
H. Black Codes
J. Central Powers
L. Black Tuesday
N. Black Power

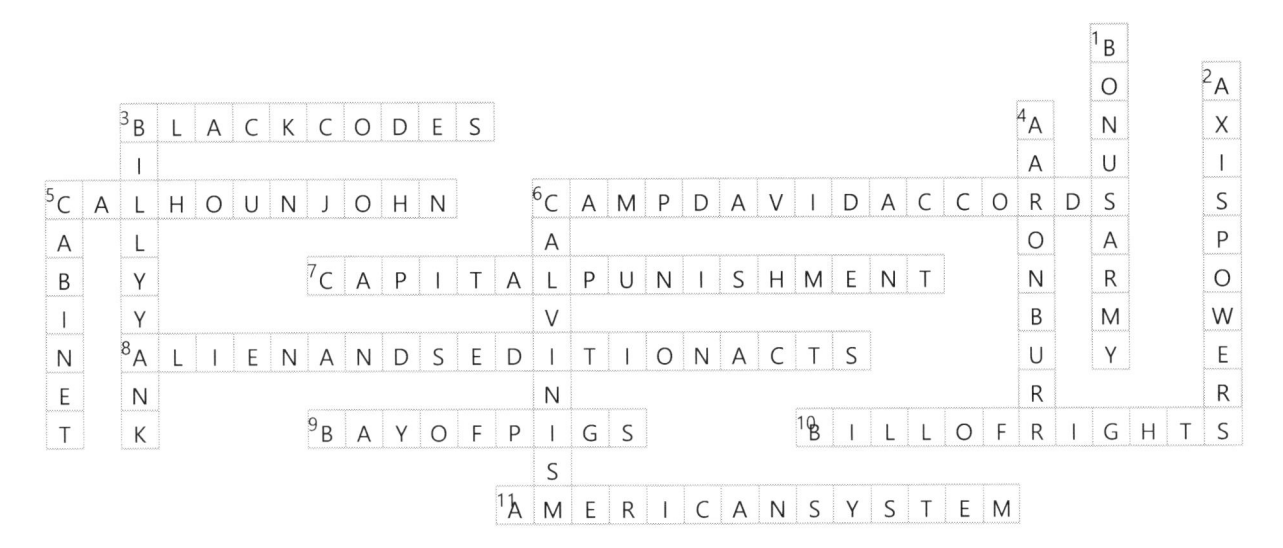

12. Using the Across and Down clues, write the correct words in the numbered grid below.

ACROSS

3. Laws passed by Southern state legislatures during Reconstruction, while Congress was out of session.
5. As vice president, Calhoun anonymously expounded the doctrine of nullification, which held that states could prevent the enforcement of a federal law within their boundaries.
6. An historic 1979 peace agreement negotiated between Egypt and Israel at the U.S. presidential retreat at Camp David, Maryland.
7. During the early nineteenth century, a movement arose to end the death penalty.
8. Passed in 1798 designed to curb criticism of the federal government.
9. A failed plan to assassinate Cuban leader Fidel Castro and liberate Cuba with a trained military force of political exiles.
10. The first ten amendments to the U.S. Constitution, which protect the rights of individuals from the powers of the national government.
11. Henry Clay's program for the national economy, which included a protective tariff to stimulate industry and a national bank to provide credit.

DOWN

1. Group of unemployed World War I veterans who marched on Washington, D.C., in June 1932 to ask for immediate payment of their war pensions.
2. In World War II, the alliance of German and Italy, and later Japan.
3. This appellation was used to refer to common soldiers serving in Union armies during the Civil War.
4. Thomas Jefferson's first vice president, who killed Alexander Hamilton in a duel in 1804.
5. This term refers to the heads of the executive departments.
6. Emphasized the power and omnipotence of God and the importance of seeking to earn saving grace and salvation.

A. Bonus Army
D. Black Codes
G. Billy Yank
J. Cabinet
M. Aaron Burr

B. American System
E. Calhoun, John
H. Bill of Rights
K. Capital Punishment
N. Bay of Pigs

C. Camp David Accords
F. Alien and Sedition Acts
I. Calvinism
L. Axis Powers

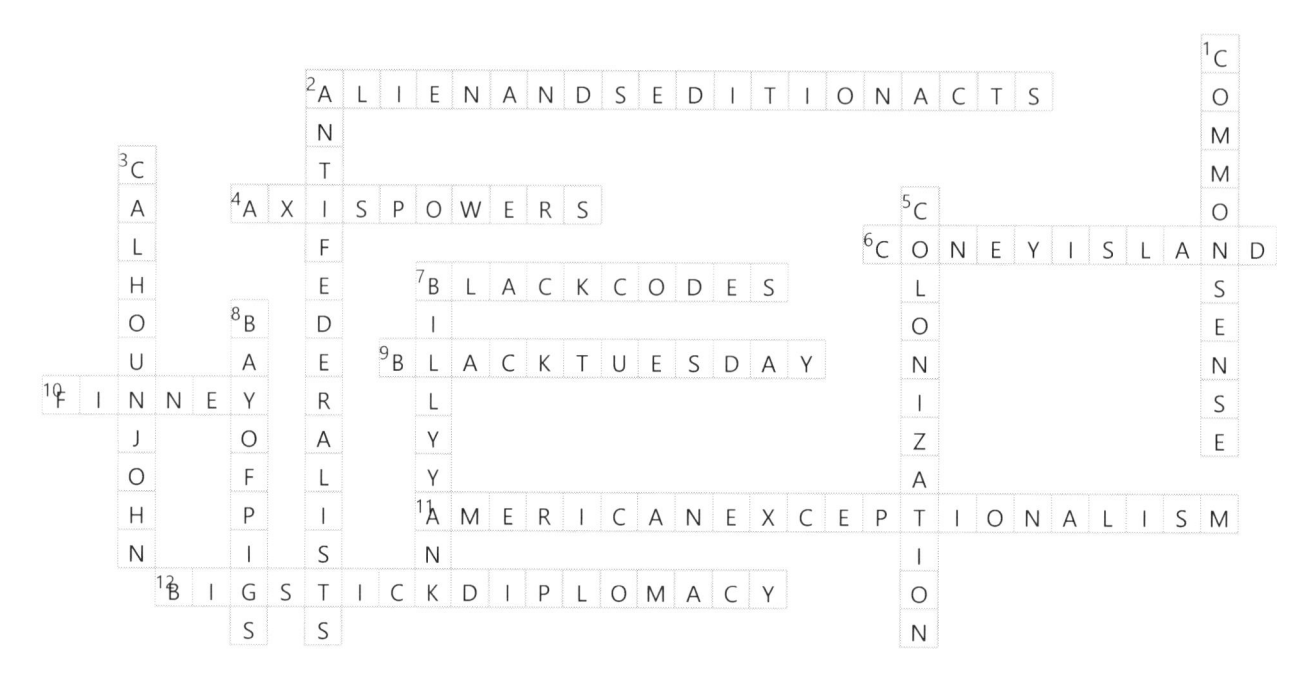

13. Using the Across and Down clues, write the correct words in the numbered grid below.

ACROSS

2. Passed in 1798 designed to curb criticism of the federal government.
4. In World War II, the alliance of German and Italy, and later Japan.
6. Popular site of New York amusement parks opening in 1890s, attracting working class Americans with rides and games celebrating abandon and instant gratification.
7. Laws passed by Southern state legislatures during Reconstruction, while Congress was out of session.
9. October 29, 1929, the day of the stock market crash that initiated the Great Depression.
10. The "father of modern revivalism," Finney devised many techniques adopted by later revival preachers. He encouraged many women to participate actively in revival.
11. Notion that America houses biologically superior people and can spread democracy to the rest of the world.
12. The proclaimed foreign policy of Theodore Roosevelt, it was based on the proverb, "Speak softly and carry a big stick,".

DOWN

1. This best-selling pamphlet by Thomas Paine, first published in 1776, denounced the British monarchy, called for American independence.
2. These were opponents of the Constitution of 1787 who sought to continue the confederation of sovereign states and to keep power as close as possible to the people.
3. As vice president, Calhoun anonymously expounded the doctrine of nullification, which held that states could prevent the enforcement of a federal law within their boundaries.
5. The effort to encourage masters to voluntarily emancipate their slaves and to resettle free blacks in Africa.
7. This appellation was used to refer to common soldiers serving in Union armies during the Civil War.
8. A failed plan to assassinate Cuban leader Fidel Castro and liberate Cuba with a trained military force of political exiles.

A. Coney Island
D. Axis Powers
G. Finney
J. American Exceptionalism
M. Common Sense
B. Alien and Sedition Acts
E. Antifederalists
H. Black Codes
K. Black Tuesday
N. Billy Yank
C. Bay of Pigs
F. Big Stick Diplomacy
I. Colonization
L. Calhoun, John

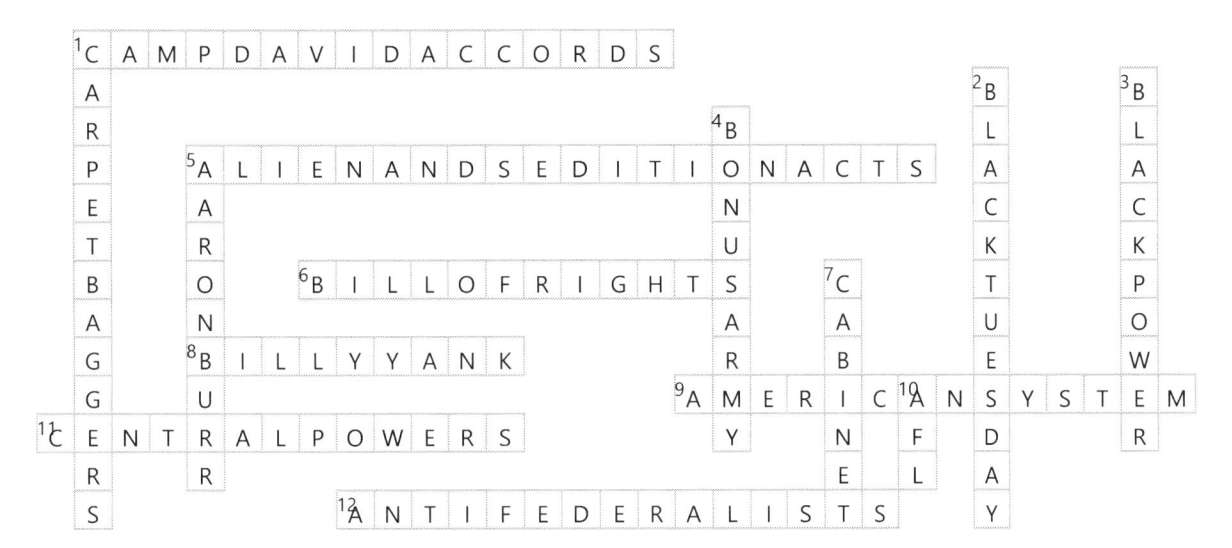

14. Using the Across and Down clues, write the correct words in the numbered grid below.

```
¹C A M P D A V I D A C C O R D S
 A                                          ²B        ³B
 R                        ⁴B                 L         L
 P   ⁵A L I E N A N D S E D I T I O N A C T S A         A
 E    A                    N                 C         C
 T    R                    U                 K         K
 B    O   ⁶B I L L O F R I G H T S  ⁷C       T         P
 A    N                    A        A        U         O
 G   ⁸B I L L Y Y A N K    R        B        E         W
 G    U                  ⁹A M E R I C ¹⁰A N S Y S T E M
¹¹C E N T R A L P O W E R S         N   F    D         R
 R    R                             E   L    A
 S            ¹²A N T I F E D E R A L I S T S Y
```

ACROSS

1. An historic 1979 peace agreement negotiated between Egypt and Israel at the U.S. presidential retreat at Camp David, Maryland.
5. Passed in 1798 designed to curb criticism of the federal government.
6. The first ten amendments to the U.S. Constitution, which protect the rights of individuals from the powers of the national government.
8. This appellation was used to refer to common soldiers serving in Union armies during the Civil War.
9. Henry Clay's program for the national economy, which included a protective tariff to stimulate industry and a national bank to provide credit.
11. In World War I, Germany and Austria-Hungary and their allies.
12. These were opponents of the Constitution of 1787 who sought to continue the confederation of sovereign states and to keep power as close as possible to the people.

DOWN

1. People who moved to the South following the Civil War and helped to bring Republican control of southern state governments during Reconstruction.
2. October 29, 1929, the day of the stock market crash that initiated the Great Depression.
3. A rallying cry for more militant blacks advocated by younger leaders beginning in the mid-1960s.
4. Group of unemployed World War I veterans who marched on Washington, D.C., in June 1932 to ask for immediate payment of their war pensions.
5. Thomas Jefferson's first vice president, who killed Alexander Hamilton in a duel in 1804.
7. This term refers to the heads of the executive departments.
10. A confederation of labor unions founded in 1886, it was composed mainly of skilled craft unions.

A. Camp David Accords
B. Aaron Burr
C. Bonus Army
D. Carpetbaggers
E. American System
F. Cabinet
G. Black Tuesday
H. Bill of Rights
I. Central Powers
J. Alien and Sedition Acts
K. Antifederalists
L. AFL
M. Black Power
N. Billy Yank

15. Using the Across and Down clues, write the correct words in the numbered grid below.

ACROSS

3. Notion that America houses biologically superior people and can spread democracy to the rest of the world.
7. A rallying cry for more militant blacks advocated by younger leaders beginning in the mid-1960s.
8. Close advisors to President Franklin Delano Roosevelt during the early days of his first term whose policy suggestions influenced much New Deal legislation.
9. The first ten amendments to the U.S. Constitution, which protect the rights of individuals from the powers of the national government.
10. The "father of modern revivalism," Finney devised many techniques adopted by later revival preachers. He encouraged many women to participate actively in revival.
11. Passed in 1798 designed to curb criticism of the federal government.
12. The process of transferring plants, animals, foods, diseases, wealth, and culture between Europe and the Americas.
13. President, 1976. His progressive racial views reflected an emergent South less concerned with racial distinctions and more concerned with economic development and political power.
14. Laws passed by Southern state legislatures during Reconstruction, while Congress was out of session.

DOWN

1. Group of unemployed World War I veterans who marched on Washington, D.C., in June 1932 to ask for immediate payment of their war pensions.
2. Immigrants who never intended to make the United States their home.
4. As vice president, Calhoun anonymously expounded the doctrine of nullification, which held that states could prevent the enforcement of a federal law within their boundaries.
5. In World War II, the alliance of German and Italy, and later Japan.
6. Literally meaning against the laws of human governance.

A. Brain Trust
B. Antinomian
C. American Exceptionalism
D. Finney
E. Black Power
F. Axis Powers
G. Alien and Sedition Acts
H. Bill of Rights
I. Carter
J. Birds of Passage
K. Columbian Exchange
L. Bonus Army
M. Black Codes
N. Calhoun, John

16. Using the Across and Down clues, write the correct words in the numbered grid below.

```
 ¹B  E  ²A  T  G  E  N  E  R  A  T  I  O  N
         X
     ³B  I  L  L  O  F  R  I  G  H  T  S
         S
 ⁴C  I  T  Y  U  P  O  N  A  H  I  L  L        ⁵C  A  M  P  D  A  V  I  D  A  ⁶C  C  O  R  D  S
         O                                                                    A
    ⁷C   W           ⁸B  L  A  C  K  C  O  D  E  S                            L
     H   E               A                                                     V
 ⁹A  M  E  R  I  C  A  N  S  Y  S  T  E  M  O  F  P  R  O  D  U  C  T  I  O  N
     N   S               O                                                     N
     N                   F                                    ¹⁰B  R  A  I  N  T  R  U  S  T
     I       ¹¹C  E  N  T  R  A  L  P  O  W  E  R  S           S
     N                   I                                      M
     G                   G
        ¹²A  L  I  E  N  A  N  D  S  E  D  I  T  I  O  N  A  C  T  S
```

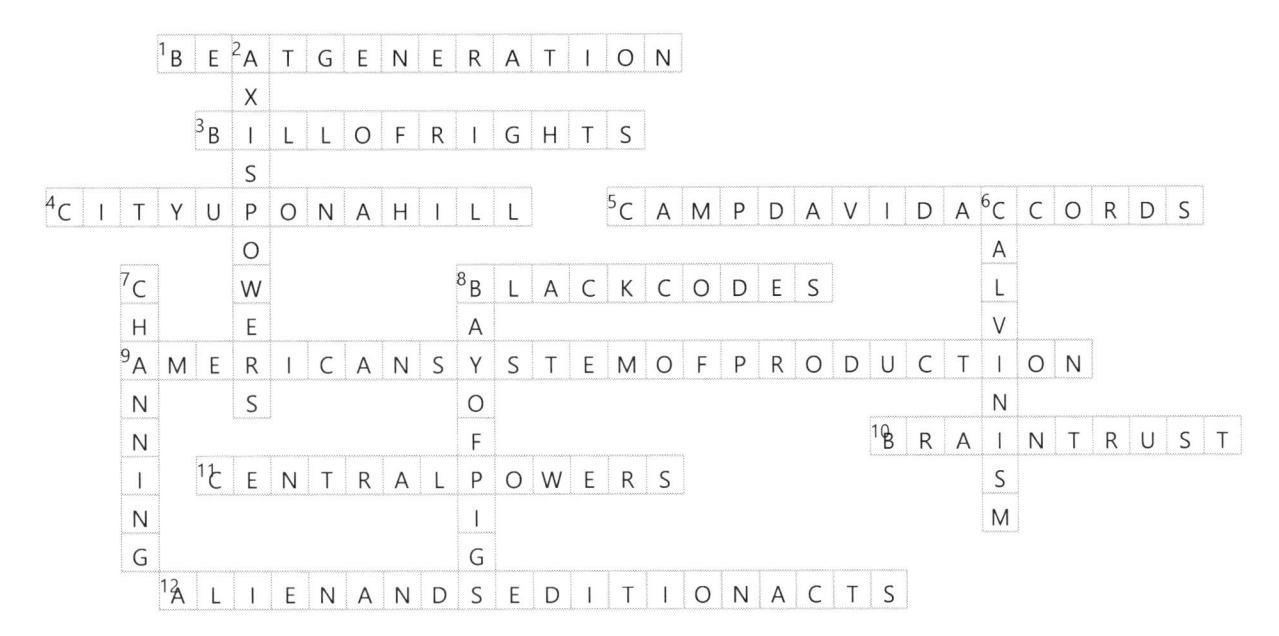

ACROSS

1. A cultural style and artistic movement of the 1950s that rejected traditional American family life and material values and celebrated African-American culture.
3. The first ten amendments to the U.S. Constitution, which protect the rights of individuals from the powers of the national government.
4. Phrase from John Winthrop's sermon, "A Model of Christian Charity," in which he challenged his fellow Puritans to build a model, ideal community in America.
5. An historic 1979 peace agreement negotiated between Egypt and Israel at the U.S. presidential retreat at Camp David, Maryland.
8. Laws passed by Southern state legislatures during Reconstruction, while Congress was out of session.
9. The high cost of labor led to the establishment of a system of mass production through the manufacture of interchangeable parts.
10. Close advisors to President Franklin Delano Roosevelt during the early days of his first term whose policy suggestions influenced much New Deal legislation.
11. In World War I, Germany and Austria-Hungary and their allies.
12. Passed in 1798 designed to curb criticism of the federal government.

DOWN

2. In World War II, the alliance of German and Italy, and later Japan.
6. Emphasized the power and omnipotence of God and the importance of seeking to earn saving grace and salvation.
7. America's leading exponent of religious liberalism, Channing was one of the founders of American Unitarianism.
8. A failed plan to assassinate Cuban leader Fidel Castro and liberate Cuba with a trained military force of political exiles.

A. Calvinism
C. Bill of Rights
E. City Upon a Hill
G. Channing
I. American System of Production
K. Beat Generation
M. Bay of Pigs

B. Brain Trust
D. Alien and Sedition Acts
F. Camp David Accords
H. Black Codes
J. Axis Powers
L. Central Powers

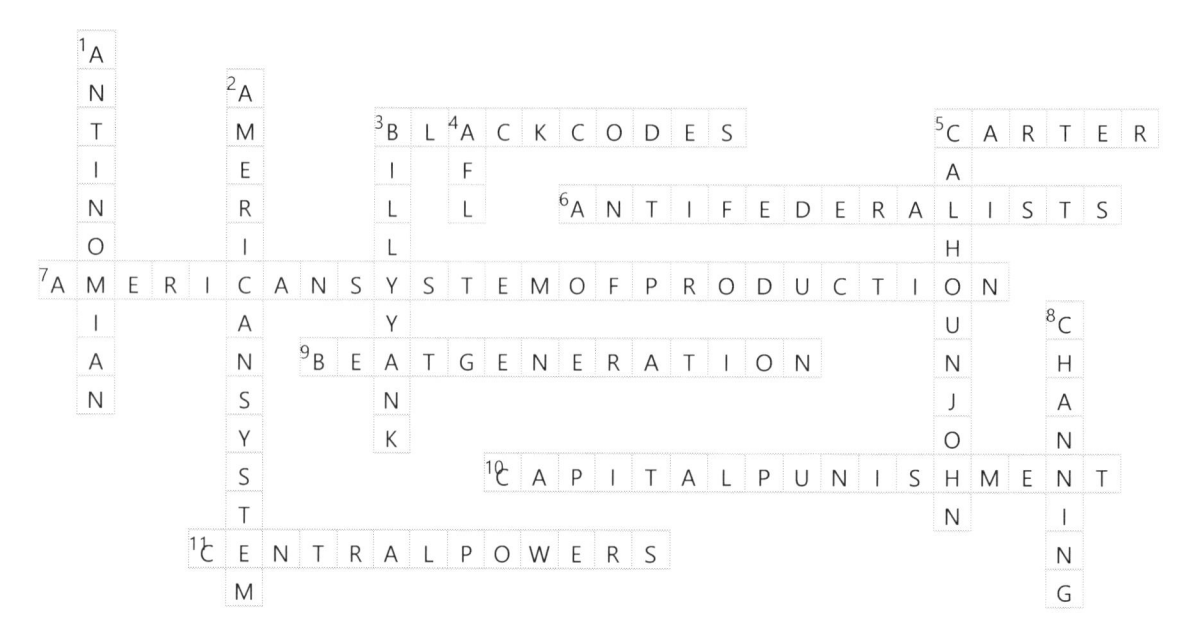

17. Using the Across and Down clues, write the correct words in the numbered grid below.

ACROSS

3. Laws passed by Southern state legislatures during Reconstruction, while Congress was out of session.
5. President, 1976. His progressive racial views reflected an emergent South less concerned with racial distinctions and more concerned with economic development and political power.
6. These were opponents of the Constitution of 1787 who sought to continue the confederation of sovereign states and to keep power as close as possible to the people.
7. The high cost of labor led to the establishment of a system of mass production through the manufacture of interchangeable parts.
9. A cultural style and artistic movement of the 1950s that rejected traditional American family life and material values and celebrated African-American culture.
10. During the early nineteenth century, a movement arose to end the death penalty.
11. In World War I, Germany and Austria-Hungary and their allies.

DOWN

1. Literally meaning against the laws of human governance.
2. Henry Clay's program for the national economy, which included a protective tariff to stimulate industry and a national bank to provide credit.
3. This appellation was used to refer to common soldiers serving in Union armies during the Civil War.
4. A confederation of labor unions founded in 1886, it was composed mainly of skilled craft unions.
5. As vice president, Calhoun anonymously expounded the doctrine of nullification, which held that states could prevent the enforcement of a federal law within their boundaries.
8. America's leading exponent of religious liberalism, Channing was one of the founders of American Unitarianism.

A. American System of Production
C. Central Powers
E. Channing
G. Black Codes
I. Calhoun, John
K. Capital Punishment
M. Antinomian

B. Carter
D. Antifederalists
F. AFL
H. American System
J. Billy Yank
L. Beat Generation

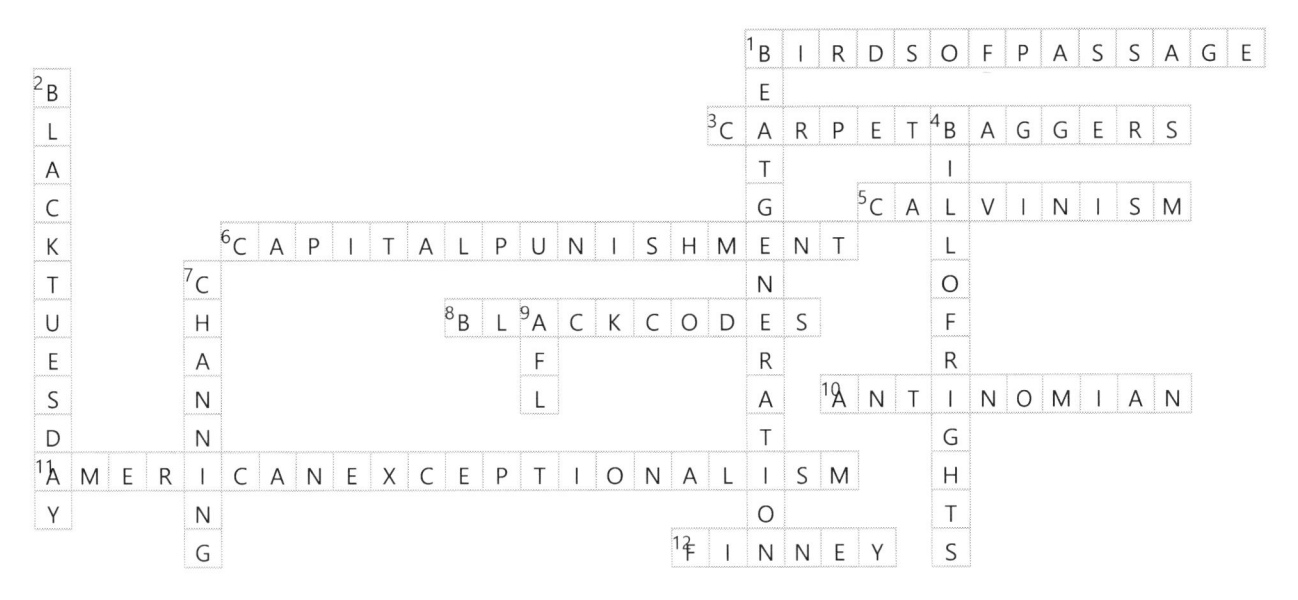

18. Using the Across and Down clues, write the correct words in the numbered grid below.

```
                                                  ¹B I R D S O F P A S S A G E
                                                   E
²B                                                ³C A R P E T ⁴B A G G E R S
 L                                                 T           I
 A                                                 G         ⁵C A L V I N I S M
 C                 ⁶C A P I T A L P U N I S H M E N T         L
 K                  ⁷C                             N          O
 T                   H            ⁸B L ⁹A C K C O D E S       F
 U                   A                 F           R          R
 E                   N                 L         ¹⁰A N T I N O M I A N
 S                   N                             T          G
 D                   I                                        H
¹¹A M E R I C A N E X C E P T I O N A L I S M                 T
 Y                   N                             O          S
                     G                           ¹²F I N N E Y
```

ACROSS

1. Immigrants who never intended to make the United States their home.
3. People who moved to the South following the Civil War and helped to bring Republican control of southern state governments during Reconstruction.
5. Emphasized the power and omnipotence of God and the importance of seeking to earn saving grace and salvation.
6. During the early nineteenth century, a movement arose to end the death penalty.
8. Laws passed by Southern state legislatures during Reconstruction, while Congress was out of session.
10. Literally meaning against the laws of human governance.
11. Notion that America houses biologically superior people and can spread democracy to the rest of the world.
12. The "father of modern revivalism," Finney devised many techniques adopted by later revival preachers. He encouraged many women to participate actively in revival.

DOWN

1. A cultural style and artistic movement of the 1950s that rejected traditional American family life and material values and celebrated African-American culture.
2. October 29, 1929, the day of the stock market crash that initiated the Great Depression.
4. The first ten amendments to the U.S. Constitution, which protect the rights of individuals from the powers of the national government.
7. America's leading exponent of religious liberalism, Channing was one of the founders of American Unitarianism.
9. A confederation of labor unions founded in 1886, it was composed mainly of skilled craft unions.

A. Carpetbaggers
D. Black Codes
G. Birds of Passage
J. American Exceptionalism
M. Antinomian

B. Channing
E. Beat Generation
H. AFL
K. Black Tuesday

C. Capital Punishment
F. Finney
I. Bill of Rights
L. Calvinism

71

19. Using the Across and Down clues, write the correct words in the numbered grid below.

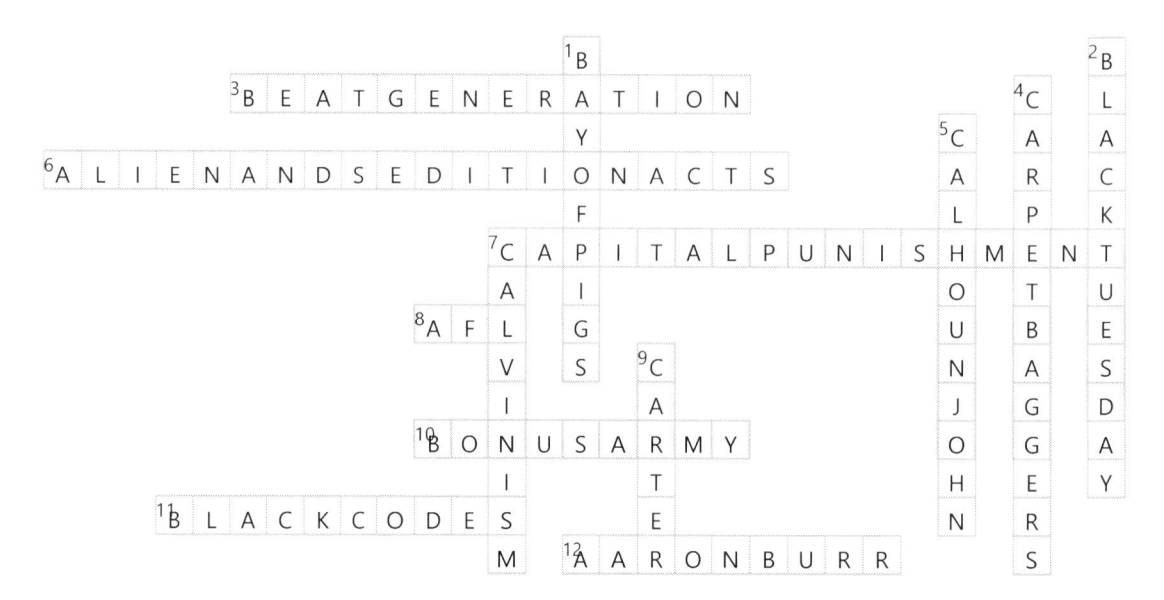

ACROSS

3. A cultural style and artistic movement of the 1950s that rejected traditional American family life and material values and celebrated African-American culture.
6. Passed in 1798 designed to curb criticism of the federal government.
7. During the early nineteenth century, a movement arose to end the death penalty.
8. A confederation of labor unions founded in 1886, it was composed mainly of skilled craft unions.
10. Group of unemployed World War I veterans who marched on Washington, D.C., in June 1932 to ask for immediate payment of their war pensions.
11. Laws passed by Southern state legislatures during Reconstruction, while Congress was out of session.
12. Thomas Jefferson's first vice president, who killed Alexander Hamilton in a duel in 1804.

DOWN

1. A failed plan to assassinate Cuban leader Fidel Castro and liberate Cuba with a trained military force of political exiles.
2. October 29, 1929, the day of the stock market crash that initiated the Great Depression.
4. People who moved to the South following the Civil War and helped to bring Republican control of southern state governments during Reconstruction.
5. As vice president, Calhoun anonymously expounded the doctrine of nullification, which held that states could prevent the enforcement of a federal law within their boundaries.
7. Emphasized the power and omnipotence of God and the importance of seeking to earn saving grace and salvation.
9. President, 1976. His progressive racial views reflected an emergent South less concerned with racial distinctions and more concerned with economic development and political power.

A. Beat Generation
B. AFL
C. Calvinism
D. Aaron Burr
E. Calhoun, John
F. Carter
G. Alien and Sedition Acts
H. Black Tuesday
I. Black Codes
J. Bay of Pigs
K. Capital Punishment
L. Carpetbaggers
M. Bonus Army

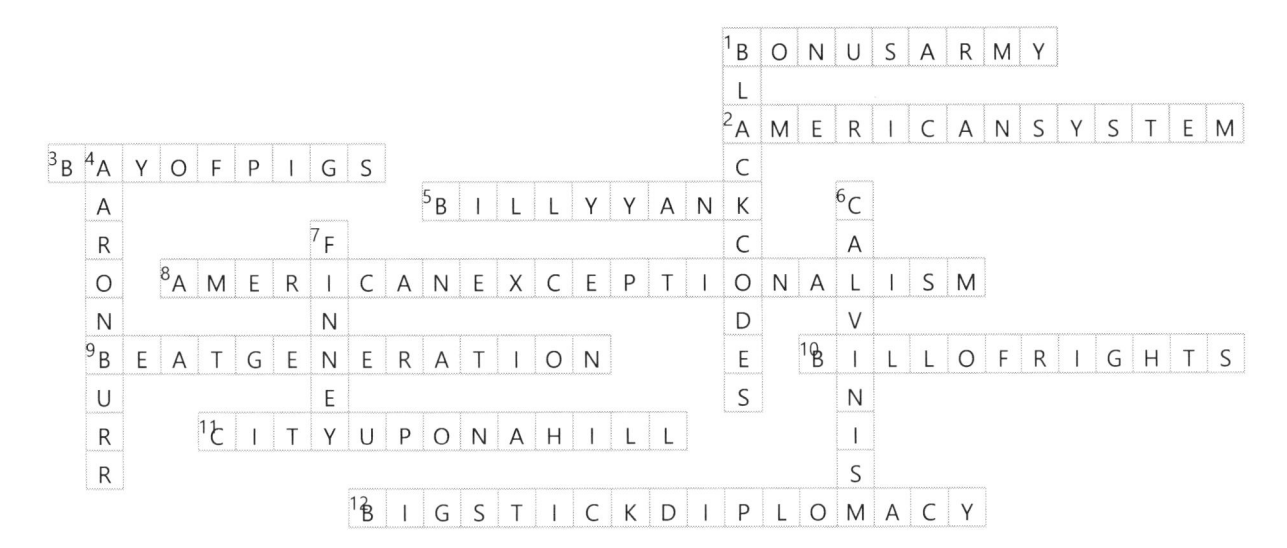

20. Using the Across and Down clues, write the correct words in the numbered grid below.

																	¹B	O	N	U	S	A	R	M	Y			
																	L											
																²A	M	E	R	I	C	A	N	S	Y	S	T	E	M
³B	⁴A	Y	O	F	P	I	G	S								C												
	A									⁵B	I	L	L	Y	Y	A	N	K		⁶C								
	R				⁷F											C				A								
	O	⁸A	M	E	R	I	C	A	N	E	X	C	E	P	T	I	O	N	A	L	I	S	M					
	N				N											D				V								
⁹B	E	A	T	G	E	N	E	R	A	T	I	O	N			E		¹⁰B	I	L	L	O	F	R	I	G	H	T	S
U					E											S		N										
R			¹¹C	I	T	Y	U	P	O	N	A	H	I	L	L			I										
R																		S										
			¹²B	I	G	S	T	I	C	K	D	I	P	L	O	M	A	C	Y									

ACROSS

1. Group of unemployed World War I veterans who marched on Washington, D.C., in June 1932 to ask for immediate payment of their war pensions.
2. Henry Clay's program for the national economy, which included a protective tariff to stimulate industry and a national bank to provide credit.
3. A failed plan to assassinate Cuban leader Fidel Castro and liberate Cuba with a trained military force of political exiles.
5. This appellation was used to refer to common soldiers serving in Union armies during the Civil War.
8. Notion that America houses biologically superior people and can spread democracy to the rest of the world.
9. A cultural style and artistic movement of the 1950s that rejected traditional American family life and material values and celebrated African-American culture.
10. The first ten amendments to the U.S. Constitution, which protect the rights of individuals from the powers of the national government.
11. Phrase from John Winthrop's sermon, "A Model of Christian Charity," in which he challenged his fellow Puritans to build a model, ideal community in America.
12. The proclaimed foreign policy of Theodore Roosevelt, it was based on the proverb, "Speak softly and carry a big stick,".

DOWN

1. Laws passed by Southern state legislatures during Reconstruction, while Congress was out of session.
4. Thomas Jefferson's first vice president, who killed Alexander Hamilton in a duel in 1804.
6. Emphasized the power and omnipotence of God and the importance of seeking to earn saving grace and salvation.
7. The "father of modern revivalism," Finney devised many techniques adopted by later revival preachers. He encouraged many women to participate actively in revival.

A. Beat Generation
D. City Upon a Hill
G. Black Codes
J. Big Stick Diplomacy
M. Bill of Rights

B. American Exceptionalism
E. Billy Yank
H. Calvinism
K. Bay of Pigs

C. Bonus Army
F. American System
I. Finney
L. Aaron Burr

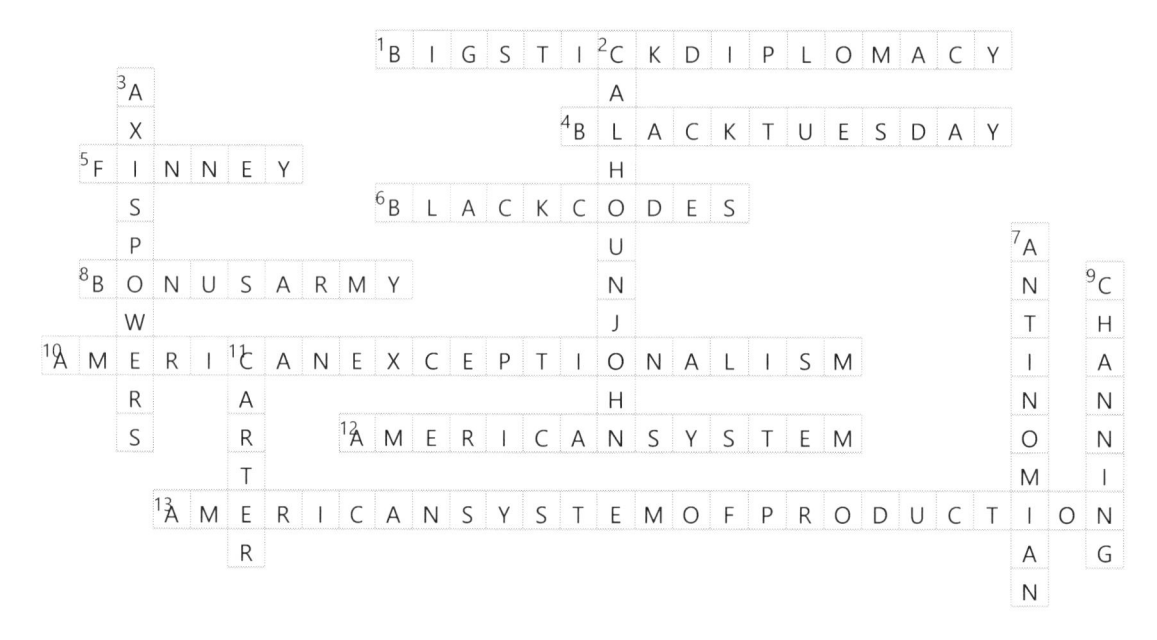

21. Using the Across and Down clues, write the correct words in the numbered grid below.

```
                          ¹B I G S T I ²C K D I P L O M A C Y
           ³A                           A
            X                          ⁴B L A C K T U E S D A Y
           ⁵F I N N E Y                 H
            S              ⁶B L A C K C O D E S
            P                           U              ⁷A
           ⁸B O N U S A R M Y           N              N     ⁹C
            W                           J              T      H
          ¹⁰A M E R I ¹¹C A N E X C E P T I O N A L I S M      A
            R         A                 H              N      N
            S         R       ¹²A M E R I C A N S Y S T E M    N
                      T                                O      I
                     ¹³A M E R I C A N S Y S T E M O F P R O D U C T I O N
                      R                                A      G
                                                       N
```

ACROSS

1. The proclaimed foreign policy of Theodore Roosevelt, it was based on the proverb, "Speak softly and carry a big stick,".
4. October 29,1929, the day of the stock market crash that initiated the Great Depression.
5. The "father of modern revivalism," Finney devised many techniques adopted by later revival preachers. He encouraged many women to participate actively in revival.
6. Laws passed by Southern state legislatures during Reconstruction, while Congress was out of session.
8. Group of unemployed World War I veterans who marched on Washington, D.C., in June 1932 to ask for immediate payment of their war pensions.
10. Notion that America houses biologically superior people and can spread democracy to the rest of the world.
12. Henry Clay's program for the national economy, which included a protective tariff to stimulate industry and a national bank to provide credit.
13. The high cost of labor led to the establishment of a system of mass production through the manufacture of interchangeable parts.

DOWN

2. As vice president, Calhoun anonymously expounded the doctrine of nullification, which held that states could prevent the enforcement of a federal law within their boundaries.
3. In World War II, the alliance of German and Italy, and later Japan.
7. Literally meaning against the laws of human governance.
9. America's leading exponent of religious liberalism, Channing was one of the founders of American Unitarianism.
11. President, 1976. His progressive racial views reflected an emergent South less concerned with racial distinctions and more concerned with economic development and political power.

A. American System of Production
C. Channing
E. Finney
G. American Exceptionalism
I. Carter
K. Antinomian
M. Black Codes

B. American System
D. Calhoun, John
F. Bonus Army
H. Axis Powers
J. Big Stick Diplomacy
L. Black Tuesday

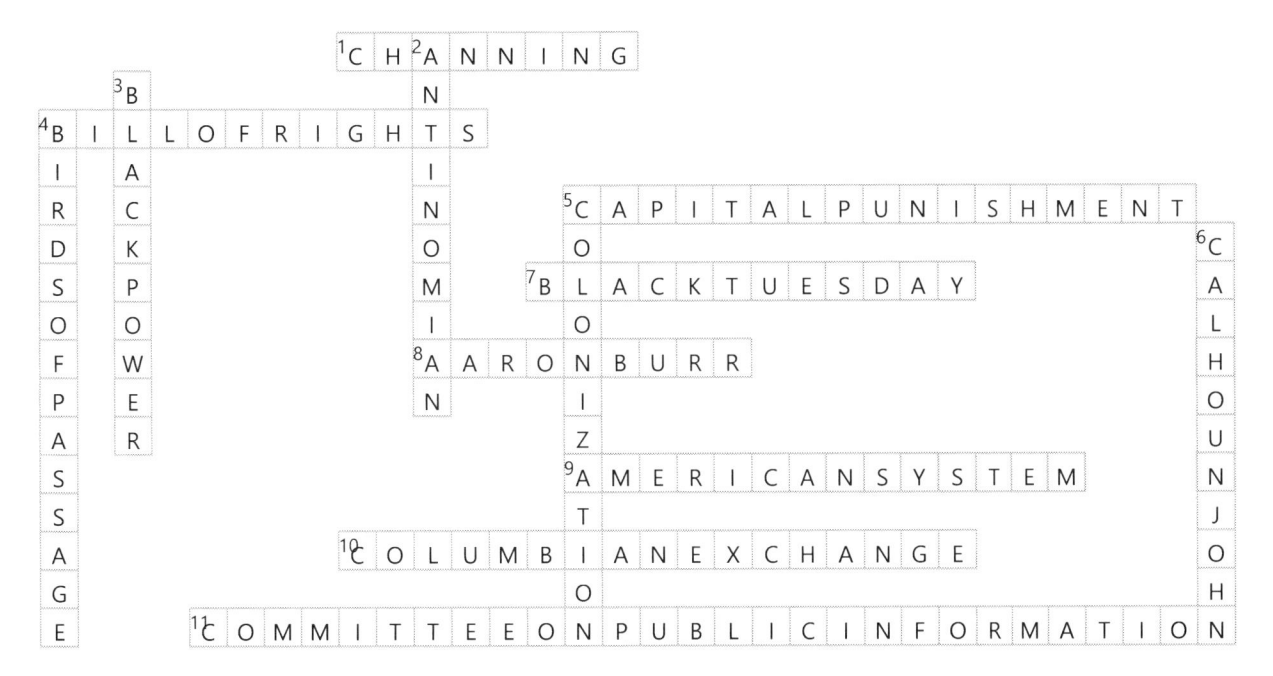

22. Using the Across and Down clues, write the correct words in the numbered grid below.

```
            ¹C  H  ²A  N  N  I  N  G
       ³B              N
  ⁴B I L L O F R I G H T S
   I   A               I
   R   C               N      ⁵C A P I T A L P U N I S H M E N T
   D   K               O       O                              ⁶C
   S   P               M   ⁷B  L A C K T U E S D A Y          A
   O   O               I       O                              L
   F   W               ⁸A A R  O N B U R R                    H
   P   E               N       I                              O
   A   R                       Z                              U
   S                           ⁹A M E R I C A N S Y S T E M   N
   S                           T                              J
   A                   ¹⁰C O L U M B I A N E X C H A N G E    O
   G                           O                              H
   E               ¹¹C O M M I T T E E O N P U B L I C I N F O R M A T I O N
```

ACROSS

1. America's leading exponent of religious liberalism, Channing was one of the founders of American Unitarianism.
4. The first ten amendments to the U.S. Constitution, which protect the rights of individuals from the powers of the national government.
5. During the early nineteenth century, a movement arose to end the death penalty.
7. October 29, 1929, the day of the stock market crash that initiated the Great Depression.
8. Thomas Jefferson's first vice president, who killed Alexander Hamilton in a duel in 1804.
9. Henry Clay's program for the national economy, which included a protective tariff to stimulate industry and a national bank to provide credit.
10. The process of transferring plants, animals, foods, diseases, wealth, and culture between Europe and the Americas.
11. U.S. propaganda agency of World War I.

DOWN

2. Literally meaning against the laws of human governance.
3. A rallying cry for more militant blacks advocated by younger leaders beginning in the mid-1960s.
4. Immigrants who never intended to make the United States their home.
5. The effort to encourage masters to voluntarily emancipate their slaves and to resettle free blacks in Africa.
6. As vice president, Calhoun anonymously expounded the doctrine of nullification, which held that states could prevent the enforcement of a federal law within their boundaries.

A. Aaron Burr
C. American System
E. Colonization
G. Bill of Rights
I. Committee on Public Information
K. Birds of Passage
M. Calhoun, John

B. Black Tuesday
D. Black Power
F. Antinomian
H. Columbian Exchange
J. Channing
L. Capital Punishment

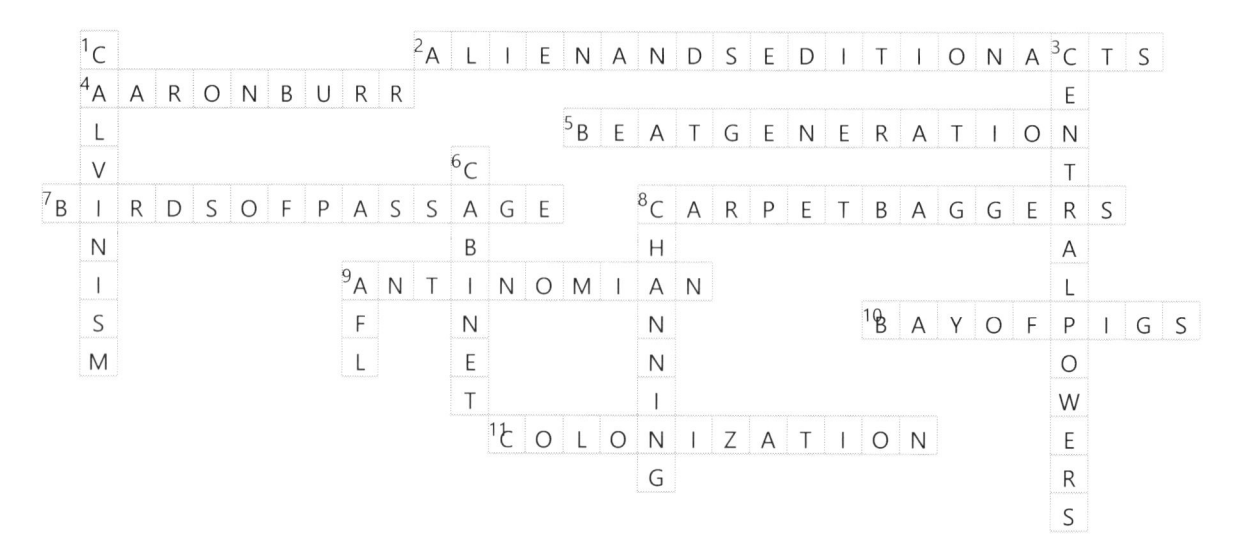

23. Using the Across and Down clues, write the correct words in the numbered grid below.

```
¹C                    ²A L I E N A N D S E D I T I O N A ³C T S
⁴A A R O N B U R R                                      E
 L                                                      N
 V                         ⁵B E A T G E N E R A T I O N
 I                 ⁶C                                   T
⁷B I R D S O F P A S S A G E      ⁸C A R P E T B A G G E R S
 N                   B             H                    A
 I                  ⁹A N T I N O M I A N                L
 S                   F             N     ¹⁰B A Y O F P I G S
 M                   L             N                    O
                     E             I                    W
                     T            ¹¹C O L O N I Z A T I O N
                                   G                    R
                                                        S
```

ACROSS

2. Passed in 1798 designed to curb criticism of the federal government.
4. Thomas Jefferson's first vice president, who killed Alexander Hamilton in a duel in 1804.
5. A cultural style and artistic movement of the 1950s that rejected traditional American family life and material values and celebrated African-American culture.
7. Immigrants who never intended to make the United States their home.
8. People who moved to the South following the Civil War and helped to bring Republican control of southern state governments during Reconstruction.
9. Literally meaning against the laws of human governance.
10. A failed plan to assassinate Cuban leader Fidel Castro and liberate Cuba with a trained military force of political exiles.
11. The effort to encourage masters to voluntarily emancipate their slaves and to resettle free blacks in Africa.

DOWN

1. Emphasized the power and omnipotence of God and the importance of seeking to earn saving grace and salvation.
3. In World War I, Germany and Austria-Hungary and their allies.
6. This term refers to the heads of the executive departments.
8. America's leading exponent of religious liberalism, Channing was one of the founders of American Unitarianism.
9. A confederation of labor unions founded in 1886, it was composed mainly of skilled craft unions.

A. Aaron Burr
B. Cabinet
C. Antinomian
D. Colonization
E. Beat Generation
F. Central Powers
G. Birds of Passage
H. Alien and Sedition Acts
I. Bay of Pigs
J. Calvinism
K. AFL
L. Channing
M. Carpetbaggers

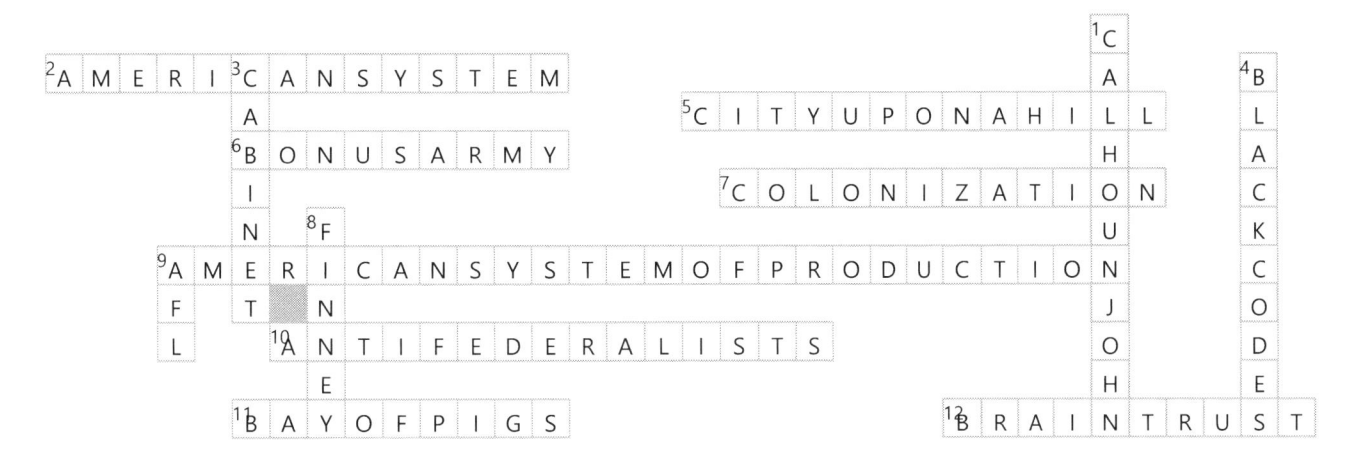

24. Using the Across and Down clues, write the correct words in the numbered grid below.

ACROSS

2. Henry Clay's program for the national economy, which included a protective tariff to stimulate industry and a national bank to provide credit.
5. Phrase from John Winthrop's sermon, "A Model of Christian Charity," in which he challenged his fellow Puritans to build a model, ideal community in America.
6. Group of unemployed World War I veterans who marched on Washington, D.C., in June 1932 to ask for immediate payment of their war pensions.
7. The effort to encourage masters to voluntarily emancipate their slaves and to resettle free blacks in Africa.
9. The high cost of labor led to the establishment of a system of mass production through the manufacture of interchangeable parts.
10. These were opponents of the Constitution of 1787 who sought to continue the confederation of sovereign states and to keep power as close as possible to the people.
11. A failed plan to assassinate Cuban leader Fidel Castro and liberate Cuba with a trained military force of political exiles.
12. Close advisors to President Franklin Delano Roosevelt during the early days of his first term whose policy suggestions influenced much New Deal legislation.

DOWN

1. As vice president, Calhoun anonymously expounded the doctrine of nullification, which held that states could prevent the enforcement of a federal law within their boundaries.
3. This term refers to the heads of the executive departments.
4. Laws passed by Southern state legislatures during Reconstruction, while Congress was out of session.
8. The "father of modern revivalism," Finney devised many techniques adopted by later revival preachers. He encouraged many women to participate actively in revival.
9. A confederation of labor unions founded in 1886, it was composed mainly of skilled craft unions.

A. Brain Trust
C. Bonus Army
E. Cabinet
G. Colonization
I. Bay of Pigs
K. Finney
M. Calhoun, John

B. Antifederalists
D. AFL
F. City Upon a Hill
H. American System
J. American System of Production
L. Black Codes

25. Using the Across and Down clues, write the correct words in the numbered grid below.

```
       ¹C ²A R P E T B A G G E R S                              ³B
    ⁴B    N                                                     L
     I    T                                                     A
     R    I                                                     C
     D    F                              ⁵B  I  L  L  Y  Y  A  N  K
     S    E                               O                     C
     O    D    ⁶A M E R I C A N E X C E P T I O N A L I S M      O
     F    E                               U                     D
     P    R    ⁷C A M P D A V I D A C C O R D S                  E
     A    A    A                          S                     S
     S    L   ⁸A A R O N B U R R    ⁹B I L L O F R I G H T S
     S    I    T                          M
    ¹⁰A X I S P O W E R S          ¹¹B A Y O F P I G S
     G    T    R
     E    S
```

ACROSS

1. People who moved to the South following the Civil War and helped to bring Republican control of southern state governments during Reconstruction.
5. This appellation was used to refer to common soldiers serving in Union armies during the Civil War.
6. Notion that America houses biologically superior people and can spread democracy to the rest of the world.
7. An historic 1979 peace agreement negotiated between Egypt and Israel at the U.S. presidential retreat at Camp David, Maryland.
8. Thomas Jefferson's first vice president, who killed Alexander Hamilton in a duel in 1804.
9. The first ten amendments to the U.S. Constitution, which protect the rights of individuals from the powers of the national government.
10. In World War II, the alliance of German and Italy, and later Japan.
11. A failed plan to assassinate Cuban leader Fidel Castro and liberate Cuba with a trained military force of political exiles.

DOWN

2. These were opponents of the Constitution of 1787 who sought to continue the confederation of sovereign states and to keep power as close as possible to the people.
3. Laws passed by Southern state legislatures during Reconstruction, while Congress was out of session.
4. Immigrants who never intended to make the United States their home.
5. Group of unemployed World War I veterans who marched on Washington, D.C., in June 1932 to ask for immediate payment of their war pensions.
7. President, 1976. His progressive racial views reflected an emergent South less concerned with racial distinctions and more concerned with economic development and political power.

A. Camp David Accords
B. Birds of Passage
C. Black Codes
D. Aaron Burr
E. American Exceptionalism
F. Antifederalists
G. Bonus Army
H. Billy Yank
I. Bay of Pigs
J. Bill of Rights
K. Carpetbaggers
L. Axis Powers
M. Carter

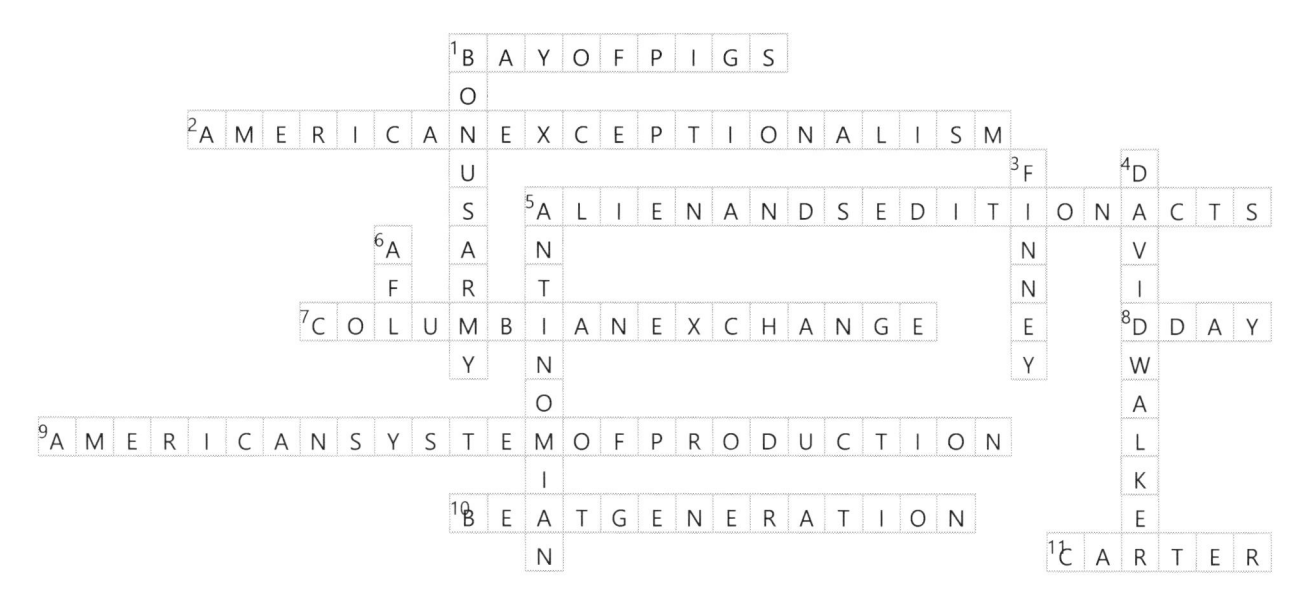

26. Using the Across and Down clues, write the correct words in the numbered grid below.

						¹B	A	Y	O	F	P	I	G	S					
						O													
²A	M	E	R	I	C	A	N	E	X	C	E	P	T	I	O	N	A	L	I	S	M
						U							³F		⁴D				
						S	⁵A	L	I	E	N	A	N	D	S	E	D	I	T	I	O	N	A	C	T	S
				⁶A		A	N							N		V			
				F		R	T							N		I			
			⁷C	O	L	U	M	B	I	A	N	E	X	C	H	A	N	G	E	E		⁸D	D	A	Y
				Y			I							Y		W			
							N									A			
⁹A	M	E	R	I	C	A	N	S	Y	S	T	E	M	O	F	P	R	O	D	U	C	T	I	O	N		L
								I								K			
							¹⁰B	E	A	T	G	E	N	E	R	A	T	I	O	N		E
								N										¹¹C	A	R	T	E	R

ACROSS

1. A failed plan to assassinate Cuban leader Fidel Castro and liberate Cuba with a trained military force of political exiles.
2. Notion that America houses biologically superior people and can spread democracy to the rest of the world.
5. Passed in 1798 designed to curb criticism of the federal government.
7. The process of transferring plants, animals, foods, diseases, wealth, and culture between Europe and the Americas.
8. June 6, 1944, the day Allied forces landed on the beaches of Normandy, in France, leading to the defeat of Germany.
9. The high cost of labor led to the establishment of a system of mass production through the manufacture of interchangeable parts.
10. A cultural style and artistic movement of the 1950s that rejected traditional American family life and material values and celebrated African-American culture.
11. President, 1976. His progressive racial views reflected an emergent South less concerned with racial distinctions and more concerned with economic development and political power.

DOWN

1. Group of unemployed World War I veterans who marched on Washington, D.C., in June 1932 to ask for immediate payment of their war pensions.
3. The "father of modern revivalism," Finney devised many techniques adopted by later revival preachers. He encouraged many women to participate actively in revival.
4. The free black author of An Appeal to the Colored Citizens of the World, which threatened violence if slavery was not abolished.
5. Literally meaning against the laws of human governance.
6. A confederation of labor unions founded in 1886, it was composed mainly of skilled craft unions.

A. Antinomian
C. Finney
E. American System of Production
G. Bay of Pigs
I. D Day
K. American Exceptionalism
M. Bonus Army
B. Carter
D. David Walker
F. Alien and Sedition Acts
H. AFL
J. Columbian Exchange
L. Beat Generation

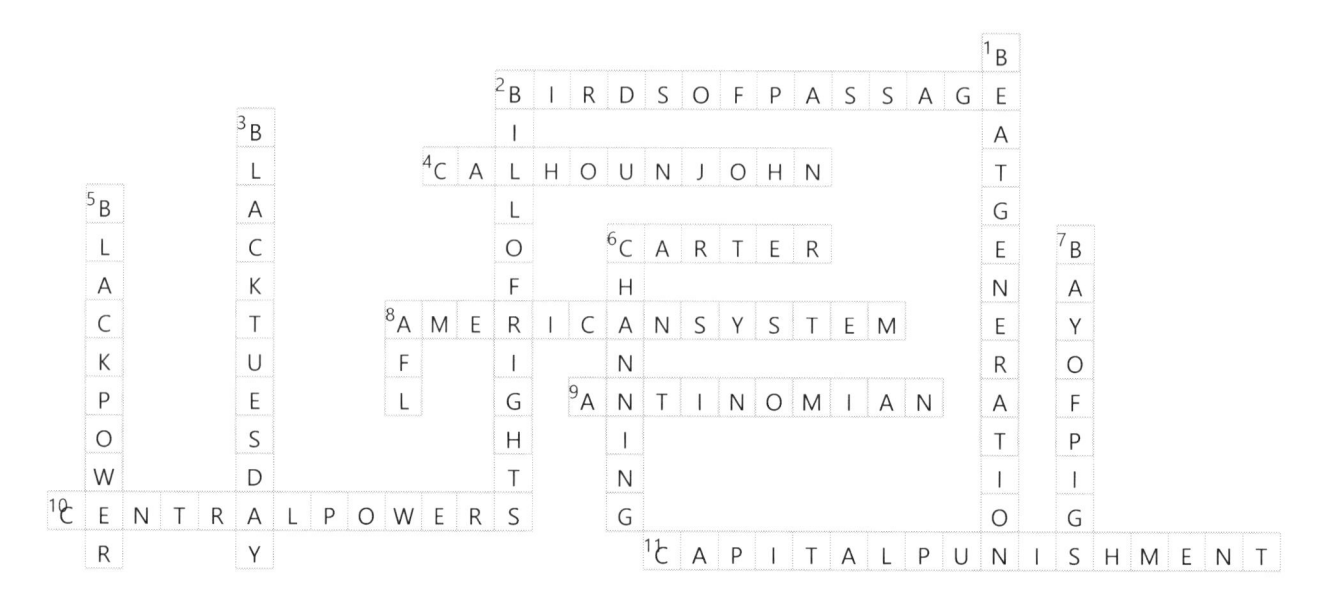

27. Using the Across and Down clues, write the correct words in the numbered grid below.

ACROSS

2. Immigrants who never intended to make the United States their home.
4. As vice president, Calhoun anonymously expounded the doctrine of nullification, which held that states could prevent the enforcement of a federal law within their boundaries.
6. President, 1976. His progressive racial views reflected an emergent South less concerned with racial distinctions and more concerned with economic development and political power.
8. Henry Clay's program for the national economy, which included a protective tariff to stimulate industry and a national bank to provide credit.
9. Literally meaning against the laws of human governance.
10. In World War I, Germany and Austria-Hungary and their allies.
11. During the early nineteenth century, a movement arose to end the death penalty.

DOWN

1. A cultural style and artistic movement of the 1950s that rejected traditional American family life and material values and celebrated African-American culture.
2. The first ten amendments to the U.S. Constitution, which protect the rights of individuals from the powers of the national government.
3. October 29,1929, the day of the stock market crash that initiated the Great Depression.
5. A rallying cry for more militant blacks advocated by younger leaders beginning in the mid-1960s.
6. America's leading exponent of religious liberalism, Channing was one of the founders of American Unitarianism.
7. A failed plan to assassinate Cuban leader Fidel Castro and liberate Cuba with a trained military force of political exiles.
8. A confederation of labor unions founded in 1886, it was composed mainly of skilled craft unions.

A. Beat Generation
B. Calhoun, John
C. Bay of Pigs
D. Black Power
E. Capital Punishment
F. Birds of Passage
G. Bill of Rights
H. Channing
I. Antinomian
J. Carter
K. AFL
L. American System
M. Black Tuesday
N. Central Powers

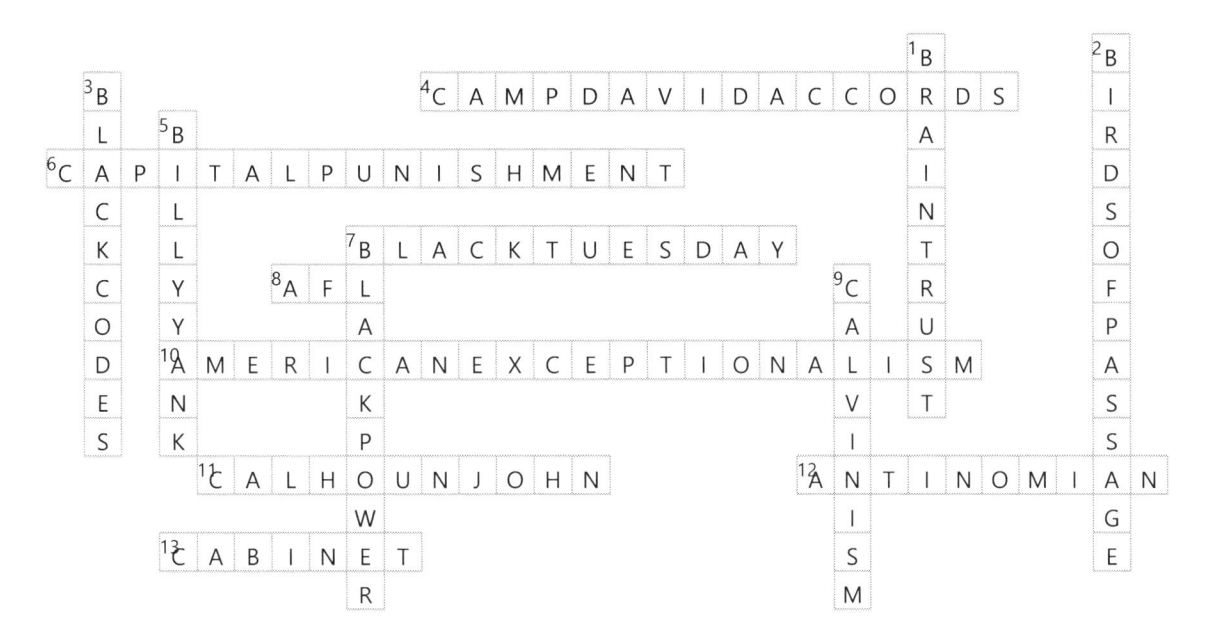

28. Using the Across and Down clues, write the correct words in the numbered grid below.

ACROSS

4. An historic 1979 peace agreement negotiated between Egypt and Israel at the U.S. presidential retreat at Camp David, Maryland.
6. During the early nineteenth century, a movement arose to end the death penalty.
7. October 29, 1929, the day of the stock market crash that initiated the Great Depression.
8. A confederation of labor unions founded in 1886, it was composed mainly of skilled craft unions.
10. Notion that America houses biologically superior people and can spread democracy to the rest of the world.
11. As vice president, Calhoun anonymously expounded the doctrine of nullification, which held that states could prevent the enforcement of a federal law within their boundaries.
12. Literally meaning against the laws of human governance.
13. This term refers to the heads of the executive departments.

DOWN

1. Close advisors to President Franklin Delano Roosevelt during the early days of his first term whose policy suggestions influenced much New Deal legislation.
2. Immigrants who never intended to make the United States their home.
3. Laws passed by Southern state legislatures during Reconstruction, while Congress was out of session.
5. This appellation was used to refer to common soldiers serving in Union armies during the Civil War.
7. A rallying cry for more militant blacks advocated by younger leaders beginning in the mid-1960s.
9. Emphasized the power and omnipotence of God and the importance of seeking to earn saving grace and salvation.

A. Camp David Accords
B. Billy Yank
C. AFL
D. Cabinet
E. Black Tuesday
F. Calhoun, John
G. Birds of Passage
H. Capital Punishment
I. Brain Trust
J. American Exceptionalism
K. Black Power
L. Antinomian
M. Calvinism
N. Black Codes

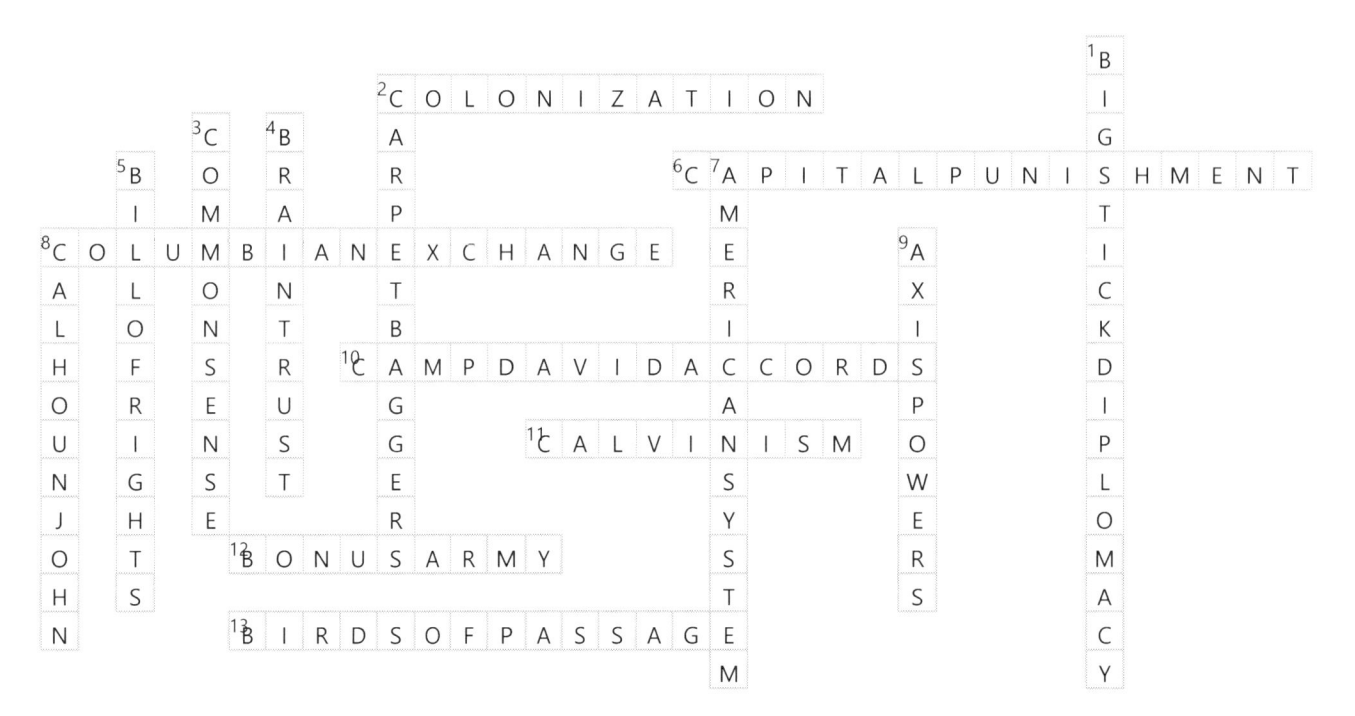

29. Using the Across and Down clues, write the correct words in the numbered grid below.

ACROSS

2. The effort to encourage masters to voluntarily emancipate their slaves and to resettle free blacks in Africa.
6. During the early nineteenth century, a movement arose to end the death penalty.
8. The process of transferring plants, animals, foods, diseases, wealth, and culture between Europe and the Americas.
10. An historic 1979 peace agreement negotiated between Egypt and Israel at the U.S. presidential retreat at Camp David, Maryland.
11. Emphasized the power and omnipotence of God and the importance of seeking to earn saving grace and salvation.
12. Group of unemployed World War I veterans who marched on Washington, D.C., in June 1932 to ask for immediate payment of their war pensions.
13. Immigrants who never intended to make the United States their home.

DOWN

1. The proclaimed foreign policy of Theodore Roosevelt, it was based on the proverb, "Speak softly and carry a big stick,".
2. People who moved to the South following the Civil War and helped to bring Republican control of southern state governments during Reconstruction.
3. This best-selling pamphlet by Thomas Paine, first published in 1776, denounced the British monarchy, called for American independence.
4. Close advisors to President Franklin Delano Roosevelt during the early days of his first term whose policy suggestions influenced much New Deal legislation.
5. The first ten amendments to the U.S. Constitution, which protect the rights of individuals from the powers of the national government.
7. Henry Clay's program for the national economy, which included a protective tariff to stimulate industry and a national bank to provide credit.
8. As vice president, Calhoun anonymously expounded the doctrine of nullification, which held that states could prevent the enforcement of a federal law within their boundaries.
9. In World War II, the alliance of German and Italy, and later Japan.

A. Calvinism
B. Bonus Army
C. Bill of Rights
D. Axis Powers
E. Capital Punishment
F. Birds of Passage
G. American System
H. Camp David Accords
I. Carpetbaggers
J. Common Sense
K. Columbian Exchange
L. Brain Trust
M. Colonization
N. Big Stick Diplomacy
O. Calhoun, John

30. Using the Across and Down clues, write the correct words in the numbered grid below.

```
            ¹C ²A P I T A L P U N I S H M E N T      ³C O L O N I Z A T I O N
               M                                      A
    ⁴C O X E Y S A R R N Y                            R  ⁵B O N U S ⁶A R M Y
     A    R                                  ⁷C       P     L         X
     B    I         ⁸C ⁹A L H O U N J O H N   A       E     A         I
     I    C             N                     L       T     C         S
     N    A             T                     V       B     K         P
     E    N      ¹⁰A L I E N A N D S E D I T I O N A C T S            O
     T    S             N                             N     G         W
          Y       ¹¹C O M M O N S E N S E     I       G     E         E
          S             M                     S       E     S         R
          T             I                     M       R     D         S
  ¹²C O P P E R H E A D S                             S     A
          M             N                                   Y
```

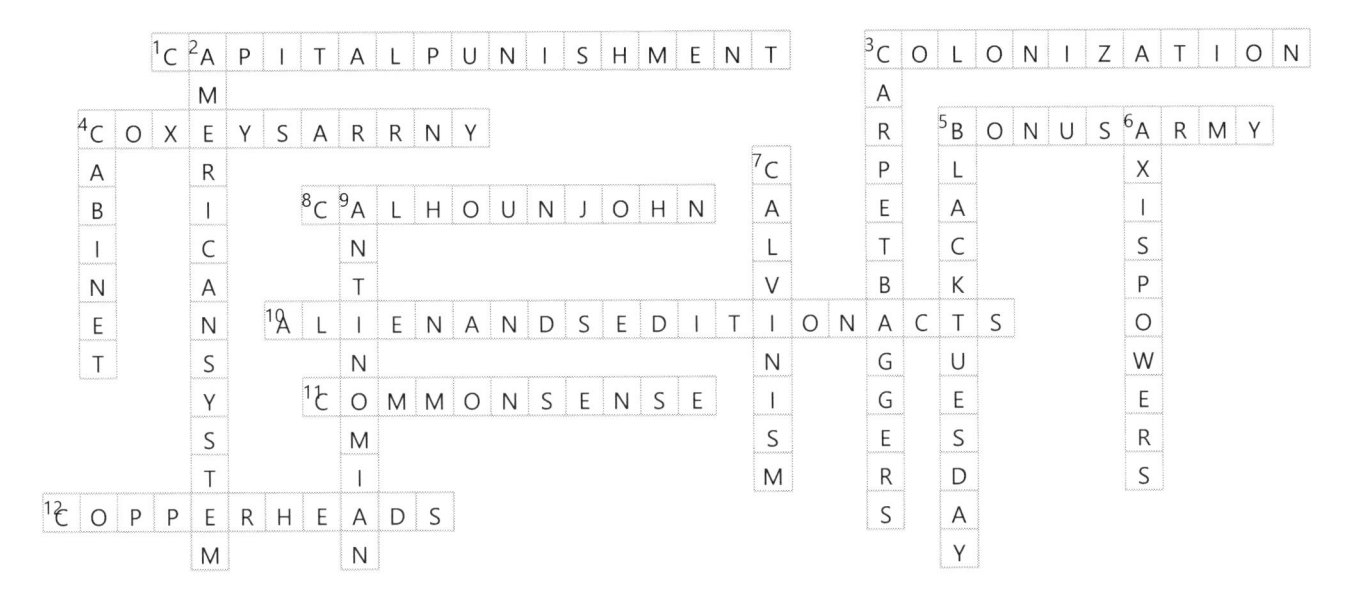

ACROSS

1. During the early nineteenth century, a movement arose to end the death penalty.
3. The effort to encourage masters to voluntarily emancipate their slaves and to resettle free blacks in Africa.
4. A movement founded to help the unemployed during the depression of the 1890s, it demanded that the federal government provide jobs and inflate the currency.
5. Group of unemployed World War I veterans who marched on Washington, D.C., in June 1932 to ask for immediate payment of their war pensions.
8. As vice president, Calhoun anonymously expounded the doctrine of nullification, which held that states could prevent the enforcement of a federal law within their boundaries.
10. Passed in 1798 designed to curb criticism of the federal government.
11. This best-selling pamphlet by Thomas Paine, first published in 1776, denounced the British monarchy, called for American independence.
12. Not every person living in the North during the Civil War favored making war against the Confederacy. Such persons came to be identified as Copperheads.

DOWN

2. Henry Clay's program for the national economy, which included a protective tariff to stimulate industry and a national bank to provide credit.
3. People who moved to the South following the Civil War and helped to bring Republican control of southern state governments during Reconstruction.
4. This term refers to the heads of the executive departments.
5. October 29, 1929, the day of the stock market crash that initiated the Great Depression.
6. In World War II, the alliance of German and Italy, and later Japan.
7. Emphasized the power and omnipotence of God and the importance of seeking to earn saving grace and salvation.
9. Literally meaning against the laws of human governance.

A. Antinomian
D. Alien and Sedition Acts
G. Calvinism
J. Black Tuesday
M. American System

B. Carpetbaggers
E. Axis Powers
H. Common Sense
K. Bonus Army
N. Cabinet

C. Calhoun, John
F. Capital Punishment
I. Copperheads
L. Coxey's Arrny
O. Colonization

Multiple Choice

From the words provided for each clue, provide the letter of the word which best matches the clue.

1. _____ Passed in 1798 designed to curb criticism of the federal government.
   A. Patrons of Husbandry   B. Alien and Sedition Acts   C. City Upon a Hill   D. Free Soil Party

2. _____ The meeting in February 1945 to determine the post-World War II world order.
   A. Fugitive Slave Law   B. Pendleton Act   C. Rationalism   D. Yalta Conference

3. _____ The practice of controlling every phase of production by owning the sources of raw materials and often the transportation facilities needed to distribute the product.
   A. Yellow Journalism   B. Vertical Integration   C. China Lobby   D. Goldwater

4. _____ The mass movement of African Americans from the South to the North during World War I.
   A. Colonization   B. Great Migration   C. First Continental Congress   D. Judicial Review

5. _____ This law allows the public and press to request declassification of government documents.
   A. Freedom of Information Act   B. Renaissance   C. Navigation System   D. Kansas Nebraska Act

6. _____ A backlash against immigration by white native-born Protestants. Nativism could be based on racial prejudice, religion, politics, and economics.
   A. Committee on Public Information   B. D Day   C. Nativism   D. Radical Republicans

7. _____ The view that the powers of the national government are limited to those described in the U.S. Constitution.
   A. D Day   B. Kissinger   C. Strict Construction   D. National Recovery Administration

8. _____ A secret organization founded in the southern states during Reconstruction to terrorize and intimidate former slaves and prevent them from voting or holding public office.
   A. Ku Klux Klan   B. Settlement House   C. David Walker   D. Garrison

9. _____ A term for hard coin, such as gold or silver, that can also back and give a fixed point of valuation to paper currencies.
   A. Rationalism   B. Populist Party   C. Specie   D. First Continental Congress

10. _____ A political party founded in 1874 to promote the issuance of legal tender paper currency not backed by precious metals in order to inflate the money supply.
    A. Renaissance   B. Greenback Party   C. Scopes Trial   D. Northwest Passage

11. _____ Civil rights activists who in 1961 demonstrated that despite a federal ban on segregated travel on interstate buses, segregation prevailed in parts of the South.
    A. Settlement House   B. Freedom Riders   C. Neutrality   D. Fireside Chats

12. _____ A group of New England intellectuals who glorified nature and believed that each person contains god-like potentialities.
    A. League of Nations   B. Rosenbergs   C. Interstate Commerce Commission   D. Transcendentalists

13. _____ Personable Soviet premier during Eisenhower's presidential term. Khrushchev condemned Stalin's purges and welcomed a melting of the Cold War.
    A. Khrushchev   B. Indulgences   C. Johnny Reb   D. American System

14. _____ President Woodrow Wilson's formula for peace after World War I.
    A. Garrison   B. Webster   C. Salutary Neglect   D. Fourteen Points

15. _____ A reform movement growing out of Jane Addams' Hull House in the late nineteenth century.
    A. Populist Party   B. Settlement House   C. Transcendentalists   D. Jazz

16. This landmark 1803 Supreme Court decision, which established the principle of judicial review.
A. Fugitive Slave Law   B. Marbury vs Madison   C. Paul Cuffe   D. Watergate

17. Alabama governor who ran for president in 1968 as a third-party candidate on the American Independent ticket
A. Rationalism   B. Joint Stock Companies   C. George Wallace   D. Protestant Reformation

18. Founder of the nation's first school to teach deaf mutes to read and write and communicate through hand signals.
A. Gallaudet   B. Horace Mann   C. Dumbbell Tenement   D. City Upon a Hill

19. The auxiliary women's unit to the U.S. army.
A. War Powers Act   B. WAC   C. Oil Crisis   D. Trust

20. Apartment buildings built to minimal codes and designed to cram the largest number of people into the smallest amount of space.
A. Henry Clay   B. Rosa Parks   C. David Walker   D. Dumbbell Tenement

21. The founder of the Mormon Church, Smith was murdered in Illinois in 1844.
A. Evangelical Revivalism   B. Electric Trolley   C. Pendleton Act   D. Joseph Smith

22. A policy of resettling eastern Indian tribes on lands west of the Mississippi River.
A. Samuel Howe   B. Removal   C. Johnny Reb   D. American System

23. Outlawed the closed shop, gave presidential power to delay strikes with a "cooling-off" period, and curtailed the political and economic power of organized labor.
A. Yellow Journalism   B. Dartmouth vs Woodward   C. Zimmermann   D. Taft Hartley

24. Public transportation for urban neighborhoods, using electric current from overhead wires.
A. China Lobby   B. Divine Right   C. Electric Trolley   D. Public Virtue

25. An antislavery political party founded in 1839.
A. Liberty Party   B. Scalawags   C. Nat Turner   D. Antifederalists

26. Parliament passed laws that allowed profit-seeking landowners to fence in their open fields to raise more sheep.
A. D Day   B. Fireside Chats   C. Enclosure Movement   D. Platt Amendment

27. This appellation was used to refer to common soldiers serving in Union armies during the Civil War.
A. Billy Yank   B. Khrushchev   C. Joseph Stalin   D. Judicial Review

28. A black Baptist preacher who led a revolt against slavery in Southampton County in southern Virginia in 1831.
A. Seward   B. Gorbachev   C. Nat Turner   D. First Continental Congress

29. The process of transferring plants, animals, foods, diseases, wealth, and culture between Europe and the Americas.
A. Columbian Exchange   B. Reagan Doctrine   C. Public Virtue   D. Oil Crisis

30. A rallying cry for more militant blacks advocated by younger leaders beginning in the mid-1960s.
A. Open Door Note   B. New Look   C. Black Power   D. Harlem Renaissance

31. America's leading exponent of religious liberalism, Channing was one of the founders of American Unitarianism.
A. Channing   B. Queensberry Rules   C. Dumbbell Tenement   D. Specie

32. A Supreme Court decision in 1896 that ruled "separate but equal" facilities for African Americans were constitutional under the Fourteenth Amendment.
A. Radical Republicans   B. Yalta Conference   C. Paul Cuffe   D. Plessy vs Ferguson

33. Herbert Hoover's program as director of the Food Administration to conserve food during World War I.
A. Equal Rights Amendment   B. Hooverizing   C. Fugitive Slave Law   D. Open Door Note

34. Six German principalities provided 30,000 soldiers to Great Britain to fight against the American rebels during the War for Independence.
A. Jefferson   B. Dartmouth vs Woodward   C. Cuban Missile Crisis   D. Hessians

35. Black student who courageously sought admission into all-white University of Mississippi in 1962. His enrollment sparked a riot instigated by a white mob.
A. Hartford Convention   B. James Meredith   C. Nativism   D. Central Powers

36. A cornerstone of good citizenship in republican states, public virtue involved the subordination of individual self-interest to serving the greater good of the whole community.
A. Fair Deal   B. Public Virtue   C. Evangelical Revivalism   D. Dumbbell Tenement

37. King and Parliament legislated a series of Navigation Acts that established England as the central hub of trade.
A. Navigation System   B. Declension   C. Lend Lease   D. Beat Generation

38. The most controversial element of the Compromise of 1850, the Fugitive Slave Law provided for the return of runaway slaves to their masters.
A. Second New Deal   B. Fugitive Slave Law   C. Equal Rights Amendment   D. McCullough vs Maryland

39. President Franklin Delano Roosevelt's program designed to bring about economic recovery and reform during the Great Depression.
A. New Look   B. New Deal   C. Scopes Trial   D. Reagan Doctrine

40. Legislation establishing mandatory insurance to be carried by employers to cover on-the-job injuries to their workers.
A. Sputnik   B. Workmens Compensation   C. Emancipation Proclamation   D. Columbian Exchange

41. A confederation of labor unions founded in 1886, it was composed mainly of skilled craft unions.
A. New South   B. AFL   C. Loose Interpretation   D. Indentured Servitude

42. An American military intervention in Panama in December 1989, which was launched against Panama's leader, Manuel Noriega, who was indicted on drug-related charges.
A. Coxey's Army   B. Antinomian   C. Indentured Servitude   D. Operation Just Cause

43. Proposed Constitutional amendment that would prohibit discrimination on the basis of gender.
A. Equal Rights Amendment   B. Khrushchev   C. Carter   D. Joseph Smith

44. As opposed to limited war, total war usually denotes a military conflict in which warfare ultimately affects the entire population, civilian as well as military.
A. Shays Rebellion   B. Total War   C. Coney Island   D. Writs of Assistance

45. An informal group of media leaders and political pundits who criticized the communist takeover of China, claiming the United States could have prevented it.
A. New South   B. Kissinger   C. China Lobby   D. Navigation System

46. Republican presidential candidate in 1964, Goldwater spearheaded an emergent conservative drive out of the South and West.
A. Goldwater   B. Freedmen's Bureau   C. Santa Anna   D. Transcendentalists

47. The primary author of the Declaration of Independence, the first secretary of state, and as president, he was responsible for the Louisiana Purchase.
A. Henry Kaiser   B. War Powers Act   C. Jefferson   D. Horace Mann

48. The economic conditions of slow economic growth, rising inflation, and flagging productivity that characterized the American economy during the 1970s.
A. Sputnik   B. Joseph Stalin   C. Stagflation   D. Non Intercourse Act

49. In World War I, Germany and Austria-Hungary and their allies.
A. Populist Party   B. Freedom Riders   C. Central Powers   D. Neutrality

50. The government in Spain gave away large tracts of conquered land in Spanish America, including whole villages of indigenous peoples, to court favorites.
A. Encomienda System   B. Hoovervilles   C. Reagan Doctrine   D. Kissinger

51. Argued in favor of establishing more democratic forms of government.
A. Radical Revolutionaries   B. American Exceptionalism   C. Cabinet   D. Seward

52. The ban of the production, sale, and consumption of alcoholic beverages.
A. Vertical Integration   B. Prohibition   C. Goldwater   D. Yellow Journalism

53. The board established in January 1942 to help mobilize the U.S. economy for war production.
A. Gospel of Wealth   B. Oil Crisis   C. Channing   D. War Production Board

54. Point Fourteen of Wilson's Fourteen Points, the proposal to establish an international organization to guarantee the territorial integrity of independent nations.
A. Tory   B. New Deal   C. Samuel Howe   D. League of Nations

55. These 85 newspaper essays, written in support of ratification of the Constitution of 1787 in New York by James Madison, Alexander Hamilton, and John Jay.
A. Populist Party   B. Lend Lease   C. American System of Production   D. Federalist Papers

56. The federal government's plan to revive industry during the Great Depression through rational planning.
A. Committee on Public Information   B. National Recovery Administration   C. Radical Republicans   D. Salutary Neglect

57. Literally meaning against the laws of human governance.
A. Hessians   B. Antinomian   C. Modern Republicanism   D. Monroe Doctrine

58. An antislavery political party founded in 1848.
A. Free Soil Party   B. Indulgences   C. Jazz   D. Kansas Nebraska Act

59. Founder of the nation's first school for the blind.
A. Capital Punishment   B. Henry Kaiser   C. Samuel Howe   D. George Wallace

60. American radicals accused of passing atomic secrets to the Soviets during World War II. Executed in 1953.
A. National Recovery Administration   B. Rosenbergs   C. Evangelical Revivalism   D. Indentured Servitude

61. Religious dissenters from England who believed that the state-supported Church of England, was too corrupt to be reformed.
A. Camp David Accords   B. Separatists   C. Renaissance   D. Workmens Compensation

62. Conflict in 1957 when governor Orval Faubus sent the Arkansas National Guard to prevent the racial integration of Little Rock's Central High School.
A. Marbury vs Madison   B. Colonization   C. Radical Revolutionaries   D. Little Rock Crisis

63. The program by which the United States provided arms and supplies to the Allies in World War II before joining the fighting.
A. Electric Trolley   B. Lend Lease   C. Dartmouth vs Woodward   D. League of Nations

64. The second stage of President Franklin Delano Roosevelt's economic recovery and reform program, launched January 4, 1935.
A. Seward   B. Writs of Assistance   C. Second New Deal   D. Paul Cuffe

65. Failed movement led by conservative Western politicians to cede federal control of western land to individual states.
A. Alien and Sedition Acts   B. Pearl Harbor   C. Antinomian   D. Sagebrush Rebellion

66. Musical style based on improvisation within a band format, combining African traditions of repetition, call and response, and strong beat with European structure.
A. Initiative and Referendum   B. Evangelical Revivalism   C. Jazz   D. Populist Party

67. Blanket search warrants used by English customs collectors in the colonies to try to catch suspected smugglers.
A. Open Door Note   B. Writs of Assistance   C. Antinomian   D. Henry Kaiser

68. Policy set forth in 1899 by Secretary of State John Hay preventing further partitioning of China by European powers and protecting the principle of free trade.
A. AFL   B. Finney   C. Reform Darwinists   D. Open Door Note

69. An early American political party opposing influence from monarchy.
A. Temperance   B. Whig Party   C. Capital Punishment   D. Free Soil Party

70. A procedure that allows citizens to propose legislation through petitions.
A. Frederick Douglass   B. Vertical Integration   C. Initiative and Referendum   D. Sherman Antitrust

71. The high cost of labor led to the establishment of a system of mass production through the manufacture of interchangeable parts.
A. Operation Just Cause   B. Patriarchal   C. American System of Production   D. Hartford Convention

72. Organization established in 1909 to fight for African-American civil rights through legal action.
A. Hartford Convention   B. Rationalism   C. Jazz   D. NAACP

73. A political party established in 1892 sought to inflate the currency with silver dollars and to establish an income tax.
A. Strict Construction   B. Populist Party   C. Joseph Stalin   D. Johnny Reb

74. The belief that God ordains certain people to amass money and use it to further God's purposes, it justified the concentration of wealth.
A. Gospel of Wealth   B. Freedmen's Bureau   C. Court Packing   D. Republicanism

75. Beginning in the 1400s, the European Renaissance represented an intellectual and cultural flowering in the arts, literature, philosophy, and the sciences.
A. AFL   B. Open Door Note   C. Renaissance   D. James Meredith

76. A religious viewpoint that rejected the Calvinist doctrines of original sin and predestination and stressed the basic goodness of human nature.
A. Encomienda System   B. Prohibition   C. Liberty Party   D. Religious Liberalism

77. Indentured servitude represented temporary service for a specified period, usually from four to seven years, to a legally designated owner.
A. Yellow Journalism   B. Finney   C. Salutary Neglect   D. Perpetual Servitude

78. Were in favor of splitting authority between their proposed strong national government and the states.
A. Federalists   B. Writs of Assistance   C. Trust   D. First Continental Congress

79. The effort to encourage masters to voluntarily emancipate their slaves and to resettle free blacks in Africa.
A. Sagebrush Rebellion   B. Yellow Journalism   C. Colonization   D. American System

80. A business model where any single entity had the power to control competition within a given industry, such as oil production.
A. Divine Right   B. Trust   C. Second New Deal   D. Religious Liberalism

81. He was an advocate of the "American System," which called for a protective tariff, a national bank, and federally funded internal improvements.
A. Federalist Papers   B. Henry Clay   C. Yellow Journalism   D. SDS

82. During the 1972 presidential campaign, burglars, tied to the Nixon White House, were caught installing eavesdropping devices in Democratic Party headquarters.
A. Hydraulic Society   B. Watergate   C. Knights of Labor   D. Scalawags

83. During the early nineteenth century, a movement arose to end the death penalty.
A. Seward   B. Capital Punishment   C. Camp David Accords   D. McCullough vs Maryland

84. The early nineteenth century's leading educational reformer, Mann led the fight for government support for public schools in Massachusetts.
A. Watergate   B. Horace Mann   C. SDS   D. American System

85. The leader of the Haitian Revolution.
A. Sharecropping   B. Louverture   C. Scopes Trial   D. Garrison

86. Advocated a canal through the Central American isthmus and a strong American naval presence in the Caribbean and Pacific.
A. Fair Deal   B. Trust   C. Large Policy   D. Joseph Stalin

87. A landmark 1819 Supreme Court decision protecting contracts.
A. Shays Rebellion   B. Dartmouth vs Woodward   C. Freedmen's Bureau   D. Walter O'Malley

88. The radical organization aimed to rid American society of poverty, racism, and violence through participatory democracy.
A. Nativism   B. Elizabeth Cady Stanton   C. Great Migration   D. SDS

89. In World War II, the alliance between the United States, Great Britain, and France.
A. Goldwater   B. Republicanism   C. Calvinism   D. Grand Alliance

90. At the time of the American Revolution, republicanism referred to the concept that sovereignty is vested in the people; the citizens of the nation.
A. Evangelical Revivalism   B. Capital Punishment   C. Republicanism   D. Kissinger

91. U.S. policy of impartiality during World Wars I and II.
A. Hessians   B. Neutrality   C. Tariff of Abominations   D. Johnny Reb

92. The national security advisor to President Nixon. A staunch anti-Communist. He was Nixon's closest associate on matters of foreign policy.
A. Hoovervilles   B. Kissinger   C. Freedom of Information Act   D. Salutary Neglect

93. The chemical-laden fog caused by automobile engines, a serious problem in southern California.
A. New Look   B. Smog   C. Dumbbell Tenement   D. Marshall Plan

94. Phrase from John Winthrop's sermon, "A Model of Christian Charity," in which he challenged his fellow Puritans to build a model, ideal community in America.
A. Specie   B. Trust   C. City Upon a Hill   D. Temperance

95. Russian satellite that successfully orbited the earth in 1957, prompting Americans to question their own values and educational system.
A. Sputnik   B. James Meredith   C. Louverture   D. Nat Turner

96. Adopted in 1964, barred a poll tax in federal elections.
A. Smog   B. Bonus Army   C. Twenty Fourth Amendment   D. Spoils System

97. A current of Protestant Christianity emphasizing personal conversion, repentance of sin, and the authority of Scripture.
A. Manumission   B. Evangelical Revivalism   C. Spirituals   D. Paul Cuffe

98. Social and political systems are denoted by power and authority residing in males, such as in the father of the family.
A. Twenty Fourth Amendment   B. D Day   C. Patriarchal   D. Antifederalists

99. African-American seamstress and active NAACP member arrested for refusing to give up her seat to a white patron in Montgomery, Alabama.
A. Tory   B. Rosa Parks   C. Central Powers   D. Stagflation

100. These companies were given the right to develop trade between England and certain geographic regions, such as Russia or India.
A. Jefferson   B. Joint Stock Companies   C. Ku Klux Klan   D. Hessians

From the words provided for each clue, provide the letter of the word which best matches the clue.

101. In World War II, the alliance of German and Italy, and later Japan.
A. Axis Powers   B. Prudence Crandall   C. Populist Party   D. Smog

102. Indentured servitude represented temporary service for a specified period, usually from four to seven years, to a legally designated owner.
A. Perpetual Servitude   B. McCullough vs Maryland   C. Emerson   D. Tariff of Abominations

103. The chemical-laden fog caused by automobile engines, a serious problem in southern California.
A. Neutrality   B. Bay of Pigs   C. Smog   D. Federalists

104. Legislation passed in 1887 to authorize the president to divide tribal land and distribute it to individual Native Americans.
A. Nationalists   B. Dawes Act   C. American System of Production   D. Webster

105. The principle that the people living in the western territories should decide whether or not to permit slavery.
A. Hartford Convention   B. Rationalism   C. Popular Sovereignty   D. Johnny Reb

106. An informal group of media leaders and political pundits who criticized the communist takeover of China, claiming the United States could have prevented it.
A. China Lobby   B. SDS   C. Bay of Pigs   D. Rosenbergs

107. The liberal reform program of President Lyndon Johnson. The program included civil rights legislation, increased public spending to help the poor, Medicare, and Medicaid.
A. Great Society   B. Thoreau   C. Progressive Party   D. Pearl Harbor

108. The economic conditions of slow economic growth, rising inflation, and flagging productivity that characterized the American economy during the 1970s.
A. Stagflation   B. Common Sense   C. Axis Powers   D. Fair Deal

109. Policy set forth in 1899 by Secretary of State John Hay preventing further partitioning of China by European powers and protecting the principle of free trade.
A. Stagflation   B. Open Door Note   C. Rationalism   D. Northwest Passage

110. Alabama governor who ran for president in 1968 as a third-party candidate on the American Independent ticket
A. Hartford Convention   B. Zimmermann   C. George Wallace   D. Social Gospel

111. Controversial 1854 legislation that opened Kansas and Nebraska to white settlement, repealed the Compromise of 1820, and led opponents to form the Republican party.
A. Second Continental Congress   B. Kansas Nebraska Act   C. Greenbacks   D. Plantation Legend

112. Literally meaning against the laws of human governance.
A. Little Rock Crisis   B. Antinomian   C. Naturalism   D. Modern Republicanism

113. Thomas Jefferson's first vice president, who killed Alexander Hamilton in a duel in 1804.
A. Queensberry Rules   B. Aaron Burr   C. American Exceptionalism   D. Deregulation

114. Russian satellite that successfully orbited the earth in 1957, prompting Americans to question their own values and educational system.
A. Queensberry Rules   B. Sputnik   C. Smog   D. SALT I

115. An organization founded in 1867 to aid farmers through its local granges.
A. Calhoun, John   B. Platt Amendment   C. Whig Party   D. Patrons of Husbandry

116. A policy of resettling eastern Indian tribes on lands west of the Mississippi River.
A. Aaron Burr   B. Removal   C. Platt Amendment   D. Guadalupe Hidalgo

117. Emphasized the power and omnipotence of God and the importance of seeking to earn saving grace and salvation.
A. Calvinism   B. Popular Sovereignty   C. Great Society   D. Goldwater

118. The process of transferring plants, animals, foods, diseases, wealth, and culture between Europe and the Americas.
A. Hooverizing   B. Gorbachev   C. New South   D. Columbian Exchange

119. A violent encounter between police and protesters in 1886 in Chicago, which led to the execution of four protest leaders.
A. Goldwater   B. Seward   C. Haymarket Square Riot   D. Social Darwinism

120. Celebrated American general removed by Truman after his criticisms of America's containment policy.
A. Copperheads   B. Freedom Riders   C. MacArthur   D. Scalawags

121. The legal principle that a criminal act should only be punished if the offender was fully capable of distinguishing right from wrong.
A. Dartmouth vs Woodward   B. Nonseparatists   C. Insanity Defense   D. Good Neighbor

122. Telegram from German Foreign Minister Arnold Zimmermann to the German ambassador to Mexico pledging a Mexican-German alliance against the United States.
A. Black Tuesday   B. Zimmermann   C. Common Sense   D. Plantation Legend

123. A North Vietnamese offensive in January 1968 against every major South Vietnamese target.
A. Neutrality   B. D Day   C. Tet Offensive   D. Bay of Pigs

124. He was an advocate of the "American System," which called for a protective tariff, a national bank, and federally funded internal improvements.
A. Sit in   B. James Madison   C. New Deal   D. Henry Clay

125. During the Age of Exploration, adventurers from England, France, and the Netherlands kept seeking an all-water route across North America.
A. China Lobby   B. Good Neighbor   C. Salutary Neglect   D. Northwest Passage

126. A political party established in 1892 sought to inflate the currency with silver dollars and to establish an income tax.
A. Flapper   B. Goldwater   C. Channing   D. Populist Party

127. June 6, 1944, the day Allied forces landed on the beaches of Normandy, in France, leading to the defeat of Germany.
A. Freedom Riders   B. Salutary Neglect   C. National Recovery Administration   D. D Day

128. A Supreme Court decision in 1896 that ruled "separate but equal" facilities for African Americans were constitutional under the Fourteenth Amendment.
A. Rosenbergs   B. Plessy vs Ferguson   C. Dartmouth vs Woodward   D. Johnny Reb

129. Applied Christian doctrines to social problems.
A. Scalawags   B. Dien Bien Phu   C. Nineteenth Amendment   D. Social Gospel

130. The view that the powers of the national government are limited to those described in the U.S. Constitution.
A. Strict Construction   B. Price Revolution   C. Bay of Pigs   D. Young

131. Literary style of the late nineteenth and early twentieth century, where the individual was a helpless victim in a world in which outside forces determined his or her fate.
A. American System of Production   B. Naturalism   C. New Look   D. Nat Turner

132. This informal group of pro-colonial rights leaders in Boston helped organize resistance against unwanted British policies, such as the Stamp Act.
A. Republicanism   B. Kansas Nebraska Act   C. Hamilton   D. Loyal Nine

133. Argued in favor of establishing more democratic forms of government.
A. Matrilineal   B. Antinomian   C. Temperance   D. Radical Revolutionaries

134. The radical organization aimed to rid American society of poverty, racism, and violence through participatory democracy.
A. George Wallace   B. Hydraulic Society   C. Khrushchev   D. SDS

135. The mass movement of African Americans from the South to the North during World War I.
A. Progressive Party   B. Large Policy   C. Great Migration   D. Sagebrush Rebellion

136. The Father of the Constitution and the Bill of Rights and a co-founder of the Jeffersonian Republican party, Madison served as president during the War of 1812.
A. Queensberry Rules   B. James Madison   C. Carpetbaggers   D. Colonization

137. Parliament passed laws that allowed profit-seeking landowners to fence in their open fields to raise more sheep.
A. Laissez faire   B. Enclosure Movement   C. Great Society   D. Yellow Journalism

138. The government in Spain gave away large tracts of conquered land in Spanish America, including whole villages of indigenous peoples, to court favorites.
A. Encomienda System   B. Washington   C. Guadalupe Hidalgo   D. Price Revolution

139. Secretary of State for Abraham Lincoln and Andrew Johnson, and advocate of a vigorous expansionism.
A. Goldwater   B. Seward   C. Colonization   D. Settlement House

140. U.S. policy of impartiality during World Wars I and II.
A. Neutrality   B. Nineteenth Amendment   C. Hooverizing   D. Evangelical Revivalism

141. A movement founded to help the unemployed during the depression of the 1890s, it demanded that the federal government provide jobs and inflate the currency.
A. Kansas Nebraska Act   B. Sputnik   C. Court Packing   D. Coxey's Arrny

142. October 29,1929, the day of the stock market crash that initiated the Great Depression.
A. James Polk   B. Hessians   C. Headright   D. Black Tuesday

143. Phrase from John Winthrop's sermon, "A Model of Christian Charity," in which he challenged his fellow Puritans to build a model, ideal community in America.
A. Antinomian   B. Nonseparatists   C. Impressment   D. City Upon a Hill

144. Spokesman for the Nation of Islam, a black religious and political organization that advocated black-owned businesses and castigated "white devils."
A. Guadalupe Hidalgo   B. Walter O'Malley   C. Malcolm X   D. Dawes Act

145. Proposed Constitutional amendment that would prohibit discrimination on the basis of gender.
A. Robert Kennedy   B. City Upon a Hill   C. Equal Rights Amendment   D. Radical Republicans

146. A political party founded by James Madison and Thomas Jefferson to combat Alexander Hamilton's fiscal policies.
A. Fireside Chats   B. Tariff of Abominations   C. Channing   D. Republicans

147. A wave of religious fervor and revivalism that swept the United States from the early nineteenth century through the Civil War.
A. Gorbachev   B. Second Great Awakening   C. Removal   D. Hoovervilles

148. The leader of the Haitian Revolution.
A. Louverture   B. Young   C. Nullification   D. Sagebrush Rebellion

149. A Virginia slave and blacksmith who organized an attempted assault against Richmond in 1800.
A. Gabriel   B. Gorbachev   C. Reagan Doctrine   D. Kansas Nebraska Act

150. Oil supply disruptions and soaring oil prices after Middle Eastern nations imposed an embargo on oil shipments to punish the West for supporting Israel in that year's Arab-Israeli war.
A. James Polk   B. Oil Crisis   C. Non Intercourse Act   D. Social Gospel

151. Appointed Chief Justice in 1801, Marshall expanded the Supreme Court's power and prestige and established the court's power of Judicial Review.
A. Political Slavery   B. James Polk   C. John Marshall   D. Johnny Reb

152. In World War I, Germany and Austria-Hungary and their allies.
A. Central Powers   B. Second Great Awakening   C. Knights of Labor   D. Large Policy

153. Notion that America houses biologically superior people and can spread democracy to the rest of the world.
A. Settlement House   B. Queensberry Rules   C. Henry Clay   D. American Exceptionalism

154. A current of Protestant Christianity emphasizing personal conversion, repentance of sin, and the authority of Scripture.
A. Jefferson   B. Tory   C. Evangelical Revivalism   D. Tet Offensive

155. The view that the national government's powers are not limited to those stated explicitly in the U.S. Constitution.
A. Implied Powers   B. SALT I   C. Black Tuesday   D. Taft Hartley

156. The leader of efforts to reform the treatment of the mentally ill.
A. Dorothea Dix   B. Neutrality   C. Camp David Accords   D. Thoreau

157. The primary author of the Declaration of Independence, the first secretary of state, and as president, he was responsible for the Louisiana Purchase.
A. Jefferson   B. Aaron Burr   C. Hessians   D. Paul Cuffe

158. President Eisenhower's domestic agenda advocated conservative spending approaches without drastically cutting back New Deal social programs.
A. Emerson B. Modern Republicanism C. Freedom Riders D. Fair Deal

159. Owner of baseball's Dodgers who oversaw their 1958 move from Brooklyn to Los Angeles.
A. Judicial Review B. Young C. Mercantilism D. Walter O'Malley

160. Republican presidential candidate in 1964, Goldwater spearheaded an emergent conservative drive out of the South and West.
A. MacArthur B. Enclosure Movement C. Nat Turner D. Goldwater

161. Shanty towns of the Great Depression, named after President Herbert Hoover.
A. Total War B. Walter O'Malley C. Hoovervilles D. Social Gospel

162. The large influx of gold and silver into Europe from Spanish America during the sixteenth century set off a three-fold rise in prices (the "great inflation").
A. Cabinet B. Price Revolution C. Coxey's Arrny D. Political Slavery

163. Investigative journalists during the Progressive Era, they wrote sensational exposes of social and political problems that helped spark the reform movements of their day.
A. Social Gospel B. Price Revolution C. Copperheads D. Muckrakers

164. Defined by historian Donald Worster as "a social order based on the intensive manipulation of water and its products in an arid setting,"
A. Hoovervilles B. Hydraulic Society C. Coxey's Arrny D. Fourteen Points

165. A massive foreign aid program to Western Europe of $17 billion over four years, beginning in 1948.
A. Marshall Plan B. Patrons of Husbandry C. Knights of Labor D. Central Powers

166. 1985 pledge of American aid to insurgent movements attempting to overthrow Soviet-back regimes in the Third World.
A. Military Reconstruction Act B. Reagan Doctrine C. Permanent Immigrants D. Tariff of Abominations

167. This term refers to the heads of the executive departments.
A. China Lobby B. Freedom Riders C. National Recovery Administration D. Cabinet

168. As vice president, Calhoun anonymously expounded the doctrine of nullification, which held that states could prevent the enforcement of a federal law within their boundaries.
A. Central Powers B. New Deal C. Calhoun, John D. Guadalupe Hidalgo

169. Blanket search warrants used by English customs collectors in the colonies to try to catch suspected smugglers.
A. Fireside Chats B. Permanent Immigrants C. Smog D. Writs of Assistance

170. Six German principalities provided 30,000 soldiers to Great Britain to fight against the American rebels during the War for Independence.
A. Robert Kennedy B. Hessians C. D Day D. Total War

171. This law allows the public and press to request declassification of government documents.
A. Total War B. Joseph Stalin C. Freedom of Information Act D. Scalawags

172. Arms control treaty signed by President Nixon and Soviet premier Leonid Brezhnev.
A. Fireside Chats B. SALT I C. Freedmen's Bureau D. Friedan

173. Immigrants who never intended to make the United States their home.
A. Marshall Plan B. Deregulation C. Birds of Passage D. Hartford Convention

174. The early nineteenth century's leading educational reformer, Mann led the fight for government support for public schools in Massachusetts.
A. Nixon Doctrine   B. Second Continental Congress   C. Khrushchev   D. Horace Mann

175. The last leader of the Soviet Union, he adopted policies of glasnost (political liberalization) and stroika (economic reform).
A. Seward   B. Freedom of Information Act   C. Mercantilism   D. Gorbachev

176. Justified the concentration of wealth and lack of governmental protection of the weak through the ideas of natural selection and survival of the fittest.
A. Prudence Crandall   B. Social Darwinism   C. Bay of Pigs   D. Prohibition

177. Radical leaders in the South during the years leading up to the Civil War, the fire-eaters were persons who took an extreme pro-slavery position.
A. Carpetbaggers   B. Fire eaters   C. New South   D. Pragmatism

178. Declared that the United States would not allow European powers to create new colonies in the Western Hemisphere or to expand the boundaries of existing colonies.
A. Tet Offensive   B. Jefferson   C. Monroe Doctrine   D. Nixon Doctrine

179. Not every person living in the North during the Civil War favored making war against the Confederacy. Such persons came to be identified as Copperheads.
A. Stamp Act Congress   B. Copperheads   C. Monroe Doctrine   D. Kansas Nebraska Act

180. A noted orator, he opposed the War of 1812 and the protectionist tariff of 1816 after his election to the House of Representatives.
A. Webster   B. Guadalupe Hidalgo   C. Billy Yank   D. Progressive Party

181. Conflict in 1957 when governor Orval Faubus sent the Arkansas National Guard to prevent the racial integration of Little Rock's Central High School.
A. Mugwumps   B. Little Rock Crisis   C. Enclosure Movement   D. Oil Crisis

182. A failed plan to assassinate Cuban leader Fidel Castro and liberate Cuba with a trained military force of political exiles.
A. Bay of Pigs   B. Renaissance   C. Separatists   D. Hooverizing

183. A law passed after the South's refusal to accept the Fourteenth Amendment in 1867, it nullified existing state governments and divided the South.
A. Coxey's Arrny   B. Little Rock Crisis   C. Carpetbaggers   D. Military Reconstruction Act

184. A labor organization founded in 1869, it called for the unity of all workers, rejected industrial capitalism, and favored cooperatively owned businesses.
A. Gabriel   B. Stagflation   C. Knights of Labor   D. Dawes Act

185. A reform movement growing out of Jane Addams' Hull House in the late nineteenth century.
A. Jefferson   B. James Polk   C. Settlement House   D. Encomienda System

186. The central banking system of the United States, established with passage of the Federal Reserve Act of 1913.
A. Antifederalists   B. Federal Reserve System   C. Walter O'Malley   D. Rationalism

187. A term of derision applied to those colonists who sought to maintain their allegiance to the British crown. Loyalists.
A. Nixon Doctrine   B. Tory   C. American System of Production   D. Mugwumps

188. The effort to encourage masters to voluntarily emancipate their slaves and to resettle free blacks in Africa.
A. Khrushchev   B. Colonization   C. Popular Sovereignty   D. Marshall Plan

189. President Franklin Delano Roosevelt's controversial plan to appoint Supreme Court justices who were sympathetic to his views, by offering retirement benefits to the sitting justices.
A. Beat Generation   B. Calvinism   C. Court Packing   D. Hooverizing

190. An amendment to an 1846 appropriations bill that would have forbade slavery from any territory acquired from Mexico.
A. Yellow Journalism   B. Wilmot Proviso   C. Camp David Accords   D. Tet Offensive

191. The main base of the U.S. Pacific fleet, which Japan attacked on December 7, 1941, forcing the United States to enter World War II.
A. Joseph Stalin   B. Enclosure Movement   C. Settlement House   D. Pearl Harbor

192. An 1828 protective tariff opposed by many Southerners.
A. Hydraulic Society   B. Tariff of Abominations   C. Freedom of Information Act   D. Pragmatism

193. An economic system built on the assumption that the world's supply of wealth is fixed and that nations must export more goods than they import.
A. John Marshall   B. Mercantilism   C. Enclosure Movement   D. Joseph Smith

194. The pre-Civil War reform movement which sought to curb the drinking of hard liquor.
A. Popular Sovereignty   B. Temperance   C. Marshall Plan   D. Hooverizing

195. A Carter era economic policy, which freed many industries from many government economic controls.
A. Deregulation   B. Queensberry Rules   C. Salutary Neglect   D. Goldwater

196. A political party established in 1912 by supporters of Theodore Roosevelt, proposed a broad program of reform.
A. Progressive Party   B. City Upon a Hill   C. Frederick Douglass   D. SDS

197. President Eisenhower's adjustment to the doctrine of containment. He advocated saving money by emphasizing nuclear over conventional weapons.
A. New Look   B. Neutrality   C. Rationalism   D. Flapper

198. A former West Indian slave who organized an attempted rebellion against slavery in Charleston, South Carolina, in 1822.
A. Denmark Vesey   B. Haymarket Square Riot   C. Joseph Smith   D. Young

199. This term signifies England's relatively benign neglect of its American colonies from about 1690 to 1760.
A. Declension   B. Salutary Neglect   C. Dawes Act   D. James Madison

200. A pencilmaker, poet, and author of the influential essay "Civil Disobedience," Thoreau sought to realize transcendentalist ideals in his personal life.
A. Colonization   B. Seward   C. Thoreau   D. Fireside Chats

From the words provided for each clue, provide the letter of the word which best matches the clue.

201. Passed in 1920, the Constitutional guarantee of women's right to vote.
A. Thoreau   B. Nineteenth Amendment   C. Sagebrush Rebellion   D. Knights of Labor

202. Sociologists who rejected the determinism of the Social Darwinists.
A. Billy Yank   B. Reform Darwinists   C. Trust   D. Religious Liberalism

203. African-American seamstress and active NAACP member arrested for refusing to give up her seat to a white patron in Montgomery, Alabama.
A. Denmark Vesey   B. Rosa Parks   C. Radical Revolutionaries   D. James Madison

96

204. An anti-foreign, anti-Catholic political party that arose following massive Irish and Catholic immigration during the late 1840s.
A. Smog B. Mercantilism C. Know Nothing Party D. Black Codes

205. Alabama governor who ran for president in 1968 as a third-party candidate on the American Independent ticket
A. Enumerated Goods B. Second New Deal C. George Wallace D. Impressment

206. A policy of resettling eastern Indian tribes on lands west of the Mississippi River.
A. Populist Party B. Nixon Doctrine C. Second Great Awakening D. Removal

207. Legal codes that defined the slaveholders' power and the slaves' status as property.
A. Perpetual Servitude B. Mugwumps C. Robert Kennedy D. Slave Codes

208. A broadly influential philosophical and intellectual movement that began in Europe during the eighteenth century.
A. Merchantilism B. Enlightenment C. Calvinism D. Farewell Address

209. American radicals accused of passing atomic secrets to the Soviets during World War II. Executed in 1953.
A. Nonseparatists B. Guadalupe Hidalgo C. Columbian Exchange D. Rosenbergs

210. Industrialist who epitomized the close relationship between government and industry in the West.
A. Plessy vs Ferguson B. Judicial Review C. Northwest Passage D. Henry Kaiser

211. The leader of the Haitian Revolution.
A. Stagflation B. Mugwumps C. Louverture D. Insanity Defense

212. A Quaker schoolteacher, she sparked controversy when she opened a school for the education of free blacks.
A. Price Revolution B. Prudence Crandall C. Black Codes D. Nixon Doctrine

213. This appellation was used to refer to common soldiers serving in Union armies during the Civil War.
A. McCullough vs Maryland B. Fireside Chats C. Billy Yank D. Louverture

214. A cornerstone of good citizenship in republican states, public virtue involved the subordination of individual self-interest to serving the greater good of the whole community.
A. Public Virtue B. Rock and Roll C. Fair Deal D. John Marshall

215. Emphasized the power and omnipotence of God and the importance of seeking to earn saving grace and salvation.
A. Calvinism B. D Day C. John Marshall D. Watergate

216. Adopted in 1964, barred a poll tax in federal elections.
A. Twenty Fourth Amendment B. Alien and Sedition Acts C. Enlightenment D. Stagflation

217. The free black author of An Appeal to the Colored Citizens of the World, which threatened violence if slavery was not abolished.
A. David Walker B. Freedom Riders C. Progressive Party D. Mercantilism

218. Defined by historian Donald Worster as "a social order based on the intensive manipulation of water and its products in an arid setting,"
A. Hydraulic Society B. Kansas Nebraska Act C. Writs of Assistance D. McCullough vs Maryland

219. All slaves in the rebellious Confederate states were to be forever free. However, slavery could continue to exist in border states that were not at war.
A. Grand Alliance B. Military Reconstruction Act C. Prohibition D. Emancipation Proclamation

220. The power of the courts to determine the constitutionality of acts of other branches of government and to declare unconstitutional acts null and void.
A. Judicial Review B. Patrons of Husbandry C. Spoils System D. Kissinger

221. 1985 pledge of American aid to insurgent movements attempting to overthrow Soviet-back regimes in the Third World.
A. Scalawags   B. Reagan Doctrine   C. Yalta Conference   D. Elizabeth Cady Stanton

222. A violent encounter between police and protesters in 1886 in Chicago, which led to the execution of four protest leaders.
A. Haymarket Square Riot   B. New Deal   C. Dartmouth vs Woodward   D. Common Sense

223. The founder of the Mormon Church, Smith was murdered in Illinois in 1844.
A. Whig Party   B. Spoils System   C. Joseph Smith   D. Northwest Passage

224. The Father of the Constitution and the Bill of Rights and a co-founder of the Jeffersonian Republican party, Madison served as president during the War of 1812.
A. James Madison   B. Deregulation   C. Writs of Assistance   D. Cuban Missile Crisis

225. A landmark 1819 Supreme Court decision protecting contracts.
A. D Day   B. Dartmouth vs Woodward   C. Thoreau   D. Northwest Passage

226. Supreme Court decision establishing Congress's power to charter a national bank and declaring unconstitutional a tax imposed by Maryland on the local branch.
A. Calvinism   B. Birds of Passage   C. Republicanism   D. McCullough vs Maryland

227. Conflict in 1957 when governor Orval Faubus sent the Arkansas National Guard to prevent the racial integration of Little Rock's Central High School.
A. Price Revolution   B. Fire eaters   C. Billy Yank   D. Little Rock Crisis

228. Religious songs composed by enslaved African Americans.
A. Calvinism   B. Birds of Passage   C. Spirituals   D. Denmark Vesey

229. During the 1972 presidential campaign, burglars, tied to the Nixon White House, were caught installing eavesdropping devices in Democratic Party headquarters.
A. Whig Party   B. Détente   C. Guadalupe Hidalgo   D. Watergate

230. A labor organization founded in 1869, it called for the unity of all workers, rejected industrial capitalism, and favored cooperatively owned businesses.
A. Spoils System   B. Patrons of Husbandry   C. Knights of Labor   D. Republicans

231. The "father of modern revivalism," Finney devised many techniques adopted by later revival preachers. He encouraged many women to participate actively in revival.
A. Marbury vs Madison   B. Sagebrush Rebellion   C. Finney   D. Rock and Roll

232. Standardized boxing rules of the late nineteenth century, creating structured three-minute rounds with one-minute rest periods.
A. Court Packing   B. Loose Interpretation   C. Great Awakening   D. Queensberry Rules

233. A law passed in 1883 to eliminate political corruption in the federal government and established the Civil Service Commission to administer competitive examinations.
A. Versailles   B. Calhoun, John   C. Pendleton Act   D. Louverture

234. This best-selling pamphlet by Thomas Paine, first published in 1776, denounced the British monarchy, called for American independence.
A. Iranian Hostage Crisis   B. Henry Kaiser   C. Eli Whitney   D. Common Sense

235. Soviet premier in the 1930s and 1940s, known for his violent purges of internal political enemies and his suspicion of Western leaders.
A. Black Tuesday   B. Joseph Stalin   C. Hoovervilles   D. Dawes Act

236. Literary style of the late nineteenth and early twentieth century, where the individual was a helpless victim in a world in which outside forces determined his or her fate.
A. Lusitania   B. Haymarket Square Riot   C. Naturalism   D. Great Migration

237. As an economic incentive to encourage English to settle in Virginia and other English colonies during the seventeenth century.
A. Farewell Address   B. Henry Kaiser   C. Headright   D. James Polk

238. Farmers from western Massachusetts rose up in rebellion against their state government in 1786 because they had failed to obtain tax relief.
A. Settlement House   B. Shays Rebellion   C. Liluokalani   D. Neutrality

239. A relaxation of tensions between the United States and the Soviet Union that was begun by President Richard M. Nixon.
A. American Exceptionalism   B. Equal Rights Amendment   C. Greenback Party   D. Détente

240. The leader of the Mormon church following Joseph Smith's murder, Young led the Mormon exodus from Illinois to the Great Salt Lake.
A. Haymarket Square Riot   B. Shays Rebellion   C. Young   D. Calvinism

241. A leading orator in the abolitionist and women's rights movements, Sojourner Truth was born into slavery in New York's Hudson River Valley and escaped in 1826.
A. Axis Powers   B. Garrison   C. Horace Mann   D. Sojourner Truth

242. The most controversial element of the Compromise of 1850, the Fugitive Slave Law provided for the return of runaway slaves to their masters.
A. Fugitive Slave Law   B. Republicanism   C. Axis Powers   D. Twenty Fourth Amendment

243. An organization established by Congress on March 3, 1865 to deal with the dislocations of the Civil War.
A. Removal   B. Little Rock Crisis   C. Alien and Sedition Acts   D. Freedmen's Bureau

244. The second stage of President Franklin Delano Roosevelt's economic recovery and reform program, launched January 4, 1935.
A. Second New Deal   B. Prohibition   C. Rosa Parks   D. Perpetual Servitude

245. June 6, 1944, the day Allied forces landed on the beaches of Normandy, in France, leading to the defeat of Germany.
A. Stamp Act Congress   B. D Day   C. Impressment   D. Finney

246. The conflict in 1962 prompted by Soviet installation of missiles on Cuba and President Kennedy's announcement to the American Public.
A. Kissinger   B. Fugitive Slave Law   C. Garrison   D. Cuban Missile Crisis

247. The early nineteenth century's leading educational reformer, Mann led the fight for government support for public schools in Massachusetts.
A. Horace Mann   B. Open Door Note   C. Total War   D. Separatists

248. His administration was marked by the acquisition of Florida (1819), the Missouri Compromise (1820), and the Monroe Doctrine (1823).
A. James Monroe   B. Writs of Assistance   C. AFL   D. Stagflation

249. A wave of religious fervor and revivalism that swept the United States from the early nineteenth century through the Civil War.
A. Greenback Party   B. Second Great Awakening   C. Deregulation   D. Beat Generation

250. The meeting in February 1945 to determine the post-World War II world order.
A. Yalta Conference   B. Denmark Vesey   C. Scopes Trial   D. New Look

251. This 1973 law required presidents to win specific authorization from Congress to engage U.S. forces in foreign combat for more than 90 days.
A. Columbian Exchange   B. War Powers Act   C. Wilmot Proviso   D. Price Revolution

252. Indentured servitude represented temporary service for a specified period, usually from four to seven years, to a legally designated owner.
A. Carpetbaggers   B. National Recovery Administration   C. Writs of Assistance   D. Perpetual Servitude

253. In World War II, the alliance of German and Italy, and later Japan.
A. Evangelical Revivalism   B. Axis Powers   C. Jazz   D. Calvinism

254. During the Age of Exploration, adventurers from England, France, and the Netherlands kept seeking an all-water route across North America.
A. Calvinism   B. Indentured Servitude   C. Black Power   D. Northwest Passage

255. The economic conditions of slow economic growth, rising inflation, and flagging productivity that characterized the American economy during the 1970s.
A. Northwest Passage   B. Sagebrush Rebellion   C. James Madison   D. Stagflation

256. Vietminh siege of 13,000 French soldiers in 1954 at a remote military outpost. The French surrender led to the 1956 elections designed to reunify Vietnam.
A. Electric Trolley   B. Stamp Act Congress   C. Stagflation   D. Dien Bien Phu

257. The auxiliary women's unit to the U.S. army.
A. WAC   B. Reagan Doctrine   C. New Look   D. Greenback Party

258. As president of the United States during the Mexican War, Polk increased American territory by a third.
A. Prudence Crandall   B. Aaron Burr   C. James Polk   D. Alien and Sedition Acts

259. The pre-Civil War reform movement which sought to curb the drinking of hard liquor.
A. Black Tuesday   B. Populist Party   C. Temperance   D. Jazz

260. Declared that the United States would not allow European powers to create new colonies in the Western Hemisphere or to expand the boundaries of existing colonies.
A. Monroe Doctrine   B. Republicans   C. Specie   D. Hydraulic Society

261. An amendment to an 1846 appropriations bill that would have forbade slavery from any territory acquired from Mexico.
A. Wilmot Proviso   B. Total War   C. Bay of Pigs   D. Santa Anna

262. The peace treaty ending the Mexican War gave the United States California, Nevada, New Mexico, Utah, and parts of Arizona, Colorado, Kansas, and Wyoming.
A. Billy Yank   B. Finney   C. Joseph Stalin   D. Guadalupe Hidalgo

263. During the early nineteenth century, a movement arose to end the death penalty.
A. Platt Amendment   B. WAC   C. Capital Punishment   D. Spoils System

264. Parliament passed laws that allowed profit-seeking landowners to fence in their open fields to raise more sheep.
A. Enclosure Movement   B. Axis Powers   C. McCullough vs Maryland   D. Black Codes

265. A confederation of labor unions founded in 1886, it was composed mainly of skilled craft unions.
A. Rosenbergs   B. Marbury vs Madison   C. AFL   D. Era of Good Feelings

266. Thomas Jefferson's first vice president, who killed Alexander Hamilton in a duel in 1804.
A. Mugwumps   B. Aaron Burr   C. Emancipation Proclamation   D. Tory

267. In World War II, the alliance between the United States, Great Britain, and France.
A. John Adams   B. Radical Revolutionaries   C. Freedom Riders   D. Grand Alliance

268. The belief that God ordains certain people to amass money and use it to further God's purposes, it justified the concentration of wealth.
A. Carpetbaggers   B. Hydraulic Society   C. Iranian Hostage Crisis   D. Gospel of Wealth

269. October 29,1929, the day of the stock market crash that initiated the Great Depression.
A. Guadalupe Hidalgo   B. Black Tuesday   C. Permanent Immigrants   D. Marbury vs Madison

270. Celebrated American general removed by Truman after his criticisms of America's containment policy.
A. Cuban Missile Crisis   B. Great Awakening   C. Watergate   D. MacArthur

271. Policy set forth in 1899 by Secretary of State John Hay preventing further partitioning of China by European powers and protecting the principle of free trade.
A. Open Door Note   B. Sharecropping   C. Insanity Defense   D. Social Gospel

272. An early American political party opposing influence from monarchy.
A. Freedmen's Bureau   B. Removal   C. Fugitive Slave Law   D. Whig Party

273. The legal principle that a criminal act should only be punished if the offender was fully capable of distinguishing right from wrong.
A. Non Intercourse Act   B. Carpetbaggers   C. Insanity Defense   D. Permanent Immigrants

274. Appointed Chief Justice in 1801, Marshall expanded the Supreme Court's power and prestige and established the court's power of Judicial Review.
A. Henry Kaiser   B. Knights of Labor   C. Nat Turner   D. John Marshall

275. President Nixon argued for "Vietnamization," the notion that the South Vietnamese would carry more of the war's combat burden.
A. Rosenbergs   B. Black Codes   C. Nixon Doctrine   D. Loose Interpretation

276. A business model where any single entity had the power to control competition within a given industry, such as oil production.
A. Open Door Note   B. Large Policy   C. Trust   D. Antifederalists

277. A Supreme Court decision in 1896 that ruled "separate but equal" facilities for African Americans were constitutional under the Fourteenth Amendment.
A. Plessy vs Ferguson   B. Judicial Review   C. Patriarchal   D. Gabriel

278. Justified the concentration of wealth and lack of governmental protection of the weak through the ideas of natural selection and survival of the fittest.
A. Temperance   B. Sputnik   C. Social Darwinism   D. Muckrakers

279. Civil rights activists who in 1961 demonstrated that despite a federal ban on segregated travel on interstate buses, segregation prevailed in parts of the South.
A. Freedom Riders   B. Matrilineal   C. Tory   D. Second Great Awakening

280. A political party founded in 1874 to promote the issuance of legal tender paper currency not backed by precious metals in order to inflate the money supply.
A. Radical Revolutionaries   B. Finney   C. Muckrakers   D. Greenback Party

281. After an early public life as a committed Cold Warrior, Kennedy ran for the Democratic nomination in 1968 as a peace candidate representative of young liberals.
A. Coxey's Army   B. Robert Kennedy   C. Strict Construction   D. Rock and Roll

282. President Franklin Delano Roosevelt's program designed to bring about economic recovery and reform during the Great Depression.
A. Manhattan Project   B. New Deal   C. New Look   D. Progressive Party

283. A political party established in 1912 by supporters of Theodore Roosevelt, proposed a broad program of reform.
A. Gospel of Wealth   B. Finney   C. Progressive Party   D. Santa Anna

284. Legislation passed in 1887 to authorize the president to divide tribal land and distribute it to individual Native Americans.
A. Khrushchev   B. Dawes Act   C. Sojourner Truth   D. Coxey's Arrny

285. Failed 1948 legislative package proposed by President Truman.
A. Fair Deal   B. Dred Scott   C. Headright   D. Navigation System

286. Public transportation for urban neighborhoods, using electric current from overhead wires.
A. Electric Trolley   B. Insanity Defense   C. Black Tuesday   D. McCullough vs Maryland

287. Immigrants coming to America to settle permanently, often due to ethnic and religious persecution at home.
A. Settlement House   B. Radical Revolutionaries   C. Santa Anna   D. Permanent Immigrants

288. An 1809 statute which replaced the Embargo of 1807. It forbade trade with Britain, France, and their possessions, but reopened trade with other countries.
A. Non Intercourse Act   B. Popular Sovereignty   C. Yalta Conference   D. Little Rock Crisis

289. Laws passed by Southern state legislatures during Reconstruction, while Congress was out of session.
A. Black Codes   B. Liliuokalani   C. Robert Kennedy   D. Alien and Sedition Acts

290. A labor system was similar to that of indentured servitude in providing a way for persons without financial means to get to America.
A. Sojourner Truth   B. McCullough vs Maryland   C. Redemptioners   D. Fair Deal

291. President Eisenhower's adjustment to the doctrine of containment. He advocated saving money by emphasizing nuclear over conventional weapons.
A. Kansas Nebraska Act   B. Insanity Defense   C. New Look   D. Iranian Hostage Crisis

292. The ban of the production, sale, and consumption of alcoholic beverages.
A. Large Policy   B. Prohibition   C. Guadalupe Hidalgo   D. Bill of Rights

293. This landmark 1803 Supreme Court decision, which established the principle of judicial review.
A. Capital Punishment   B. Great Awakening   C. Mercantilism   D. Marbury vs Madison

294. A reform faction of the Republican party in the 1870s and 1880s, they crusaded for honest and effective government and some supported Democratic reform candidates.
A. Spirituals   B. Scopes Trial   C. City Upon a Hill   D. Mugwumps

295. Failed movement led by conservative Western politicians to cede federal control of western land to individual states.
A. Sit in   B. New South   C. Sagebrush Rebellion   D. Stamp Act Congress

296. Social and political systems are denoted by power and authority residing in males, such as in the father of the family.
A. Kissinger   B. Tory   C. Patriarchal   D. Emancipation Proclamation

297. The program by which the United States provided arms and supplies to the Allies in World War II before joining the fighting.
A. Détente   B. Watergate   C. Lend Lease   D. Plessy vs Ferguson

298. Personable Soviet premier during Eisenhower's presidential term. Khrushchev condemned Stalin's purges and welcomed a melting of the Cold War.
A. Large Policy   B. Khrushchev   C. Hoovervilles   D. Beat Generation

299. A rallying cry for more militant blacks advocated by younger leaders beginning in the mid-1960s.
A. Court Packing   B. Black Power   C. Separatists   D. Stamp Act Congress

300. The national security advisor to President Nixon. A staunch anti-Communist. He was Nixon's closest associate on matters of foreign policy.
A. Laissez faire   B. Carpetbaggers   C. Social Darwinism   D. Kissinger

From the words provided for each clue, provide the letter of the word which best matches the clue.

1. __B__ Passed in 1798 designed to curb criticism of the federal government.
   A. Patrons of Husbandry   B. Alien and Sedition Acts   C. City Upon a Hill   D. Free Soil Party

2. __D__ The meeting in February 1945 to determine the post-World War II world order.
   A. Fugitive Slave Law   B. Pendleton Act   C. Rationalism   D. Yalta Conference

3. __B__ The practice of controlling every phase of production by owning the sources of raw materials and often the transportation facilities needed to distribute the product.
   A. Yellow Journalism   B. Vertical Integration   C. China Lobby   D. Goldwater

4. __B__ The mass movement of African Americans from the South to the North during World War I.
   A. Colonization   B. Great Migration   C. First Continental Congress   D. Judicial Review

5. __A__ This law allows the public and press to request declassification of government documents.
   A. Freedom of Information Act   B. Renaissance   C. Navigation System   D. Kansas Nebraska Act

6. __C__ A backlash against immigration by white native-born Protestants. Nativism could be based on racial prejudice, religion, politics, and economics.
   A. Committee on Public Information   B. D Day   C. Nativism   D. Radical Republicans

7. __C__ The view that the powers of the national government are limited to those described in the U.S. Constitution.
   A. D Day   B. Kissinger   C. Strict Construction   D. National Recovery Administration

8. __A__ A secret organization founded in the southern states during Reconstruction to terrorize and intimidate former slaves and prevent them from voting or holding public office.
   A. Ku Klux Klan   B. Settlement House   C. David Walker   D. Garrison

9. __C__ A term for hard coin, such as gold or silver, that can also back and give a fixed point of valuation to paper currencies.
   A. Rationalism   B. Populist Party   C. Specie   D. First Continental Congress

10. __B__ A political party founded in 1874 to promote the issuance of legal tender paper currency not backed by precious metals in order to inflate the money supply.
    A. Renaissance   B. Greenback Party   C. Scopes Trial   D. Northwest Passage

11. __B__ Civil rights activists who in 1961 demonstrated that despite a federal ban on segregated travel on interstate buses, segregation prevailed in parts of the South.
    A. Settlement House   B. Freedom Riders   C. Neutrality   D. Fireside Chats

12. __D__ A group of New England intellectuals who glorified nature and believed that each person contains god-like potentialities.
    A. League of Nations   B. Rosenbergs   C. Interstate Commerce Commission   D. Transcendentalists

13. __A__ Personable Soviet premier during Eisenhower's presidential term. Khrushchev condemned Stalin's purges and welcomed a melting of the Cold War.
    A. Khrushchev   B. Indulgences   C. Johnny Reb   D. American System

14. __D__ President Woodrow Wilson's formula for peace after World War I.
    A. Garrison   B. Webster   C. Salutary Neglect   D. Fourteen Points

15. __B__ A reform movement growing out of Jane Addams' Hull House in the late nineteenth century.
    A. Populist Party   B. Settlement House   C. Transcendentalists   D. Jazz

16. B This landmark 1803 Supreme Court decision, which established the principle of judicial review.
A. Fugitive Slave Law   B. Marbury vs Madison   C. Paul Cuffe   D. Watergate

17. C Alabama governor who ran for president in 1968 as a third-party candidate on the American Independent ticket
A. Rationalism   B. Joint Stock Companies   C. George Wallace   D. Protestant Reformation

18. A Founder of the nation's first school to teach deaf mutes to read and write and communicate through hand signals.
A. Gallaudet   B. Horace Mann   C. Dumbbell Tenement   D. City Upon a Hill

19. B The auxiliary women's unit to the U.S. army.
A. War Powers Act   B. WAC   C. Oil Crisis   D. Trust

20. D Apartment buildings built to minimal codes and designed to cram the largest number of people into the smallest amount of space.
A. Henry Clay   B. Rosa Parks   C. David Walker   D. Dumbbell Tenement

21. D The founder of the Mormon Church, Smith was murdered in Illinois in 1844.
A. Evangelical Revivalism   B. Electric Trolley   C. Pendleton Act   D. Joseph Smith

22. B A policy of resettling eastern Indian tribes on lands west of the Mississippi River.
A. Samuel Howe   B. Removal   C. Johnny Reb   D. American System

23. D Outlawed the closed shop, gave presidential power to delay strikes with a "cooling-off" period, and curtailed the political and economic power of organized labor.
A. Yellow Journalism   B. Dartmouth vs Woodward   C. Zimmermann   D. Taft Hartley

24. C Public transportation for urban neighborhoods, using electric current from overhead wires.
A. China Lobby   B. Divine Right   C. Electric Trolley   D. Public Virtue

25. A An antislavery political party founded in 1839.
A. Liberty Party   B. Scalawags   C. Nat Turner   D. Antifederalists

26. C Parliament passed laws that allowed profit-seeking landowners to fence in their open fields to raise more sheep.
A. D Day   B. Fireside Chats   C. Enclosure Movement   D. Platt Amendment

27. A This appellation was used to refer to common soldiers serving in Union armies during the Civil War.
A. Billy Yank   B. Khrushchev   C. Joseph Stalin   D. Judicial Review

28. C A black Baptist preacher who led a revolt against slavery in Southampton County in southern Virginia in 1831.
A. Seward   B. Gorbachev   C. Nat Turner   D. First Continental Congress

29. A The process of transferring plants, animals, foods, diseases, wealth, and culture between Europe and the Americas.
A. Columbian Exchange   B. Reagan Doctrine   C. Public Virtue   D. Oil Crisis

30. C A rallying cry for more militant blacks advocated by younger leaders beginning in the mid-1960s.
A. Open Door Note   B. New Look   C. Black Power   D. Harlem Renaissance

31. A America's leading exponent of religious liberalism, Channing was one of the founders of American Unitarianism.
A. Channing   B. Queensberry Rules   C. Dumbbell Tenement   D. Specie

32. D A Supreme Court decision in 1896 that ruled "separate but equal" facilities for African Americans were constitutional under the Fourteenth Amendment.
A. Radical Republicans   B. Yalta Conference   C. Paul Cuffe   D. Plessy vs Ferguson

33. **B** Herbert Hoover's program as director of the Food Administration to conserve food during World War I.
A. Equal Rights Amendment   B. Hooverizing   C. Fugitive Slave Law   D. Open Door Note

34. **D** Six German principalities provided 30,000 soldiers to Great Britain to fight against the American rebels during the War for Independence.
A. Jefferson   B. Dartmouth vs Woodward   C. Cuban Missile Crisis   D. Hessians

35. **B** Black student who courageously sought admission into all-white University of Mississippi in 1962. His enrollment sparked a riot instigated by a white mob.
A. Hartford Convention   B. James Meredith   C. Nativism   D. Central Powers

36. **B** A cornerstone of good citizenship in republican states, public virtue involved the subordination of individual self-interest to serving the greater good of the whole community.
A. Fair Deal   B. Public Virtue   C. Evangelical Revivalism   D. Dumbbell Tenement

37. **A** King and Parliament legislated a series of Navigation Acts that established England as the central hub of trade.
A. Navigation System   B. Declension   C. Lend Lease   D. Beat Generation

38. **B** The most controversial element of the Compromise of 1850, the Fugitive Slave Law provided for the return of runaway slaves to their masters.
A. Second New Deal   B. Fugitive Slave Law   C. Equal Rights Amendment   D. McCullough vs Maryland

39. **B** President Franklin Delano Roosevelt's program designed to bring about economic recovery and reform during the Great Depression.
A. New Look   B. New Deal   C. Scopes Trial   D. Reagan Doctrine

40. **B** Legislation establishing mandatory insurance to be carried by employers to cover on-the-job injuries to their workers.
A. Sputnik   B. Workmens Compensation   C. Emancipation Proclamation   D. Columbian Exchange

41. **B** A confederation of labor unions founded in 1886, it was composed mainly of skilled craft unions.
A. New South   B. AFL   C. Loose Interpretation   D. Indentured Servitude

42. **D** An American military intervention in Panama in December 1989, which was launched against Panama's leader, Manuel Noriega, who was indicted on drug-related charges.
A. Coxey's Arrny   B. Antinomian   C. Indentured Servitude   D. Operation Just Cause

43. **A** Proposed Constitutional amendment that would prohibit discrimination on the basis of gender.
A. Equal Rights Amendment   B. Khrushchev   C. Carter   D. Joseph Smith

44. **B** As opposed to limited war, total war usually denotes a military conflict in which warfare ultimately affects the entire population, civilian as well as military.
A. Shays Rebellion   B. Total War   C. Coney Island   D. Writs of Assistance

45. **C** An informal group of media leaders and political pundits who criticized the communist takeover of China, claiming the United States could have prevented it.
A. New South   B. Kissinger   C. China Lobby   D. Navigation System

46. **A** Republican presidential candidate in 1964, Goldwater spearheaded an emergent conservative drive out of the South and West.
A. Goldwater   B. Freedmen's Bureau   C. Santa Anna   D. Transcendentalists

47. **C** The primary author of the Declaration of Independence, the first secretary of state, and as president, he was responsible for the Louisiana Purchase.
A. Henry Kaiser   B. War Powers Act   C. Jefferson   D. Horace Mann

48. C The economic conditions of slow economic growth, rising inflation, and flagging productivity that characterized the American economy during the 1970s.
A. Sputnik   B. Joseph Stalin   C. Stagflation   D. Non Intercourse Act

49. C In World War I, Germany and Austria-Hungary and their allies.
A. Populist Party   B. Freedom Riders   C. Central Powers   D. Neutrality

50. A The government in Spain gave away large tracts of conquered land in Spanish America, including whole villages of indigenous peoples, to court favorites.
A. Encomienda System   B. Hoovervilles   C. Reagan Doctrine   D. Kissinger

51. A Argued in favor of establishing more democratic forms of government.
A. Radical Revolutionaries   B. American Exceptionalism   C. Cabinet   D. Seward

52. B The ban of the production, sale, and consumption of alcoholic beverages.
A. Vertical Integration   B. Prohibition   C. Goldwater   D. Yellow Journalism

53. D The board established in January 1942 to help mobilize the U.S. economy for war production.
A. Gospel of Wealth   B. Oil Crisis   C. Channing   D. War Production Board

54. D Point Fourteen of Wilson's Fourteen Points, the proposal to establish an international organization to guarantee the territorial integrity of independent nations.
A. Tory   B. New Deal   C. Samuel Howe   D. League of Nations

55. D These 85 newspaper essays, written in support of ratification of the Constitution of 1787 in New York by James Madison, Alexander Hamilton, and John Jay.
A. Populist Party   B. Lend Lease   C. American System of Production   D. Federalist Papers

56. B The federal government's plan to revive industry during the Great Depression through rational planning.
A. Committee on Public Information   B. National Recovery Administration   C. Radical Republicans   D. Salutary Neglect

57. B Literally meaning against the laws of human governance.
A. Hessians   B. Antinomian   C. Modern Republicanism   D. Monroe Doctrine

58. A An antislavery political party founded in 1848.
A. Free Soil Party   B. Indulgences   C. Jazz   D. Kansas Nebraska Act

59. C Founder of the nation's first school for the blind.
A. Capital Punishment   B. Henry Kaiser   C. Samuel Howe   D. George Wallace

60. B American radicals accused of passing atomic secrets to the Soviets during World War II. Executed in 1953.
A. National Recovery Administration   B. Rosenbergs   C. Evangelical Revivalism   D. Indentured Servitude

61. B Religious dissenters from England who believed that the state-supported Church of England, was too corrupt to be reformed.
A. Camp David Accords   B. Separatists   C. Renaissance   D. Workmens Compensation

62. D Conflict in 1957 when governor Orval Faubus sent the Arkansas National Guard to prevent the racial integration of Little Rock's Central High School.
A. Marbury vs Madison   B. Colonization   C. Radical Revolutionaries   D. Little Rock Crisis

63. B The program by which the United States provided arms and supplies to the Allies in World War II before joining the fighting.
A. Electric Trolley   B. Lend Lease   C. Dartmouth vs Woodward   D. League of Nations

64. C The second stage of President Franklin Delano Roosevelt's economic recovery and reform program, launched January 4, 1935.
A. Seward   B. Writs of Assistance   C. Second New Deal   D. Paul Cuffe

65. D Failed movement led by conservative Western politicians to cede federal control of western land to individual states.
A. Alien and Sedition Acts   B. Pearl Harbor   C. Antinomian   D. Sagebrush Rebellion

66. C Musical style based on improvisation within a band format, combining African traditions of repetition, call and response, and strong beat with European structure.
A. Initiative and Referendum   B. Evangelical Revivalism   C. Jazz   D. Populist Party

67. B Blanket search warrants used by English customs collectors in the colonies to try to catch suspected smugglers.
A. Open Door Note   B. Writs of Assistance   C. Antinomian   D. Henry Kaiser

68. D Policy set forth in 1899 by Secretary of State John Hay preventing further partitioning of China by European powers and protecting the principle of free trade.
A. AFL   B. Finney   C. Reform Darwinists   D. Open Door Note

69. B An early American political party opposing influence from monarchy.
A. Temperance   B. Whig Party   C. Capital Punishment   D. Free Soil Party

70. C A procedure that allows citizens to propose legislation through petitions.
A. Frederick Douglass   B. Vertical Integration   C. Initiative and Referendum   D. Sherman Antitrust

71. C The high cost of labor led to the establishment of a system of mass production through the manufacture of interchangeable parts.
A. Operation Just Cause   B. Patriarchal   C. American System of Production   D. Hartford Convention

72. D Organization established in 1909 to fight for African-American civil rights through legal action.
A. Hartford Convention   B. Rationalism   C. Jazz   D. NAACP

73. B A political party established in 1892 sought to inflate the currency with silver dollars and to establish an income tax.
A. Strict Construction   B. Populist Party   C. Joseph Stalin   D. Johnny Reb

74. A The belief that God ordains certain people to amass money and use it to further God's purposes, it justified the concentration of wealth.
A. Gospel of Wealth   B. Freedmen's Bureau   C. Court Packing   D. Republicanism

75. C Beginning in the 1400s, the European Renaissance represented an intellectual and cultural flowering in the arts, literature, philosophy, and the sciences.
A. AFL   B. Open Door Note   C. Renaissance   D. James Meredith

76. D A religious viewpoint that rejected the Calvinist doctrines of original sin and predestination and stressed the basic goodness of human nature.
A. Encomienda System   B. Prohibition   C. Liberty Party   D. Religious Liberalism

77. D Indentured servitude represented temporary service for a specified period, usually from four to seven years, to a legally designated owner.
A. Yellow Journalism   B. Finney   C. Salutary Neglect   D. Perpetual Servitude

78. A Were in favor of splitting authority between their proposed strong national government and the states.
A. Federalists   B. Writs of Assistance   C. Trust   D. First Continental Congress

79. C The effort to encourage masters to voluntarily emancipate their slaves and to resettle free blacks in Africa.
A. Sagebrush Rebellion   B. Yellow Journalism   C. Colonization   D. American System

80. B A business model where any single entity had the power to control competition within a given industry, such as oil production.
A. Divine Right   B. Trust   C. Second New Deal   D. Religious Liberalism

81. B He was an advocate of the "American System," which called for a protective tariff, a national bank, and federally funded internal improvements.
A. Federalist Papers   B. Henry Clay   C. Yellow Journalism   D. SDS

82. B During the 1972 presidential campaign, burglars, tied to the Nixon White House, were caught installing eavesdropping devices in Democratic Party headquarters.
A. Hydraulic Society   B. Watergate   C. Knights of Labor   D. Scalawags

83. B During the early nineteenth century, a movement arose to end the death penalty.
A. Seward   B. Capital Punishment   C. Camp David Accords   D. McCullough vs Maryland

84. B The early nineteenth century's leading educational reformer, Mann led the fight for government support for public schools in Massachusetts.
A. Watergate   B. Horace Mann   C. SDS   D. American System

85. B The leader of the Haitian Revolution.
A. Sharecropping   B. Louverture   C. Scopes Trial   D. Garrison

86. C Advocated a canal through the Central American isthmus and a strong American naval presence in the Caribbean and Pacific.
A. Fair Deal   B. Trust   C. Large Policy   D. Joseph Stalin

87. B A landmark 1819 Supreme Court decision protecting contracts.
A. Shays Rebellion   B. Dartmouth vs Woodward   C. Freedmen's Bureau   D. Walter O'Malley

88. D The radical organization aimed to rid American society of poverty, racism, and violence through participatory democracy.
A. Nativism   B. Elizabeth Cady Stanton   C. Great Migration   D. SDS

89. D In World War II, the alliance between the United States, Great Britain, and France.
A. Goldwater   B. Republicanism   C. Calvinism   D. Grand Alliance

90. C At the time of the American Revolution, republicanism referred to the concept that sovereignty is vested in the people; the citizens of the nation.
A. Evangelical Revivalism   B. Capital Punishment   C. Republicanism   D. Kissinger

91. B U.S. policy of impartiality during World Wars I and II.
A. Hessians   B. Neutrality   C. Tariff of Abominations   D. Johnny Reb

92. B The national security advisor to President Nixon. A staunch anti-Communist. He was Nixon's closest associate on matters of foreign policy.
A. Hoovervilles   B. Kissinger   C. Freedom of Information Act   D. Salutary Neglect

93. B The chemical-laden fog caused by automobile engines, a serious problem in southern California.
A. New Look   B. Smog   C. Dumbbell Tenement   D. Marshall Plan

94. C Phrase from John Winthrop's sermon, "A Model of Christian Charity," in which he challenged his fellow Puritans to build a model, ideal community in America.
A. Specie   B. Trust   C. City Upon a Hill   D. Temperance

95. A Russian satellite that successfully orbited the earth in 1957, prompting Americans to question their own values and educational system.
A. Sputnik   B. James Meredith   C. Louverture   D. Nat Turner

96. C Adopted in 1964, barred a poll tax in federal elections.
A. Smog   B. Bonus Army   C. Twenty Fourth Amendment   D. Spoils System

97. B A current of Protestant Christianity emphasizing personal conversion, repentance of sin, and the authority of Scripture.
A. Manumission   B. Evangelical Revivalism   C. Spirituals   D. Paul Cuffe

98. C Social and political systems are denoted by power and authority residing in males, such as in the father of the family.
A. Twenty Fourth Amendment   B. D Day   C. Patriarchal   D. Antifederalists

99. B African-American seamstress and active NAACP member arrested for refusing to give up her seat to a white patron in Montgomery, Alabama.
A. Tory   B. Rosa Parks   C. Central Powers   D. Stagflation

100. B These companies were given the right to develop trade between England and certain geographic regions, such as Russia or India.
A. Jefferson   B. Joint Stock Companies   C. Ku Klux Klan   D. Hessians

From the words provided for each clue, provide the letter of the word which best matches the clue.

101. A In World War II, the alliance of German and Italy, and later Japan.
A. Axis Powers   B. Prudence Crandall   C. Populist Party   D. Smog

102. A Indentured servitude represented temporary service for a specified period, usually from four to seven years, to a legally designated owner.
A. Perpetual Servitude   B. McCullough vs Maryland   C. Emerson   D. Tariff of Abominations

103. C The chemical-laden fog caused by automobile engines, a serious problem in southern California.
A. Neutrality   B. Bay of Pigs   C. Smog   D. Federalists

104. B Legislation passed in 1887 to authorize the president to divide tribal land and distribute it to individual Native Americans.
A. Nationalists   B. Dawes Act   C. American System of Production   D. Webster

105. C The principle that the people living in the western territories should decide whether or not to permit slavery.
A. Hartford Convention   B. Rationalism   C. Popular Sovereignty   D. Johnny Reb

106. A An informal group of media leaders and political pundits who criticized the communist takeover of China, claiming the United States could have prevented it.
A. China Lobby   B. SDS   C. Bay of Pigs   D. Rosenbergs

107. A The liberal reform program of President Lyndon Johnson. The program included civil rights legislation, increased public spending to help the poor, Medicare, and Medicaid.
A. Great Society   B. Thoreau   C. Progressive Party   D. Pearl Harbor

108. A The economic conditions of slow economic growth, rising inflation, and flagging productivity that characterized the American economy during the 1970s.
A. Stagflation   B. Common Sense   C. Axis Powers   D. Fair Deal

109. B Policy set forth in 1899 by Secretary of State John Hay preventing further partitioning of China by European powers and protecting the principle of free trade.
A. Stagflation   B. Open Door Note   C. Rationalism   D. Northwest Passage

110. C Alabama governor who ran for president in 1968 as a third-party candidate on the American Independent ticket
A. Hartford Convention   B. Zimmermann   C. George Wallace   D. Social Gospel

111. B Controversial 1854 legislation that opened Kansas and Nebraska to white settlement, repealed the Compromise of 1820, and led opponents to form the Republican party.
A. Second Continental Congress   B. Kansas Nebraska Act   C. Greenbacks   D. Plantation Legend

112. B Literally meaning against the laws of human governance.
A. Little Rock Crisis   B. Antinomian   C. Naturalism   D. Modern Republicanism

113. B Thomas Jefferson's first vice president, who killed Alexander Hamilton in a duel in 1804.
A. Queensberry Rules   B. Aaron Burr   C. American Exceptionalism   D. Deregulation

114. B Russian satellite that successfully orbited the earth in 1957, prompting Americans to question their own values and educational system.
A. Queensberry Rules   B. Sputnik   C. Smog   D. SALT I

115. D An organization founded in 1867 to aid farmers through its local granges.
A. Calhoun, John   B. Platt Amendment   C. Whig Party   D. Patrons of Husbandry

116. B A policy of resettling eastern Indian tribes on lands west of the Mississippi River.
A. Aaron Burr   B. Removal   C. Platt Amendment   D. Guadalupe Hidalgo

117. A Emphasized the power and omnipotence of God and the importance of seeking to earn saving grace and salvation.
A. Calvinism   B. Popular Sovereignty   C. Great Society   D. Goldwater

118. D The process of transferring plants, animals, foods, diseases, wealth, and culture between Europe and the Americas.
A. Hooverizing   B. Gorbachev   C. New South   D. Columbian Exchange

119. C A violent encounter between police and protesters in 1886 in Chicago, which led to the execution of four protest leaders.
A. Goldwater   B. Seward   C. Haymarket Square Riot   D. Social Darwinism

120. C Celebrated American general removed by Truman after his criticisms of America's containment policy.
A. Copperheads   B. Freedom Riders   C. MacArthur   D. Scalawags

121. C The legal principle that a criminal act should only be punished if the offender was fully capable of distinguishing right from wrong.
A. Dartmouth vs Woodward   B. Nonseparatists   C. Insanity Defense   D. Good Neighbor

122. B Telegram from German Foreign Minister Arnold Zimmermann to the German ambassador to Mexico pledging a Mexican-German alliance against the United States.
A. Black Tuesday   B. Zimmermann   C. Common Sense   D. Plantation Legend

123. C A North Vietnamese offensive in January 1968 against every major South Vietnamese target.
A. Neutrality   B. D Day   C. Tet Offensive   D. Bay of Pigs

124. D He was an advocate of the "American System," which called for a protective tariff, a national bank, and federally funded internal improvements.
A. Sit in   B. James Madison   C. New Deal   D. Henry Clay

125. D During the Age of Exploration, adventurers from England, France, and the Netherlands kept seeking an all-water route across North America.
A. China Lobby   B. Good Neighbor   C. Salutary Neglect   D. Northwest Passage

126. D A political party established in 1892 sought to inflate the currency with silver dollars and to establish an income tax.
A. Flapper   B. Goldwater   C. Channing   D. Populist Party

127. D June 6, 1944, the day Allied forces landed on the beaches of Normandy, in France, leading to the defeat of Germany.
A. Freedom Riders   B. Salutary Neglect   C. National Recovery Administration   D. D Day

128. B A Supreme Court decision in 1896 that ruled "separate but equal" facilities for African Americans were constitutional under the Fourteenth Amendment.
A. Rosenbergs   B. Plessy vs Ferguson   C. Dartmouth vs Woodward   D. Johnny Reb

129. D Applied Christian doctrines to social problems.
A. Scalawags   B. Dien Bien Phu   C. Nineteenth Amendment   D. Social Gospel

130. A The view that the powers of the national government are limited to those described in the U.S. Constitution.
A. Strict Construction   B. Price Revolution   C. Bay of Pigs   D. Young

131. B Literary style of the late nineteenth and early twentieth century, where the individual was a helpless victim in a world in which outside forces determined his or her fate.
A. American System of Production   B. Naturalism   C. New Look   D. Nat Turner

132. D This informal group of pro-colonial rights leaders in Boston helped organize resistance against unwanted British policies, such as the Stamp Act.
A. Republicanism   B. Kansas Nebraska Act   C. Hamilton   D. Loyal Nine

133. D Argued in favor of establishing more democratic forms of government.
A. Matrilineal   B. Antinomian   C. Temperance   D. Radical Revolutionaries

134. D The radical organization aimed to rid American society of poverty, racism, and violence through participatory democracy.
A. George Wallace   B. Hydraulic Society   C. Khrushchev   D. SDS

135. C The mass movement of African Americans from the South to the North during World War I.
A. Progressive Party   B. Large Policy   C. Great Migration   D. Sagebrush Rebellion

136. B The Father of the Constitution and the Bill of Rights and a co-founder of the Jeffersonian Republican party, Madison served as president during the War of 1812.
A. Queensberry Rules   B. James Madison   C. Carpetbaggers   D. Colonization

137. B Parliament passed laws that allowed profit-seeking landowners to fence in their open fields to raise more sheep.
A. Laissez faire   B. Enclosure Movement   C. Great Society   D. Yellow Journalism

138. A The government in Spain gave away large tracts of conquered land in Spanish America, including whole villages of indigenous peoples, to court favorites.
A. Encomienda System   B. Washington   C. Guadalupe Hidalgo   D. Price Revolution

139. B Secretary of State for Abraham Lincoln and Andrew Johnson, and advocate of a vigorous expansionism.
A. Goldwater   B. Seward   C. Colonization   D. Settlement House

140. A U.S. policy of impartiality during World Wars I and II.
A. Neutrality   B. Nineteenth Amendment   C. Hooverizing   D. Evangelical Revivalism

141. D A movement founded to help the unemployed during the depression of the 1890s, it demanded that the federal government provide jobs and inflate the currency.
A. Kansas Nebraska Act   B. Sputnik   C. Court Packing   D. Coxey's Arrny

142. __D__ October 29, 1929, the day of the stock market crash that initiated the Great Depression.
A. James Polk   B. Hessians   C. Headright   D. Black Tuesday

143. __D__ Phrase from John Winthrop's sermon, "A Model of Christian Charity," in which he challenged his fellow Puritans to build a model, ideal community in America.
A. Antinomian   B. Nonseparatists   C. Impressment   D. City Upon a Hill

144. __C__ Spokesman for the Nation of Islam, a black religious and political organization that advocated black-owned businesses and castigated "white devils."
A. Guadalupe Hidalgo   B. Walter O'Malley   C. Malcolm X   D. Dawes Act

145. __C__ Proposed Constitutional amendment that would prohibit discrimination on the basis of gender.
A. Robert Kennedy   B. City Upon a Hill   C. Equal Rights Amendment   D. Radical Republicans

146. __D__ A political party founded by James Madison and Thomas Jefferson to combat Alexander Hamilton's fiscal policies.
A. Fireside Chats   B. Tariff of Abominations   C. Channing   D. Republicans

147. __B__ A wave of religious fervor and revivalism that swept the United States from the early nineteenth century through the Civil War.
A. Gorbachev   B. Second Great Awakening   C. Removal   D. Hoovervilles

148. __A__ The leader of the Haitian Revolution.
A. Louverture   B. Young   C. Nullification   D. Sagebrush Rebellion

149. __A__ A Virginia slave and blacksmith who organized an attempted assault against Richmond in 1800.
A. Gabriel   B. Gorbachev   C. Reagan Doctrine   D. Kansas Nebraska Act

150. __B__ Oil supply disruptions and soaring oil prices after Middle Eastern nations imposed an embargo on oil shipments to punish the West for supporting Israel in that year's Arab-Israeli war.
A. James Polk   B. Oil Crisis   C. Non Intercourse Act   D. Social Gospel

151. __C__ Appointed Chief Justice in 1801, Marshall expanded the Supreme Court's power and prestige and established the court's power of Judicial Review.
A. Political Slavery   B. James Polk   C. John Marshall   D. Johnny Reb

152. __A__ In World War I, Germany and Austria-Hungary and their allies.
A. Central Powers   B. Second Great Awakening   C. Knights of Labor   D. Large Policy

153. __D__ Notion that America houses biologically superior people and can spread democracy to the rest of the world.
A. Settlement House   B. Queensberry Rules   C. Henry Clay   D. American Exceptionalism

154. __C__ A current of Protestant Christianity emphasizing personal conversion, repentance of sin, and the authority of Scripture.
A. Jefferson   B. Tory   C. Evangelical Revivalism   D. Tet Offensive

155. __A__ The view that the national government's powers are not limited to those stated explicitly in the U.S. Constitution.
A. Implied Powers   B. SALT I   C. Black Tuesday   D. Taft Hartley

156. __A__ The leader of efforts to reform the treatment of the mentally ill.
A. Dorothea Dix   B. Neutrality   C. Camp David Accords   D. Thoreau

157. __A__ The primary author of the Declaration of Independence, the first secretary of state, and as president, he was responsible for the Louisiana Purchase.
A. Jefferson   B. Aaron Burr   C. Hessians   D. Paul Cuffe

158. B President Eisenhower's domestic agenda advocated conservative spending approaches without drastically cutting back New Deal social programs.
A. Emerson   B. Modern Republicanism   C. Freedom Riders   D. Fair Deal

159. D Owner of baseball's Dodgers who oversaw their 1958 move from Brooklyn to Los Angeles.
A. Judicial Review   B. Young   C. Mercantilism   D. Walter O'Malley

160. D Republican presidential candidate in 1964, Goldwater spearheaded an emergent conservative drive out of the South and West.
A. MacArthur   B. Enclosure Movement   C. Nat Turner   D. Goldwater

161. C Shanty towns of the Great Depression, named after President Herbert Hoover.
A. Total War   B. Walter O'Malley   C. Hoovervilles   D. Social Gospel

162. B The large influx of gold and silver into Europe from Spanish America during the sixteenth century set off a three-fold rise in prices (the "great inflation").
A. Cabinet   B. Price Revolution   C. Coxey's Arrny   D. Political Slavery

163. D Investigative journalists during the Progressive Era, they wrote sensational exposes of social and political problems that helped spark the reform movements of their day.
A. Social Gospel   B. Price Revolution   C. Copperheads   D. Muckrakers

164. B Defined by historian Donald Worster as "a social order based on the intensive manipulation of water and its products in an arid setting,"
A. Hoovervilles   B. Hydraulic Society   C. Coxey's Arrny   D. Fourteen Points

165. A A massive foreign aid program to Western Europe of $17 billion over four years, beginning in 1948.
A. Marshall Plan   B. Patrons of Husbandry   C. Knights of Labor   D. Central Powers

166. B 1985 pledge of American aid to insurgent movements attempting to overthrow Soviet-back regimes in the Third World.
A. Military Reconstruction Act   B. Reagan Doctrine   C. Permanent Immigrants   D. Tariff of Abominations

167. D This term refers to the heads of the executive departments.
A. China Lobby   B. Freedom Riders   C. National Recovery Administration   D. Cabinet

168. C As vice president, Calhoun anonymously expounded the doctrine of nullification, which held that states could prevent the enforcement of a federal law within their boundaries.
A. Central Powers   B. New Deal   C. Calhoun, John   D. Guadalupe Hidalgo

169. D Blanket search warrants used by English customs collectors in the colonies to try to catch suspected smugglers.
A. Fireside Chats   B. Permanent Immigrants   C. Smog   D. Writs of Assistance

170. B Six German principalities provided 30,000 soldiers to Great Britain to fight against the American rebels during the War for Independence.
A. Robert Kennedy   B. Hessians   C. D Day   D. Total War

171. C This law allows the public and press to request declassification of government documents.
A. Total War   B. Joseph Stalin   C. Freedom of Information Act   D. Scalawags

172. B Arms control treaty signed by President Nixon and Soviet premier Leonid Brezhnev.
A. Fireside Chats   B. SALT I   C. Freedmen's Bureau   D. Friedan

173. C Immigrants who never intended to make the United States their home.
A. Marshall Plan   B. Deregulation   C. Birds of Passage   D. Hartford Convention

174. D The early nineteenth century's leading educational reformer, Mann led the fight for government support for public schools in Massachusetts.
A. Nixon Doctrine   B. Second Continental Congress   C. Khrushchev   D. Horace Mann

175. D The last leader of the Soviet Union, he adopted policies of glasnost (political liberalization) and stroika (economic reform).
A. Seward   B. Freedom of Information Act   C. Mercantilism   D. Gorbachev

176. B Justified the concentration of wealth and lack of governmental protection of the weak through the ideas of natural selection and survival of the fittest.
A. Prudence Crandall   B. Social Darwinism   C. Bay of Pigs   D. Prohibition

177. B Radical leaders in the South during the years leading up to the Civil War, the fire-eaters were persons who took an extreme pro-slavery position.
A. Carpetbaggers   B. Fire eaters   C. New South   D. Pragmatism

178. C Declared that the United States would not allow European powers to create new colonies in the Western Hemisphere or to expand the boundaries of existing colonies.
A. Tet Offensive   B. Jefferson   C. Monroe Doctrine   D. Nixon Doctrine

179. B Not every person living in the North during the Civil War favored making war against the Confederacy. Such persons came to be identified as Copperheads.
A. Stamp Act Congress   B. Copperheads   C. Monroe Doctrine   D. Kansas Nebraska Act

180. A A noted orator, he opposed the War of 1812 and the protectionist tariff of 1816 after his election to the House of Representatives.
A. Webster   B. Guadalupe Hidalgo   C. Billy Yank   D. Progressive Party

181. B Conflict in 1957 when governor Orval Faubus sent the Arkansas National Guard to prevent the racial integration of Little Rock's Central High School.
A. Mugwumps   B. Little Rock Crisis   C. Enclosure Movement   D. Oil Crisis

182. A A failed plan to assassinate Cuban leader Fidel Castro and liberate Cuba with a trained military force of political exiles.
A. Bay of Pigs   B. Renaissance   C. Separatists   D. Hooverizing

183. D A law passed after the South's refusal to accept the Fourteenth Amendment in 1867, it nullified existing state governments and divided the South.
A. Coxey's Arrny   B. Little Rock Crisis   C. Carpetbaggers   D. Military Reconstruction Act

184. C A labor organization founded in 1869, it called for the unity of all workers, rejected industrial capitalism, and favored cooperatively owned businesses.
A. Gabriel   B. Stagflation   C. Knights of Labor   D. Dawes Act

185. C A reform movement growing out of Jane Addams' Hull House in the late nineteenth century.
A. Jefferson   B. James Polk   C. Settlement House   D. Encomienda System

186. B The central banking system of the United States, established with passage of the Federal Reserve Act of 1913.
A. Antifederalists   B. Federal Reserve System   C. Walter O'Malley   D. Rationalism

187. B A term of derision applied to those colonists who sought to maintain their allegiance to the British crown. Loyalists.
A. Nixon Doctrine   B. Tory   C. American System of Production   D. Mugwumps

188. B The effort to encourage masters to voluntarily emancipate their slaves and to resettle free blacks in Africa.
A. Khrushchev   B. Colonization   C. Popular Sovereignty   D. Marshall Plan

189. __C__ President Franklin Delano Roosevelt's controversial plan to appoint Supreme Court justices who were sympathetic to his views, by offering retirement benefits to the sitting justices.
A. Beat Generation   B. Calvinism   C. Court Packing   D. Hooverizing

190. __B__ An amendment to an 1846 appropriations bill that would have forbade slavery from any territory acquired from Mexico.
A. Yellow Journalism   B. Wilmot Proviso   C. Camp David Accords   D. Tet Offensive

191. __D__ The main base of the U.S. Pacific fleet, which Japan attacked on December 7, 1941, forcing the United States to enter World War II.
A. Joseph Stalin   B. Enclosure Movement   C. Settlement House   D. Pearl Harbor

192. __B__ An 1828 protective tariff opposed by many Southerners.
A. Hydraulic Society   B. Tariff of Abominations   C. Freedom of Information Act   D. Pragmatism

193. __B__ An economic system built on the assumption that the world's supply of wealth is fixed and that nations must export more goods than they import.
A. John Marshall   B. Mercantilism   C. Enclosure Movement   D. Joseph Smith

194. __B__ The pre-Civil War reform movement which sought to curb the drinking of hard liquor.
A. Popular Sovereignty   B. Temperance   C. Marshall Plan   D. Hooverizing

195. __A__ A Carter era economic policy, which freed many industries from many government economic controls.
A. Deregulation   B. Queensberry Rules   C. Salutary Neglect   D. Goldwater

196. __A__ A political party established in 1912 by supporters of Theodore Roosevelt, proposed a broad program of reform.
A. Progressive Party   B. City Upon a Hill   C. Frederick Douglass   D. SDS

197. __A__ President Eisenhower's adjustment to the doctrine of containment. He advocated saving money by emphasizing nuclear over conventional weapons.
A. New Look   B. Neutrality   C. Rationalism   D. Flapper

198. __A__ A former West Indian slave who organized an attempted rebellion against slavery in Charleston, South Carolina, in 1822.
A. Denmark Vesey   B. Haymarket Square Riot   C. Joseph Smith   D. Young

199. __B__ This term signifies England's relatively benign neglect of its American colonies from about 1690 to 1760.
A. Declension   B. Salutary Neglect   C. Dawes Act   D. James Madison

200. __C__ A pencilmaker, poet, and author of the influential essay "Civil Disobedience," Thoreau sought to realize transcendentalist ideals in his personal life.
A. Colonization   B. Seward   C. Thoreau   D. Fireside Chats

From the words provided for each clue, provide the letter of the word which best matches the clue.

201. __B__ Passed in 1920, the Constitutional guarantee of women's right to vote.
A. Thoreau   B. Nineteenth Amendment   C. Sagebrush Rebellion   D. Knights of Labor

202. __B__ Sociologists who rejected the determinism of the Social Darwinists.
A. Billy Yank   B. Reform Darwinists   C. Trust   D. Religious Liberalism

203. __B__ African-American seamstress and active NAACP member arrested for refusing to give up her seat to a white patron in Montgomery, Alabama.
A. Denmark Vesey   B. Rosa Parks   C. Radical Revolutionaries   D. James Madison

204. C An anti-foreign, anti-Catholic political party that arose following massive Irish and Catholic immigration during the late 1840s.
A. Smog   B. Mercantilism   C. Know Nothing Party   D. Black Codes

205. C Alabama governor who ran for president in 1968 as a third-party candidate on the American Independent ticket
A. Enumerated Goods   B. Second New Deal   C. George Wallace   D. Impressment

206. D A policy of resettling eastern Indian tribes on lands west of the Mississippi River.
A. Populist Party   B. Nixon Doctrine   C. Second Great Awakening   D. Removal

207. D Legal codes that defined the slaveholders' power and the slaves' status as property.
A. Perpetual Servitude   B. Mugwumps   C. Robert Kennedy   D. Slave Codes

208. B A broadly influential philosophical and intellectual movement that began in Europe during the eighteenth century.
A. Merchantilism   B. Enlightenment   C. Calvinism   D. Farewell Address

209. D American radicals accused of passing atomic secrets to the Soviets during World War II. Executed in 1953.
A. Nonseparatists   B. Guadalupe Hidalgo   C. Columbian Exchange   D. Rosenbergs

210. D Industrialist who epitomized the close relationship between government and industry in the West.
A. Plessy vs Ferguson   B. Judicial Review   C. Northwest Passage   D. Henry Kaiser

211. C The leader of the Haitian Revolution.
A. Stagflation   B. Mugwumps   C. Louverture   D. Insanity Defense

212. B A Quaker schoolteacher, she sparked controversy when she opened a school for the education of free blacks.
A. Price Revolution   B. Prudence Crandall   C. Black Codes   D. Nixon Doctrine

213. C This appellation was used to refer to common soldiers serving in Union armies during the Civil War.
A. McCullough vs Maryland   B. Fireside Chats   C. Billy Yank   D. Louverture

214. A A cornerstone of good citizenship in republican states, public virtue involved the subordination of individual self-interest to serving the greater good of the whole community.
A. Public Virtue   B. Rock and Roll   C. Fair Deal   D. John Marshall

215. A Emphasized the power and omnipotence of God and the importance of seeking to earn saving grace and salvation.
A. Calvinism   B. D Day   C. John Marshall   D. Watergate

216. A Adopted in 1964, barred a poll tax in federal elections.
A. Twenty Fourth Amendment   B. Alien and Sedition Acts   C. Enlightenment   D. Stagflation

217. A The free black author of An Appeal to the Colored Citizens of the World, which threatened violence if slavery was not abolished.
A. David Walker   B. Freedom Riders   C. Progressive Party   D. Mercantilism

218. A Defined by historian Donald Worster as "a social order based on the intensive manipulation of water and its products in an arid setting,"
A. Hydraulic Society   B. Kansas Nebraska Act   C. Writs of Assistance   D. McCullough vs Maryland

219. D All slaves in the rebellious Confederate states were to be forever free. However, slavery could continue to exist in border states that were not at war.
A. Grand Alliance   B. Military Reconstruction Act   C. Prohibition   D. Emancipation Proclamation

220. A The power of the courts to determine the constitutionality of acts of other branches of government and to declare unconstitutional acts null and void.
A. Judicial Review   B. Patrons of Husbandry   C. Spoils System   D. Kissinger

221. B — 1985 pledge of American aid to insurgent movements attempting to overthrow Soviet-back regimes in the Third World.
A. Scalawags   B. Reagan Doctrine   C. Yalta Conference   D. Elizabeth Cady Stanton

222. A — A violent encounter between police and protesters in 1886 in Chicago, which led to the execution of four protest leaders.
A. Haymarket Square Riot   B. New Deal   C. Dartmouth vs Woodward   D. Common Sense

223. C — The founder of the Mormon Church, Smith was murdered in Illinois in 1844.
A. Whig Party   B. Spoils System   C. Joseph Smith   D. Northwest Passage

224. A — The Father of the Constitution and the Bill of Rights and a co-founder of the Jeffersonian Republican party, Madison served as president during the War of 1812.
A. James Madison   B. Deregulation   C. Writs of Assistance   D. Cuban Missile Crisis

225. B — A landmark 1819 Supreme Court decision protecting contracts.
A. D Day   B. Dartmouth vs Woodward   C. Thoreau   D. Northwest Passage

226. D — Supreme Court decision establishing Congress's power to charter a national bank and declaring unconstitutional a tax imposed by Maryland on the local branch.
A. Calvinism   B. Birds of Passage   C. Republicanism   D. McCullough vs Maryland

227. D — Conflict in 1957 when governor Orval Faubus sent the Arkansas National Guard to prevent the racial integration of Little Rock's Central High School.
A. Price Revolution   B. Fire eaters   C. Billy Yank   D. Little Rock Crisis

228. C — Religious songs composed by enslaved African Americans.
A. Calvinism   B. Birds of Passage   C. Spirituals   D. Denmark Vesey

229. D — During the 1972 presidential campaign, burglars, tied to the Nixon White House, were caught installing eavesdropping devices in Democratic Party headquarters.
A. Whig Party   B. Détente   C. Guadalupe Hidalgo   D. Watergate

230. C — A labor organization founded in 1869, it called for the unity of all workers, rejected industrial capitalism, and favored cooperatively owned businesses.
A. Spoils System   B. Patrons of Husbandry   C. Knights of Labor   D. Republicans

231. C — The "father of modern revivalism," Finney devised many techniques adopted by later revival preachers. He encouraged many women to participate actively in revival.
A. Marbury vs Madison   B. Sagebrush Rebellion   C. Finney   D. Rock and Roll

232. D — Standardized boxing rules of the late nineteenth century, creating structured three-minute rounds with one-minute rest periods.
A. Court Packing   B. Loose Interpretation   C. Great Awakening   D. Queensberry Rules

233. C — A law passed in 1883 to eliminate political corruption in the federal government and established the Civil Service Commission to administer competitive examinations.
A. Versailles   B. Calhoun, John   C. Pendleton Act   D. Louverture

234. D — This best-selling pamphlet by Thomas Paine, first published in 1776, denounced the British monarchy, called for American independence.
A. Iranian Hostage Crisis   B. Henry Kaiser   C. Eli Whitney   D. Common Sense

235. B — Soviet premier in the 1930s and 1940s, known for his violent purges of internal political enemies and his suspicion of Western leaders.
A. Black Tuesday   B. Joseph Stalin   C. Hoovervilles   D. Dawes Act

236. C Literary style of the late nineteenth and early twentieth century, where the individual was a helpless victim in a world in which outside forces determined his or her fate.
A. Lusitania B. Haymarket Square Riot C. Naturalism D. Great Migration

237. C As an economic incentive to encourage English to settle in Virginia and other English colonies during the seventeenth century.
A. Farewell Address B. Henry Kaiser C. Headright D. James Polk

238. B Farmers from western Massachusetts rose up in rebellion against their state government in 1786 because they had failed to obtain tax relief.
A. Settlement House B. Shays Rebellion C. Liluokalani D. Neutrality

239. D A relaxation of tensions between the United States and the Soviet Union that was begun by President Richard M. Nixon.
A. American Exceptionalism B. Equal Rights Amendment C. Greenback Party D. Détente

240. C The leader of the Mormon church following Joseph Smith's murder, Young led the Mormon exodus from Illinois to the Great Salt Lake.
A. Haymarket Square Riot B. Shays Rebellion C. Young D. Calvinism

241. D A leading orator in the abolitionist and women's rights movements, Sojourner Truth was born into slavery in New York's Hudson River Valley and escaped in 1826.
A. Axis Powers B. Garrison C. Horace Mann D. Sojourner Truth

242. A The most controversial element of the Compromise of 1850, the Fugitive Slave Law provided for the return of runaway slaves to their masters.
A. Fugitive Slave Law B. Republicanism C. Axis Powers D. Twenty Fourth Amendment

243. D An organization established by Congress on March 3, 1865 to deal with the dislocations of the Civil War.
A. Removal B. Little Rock Crisis C. Alien and Sedition Acts D. Freedmen's Bureau

244. A The second stage of President Franklin Delano Roosevelt's economic recovery and reform program, launched January 4, 1935.
A. Second New Deal B. Prohibition C. Rosa Parks D. Perpetual Servitude

245. B June 6, 1944, the day Allied forces landed on the beaches of Normandy, in France, leading to the defeat of Germany.
A. Stamp Act Congress B. D Day C. Impressment D. Finney

246. D The conflict in 1962 prompted by Soviet installation of missiles on Cuba and President Kennedy's announcement to the American Public.
A. Kissinger B. Fugitive Slave Law C. Garrison D. Cuban Missile Crisis

247. A The early nineteenth century's leading educational reformer, Mann led the fight for government support for public schools in Massachusetts.
A. Horace Mann B. Open Door Note C. Total War D. Separatists

248. A His administration was marked by the acquisition of Florida (1819), the Missouri Compromise (1820), and the Monroe Doctrine (1823).
A. James Monroe B. Writs of Assistance C. AFL D. Stagflation

249. B A wave of religious fervor and revivalism that swept the United States from the early nineteenth century through the Civil War.
A. Greenback Party B. Second Great Awakening C. Deregulation D. Beat Generation

250. A The meeting in February 1945 to determine the post-World War II world order.
A. Yalta Conference B. Denmark Vesey C. Scopes Trial D. New Look

251. **B** This 1973 law required presidents to win specific authorization from Congress to engage U.S. forces in foreign combat for more than 90 days.
A. Columbian Exchange   B. War Powers Act   C. Wilmot Proviso   D. Price Revolution

252. **D** Indentured servitude represented temporary service for a specified period, usually from four to seven years, to a legally designated owner.
A. Carpetbaggers   B. National Recovery Administration   C. Writs of Assistance   D. Perpetual Servitude

253. **B** In World War II, the alliance of German and Italy, and later Japan.
A. Evangelical Revivalism   B. Axis Powers   C. Jazz   D. Calvinism

254. **D** During the Age of Exploration, adventurers from England, France, and the Netherlands kept seeking an all-water route across North America.
A. Calvinism   B. Indentured Servitude   C. Black Power   D. Northwest Passage

255. **D** The economic conditions of slow economic growth, rising inflation, and flagging productivity that characterized the American economy during the 1970s.
A. Northwest Passage   B. Sagebrush Rebellion   C. James Madison   D. Stagflation

256. **D** Vietminh siege of 13,000 French soldiers in 1954 at a remote military outpost. The French surrender led to the 1956 elections designed to reunify Vietnam.
A. Electric Trolley   B. Stamp Act Congress   C. Stagflation   D. Dien Bien Phu

257. **A** The auxiliary women's unit to the U.S. army.
A. WAC   B. Reagan Doctrine   C. New Look   D. Greenback Party

258. **C** As president of the United States during the Mexican War, Polk increased American territory by a third.
A. Prudence Crandall   B. Aaron Burr   C. James Polk   D. Alien and Sedition Acts

259. **C** The pre-Civil War reform movement which sought to curb the drinking of hard liquor.
A. Black Tuesday   B. Populist Party   C. Temperance   D. Jazz

260. **A** Declared that the United States would not allow European powers to create new colonies in the Western Hemisphere or to expand the boundaries of existing colonies.
A. Monroe Doctrine   B. Republicans   C. Specie   D. Hydraulic Society

261. **A** An amendment to an 1846 appropriations bill that would have forbade slavery from any territory acquired from Mexico.
A. Wilmot Proviso   B. Total War   C. Bay of Pigs   D. Santa Anna

262. **D** The peace treaty ending the Mexican War gave the United States California, Nevada, New Mexico, Utah, and parts of Arizona, Colorado, Kansas, and Wyoming.
A. Billy Yank   B. Finney   C. Joseph Stalin   D. Guadalupe Hidalgo

263. **C** During the early nineteenth century, a movement arose to end the death penalty.
A. Platt Amendment   B. WAC   C. Capital Punishment   D. Spoils System

264. **A** Parliament passed laws that allowed profit-seeking landowners to fence in their open fields to raise more sheep.
A. Enclosure Movement   B. Axis Powers   C. McCullough vs Maryland   D. Black Codes

265. **C** A confederation of labor unions founded in 1886, it was composed mainly of skilled craft unions.
A. Rosenbergs   B. Marbury vs Madison   C. AFL   D. Era of Good Feelings

266. **B** Thomas Jefferson's first vice president, who killed Alexander Hamilton in a duel in 1804.
A. Mugwumps   B. Aaron Burr   C. Emancipation Proclamation   D. Tory

267. D In World War II, the alliance between the United States, Great Britain, and France.
A. John Adams   B. Radical Revolutionaries   C. Freedom Riders   D. Grand Alliance

268. D The belief that God ordains certain people to amass money and use it to further God's purposes, it justified the concentration of wealth.
A. Carpetbaggers   B. Hydraulic Society   C. Iranian Hostage Crisis   D. Gospel of Wealth

269. B October 29, 1929, the day of the stock market crash that initiated the Great Depression.
A. Guadalupe Hidalgo   B. Black Tuesday   C. Permanent Immigrants   D. Marbury vs Madison

270. D Celebrated American general removed by Truman after his criticisms of America's containment policy.
A. Cuban Missile Crisis   B. Great Awakening   C. Watergate   D. MacArthur

271. A Policy set forth in 1899 by Secretary of State John Hay preventing further partitioning of China by European powers and protecting the principle of free trade.
A. Open Door Note   B. Sharecropping   C. Insanity Defense   D. Social Gospel

272. D An early American political party opposing influence from monarchy.
A. Freedmen's Bureau   B. Removal   C. Fugitive Slave Law   D. Whig Party

273. C The legal principle that a criminal act should only be punished if the offender was fully capable of distinguishing right from wrong.
A. Non Intercourse Act   B. Carpetbaggers   C. Insanity Defense   D. Permanent Immigrants

274. D Appointed Chief Justice in 1801, Marshall expanded the Supreme Court's power and prestige and established the court's power of Judicial Review.
A. Henry Kaiser   B. Knights of Labor   C. Nat Turner   D. John Marshall

275. C President Nixon argued for "Vietnamization," the notion that the South Vietnamese would carry more of the war's combat burden.
A. Rosenbergs   B. Black Codes   C. Nixon Doctrine   D. Loose Interpretation

276. C A business model where any single entity had the power to control competition within a given industry, such as oil production.
A. Open Door Note   B. Large Policy   C. Trust   D. Antifederalists

277. A A Supreme Court decision in 1896 that ruled "separate but equal" facilities for African Americans were constitutional under the Fourteenth Amendment.
A. Plessy vs Ferguson   B. Judicial Review   C. Patriarchal   D. Gabriel

278. C Justified the concentration of wealth and lack of governmental protection of the weak through the ideas of natural selection and survival of the fittest.
A. Temperance   B. Sputnik   C. Social Darwinism   D. Muckrakers

279. A Civil rights activists who in 1961 demonstrated that despite a federal ban on segregated travel on interstate buses, segregation prevailed in parts of the South.
A. Freedom Riders   B. Matrilineal   C. Tory   D. Second Great Awakening

280. D A political party founded in 1874 to promote the issuance of legal tender paper currency not backed by precious metals in order to inflate the money supply.
A. Radical Revolutionaries   B. Finney   C. Muckrakers   D. Greenback Party

281. B After an early public life as a committed Cold Warrior, Kennedy ran for the Democratic nomination in 1968 as a peace candidate representative of young liberals.
A. Coxey's Army   B. Robert Kennedy   C. Strict Construction   D. Rock and Roll

282. **B** — President Franklin Delano Roosevelt's program designed to bring about economic recovery and reform during the Great Depression.
A. Manhattan Project B. New Deal C. New Look D. Progressive Party

283. **C** — A political party established in 1912 by supporters of Theodore Roosevelt, proposed a broad program of reform.
A. Gospel of Wealth B. Finney C. Progressive Party D. Santa Anna

284. **B** — Legislation passed in 1887 to authorize the president to divide tribal land and distribute it to individual Native Americans.
A. Khrushchev B. Dawes Act C. Sojourner Truth D. Coxey's Arrny

285. **A** — Failed 1948 legislative package proposed by President Truman.
A. Fair Deal B. Dred Scott C. Headright D. Navigation System

286. **A** — Public transportation for urban neighborhoods, using electric current from overhead wires.
A. Electric Trolley B. Insanity Defense C. Black Tuesday D. McCullough vs Maryland

287. **D** — Immigrants coming to America to settle permanently, often due to ethnic and religious persecution at home.
A. Settlement House B. Radical Revolutionaries C. Santa Anna D. Permanent Immigrants

288. **A** — An 1809 statute which replaced the Embargo of 1807. It forbade trade with Britain, France, and their possessions, but reopened trade with other countries.
A. Non Intercourse Act B. Popular Sovereignty C. Yalta Conference D. Little Rock Crisis

289. **A** — Laws passed by Southern state legislatures during Reconstruction, while Congress was out of session.
A. Black Codes B. Liluokalani C. Robert Kennedy D. Alien and Sedition Acts

290. **C** — A labor system was similar to that of indentured servitude in providing a way for persons without financial means to get to America.
A. Sojourner Truth B. McCullough vs Maryland C. Redemptioners D. Fair Deal

291. **C** — President Eisenhower's adjustment to the doctrine of containment. He advocated saving money by emphasizing nuclear over conventional weapons.
A. Kansas Nebraska Act B. Insanity Defense C. New Look D. Iranian Hostage Crisis

292. **B** — The ban of the production, sale, and consumption of alcoholic beverages.
A. Large Policy B. Prohibition C. Guadalupe Hidalgo D. Bill of Rights

293. **D** — This landmark 1803 Supreme Court decision, which established the principle of judicial review.
A. Capital Punishment B. Great Awakening C. Mercantilism D. Marbury vs Madison

294. **D** — A reform faction of the Republican party in the 1870s and 1880s, they crusaded for honest and effective government and some supported Democratic reform candidates.
A. Spirituals B. Scopes Trial C. City Upon a Hill D. Mugwumps

295. **C** — Failed movement led by conservative Western politicians to cede federal control of western land to individual states.
A. Sit in B. New South C. Sagebrush Rebellion D. Stamp Act Congress

296. **C** — Social and political systems are denoted by power and authority residing in males, such as in the father of the family.
A. Kissinger B. Tory C. Patriarchal D. Emancipation Proclamation

297. **C** — The program by which the United States provided arms and supplies to the Allies in World War II before joining the fighting.
A. Détente B. Watergate C. Lend Lease D. Plessy vs Ferguson

298. B Personable Soviet premier during Eisenhower's presidential term. Khrushchev condemned Stalin's purges and welcomed a melting of the Cold War.
A. Large Policy   B. Khrushchev   C. Hoovervilles   D. Beat Generation

299. B A rallying cry for more militant blacks advocated by younger leaders beginning in the mid-1960s.
A. Court Packing   B. Black Power   C. Separatists   D. Stamp Act Congress

300. D The national security advisor to President Nixon. A staunch anti-Communist. He was Nixon's closest associate on matters of foreign policy.
A. Laissez faire   B. Carpetbaggers   C. Social Darwinism   D. Kissinger

Matching
Provide the word that best matches each clue.

1. _____ This appellation was used to refer to common soldiers serving in Union armies during the Civil War.

2. _____ Henry Clay's program for the national economy, which included a protective tariff to stimulate industry and a national bank to provide credit.

3. _____ This term refers to the heads of the executive departments.

4. _____ During the early nineteenth century, a movement arose to end the death penalty.

5. _____ The process of transferring plants, animals, foods, diseases, wealth, and culture between Europe and the Americas.

6. _____ Popular site of New York amusement parks opening in 1890s, attracting working class Americans with rides and games celebrating abandon and instant gratification.

7. _____ A confederation of labor unions founded in 1886, it was composed mainly of skilled craft unions.

8. _____ A movement founded to help the unemployed during the depression of the 1890s, it demanded that the federal government provide jobs and inflate the currency.

9. _____ A landmark 1819 Supreme Court decision protecting contracts.

10. _____ Phrase from John Winthrop's sermon, "A Model of Christian Charity," in which he challenged his fellow Puritans to build a model, ideal community in America.

11. _____ These were opponents of the Constitution of 1787 who sought to continue the confederation of sovereign states and to keep power as close as possible to the people.

12. _____ America's leading exponent of religious liberalism, Channing was one of the founders of American Unitarianism.

13. _____ The conflict in 1962 prompted by Soviet installation of missiles on Cuba and President Kennedy's announcement to the American Public.

14. _____ The proclaimed foreign policy of Theodore Roosevelt, it was based on the proverb, "Speak softly and carry a big stick,".

15. _____ A relaxation of tensions between the United States and the Soviet Union that was begun by President Richard M. Nixon.

16. _____ A Missouri slave, Scott sued for his freedom on the grounds that his master had taken him onto free soil.

17. _____ An historic 1979 peace agreement negotiated between Egypt and Israel at the U.S. presidential retreat at Camp David, Maryland.

18. _____ The effort to encourage masters to voluntarily emancipate their slaves and to resettle free blacks in Africa.

19. _____ This best-selling pamphlet by Thomas Paine, first published in 1776, denounced the British monarchy, called for American independence.

20. _____ Close advisors to President Franklin Delano Roosevelt during the early days of his first term whose policy suggestions influenced much New Deal legislation.

21. _____ U.S. propaganda agency of World War I.

22. _____ The "father of modern revivalism," Finney devised many techniques adopted by later revival preachers. He encouraged many women to participate actively in revival.

23. _____ A failed plan to assassinate Cuban leader Fidel Castro and liberate Cuba with a trained military force of political exiles.

24. _____ Laws passed by Southern state legislatures during Reconstruction, while Congress was out of session.

25. _____ Literally meaning against the laws of human governance.

A. Bay of Pigs   B. Brain Trust

125

C. Dartmouth vs Woodward
E. Columbian Exchange
G. Cuban Missile Crisis
I. Camp David Accords
K. Black Codes
M. Coxey's Arrny
O. American System
Q. Common Sense
S. Antifederalists
U. Channing
W. Détente
Y. Antinomian

D. Colonization
F. Cabinet
H. AFL
J. Committee on Public Information
L. Capital Punishment
N. Dred Scott
P. City Upon a Hill
R. Coney Island
T. Billy Yank
V. Finney
X. Big Stick Diplomacy

Provide the word that best matches each clue.

26. _____ The effort to encourage masters to voluntarily emancipate their slaves and to resettle free blacks in Africa.

27. _____ Laws passed by Southern state legislatures during Reconstruction, while Congress was out of session.

28. _____ Henry Clay's program for the national economy, which included a protective tariff to stimulate industry and a national bank to provide credit.

29. _____ In World War II, the alliance of German and Italy, and later Japan.

30. _____ A landmark 1819 Supreme Court decision protecting contracts.

31. _____ Emphasized the power and omnipotence of God and the importance of seeking to earn saving grace and salvation.

32. _____ A rallying cry for more militant blacks advocated by younger leaders beginning in the mid-1960s.

33. _____ Thomas Jefferson's first vice president, who killed Alexander Hamilton in a duel in 1804.

34. _____ Close advisors to President Franklin Delano Roosevelt during the early days of his first term whose policy suggestions influenced much New Deal legislation.

35. _____ Phrase from John Winthrop's sermon, "A Model of Christian Charity," in which he challenged his fellow Puritans to build a model, ideal community in America.

36. _____ President Franklin Delano Roosevelt's controversial plan to appoint Supreme Court justices who were sympathetic to his views, by offering retirement benefits to the sitting justices.

37. _____ Legislation passed in 1887 to authorize the president to divide tribal land and distribute it to individual Native Americans.

38. _____ This term refers to the heads of the executive departments.

39. _____ As vice president, Calhoun anonymously expounded the doctrine of nullification, which held that states could prevent the enforcement of a federal law within their boundaries.

40. _____ A failed plan to assassinate Cuban leader Fidel Castro and liberate Cuba with a trained military force of political exiles.

41. _____ U.S. propaganda agency of World War I.

42. _____ People who moved to the South following the Civil War and helped to bring Republican control of southern state governments during Reconstruction.

43. _____ The proclaimed foreign policy of Theodore Roosevelt, it was based on the proverb, "Speak softly and carry a big stick,".

44. _____ These were opponents of the Constitution of 1787 who sought to continue the confederation of sovereign states and to keep power as close as possible to the people.

45. _____ This best-selling pamphlet by Thomas Paine, first published in 1776, denounced the British monarchy, called for American independence.

46. _____ A confederation of labor unions founded in 1886, it was composed mainly of skilled craft unions.

47. _____ President, 1976. His progressive racial views reflected an emergent South less concerned with racial distinctions and more concerned with economic development and political power.

48. _____ An historic 1979 peace agreement negotiated between Egypt and Israel at the U.S. presidential retreat at Camp David, Maryland.

49. _____ A relaxation of tensions between the United States and the Soviet Union that was begun by President Richard M. Nixon.

50. _____ America's leading exponent of religious liberalism, Channing was one of the founders of American Unitarianism.

- A. Colonization
- B. Black Codes
- C. American System
- D. Channing
- E. Détente
- F. Brain Trust
- G. Bay of Pigs
- H. Black Power
- I. Common Sense
- J. Camp David Accords
- K. City Upon a Hill
- L. Aaron Burr
- M. Calvinism
- N. Antifederalists
- O. Dawes Act
- P. Axis Powers
- Q. Committee on Public Information
- R. Cabinet
- S. Calhoun, John
- T. AFL
- U. Court Packing
- V. Carter
- W. Big Stick Diplomacy
- X. Dartmouth vs Woodward
- Y. Carpetbaggers

Provide the word that best matches each clue.

51. _____ This term refers to the heads of the executive departments.

52. _____ The conflict in 1962 prompted by Soviet installation of missiles on Cuba and President Kennedy's announcement to the American Public.

53. _____ During the early nineteenth century, a movement arose to end the death penalty.

54. _____ A former West Indian slave who organized an attempted rebellion against slavery in Charleston, South Carolina, in 1822.

55. _____ Henry Clay's program for the national economy, which included a protective tariff to stimulate industry and a national bank to provide credit.

56. _____ A confederation of labor unions founded in 1886, it was composed mainly of skilled craft unions.

57. _____ A landmark 1819 Supreme Court decision protecting contracts.

58. _____ A rallying cry for more militant blacks advocated by younger leaders beginning in the mid-1960s.

59. _____ Public transportation for urban neighborhoods, using electric current from overhead wires.

60. _____ The process of transferring plants, animals, foods, diseases, wealth, and culture between Europe and the Americas.

61. _____ The proclaimed foreign policy of Theodore Roosevelt, it was based on the proverb, "Speak softly and carry a big stick,".

62. _____ These were opponents of the Constitution of 1787 who sought to continue the confederation of sovereign states and to keep power as close as possible to the people.

63. _____ America's leading exponent of religious liberalism, Channing was one of the founders of American Unitarianism.

64. _____ Emphasized the power and omnipotence of God and the importance of seeking to earn saving grace and salvation.

65. _____ An historic 1979 peace agreement negotiated between Egypt and Israel at the U.S. presidential retreat at Camp David, Maryland.

66. _____ People who moved to the South following the Civil War and helped to bring Republican control of southern state governments during Reconstruction.

67. _____ A cultural style and artistic movement of the 1950s that rejected traditional American family life and material values and celebrated African-American culture.

68. _____ This best-selling pamphlet by Thomas Paine, first published in 1776, denounced the British monarchy, called for American independence.

69. _____ Legislation passed in 1887 to authorize the president to divide tribal land and distribute it to individual Native Americans.

70. _____ Vietminh siege of 13,000 French soldiers in 1954 at a remote military outpost. The French surrender led to the 1956 elections designed to reunify Vietnam.

71. _____ June 6, 1944, the day Allied forces landed on the beaches of Normandy, in France, leading to the defeat of Germany.

72. _____ Laws passed by Southern state legislatures during Reconstruction, while Congress was out of session.

73. _____ Group of unemployed World War I veterans who marched on Washington, D.C., in June 1932 to ask for immediate payment of their war pensions.

74. _____ Not every person living in the North during the Civil War favored making war against the Confederacy. Such persons came to be identified as Copperheads.

75. _____ A Missouri slave, Scott sued for his freedom on the grounds that his master had taken him onto free soil.

A. Bonus Army
B. Denmark Vesey
C. Beat Generation
D. Dartmouth vs Woodward
E. Black Codes
F. Antifederalists
G. Big Stick Diplomacy
H. Common Sense
I. AFL
J. Channing
K. Dred Scott
L. D Day
M. Dawes Act
N. Camp David Accords
O. Cabinet
P. Capital Punishment
Q. Dien Bien Phu
R. American System
S. Columbian Exchange
T. Black Power
U. Calvinism
V. Copperheads
W. Cuban Missile Crisis
X. Electric Trolley
Y. Carpetbaggers

Provide the word that best matches each clue.

76. _____ This best-selling pamphlet by Thomas Paine, first published in 1776, denounced the British monarchy, called for American independence.

77. _____ A term associated with the Massachusetts Bay Colony, referring to the declining zeal of later generations or movement away from the utopian ideals of those Puritan leaders.

78. _____ June 6, 1944, the day Allied forces landed on the beaches of Normandy, in France, leading to the defeat of Germany.

79. _____ Thomas Jefferson's first vice president, who killed Alexander Hamilton in a duel in 1804.

80. _____ Group of unemployed World War I veterans who marched on Washington, D.C., in June 1932 to ask for immediate payment of their war pensions.

81. _____ President, 1976. His progressive racial views reflected an emergent South less concerned with racial distinctions and more concerned with economic development and political power.

82. _____ Immigrants who never intended to make the United States their home.

83. _____ Henry Clay's program for the national economy, which included a protective tariff to stimulate industry and a national bank to provide credit.

84. _____ The free black author of An Appeal to the Colored Citizens of the World, which threatened violence if slavery was not abolished.

85. _____ The "father of modern revivalism," Finney devised many techniques adopted by later revival preachers. He encouraged many women to participate actively in revival.

86. _____ A movement founded to help the unemployed during the depression of the 1890s, it demanded that the federal government provide jobs and inflate the currency.

87. _____ The first ten amendments to the U.S. Constitution, which protect the rights of individuals from the powers of the national government.

88. _____ Legislation passed in 1887 to authorize the president to divide tribal land and distribute it to individual Native Americans.

89. _____ A cultural style and artistic movement of the 1950s that rejected traditional American family life and material values and celebrated African-American culture.

90. _____ The process of transferring plants, animals, foods, diseases, wealth, and culture between Europe and the Americas.

91. _____ People who moved to the South following the Civil War and helped to bring Republican control of southern state governments during Reconstruction.

92. _____ The proclaimed foreign policy of Theodore Roosevelt, it was based on the proverb, "Speak softly and carry a big stick,".

93. _____ These were opponents of the Constitution of 1787 who sought to continue the confederation of sovereign states and to keep power as close as possible to the people.

94. _____ Emphasized the power and omnipotence of God and the importance of seeking to earn saving grace and salvation.

95. _____ As vice president, Calhoun anonymously expounded the doctrine of nullification, which held that states could prevent the enforcement of a federal law within their boundaries.

96. _____ Notion that America houses biologically superior people and can spread democracy to the rest of the world.

97. _____ During the early nineteenth century, a movement arose to end the death penalty.

98. _____ The conflict in 1962 prompted by Soviet installation of missiles on Cuba and President Kennedy's announcement to the American Public.

99. _____ The high cost of labor led to the establishment of a system of mass production through the manufacture of interchangeable parts.

100. _____ A former West Indian slave who organized an attempted rebellion against slavery in Charleston, South Carolina, in 1822.

A. Coxey's Arrny
B. Declension
C. Cuban Missile Crisis
D. Columbian Exchange
E. Big Stick Diplomacy
F. Dawes Act
G. David Walker
H. Finney
I. Carter
J. American System of Production
K. Denmark Vesey
L. Common Sense
M. Calvinism
N. Carpetbaggers
O. Capital Punishment
P. Bonus Army
Q. American System
R. American Exceptionalism
S. D Day
T. Aaron Burr
U. Birds of Passage
V. Bill of Rights
W. Calhoun, John
X. Beat Generation
Y. Antifederalists

Provide the word that best matches each clue.

101. _____ As vice president, Calhoun anonymously expounded the doctrine of nullification, which held that states could prevent the enforcement of a federal law within their boundaries.

102. _____ This best-selling pamphlet by Thomas Paine, first published in 1776, denounced the British monarchy, called for American independence.

103. _____ The "father of modern revivalism," Finney devised many techniques adopted by later revival preachers. He encouraged many women to participate actively in revival.

104. _____ Laws passed by Southern state legislatures during Reconstruction, while Congress was out of session.

105. _____ In World War II, the alliance of German and Italy, and later Japan.

106. _____ June 6, 1944, the day Allied forces landed on the beaches of Normandy, in France, leading to the defeat of Germany.

107. _____ A movement founded to help the unemployed during the depression of the 1890s, it demanded that the federal government provide jobs and inflate the currency.

108. _____ Henry Clay's program for the national economy, which included a protective tariff to stimulate industry and a national bank to provide credit.

109. _____ The proclaimed foreign policy of Theodore Roosevelt, it was based on the proverb, "Speak softly and carry a big stick,".

110. _____ An historic 1979 peace agreement negotiated between Egypt and Israel at the U.S. presidential retreat at Camp David, Maryland.

111. _____ America's leading exponent of religious liberalism, Channing was one of the founders of American Unitarianism.

112. _____ U.S. propaganda agency of World War I.

113. _____ Group of unemployed World War I veterans who marched on Washington, D.C., in June 1932 to ask for immediate payment of their war pensions.

114. _____ This term refers to the heads of the executive departments.

115. _____ Literally meaning against the laws of human governance.

116. _____ A confederation of labor unions founded in 1886, it was composed mainly of skilled craft unions.

117. _____ Emphasized the power and omnipotence of God and the importance of seeking to earn saving grace and salvation.

118. _____ The effort to encourage masters to voluntarily emancipate their slaves and to resettle free blacks in Africa.

119. _____ People who moved to the South following the Civil War and helped to bring Republican control of southern state governments during Reconstruction.

120. _____ President, 1976. His progressive racial views reflected an emergent South less concerned with racial distinctions and more concerned with economic development and political power.

121. _____ Popular site of New York amusement parks opening in 1890s, attracting working class Americans with rides and games celebrating abandon and instant gratification.

122. _____ The high cost of labor led to the establishment of a system of mass production through the manufacture of interchangeable parts.

123. _____ Legislation passed in 1887 to authorize the president to divide tribal land and distribute it to individual Native Americans.

124. _____ Not every person living in the North during the Civil War favored making war against the Confederacy. Such persons came to be identified as Copperheads.

125. _____ President Franklin Delano Roosevelt's controversial plan to appoint Supreme Court justices who were sympathetic to his views, by offering retirement benefits to the sitting justices.

A. Finney
B. Copperheads
C. Carpetbaggers
D. Coney Island
E. Calhoun, John
F. Antinomian
G. Common Sense
H. Cabinet

I. American System of Production
K. Court Packing
M. Committee on Public Information
O. Bonus Army
Q. D Day
S. Carter
U. Colonization
W. Channing
Y. Black Codes

J. Big Stick Diplomacy
L. Coxey's Arrny
N. AFL
P. Dawes Act
R. American System
T. Axis Powers
V. Calvinism
X. Camp David Accords

Provide the word that best matches each clue.

126. _____ During the early nineteenth century, a movement arose to end the death penalty.

127. _____ Phrase from John Winthrop's sermon, "A Model of Christian Charity," in which he challenged his fellow Puritans to build a model, ideal community in America.

128. _____ A rallying cry for more militant blacks advocated by younger leaders beginning in the mid-1960s.

129. _____ The high cost of labor led to the establishment of a system of mass production through the manufacture of interchangeable parts.

130. _____ A cultural style and artistic movement of the 1950s that rejected traditional American family life and material values and celebrated African-American culture.

131. _____ Emphasized the power and omnipotence of God and the importance of seeking to earn saving grace and salvation.

132. _____ The "father of modern revivalism," Finney devised many techniques adopted by later revival preachers. He encouraged many women to participate actively in revival.

133. _____ An historic 1979 peace agreement negotiated between Egypt and Israel at the U.S. presidential retreat at Camp David, Maryland.

134. _____ A movement founded to help the unemployed during the depression of the 1890s, it demanded that the federal government provide jobs and inflate the currency.

135. _____ Immigrants who never intended to make the United States their home.

136. _____ This best-selling pamphlet by Thomas Paine, first published in 1776, denounced the British monarchy, called for American independence.

137. _____ The effort to encourage masters to voluntarily emancipate their slaves and to resettle free blacks in Africa.

138. _____ October 29, 1929, the day of the stock market crash that initiated the Great Depression.

139. _____ Passed in 1798 designed to curb criticism of the federal government.

140. _____ This appellation was used to refer to common soldiers serving in Union armies during the Civil War.

141. _____ America's leading exponent of religious liberalism, Channing was one of the founders of American Unitarianism.

142. _____ A failed plan to assassinate Cuban leader Fidel Castro and liberate Cuba with a trained military force of political exiles.

143. _____ The proclaimed foreign policy of Theodore Roosevelt, it was based on the proverb, "Speak softly and carry a big stick,".

144. _____ Notion that America houses biologically superior people and can spread democracy to the rest of the world.

145. _____ This term refers to the heads of the executive departments.

146. _____ Henry Clay's program for the national economy, which included a protective tariff to stimulate industry and a national bank to provide credit.

147. _____ Thomas Jefferson's first vice president, who killed Alexander Hamilton in a duel in 1804.

148. _____ People who moved to the South following the Civil War and helped to bring Republican control of southern state governments during Reconstruction.

149. _____ These were opponents of the Constitution of 1787 who sought to continue the confederation of sovereign states and to keep power as close as possible to the people.

150. _____ The process of transferring plants, animals, foods, diseases, wealth, and culture between Europe and the Americas.

A. Black Power
C. American System
E. Carpetbaggers
G. City Upon a Hill
I. American Exceptionalism
K. Coxey's Arrny
M. Capital Punishment
O. Colonization
Q. Antifederalists
S. Black Tuesday
U. Beat Generation
W. Camp David Accords
Y. Common Sense

B. Cabinet
D. Calvinism
F. Aaron Burr
H. Big Stick Diplomacy
J. Bay of Pigs
L. Alien and Sedition Acts
N. American System of Production
P. Channing
R. Columbian Exchange
T. Birds of Passage
V. Finney
X. Billy Yank

Provide the word that best matches each clue.

151. _____ This best-selling pamphlet by Thomas Paine, first published in 1776, denounced the British monarchy, called for American independence.

152. _____ In World War I, Germany and Austria-Hungary and their allies.

153. _____ President, 1976. His progressive racial views reflected an emergent South less concerned with racial distinctions and more concerned with economic development and political power.

154. _____ Legislation passed in 1887 to authorize the president to divide tribal land and distribute it to individual Native Americans.

155. _____ In World War II, the alliance of German and Italy, and later Japan.

156. _____ Passed in 1798 designed to curb criticism of the federal government.

157. _____ Henry Clay's program for the national economy, which included a protective tariff to stimulate industry and a national bank to provide credit.

158. _____ A relaxation of tensions between the United States and the Soviet Union that was begun by President Richard M. Nixon.

159. _____ The free black author of An Appeal to the Colored Citizens of the World, which threatened violence if slavery was not abolished.

160. _____ Group of unemployed World War I veterans who marched on Washington, D.C., in June 1932 to ask for immediate payment of their war pensions.

161. _____ Popular site of New York amusement parks opening in 1890s, attracting working class Americans with rides and games celebrating abandon and instant gratification.

162. _____ Immigrants who never intended to make the United States their home.

163. _____ The effort to encourage masters to voluntarily emancipate their slaves and to resettle free blacks in Africa.

164. _____ June 6, 1944, the day Allied forces landed on the beaches of Normandy, in France, leading to the defeat of Germany.

165. _____ Vietminh siege of 13,000 French soldiers in 1954 at a remote military outpost. The French surrender led to the 1956 elections designed to reunify Vietnam.

166. _____ U.S. propaganda agency of World War I.

167. _____ Laws passed by Southern state legislatures during Reconstruction, while Congress was out of session.

168. _____ As vice president, Calhoun anonymously expounded the doctrine of nullification, which held that states could prevent the enforcement of a federal law within their boundaries.

169. _____ A confederation of labor unions founded in 1886, it was composed mainly of skilled craft unions.

170. _____ Emphasized the power and omnipotence of God and the importance of seeking to earn saving grace and salvation.

171. _____ Phrase from John Winthrop's sermon, "A Model of Christian Charity," in which he challenged his fellow Puritans to build a model, ideal community in America.

172. _____ A movement founded to help the unemployed during the depression of the 1890s, it demanded that the federal government provide jobs and inflate the currency.

173. _____ This appellation was used to refer to common soldiers serving in Union armies during the Civil War.

174. _____ This term refers to the heads of the executive departments.

175. _____ America's leading exponent of religious liberalism, Channing was one of the founders of American Unitarianism.

A. Billy Yank
B. D Day
C. Channing
D. AFL
E. Carter
F. Central Powers
G. Coxey's Army
H. City Upon a Hill
I. Calvinism
J. Coney Island
K. Cabinet
L. Black Codes
M. Bonus Army
N. Axis Powers
O. Common Sense
P. David Walker
Q. Dien Bien Phu
R. Colonization
S. Détente
T. Alien and Sedition Acts
U. Dawes Act
V. Calhoun, John
W. Committee on Public Information
X. Birds of Passage
Y. American System

Provide the word that best matches each clue.

176. _____ This term refers to the heads of the executive departments.

177. _____ Henry Clay's program for the national economy, which included a protective tariff to stimulate industry and a national bank to provide credit.

178. _____ The high cost of labor led to the establishment of a system of mass production through the manufacture of interchangeable parts.

179. _____ An historic 1979 peace agreement negotiated between Egypt and Israel at the U.S. presidential retreat at Camp David, Maryland.

180. _____ In World War II, the alliance of German and Italy, and later Japan.

181. _____ Thomas Jefferson's first vice president, who killed Alexander Hamilton in a duel in 1804.

182. _____ People who moved to the South following the Civil War and helped to bring Republican control of southern state governments during Reconstruction.

183. _____ A failed plan to assassinate Cuban leader Fidel Castro and liberate Cuba with a trained military force of political exiles.

184. _____ Legislation passed in 1887 to authorize the president to divide tribal land and distribute it to individual Native Americans.

185. _____ Immigrants who never intended to make the United States their home.

186. _____ In World War I, Germany and Austria-Hungary and their allies.

187. _____ This best-selling pamphlet by Thomas Paine, first published in 1776, denounced the British monarchy, called for American independence.

188. _____ A movement founded to help the unemployed during the depression of the 1890s, it demanded that the federal government provide jobs and inflate the currency.

189. _____ These were opponents of the Constitution of 1787 who sought to continue the confederation of sovereign states and to keep power as close as possible to the people.

190. _____ President Franklin Delano Roosevelt's controversial plan to appoint Supreme Court justices who were sympathetic to his views, by offering retirement benefits to the sitting justices.

191. _____ The effort to encourage masters to voluntarily emancipate their slaves and to resettle free blacks in Africa.

192. _____ A landmark 1819 Supreme Court decision protecting contracts.

193. _____ This appellation was used to refer to common soldiers serving in Union armies during the Civil War.

194. _____ Popular site of New York amusement parks opening in 1890s, attracting working class Americans with rides and games celebrating abandon and instant gratification.

195. _____ A confederation of labor unions founded in 1886, it was composed mainly of skilled craft unions.

196. _____ Group of unemployed World War I veterans who marched on Washington, D.C., in June 1932 to ask for immediate payment of their war pensions.

197. _____ America's leading exponent of religious liberalism, Channing was one of the founders of American Unitarianism.

198. _____ The conflict in 1962 prompted by Soviet installation of missiles on Cuba and President Kennedy's announcement to the American Public.

199. _____ Literally meaning against the laws of human governance.

200. _____ President, 1976. His progressive racial views reflected an emergent South less concerned with racial distinctions and more concerned with economic development and political power.

A. Camp David Accords
C. Common Sense
E. Channing
G. Cabinet
I. Cuban Missile Crisis
K. Axis Powers

B. Carter
D. Bonus Army
F. Court Packing
H. Birds of Passage
J. Coney Island
L. Coxey's Arrny

141

M. AFL
O. Antifederalists
Q. Central Powers
S. Bay of Pigs
U. Billy Yank
W. Colonization
Y. Dartmouth vs Woodward

N. Antinomian
P. Aaron Burr
R. American System
T. Carpetbaggers
V. American System of Production
X. Dawes Act

Provide the word that best matches each clue.

201. _____ This best-selling pamphlet by Thomas Paine, first published in 1776, denounced the British monarchy, called for American independence.

202. _____ A cultural style and artistic movement of the 1950s that rejected traditional American family life and material values and celebrated African-American culture.

203. _____ A landmark 1819 Supreme Court decision protecting contracts.

204. _____ A Carter era economic policy, which freed many industries from many government economic controls.

205. _____ Notion that America houses biologically superior people and can spread democracy to the rest of the world.

206. _____ President Franklin Delano Roosevelt's controversial plan to appoint Supreme Court justices who were sympathetic to his views, by offering retirement benefits to the sitting justices.

207. _____ The "father of modern revivalism," Finney devised many techniques adopted by later revival preachers. He encouraged many women to participate actively in revival.

208. _____ June 6, 1944, the day Allied forces landed on the beaches of Normandy, in France, leading to the defeat of Germany.

209. _____ The process of transferring plants, animals, foods, diseases, wealth, and culture between Europe and the Americas.

210. _____ This appellation was used to refer to common soldiers serving in Union armies during the Civil War.

211. _____ America's leading exponent of religious liberalism, Channing was one of the founders of American Unitarianism.

212. _____ The effort to encourage masters to voluntarily emancipate their slaves and to resettle free blacks in Africa.

213. _____ Close advisors to President Franklin Delano Roosevelt during the early days of his first term whose policy suggestions influenced much New Deal legislation.

214. _____ In World War II, the alliance of German and Italy, and later Japan.

215. _____ President, 1976. His progressive racial views reflected an emergent South less concerned with racial distinctions and more concerned with economic development and political power.

216. _____ People who moved to the South following the Civil War and helped to bring Republican control of southern state governments during Reconstruction.

217. _____ The high cost of labor led to the establishment of a system of mass production through the manufacture of interchangeable parts.

218. _____ A former West Indian slave who organized an attempted rebellion against slavery in Charleston, South Carolina, in 1822.

219. _____ U.S. propaganda agency of World War I.

220. _____ A confederation of labor unions founded in 1886, it was composed mainly of skilled craft unions.

221. _____ Group of unemployed World War I veterans who marched on Washington, D.C., in June 1932 to ask for immediate payment of their war pensions.

222. _____ The proclaimed foreign policy of Theodore Roosevelt, it was based on the proverb, "Speak softly and carry a big stick,".

223. _____ A failed plan to assassinate Cuban leader Fidel Castro and liberate Cuba with a trained military force of political exiles.

224. _____ A rallying cry for more militant blacks advocated by younger leaders beginning in the mid-1960s.

225. _____ These were opponents of the Constitution of 1787 who sought to continue the confederation of sovereign states and to keep power as close as possible to the people.

A. Dartmouth vs Woodward
B. Black Power
C. Bonus Army
D. Beat Generation
E. AFL
F. Bay of Pigs
G. Billy Yank
H. Channing
I. Finney
J. Colonization
K. American System of Production
L. Carpetbaggers
M. Committee on Public Information
N. Columbian Exchange
O. American Exceptionalism
P. Common Sense
Q. Brain Trust
R. Deregulation
S. Antifederalists
T. Big Stick Diplomacy
U. Axis Powers
V. Carter
W. D Day
X. Court Packing
Y. Denmark Vesey

Provide the word that best matches each clue.

226. _____ June 6, 1944, the day Allied forces landed on the beaches of Normandy, in France, leading to the defeat of Germany.

227. _____ Phrase from John Winthrop's sermon, "A Model of Christian Charity," in which he challenged his fellow Puritans to build a model, ideal community in America.

228. _____ The proclaimed foreign policy of Theodore Roosevelt, it was based on the proverb, "Speak softly and carry a big stick,".

229. _____ The free black author of An Appeal to the Colored Citizens of the World, which threatened violence if slavery was not abolished.

230. _____ The effort to encourage masters to voluntarily emancipate their slaves and to resettle free blacks in Africa.

231. _____ Henry Clay's program for the national economy, which included a protective tariff to stimulate industry and a national bank to provide credit.

232. _____ America's leading exponent of religious liberalism, Channing was one of the founders of American Unitarianism.

233. _____ A former West Indian slave who organized an attempted rebellion against slavery in Charleston, South Carolina, in 1822.

234. _____ Immigrants who never intended to make the United States their home.

235. _____ A relaxation of tensions between the United States and the Soviet Union that was begun by President Richard M. Nixon.

236. _____ This best-selling pamphlet by Thomas Paine, first published in 1776, denounced the British monarchy, called for American independence.

237. _____ The leader of efforts to reform the treatment of the mentally ill.

238. _____ Not every person living in the North during the Civil War favored making war against the Confederacy. Such persons came to be identified as Copperheads.

239. _____ The first ten amendments to the U.S. Constitution, which protect the rights of individuals from the powers of the national government.

240. _____ Passed in 1798 designed to curb criticism of the federal government.

241. _____ An historic 1979 peace agreement negotiated between Egypt and Israel at the U.S. presidential retreat at Camp David, Maryland.

242. _____ Literally meaning against the laws of human governance.

243. _____ A movement founded to help the unemployed during the depression of the 1890s, it demanded that the federal government provide jobs and inflate the currency.

244. _____ Thomas Jefferson's first vice president, who killed Alexander Hamilton in a duel in 1804.

245. _____ A confederation of labor unions founded in 1886, it was composed mainly of skilled craft unions.

246. _____ This term refers to the heads of the executive departments.

247. _____ These were opponents of the Constitution of 1787 who sought to continue the confederation of sovereign states and to keep power as close as possible to the people.

248. _____ During the early nineteenth century, a movement arose to end the death penalty.

249. _____ A landmark 1819 Supreme Court decision protecting contracts.

250. _____ Popular site of New York amusement parks opening in 1890s, attracting working class Americans with rides and games celebrating abandon and instant gratification.

A. D Day
B. Alien and Sedition Acts
C. Capital Punishment
D. Dartmouth vs Woodward
E. AFL
F. Common Sense
G. Camp David Accords
H. American System
I. Denmark Vesey
J. Copperheads
K. Antinomian
L. Birds of Passage
M. David Walker
N. Channing
O. Dorothea Dix
P. Détente
Q. Coney Island
R. City Upon a Hill
S. Aaron Burr
T. Antifederalists
U. Big Stick Diplomacy
V. Bill of Rights
W. Coxey's Arrny
X. Colonization
Y. Cabinet

Provide the word that best matches each clue.

251. _____ Not every person living in the North during the Civil War favored making war against the Confederacy. Such persons came to be identified as Copperheads.

252. _____ The first ten amendments to the U.S. Constitution, which protect the rights of individuals from the powers of the national government.

253. _____ June 6, 1944, the day Allied forces landed on the beaches of Normandy, in France, leading to the defeat of Germany.

254. _____ Thomas Jefferson's first vice president, who killed Alexander Hamilton in a duel in 1804.

255. _____ The "father of modern revivalism," Finney devised many techniques adopted by later revival preachers. He encouraged many women to participate actively in revival.

256. _____ A movement founded to help the unemployed during the depression of the 1890s, it demanded that the federal government provide jobs and inflate the currency.

257. _____ America's leading exponent of religious liberalism, Channing was one of the founders of American Unitarianism.

258. _____ The high cost of labor led to the establishment of a system of mass production through the manufacture of interchangeable parts.

259. _____ These were opponents of the Constitution of 1787 who sought to continue the confederation of sovereign states and to keep power as close as possible to the people.

260. _____ U.S. propaganda agency of World War I.

261. _____ A failed plan to assassinate Cuban leader Fidel Castro and liberate Cuba with a trained military force of political exiles.

262. _____ Phrase from John Winthrop's sermon, "A Model of Christian Charity," in which he challenged his fellow Puritans to build a model, ideal community in America.

263. _____ A confederation of labor unions founded in 1886, it was composed mainly of skilled craft unions.

264. _____ A former West Indian slave who organized an attempted rebellion against slavery in Charleston, South Carolina, in 1822.

265. _____ President Franklin Delano Roosevelt's controversial plan to appoint Supreme Court justices who were sympathetic to his views, by offering retirement benefits to the sitting justices.

266. _____ People who moved to the South following the Civil War and helped to bring Republican control of southern state governments during Reconstruction.

267. _____ Henry Clay's program for the national economy, which included a protective tariff to stimulate industry and a national bank to provide credit.

268. _____ Popular site of New York amusement parks opening in 1890s, attracting working class Americans with rides and games celebrating abandon and instant gratification.

269. _____ President, 1976. His progressive racial views reflected an emergent South less concerned with racial distinctions and more concerned with economic development and political power.

270. _____ A rallying cry for more militant blacks advocated by younger leaders beginning in the mid-1960s.

271. _____ Close advisors to President Franklin Delano Roosevelt during the early days of his first term whose policy suggestions influenced much New Deal legislation.

272. _____ As vice president, Calhoun anonymously expounded the doctrine of nullification, which held that states could prevent the enforcement of a federal law within their boundaries.

273. _____ During the early nineteenth century, a movement arose to end the death penalty.

274. _____ A cultural style and artistic movement of the 1950s that rejected traditional American family life and material values and celebrated African-American culture.

275. _____ Legislation passed in 1887 to authorize the president to divide tribal land and distribute it to individual Native Americans.

A. Finney
C. American System
E. Channing
G. American System of Production
I. D Day
K. Coxey's Army
M. Antifederalists
O. Capital Punishment
Q. Carter
S. Bay of Pigs
U. Copperheads
W. Aaron Burr
Y. Carpetbaggers

B. Beat Generation
D. Court Packing
F. AFL
H. Brain Trust
J. Calhoun, John
L. Dawes Act
N. Bill of Rights
P. Denmark Vesey
R. Black Power
T. Coney Island
V. City Upon a Hill
X. Committee on Public Information

Provide the word that best matches each clue.

276. _____ The process of transferring plants, animals, foods, diseases, wealth, and culture between Europe and the Americas.

277. _____ This term refers to the heads of the executive departments.

278. _____ A landmark 1819 Supreme Court decision protecting contracts.

279. _____ Immigrants who never intended to make the United States their home.

280. _____ The free black author of An Appeal to the Colored Citizens of the World, which threatened violence if slavery was not abolished.

281. _____ The first ten amendments to the U.S. Constitution, which protect the rights of individuals from the powers of the national government.

282. _____ America's leading exponent of religious liberalism, Channing was one of the founders of American Unitarianism.

283. _____ A term associated with the Massachusetts Bay Colony, referring to the declining zeal of later generations or movement away from the utopian ideals of those Puritan leaders.

284. _____ Literally meaning against the laws of human governance.

285. _____ A rallying cry for more militant blacks advocated by younger leaders beginning in the mid-1960s.

286. _____ People who moved to the South following the Civil War and helped to bring Republican control of southern state governments during Reconstruction.

287. _____ Not every person living in the North during the Civil War favored making war against the Confederacy. Such persons came to be identified as Copperheads.

288. _____ Emphasized the power and omnipotence of God and the importance of seeking to earn saving grace and salvation.

289. _____ Legislation passed in 1887 to authorize the president to divide tribal land and distribute it to individual Native Americans.

290. _____ A confederation of labor unions founded in 1886, it was composed mainly of skilled craft unions.

291. _____ U.S. propaganda agency of World War I.

292. _____ A movement founded to help the unemployed during the depression of the 1890s, it demanded that the federal government provide jobs and inflate the currency.

293. _____ Thomas Jefferson's first vice president, who killed Alexander Hamilton in a duel in 1804.

294. _____ President, 1976. His progressive racial views reflected an emergent South less concerned with racial distinctions and more concerned with economic development and political power.

295. _____ Henry Clay's program for the national economy, which included a protective tariff to stimulate industry and a national bank to provide credit.

296. _____ Popular site of New York amusement parks opening in 1890s, attracting working class Americans with rides and games celebrating abandon and instant gratification.

297. _____ Notion that America houses biologically superior people and can spread democracy to the rest of the world.

298. _____ In World War I, Germany and Austria-Hungary and their allies.

299. _____ President Franklin Delano Roosevelt's controversial plan to appoint Supreme Court justices who were sympathetic to his views, by offering retirement benefits to the sitting justices.

300. _____ As vice president, Calhoun anonymously expounded the doctrine of nullification, which held that states could prevent the enforcement of a federal law within their boundaries.

A. Central Powers
C. Declension
E. AFL
G. Calhoun, John
I. Coney Island

B. Channing
D. Coxey's Arrny
F. American System
H. Carpetbaggers
J. Aaron Burr

150

K. Birds of Passage
M. Dawes Act
O. Committee on Public Information
Q. David Walker
S. Dartmouth vs Woodward
U. Carter
W. Columbian Exchange
Y. Antinomian

L. American Exceptionalism
N. Black Power
P. Bill of Rights
R. Cabinet
T. Court Packing
V. Copperheads
X. Calvinism

Provide the word that best matches each clue.

1. BILLY YANK — This appellation was used to refer to common soldiers serving in Union armies during the Civil War.

2. AMERICAN SYSTEM — Henry Clay's program for the national economy, which included a protective tariff to stimulate industry and a national bank to provide credit.

3. CABINET — This term refers to the heads of the executive departments.

4. CAPITAL PUNISHMENT — During the early nineteenth century, a movement arose to end the death penalty.

5. COLUMBIAN EXCHANGE — The process of transferring plants, animals, foods, diseases, wealth, and culture between Europe and the Americas.

6. CONEY ISLAND — Popular site of New York amusement parks opening in 1890s, attracting working class Americans with rides and games celebrating abandon and instant gratification.

7. AFL — A confederation of labor unions founded in 1886, it was composed mainly of skilled craft unions.

8. COXEY'S ARRNY — A movement founded to help the unemployed during the depression of the 1890s, it demanded that the federal government provide jobs and inflate the currency.

9. DARTMOUTH VS WOODWARD — A landmark 1819 Supreme Court decision protecting contracts.

10. CITY UPON A HILL — Phrase from John Winthrop's sermon, "A Model of Christian Charity," in which he challenged his fellow Puritans to build a model, ideal community in America.

11. ANTIFEDERALISTS — These were opponents of the Constitution of 1787 who sought to continue the confederation of sovereign states and to keep power as close as possible to the people.

12. CHANNING — America's leading exponent of religious liberalism, Channing was one of the founders of American Unitarianism.

13. CUBAN MISSILE CRISIS — The conflict in 1962 prompted by Soviet installation of missiles on Cuba and President Kennedy's announcement to the American Public.

14. BIG STICK DIPLOMACY — The proclaimed foreign policy of Theodore Roosevelt, it was based on the proverb, "Speak softly and carry a big stick,".

15. DÉTENTE — A relaxation of tensions between the United States and the Soviet Union that was begun by President Richard M. Nixon.

16. DRED SCOTT — A Missouri slave, Scott sued for his freedom on the grounds that his master had taken him onto free soil.

17. CAMP DAVID ACCORDS — An historic 1979 peace agreement negotiated between Egypt and Israel at the U.S. presidential retreat at Camp David, Maryland.

18. COLONIZATION — The effort to encourage masters to voluntarily emancipate their slaves and to resettle free blacks in Africa.

19. COMMON SENSE — This best-selling pamphlet by Thomas Paine, first published in 1776, denounced the British monarchy, called for American independence.

20. BRAIN TRUST — Close advisors to President Franklin Delano Roosevelt during the early days of his first term whose policy suggestions influenced much New Deal legislation.

21. COMMITTEE ON PUBLIC INFORMATION — U.S. propaganda agency of World War I.

22. FINNEY — The "father of modern revivalism," Finney devised many techniques adopted by later revival preachers. He encouraged many women to participate actively in revival.

23. BAY OF PIGS — A failed plan to assassinate Cuban leader Fidel Castro and liberate Cuba with a trained military force of political exiles.

24. BLACK CODES — Laws passed by Southern state legislatures during Reconstruction, while Congress was out of session.

25. ANTINOMIAN — Literally meaning against the laws of human governance.

A. Bay of Pigs

B. Brain Trust

- C. Dartmouth vs Woodward
- D. Colonization
- E. Columbian Exchange
- F. Cabinet
- G. Cuban Missile Crisis
- H. AFL
- I. Camp David Accords
- J. Committee on Public Information
- K. Black Codes
- L. Capital Punishment
- M. Coxey's Army
- N. Dred Scott
- O. American System
- P. City Upon a Hill
- Q. Common Sense
- R. Coney Island
- S. Antifederalists
- T. Billy Yank
- U. Channing
- V. Finney
- W. Détente
- X. Big Stick Diplomacy
- Y. Antinomian

Provide the word that best matches each clue.

26. COLONIZATION — The effort to encourage masters to voluntarily emancipate their slaves and to resettle free blacks in Africa.

27. BLACK CODES — Laws passed by Southern state legislatures during Reconstruction, while Congress was out of session.

28. AMERICAN SYSTEM — Henry Clay's program for the national economy, which included a protective tariff to stimulate industry and a national bank to provide credit.

29. AXIS POWERS — In World War II, the alliance of German and Italy, and later Japan.

30. DARTMOUTH VS WOODWARD — A landmark 1819 Supreme Court decision protecting contracts.

31. CALVINISM — Emphasized the power and omnipotence of God and the importance of seeking to earn saving grace and salvation.

32. BLACK POWER — A rallying cry for more militant blacks advocated by younger leaders beginning in the mid-1960s.

33. AARON BURR — Thomas Jefferson's first vice president, who killed Alexander Hamilton in a duel in 1804.

34. BRAIN TRUST — Close advisors to President Franklin Delano Roosevelt during the early days of his first term whose policy suggestions influenced much New Deal legislation.

35. CITY UPON A HILL — Phrase from John Winthrop's sermon, "A Model of Christian Charity," in which he challenged his fellow Puritans to build a model, ideal community in America.

36.	COURT PACKING	President Franklin Delano Roosevelt's controversial plan to appoint Supreme Court justices who were sympathetic to his views, by offering retirement benefits to the sitting justices.
37.	DAWES ACT	Legislation passed in 1887 to authorize the president to divide tribal land and distribute it to individual Native Americans.
38.	CABINET	This term refers to the heads of the executive departments.
39.	CALHOUN, JOHN	As vice president, Calhoun anonymously expounded the doctrine of nullification, which held that states could prevent the enforcement of a federal law within their boundaries.
40.	BAY OF PIGS	A failed plan to assassinate Cuban leader Fidel Castro and liberate Cuba with a trained military force of political exiles.
41.	COMMITTEE ON PUBLIC INFORMATION	U.S. propaganda agency of World War I.
42.	CARPETBAGGERS	People who moved to the South following the Civil War and helped to bring Republican control of southern state governments during Reconstruction.
43.	BIG STICK DIPLOMACY	The proclaimed foreign policy of Theodore Roosevelt, it was based on the proverb, "Speak softly and carry a big stick,".
44.	ANTIFEDERALISTS	These were opponents of the Constitution of 1787 who sought to continue the confederation of sovereign states and to keep power as close as possible to the people.
45.	COMMON SENSE	This best-selling pamphlet by Thomas Paine, first published in 1776, denounced the British monarchy, called for American independence.
46.	AFL	A confederation of labor unions founded in 1886, it was composed mainly of skilled craft unions.
47.	CARTER	President, 1976. His progressive racial views reflected an emergent South less concerned with racial distinctions and more concerned with economic development and political power.

48. CAMP DAVID ACCORDS — An historic 1979 peace agreement negotiated between Egypt and Israel at the U.S. presidential retreat at Camp David, Maryland.

49. DÉTENTE — A relaxation of tensions between the United States and the Soviet Union that was begun by President Richard M. Nixon.

50. CHANNING — America's leading exponent of religious liberalism, Channing was one of the founders of American Unitarianism.

A. Colonization
B. Black Codes
C. American System
D. Channing
E. Détente
F. Brain Trust
G. Bay of Pigs
H. Black Power
I. Common Sense
J. Camp David Accords
K. City Upon a Hill
L. Aaron Burr
M. Calvinism
N. Antifederalists
O. Dawes Act
P. Axis Powers
Q. Committee on Public Information
R. Cabinet
S. Calhoun, John
T. AFL
U. Court Packing
V. Carter
W. Big Stick Diplomacy
X. Dartmouth vs Woodward
Y. Carpetbaggers

Provide the word that best matches each clue.

51. CABINET — This term refers to the heads of the executive departments.

52. CUBAN MISSILE CRISIS — The conflict in 1962 prompted by Soviet installation of missiles on Cuba and President Kennedy's announcement to the American Public.

53. CAPITAL PUNISHMENT — During the early nineteenth century, a movement arose to end the death penalty.

54. DENMARK VESEY — A former West Indian slave who organized an attempted rebellion against slavery in Charleston, South Carolina, in 1822.

55. AMERICAN SYSTEM — Henry Clay's program for the national economy, which included a protective tariff to stimulate industry and a national bank to provide credit.

56. AFL — A confederation of labor unions founded in 1886, it was composed mainly of skilled craft unions.

57. DARTMOUTH VS WOODWARD — A landmark 1819 Supreme Court decision protecting contracts.

58. BLACK POWER — A rallying cry for more militant blacks advocated by younger leaders beginning in the mid-1960s.

59. ELECTRIC TROLLEY — Public transportation for urban neighborhoods, using electric current from overhead wires.

60. COLUMBIAN EXCHANGE — The process of transferring plants, animals, foods, diseases, wealth, and culture between Europe and the Americas.

61. BIG STICK DIPLOMACY — The proclaimed foreign policy of Theodore Roosevelt, it was based on the proverb, "Speak softly and carry a big stick,".

62. ANTIFEDERALISTS — These were opponents of the Constitution of 1787 who sought to continue the confederation of sovereign states and to keep power as close as possible to the people.

63. CHANNING — America's leading exponent of religious liberalism, Channing was one of the founders of American Unitarianism.

64. CALVINISM — Emphasized the power and omnipotence of God and the importance of seeking to earn saving grace and salvation.

65. CAMP DAVID ACCORDS — An historic 1979 peace agreement negotiated between Egypt and Israel at the U.S. presidential retreat at Camp David, Maryland.

66. CARPETBAGGERS — People who moved to the South following the Civil War and helped to bring Republican control of southern state governments during Reconstruction.

67. BEAT GENERATION — A cultural style and artistic movement of the 1950s that rejected traditional American family life and material values and celebrated African-American culture.

68. COMMON SENSE — This best-selling pamphlet by Thomas Paine, first published in 1776, denounced the British monarchy, called for American independence.

69. DAWES ACT — Legislation passed in 1887 to authorize the president to divide tribal land and distribute it to individual Native Americans.

70. DIEN BIEN PHU — Vietminh siege of 13,000 French soldiers in 1954 at a remote military outpost. The French surrender led to the 1956 elections designed to reunify Vietnam.

71. D DAY — June 6, 1944, the day Allied forces landed on the beaches of Normandy, in France, leading to the defeat of Germany.

72. BLACK CODES — Laws passed by Southern state legislatures during Reconstruction, while Congress was out of session.

73. BONUS ARMY — Group of unemployed World War I veterans who marched on Washington, D.C., in June 1932 to ask for immediate payment of their war pensions.

74. COPPERHEADS — Not every person living in the North during the Civil War favored making war against the Confederacy. Such persons came to be identified as Copperheads.

75. DRED SCOTT — A Missouri slave, Scott sued for his freedom on the grounds that his master had taken him onto free soil.

- A. Bonus Army
- B. Denmark Vesey
- C. Beat Generation
- D. Dartmouth vs Woodward
- E. Black Codes
- F. Antifederalists
- G. Big Stick Diplomacy
- H. Common Sense
- I. AFL
- J. Channing
- K. Dred Scott
- L. D Day
- M. Dawes Act
- N. Camp David Accords
- O. Cabinet
- P. Capital Punishment
- Q. Dien Bien Phu
- R. American System
- S. Columbian Exchange
- T. Black Power
- U. Calvinism
- V. Copperheads
- W. Cuban Missile Crisis
- X. Electric Trolley
- Y. Carpetbaggers

Provide the word that best matches each clue.

76. COMMON SENSE — This best-selling pamphlet by Thomas Paine, first published in 1776, denounced the British monarchy, called for American independence.

77. DECLENSION — A term associated with the Massachusetts Bay Colony, referring to the declining zeal of later generations or movement away from the utopian ideals of those Puritan leaders.

78. D DAY — June 6, 1944, the day Allied forces landed on the beaches of Normandy, in France, leading to the defeat of Germany.

79. AARON BURR — Thomas Jefferson's first vice president, who killed Alexander Hamilton in a duel in 1804.

80. BONUS ARMY — Group of unemployed World War I veterans who marched on Washington, D.C., in June 1932 to ask for immediate payment of their war pensions.

81. CARTER — President, 1976. His progressive racial views reflected an emergent South less concerned with racial distinctions and more concerned with economic development and political power.

82.	BIRDS OF PASSAGE	Immigrants who never intended to make the United States their home.
83.	AMERICAN SYSTEM	Henry Clay's program for the national economy, which included a protective tariff to stimulate industry and a national bank to provide credit.
84.	DAVID WALKER	The free black author of An Appeal to the Colored Citizens of the World, which threatened violence if slavery was not abolished.
85.	FINNEY	The "father of modern revivalism," Finney devised many techniques adopted by later revival preachers. He encouraged many women to participate actively in revival.
86.	COXEY'S ARRNY	A movement founded to help the unemployed during the depression of the 1890s, it demanded that the federal government provide jobs and inflate the currency.
87.	BILL OF RIGHTS	The first ten amendments to the U.S. Constitution, which protect the rights of individuals from the powers of the national government.
88.	DAWES ACT	Legislation passed in 1887 to authorize the president to divide tribal land and distribute it to individual Native Americans.
89.	BEAT GENERATION	A cultural style and artistic movement of the 1950s that rejected traditional American family life and material values and celebrated African-American culture.
90.	COLUMBIAN EXCHANGE	The process of transferring plants, animals, foods, diseases, wealth, and culture between Europe and the Americas.
91.	CARPETBAGGERS	People who moved to the South following the Civil War and helped to bring Republican control of southern state governments during Reconstruction.
92.	BIG STICK DIPLOMACY	The proclaimed foreign policy of Theodore Roosevelt, it was based on the proverb, "Speak softly and carry a big stick,".
93.	ANTIFEDERALISTS	These were opponents of the Constitution of 1787 who sought to continue the confederation of sovereign states and to keep power as close as possible to the people.

94. CALVINISM	Emphasized the power and omnipotence of God and the importance of seeking to earn saving grace and salvation.
95. CALHOUN, JOHN	As vice president, Calhoun anonymously expounded the doctrine of nullification, which held that states could prevent the enforcement of a federal law within their boundaries.
96. AMERICAN EXCEPTIONALISM	Notion that America houses biologically superior people and can spread democracy to the rest of the world.
97. CAPITAL PUNISHMENT	During the early nineteenth century, a movement arose to end the death penalty.
98. CUBAN MISSILE CRISIS	The conflict in 1962 prompted by Soviet installation of missiles on Cuba and President Kennedy's announcement to the American Public.
99. AMERICAN SYSTEM OF PRODUCTION	The high cost of labor led to the establishment of a system of mass production through the manufacture of interchangeable parts.
100. DENMARK VESEY	A former West Indian slave who organized an attempted rebellion against slavery in Charleston, South Carolina, in 1822.

A. Coxey's Arrny
B. Declension
C. Cuban Missile Crisis
D. Columbian Exchange
E. Big Stick Diplomacy
F. Dawes Act
G. David Walker
H. Finney
I. Carter
J. American System of Production
K. Denmark Vesey
L. Common Sense
M. Calvinism
N. Carpetbaggers
O. Capital Punishment
P. Bonus Army
Q. American System
R. American Exceptionalism
S. D Day
T. Aaron Burr
U. Birds of Passage
V. Bill of Rights
W. Calhoun, John
X. Beat Generation
Y. Antifederalists

Provide the word that best matches each clue.

101. CALHOUN, JOHN	As vice president, Calhoun anonymously expounded the doctrine of nullification, which held that states could prevent the enforcement of a federal law within their boundaries.

102. COMMON SENSE — This best-selling pamphlet by Thomas Paine, first published in 1776, denounced the British monarchy, called for American independence.

103. FINNEY — The "father of modern revivalism," Finney devised many techniques adopted by later revival preachers. He encouraged many women to participate actively in revival.

104. BLACK CODES — Laws passed by Southern state legislatures during Reconstruction, while Congress was out of session.

105. AXIS POWERS — In World War II, the alliance of German and Italy, and later Japan.

106. D DAY — June 6, 1944, the day Allied forces landed on the beaches of Normandy, in France, leading to the defeat of Germany.

107. COXEY'S ARRNY — A movement founded to help the unemployed during the depression of the 1890s, it demanded that the federal government provide jobs and inflate the currency.

108. AMERICAN SYSTEM — Henry Clay's program for the national economy, which included a protective tariff to stimulate industry and a national bank to provide credit.

109. BIG STICK DIPLOMACY — The proclaimed foreign policy of Theodore Roosevelt, it was based on the proverb, "Speak softly and carry a big stick,".

110. CAMP DAVID ACCORDS — An historic 1979 peace agreement negotiated between Egypt and Israel at the U.S. presidential retreat at Camp David, Maryland.

111. CHANNING — America's leading exponent of religious liberalism, Channing was one of the founders of American Unitarianism.

112. COMMITTEE ON PUBLIC INFORMATION — U.S. propaganda agency of World War I.

113. BONUS ARMY — Group of unemployed World War I veterans who marched on Washington, D.C., in June 1932 to ask for immediate payment of their war pensions.

114. CABINET — This term refers to the heads of the executive departments.

115. ANTINOMIAN — Literally meaning against the laws of human governance.

116. AFL — A confederation of labor unions founded in 1886, it was composed mainly of skilled craft unions.

117. CALVINISM — Emphasized the power and omnipotence of God and the importance of seeking to earn saving grace and salvation.

118. COLONIZATION — The effort to encourage masters to voluntarily emancipate their slaves and to resettle free blacks in Africa.

119. CARPETBAGGERS — People who moved to the South following the Civil War and helped to bring Republican control of southern state governments during Reconstruction.

120. CARTER — President, 1976. His progressive racial views reflected an emergent South less concerned with racial distinctions and more concerned with economic development and political power.

121. CONEY ISLAND — Popular site of New York amusement parks opening in 1890s, attracting working class Americans with rides and games celebrating abandon and instant gratification.

122. AMERICAN SYSTEM OF PRODUCTION — The high cost of labor led to the establishment of a system of mass production through the manufacture of interchangeable parts.

123. DAWES ACT — Legislation passed in 1887 to authorize the president to divide tribal land and distribute it to individual Native Americans.

124. COPPERHEADS — Not every person living in the North during the Civil War favored making war against the Confederacy. Such persons came to be identified as Copperheads.

125. COURT PACKING — President Franklin Delano Roosevelt's controversial plan to appoint Supreme Court justices who were sympathetic to his views, by offering retirement benefits to the sitting justices.

A. Finney
C. Carpetbaggers
E. Calhoun, John
G. Common Sense
B. Copperheads
D. Coney Island
F. Antinomian
H. Cabinet

I. American System of Production
K. Court Packing
M. Committee on Public Information
O. Bonus Army
Q. D Day
S. Carter
U. Colonization
W. Channing
Y. Black Codes

J. Big Stick Diplomacy
L. Coxey's Arrny
N. AFL
P. Dawes Act
R. American System
T. Axis Powers
V. Calvinism
X. Camp David Accords

Provide the word that best matches each clue.

126. CAPITAL PUNISHMENT — During the early nineteenth century, a movement arose to end the death penalty.

127. CITY UPON A HILL — Phrase from John Winthrop's sermon, "A Model of Christian Charity," in which he challenged his fellow Puritans to build a model, ideal community in America.

128. BLACK POWER — A rallying cry for more militant blacks advocated by younger leaders beginning in the mid-1960s.

129. AMERICAN SYSTEM OF PRODUCTION — The high cost of labor led to the establishment of a system of mass production through the manufacture of interchangeable parts.

130. BEAT GENERATION — A cultural style and artistic movement of the 1950s that rejected traditional American family life and material values and celebrated African-American culture.

131. CALVINISM — Emphasized the power and omnipotence of God and the importance of seeking to earn saving grace and salvation.

132. FINNEY — The "father of modern revivalism," Finney devised many techniques adopted by later revival preachers. He encouraged many women to participate actively in revival.

133. CAMP DAVID ACCORDS — An historic 1979 peace agreement negotiated between Egypt and Israel at the U.S. presidential retreat at Camp David, Maryland.

134. COXEY'S ARRNY — A movement founded to help the unemployed during the depression of the 1890s, it demanded that the federal government provide jobs and inflate the currency.

135.	BIRDS OF PASSAGE	Immigrants who never intended to make the United States their home.
136.	COMMON SENSE	This best-selling pamphlet by Thomas Paine, first published in 1776, denounced the British monarchy, called for American independence.
137.	COLONIZATION	The effort to encourage masters to voluntarily emancipate their slaves and to resettle free blacks in Africa.
138.	BLACK TUESDAY	October 29,1929, the day of the stock market crash that initiated the Great Depression.
139.	ALIEN AND SEDITION ACTS	Passed in 1798 designed to curb criticism of the federal government.
140.	BILLY YANK	This appellation was used to refer to common soldiers serving in Union armies during the Civil War.
141.	CHANNING	America's leading exponent of religious liberalism, Channing was one of the founders of American Unitarianism.
142.	BAY OF PIGS	A failed plan to assassinate Cuban leader Fidel Castro and liberate Cuba with a trained military force of political exiles.
143.	BIG STICK DIPLOMACY	The proclaimed foreign policy of Theodore Roosevelt, it was based on the proverb, "Speak softly and carry a big stick,".
144.	AMERICAN EXCEPTIONALISM	Notion that America houses biologically superior people and can spread democracy to the rest of the world.
145.	CABINET	This term refers to the heads of the executive departments.
146.	AMERICAN SYSTEM	Henry Clay's program for the national economy, which included a protective tariff to stimulate industry and a national bank to provide credit.
147.	AARON BURR	Thomas Jefferson's first vice president, who killed Alexander Hamilton in a duel in 1804.
148.	CARPETBAGGERS	People who moved to the South following the Civil War and helped to bring Republican control of southern state governments during Reconstruction.

149. ANTIFEDERALISTS — These were opponents of the Constitution of 1787 who sought to continue the confederation of sovereign states and to keep power as close as possible to the people.

150. COLUMBIAN EXCHANGE — The process of transferring plants, animals, foods, diseases, wealth, and culture between Europe and the Americas.

A. Black Power
C. American System
E. Carpetbaggers
G. City Upon a Hill
I. American Exceptionalism
K. Coxey's Arrny
M. Capital Punishment
O. Colonization
Q. Antifederalists
S. Black Tuesday
U. Beat Generation
W. Camp David Accords
Y. Common Sense

B. Cabinet
D. Calvinism
F. Aaron Burr
H. Big Stick Diplomacy
J. Bay of Pigs
L. Alien and Sedition Acts
N. American System of Production
P. Channing
R. Columbian Exchange
T. Birds of Passage
V. Finney
X. Billy Yank

Provide the word that best matches each clue.

151. COMMON SENSE — This best-selling pamphlet by Thomas Paine, first published in 1776, denounced the British monarchy, called for American independence.

152. CENTRAL POWERS — In World War I, Germany and Austria-Hungary and their allies.

153. CARTER — President, 1976. His progressive racial views reflected an emergent South less concerned with racial distinctions and more concerned with economic development and political power.

154. DAWES ACT — Legislation passed in 1887 to authorize the president to divide tribal land and distribute it to individual Native Americans.

155. AXIS POWERS — In World War II, the alliance of German and Italy, and later Japan.

156. ALIEN AND SEDITION ACTS — Passed in 1798 designed to curb criticism of the federal government.

157. AMERICAN SYSTEM	Henry Clay's program for the national economy, which included a protective tariff to stimulate industry and a national bank to provide credit.
158. DÉTENTE	A relaxation of tensions between the United States and the Soviet Union that was begun by President Richard M. Nixon.
159. DAVID WALKER	The free black author of An Appeal to the Colored Citizens of the World, which threatened violence if slavery was not abolished.
160. BONUS ARMY	Group of unemployed World War I veterans who marched on Washington, D.C., in June 1932 to ask for immediate payment of their war pensions.
161. CONEY ISLAND	Popular site of New York amusement parks opening in 1890s, attracting working class Americans with rides and games celebrating abandon and instant gratification.
162. BIRDS OF PASSAGE	Immigrants who never intended to make the United States their home.
163. COLONIZATION	The effort to encourage masters to voluntarily emancipate their slaves and to resettle free blacks in Africa.
164. D DAY	June 6, 1944, the day Allied forces landed on the beaches of Normandy, in France, leading to the defeat of Germany.
165. DIEN BIEN PHU	Vietminh siege of 13,000 French soldiers in 1954 at a remote military outpost. The French surrender led to the 1956 elections designed to reunify Vietnam.
166. COMMITTEE ON PUBLIC INFORMATION	U.S. propaganda agency of World War I.
167. BLACK CODES	Laws passed by Southern state legislatures during Reconstruction, while Congress was out of session.
168. CALHOUN, JOHN	As vice president, Calhoun anonymously expounded the doctrine of nullification, which held that states could prevent the enforcement of a federal law within their boundaries.
169. AFL	A confederation of labor unions founded in 1886, it was composed mainly of skilled craft unions.

170. CALVINISM — Emphasized the power and omnipotence of God and the importance of seeking to earn saving grace and salvation.

171. CITY UPON A HILL — Phrase from John Winthrop's sermon, "A Model of Christian Charity," in which he challenged his fellow Puritans to build a model, ideal community in America.

172. COXEY'S ARRNY — A movement founded to help the unemployed during the depression of the 1890s, it demanded that the federal government provide jobs and inflate the currency.

173. BILLY YANK — This appellation was used to refer to common soldiers serving in Union armies during the Civil War.

174. CABINET — This term refers to the heads of the executive departments.

175. CHANNING — America's leading exponent of religious liberalism, Channing was one of the founders of American Unitarianism.

- A. Billy Yank
- B. D Day
- C. Channing
- D. AFL
- E. Carter
- F. Central Powers
- G. Coxey's Arrny
- H. City Upon a Hill
- I. Calvinism
- J. Coney Island
- K. Cabinet
- L. Black Codes
- M. Bonus Army
- N. Axis Powers
- O. Common Sense
- P. David Walker
- Q. Dien Bien Phu
- R. Colonization
- S. Détente
- T. Alien and Sedition Acts
- U. Dawes Act
- V. Calhoun, John
- W. Committee on Public Information
- X. Birds of Passage
- Y. American System

Provide the word that best matches each clue.

176. CABINET — This term refers to the heads of the executive departments.

177. AMERICAN SYSTEM — Henry Clay's program for the national economy, which included a protective tariff to stimulate industry and a national bank to provide credit.

178.	AMERICAN SYSTEM OF PRODUCTION	The high cost of labor led to the establishment of a system of mass production through the manufacture of interchangeable parts.
179.	CAMP DAVID ACCORDS	An historic 1979 peace agreement negotiated between Egypt and Israel at the U.S. presidential retreat at Camp David, Maryland.
180.	AXIS POWERS	In World War II, the alliance of German and Italy, and later Japan.
181.	AARON BURR	Thomas Jefferson's first vice president, who killed Alexander Hamilton in a duel in 1804.
182.	CARPETBAGGERS	People who moved to the South following the Civil War and helped to bring Republican control of southern state governments during Reconstruction.
183.	BAY OF PIGS	A failed plan to assassinate Cuban leader Fidel Castro and liberate Cuba with a trained military force of political exiles.
184.	DAWES ACT	Legislation passed in 1887 to authorize the president to divide tribal land and distribute it to individual Native Americans.
185.	BIRDS OF PASSAGE	Immigrants who never intended to make the United States their home.
186.	CENTRAL POWERS	In World War I, Germany and Austria-Hungary and their allies.
187.	COMMON SENSE	This best-selling pamphlet by Thomas Paine, first published in 1776, denounced the British monarchy, called for American independence.
188.	COXEY'S ARRNY	A movement founded to help the unemployed during the depression of the 1890s, it demanded that the federal government provide jobs and inflate the currency.
189.	ANTIFEDERALISTS	These were opponents of the Constitution of 1787 who sought to continue the confederation of sovereign states and to keep power as close as possible to the people.

190. COURT PACKING — President Franklin Delano Roosevelt's controversial plan to appoint Supreme Court justices who were sympathetic to his views, by offering retirement benefits to the sitting justices.

191. COLONIZATION — The effort to encourage masters to voluntarily emancipate their slaves and to resettle free blacks in Africa.

192. DARTMOUTH VS WOODWARD — A landmark 1819 Supreme Court decision protecting contracts.

193. BILLY YANK — This appellation was used to refer to common soldiers serving in Union armies during the Civil War.

194. CONEY ISLAND — Popular site of New York amusement parks opening in 1890s, attracting working class Americans with rides and games celebrating abandon and instant gratification.

195. AFL — A confederation of labor unions founded in 1886, it was composed mainly of skilled craft unions.

196. BONUS ARMY — Group of unemployed World War I veterans who marched on Washington, D.C., in June 1932 to ask for immediate payment of their war pensions.

197. CHANNING — America's leading exponent of religious liberalism, Channing was one of the founders of American Unitarianism.

198. CUBAN MISSILE CRISIS — The conflict in 1962 prompted by Soviet installation of missiles on Cuba and President Kennedy's announcement to the American Public.

199. ANTINOMIAN — Literally meaning against the laws of human governance.

200. CARTER — President, 1976. His progressive racial views reflected an emergent South less concerned with racial distinctions and more concerned with economic development and political power.

A. Camp David Accords
B. Carter
C. Common Sense
D. Bonus Army
E. Channing
F. Court Packing
G. Cabinet
H. Birds of Passage
I. Cuban Missile Crisis
J. Coney Island
K. Axis Powers
L. Coxey's Arrny

- M. AFL
- O. Antifederalists
- Q. Central Powers
- S. Bay of Pigs
- U. Billy Yank
- W. Colonization
- Y. Dartmouth vs Woodward
- N. Antinomian
- P. Aaron Burr
- R. American System
- T. Carpetbaggers
- V. American System of Production
- X. Dawes Act

Provide the word that best matches each clue.

201. COMMON SENSE — This best-selling pamphlet by Thomas Paine, first published in 1776, denounced the British monarchy, called for American independence.

202. BEAT GENERATION — A cultural style and artistic movement of the 1950s that rejected traditional American family life and material values and celebrated African-American culture.

203. DARTMOUTH VS WOODWARD — A landmark 1819 Supreme Court decision protecting contracts.

204. DEREGULATION — A Carter era economic policy, which freed many industries from many government economic controls.

205. AMERICAN EXCEPTIONALISM — Notion that America houses biologically superior people and can spread democracy to the rest of the world.

206. COURT PACKING — President Franklin Delano Roosevelt's controversial plan to appoint Supreme Court justices who were sympathetic to his views, by offering retirement benefits to the sitting justices.

207. FINNEY — The "father of modern revivalism," Finney devised many techniques adopted by later revival preachers. He encouraged many women to participate actively in revival.

208. D DAY — June 6, 1944, the day Allied forces landed on the beaches of Normandy, in France, leading to the defeat of Germany.

209. COLUMBIAN EXCHANGE — The process of transferring plants, animals, foods, diseases, wealth, and culture between Europe and the Americas.

210. BILLY YANK — This appellation was used to refer to common soldiers serving in Union armies during the Civil War.

211. CHANNING — America's leading exponent of religious liberalism, Channing was one of the founders of American Unitarianism.

212. COLONIZATION — The effort to encourage masters to voluntarily emancipate their slaves and to resettle free blacks in Africa.

213. BRAIN TRUST — Close advisors to President Franklin Delano Roosevelt during the early days of his first term whose policy suggestions influenced much New Deal legislation.

214. AXIS POWERS — In World War II, the alliance of German and Italy, and later Japan.

215. CARTER — President, 1976. His progressive racial views reflected an emergent South less concerned with racial distinctions and more concerned with economic development and political power.

216. CARPETBAGGERS — People who moved to the South following the Civil War and helped to bring Republican control of southern state governments during Reconstruction.

217. AMERICAN SYSTEM OF PRODUCTION — The high cost of labor led to the establishment of a system of mass production through the manufacture of interchangeable parts.

218. DENMARK VESEY — A former West Indian slave who organized an attempted rebellion against slavery in Charleston, South Carolina, in 1822.

219. COMMITTEE ON PUBLIC INFORMATION — U.S. propaganda agency of World War I.

220. AFL — A confederation of labor unions founded in 1886, it was composed mainly of skilled craft unions.

221. BONUS ARMY — Group of unemployed World War I veterans who marched on Washington, D.C., in June 1932 to ask for immediate payment of their war pensions.

222. BIG STICK DIPLOMACY — The proclaimed foreign policy of Theodore Roosevelt, it was based on the proverb, "Speak softly and carry a big stick,".

223. BAY OF PIGS — A failed plan to assassinate Cuban leader Fidel Castro and liberate Cuba with a trained military force of political exiles.

224. BLACK POWER — A rallying cry for more militant blacks advocated by younger leaders beginning in the mid-1960s.

225. ANTIFEDERALISTS — These were opponents of the Constitution of 1787 who sought to continue the confederation of sovereign states and to keep power as close as possible to the people.

A. Dartmouth vs Woodward
B. Black Power
C. Bonus Army
D. Beat Generation
E. AFL
F. Bay of Pigs
G. Billy Yank
H. Channing
I. Finney
J. Colonization
K. American System of Production
L. Carpetbaggers
M. Committee on Public Information
N. Columbian Exchange
O. American Exceptionalism
P. Common Sense
Q. Brain Trust
R. Deregulation
S. Antifederalists
T. Big Stick Diplomacy
U. Axis Powers
V. Carter
W. D Day
X. Court Packing
Y. Denmark Vesey

Provide the word that best matches each clue.

226. D DAY — June 6, 1944, the day Allied forces landed on the beaches of Normandy, in France, leading to the defeat of Germany.

227. CITY UPON A HILL — Phrase from John Winthrop's sermon, "A Model of Christian Charity," in which he challenged his fellow Puritans to build a model, ideal community in America.

228. BIG STICK DIPLOMACY — The proclaimed foreign policy of Theodore Roosevelt, it was based on the proverb, "Speak softly and carry a big stick,".

229. DAVID WALKER — The free black author of An Appeal to the Colored Citizens of the World, which threatened violence if slavery was not abolished.

230. COLONIZATION — The effort to encourage masters to voluntarily emancipate their slaves and to resettle free blacks in Africa.

231. AMERICAN SYSTEM — Henry Clay's program for the national economy, which included a protective tariff to stimulate industry and a national bank to provide credit.

232. CHANNING — America's leading exponent of religious liberalism, Channing was one of the founders of American Unitarianism.

233.	DENMARK VESEY	A former West Indian slave who organized an attempted rebellion against slavery in Charleston, South Carolina, in 1822.
234.	BIRDS OF PASSAGE	Immigrants who never intended to make the United States their home.
235.	DÉTENTE	A relaxation of tensions between the United States and the Soviet Union that was begun by President Richard M. Nixon.
236.	COMMON SENSE	This best-selling pamphlet by Thomas Paine, first published in 1776, denounced the British monarchy, called for American independence.
237.	DOROTHEA DIX	The leader of efforts to reform the treatment of the mentally ill.
238.	COPPERHEADS	Not every person living in the North during the Civil War favored making war against the Confederacy. Such persons came to be identified as Copperheads.
239.	BILL OF RIGHTS	The first ten amendments to the U.S. Constitution, which protect the rights of individuals from the powers of the national government.
240.	ALIEN AND SEDITION ACTS	Passed in 1798 designed to curb criticism of the federal government.
241.	CAMP DAVID ACCORDS	An historic 1979 peace agreement negotiated between Egypt and Israel at the U.S. presidential retreat at Camp David, Maryland.
242.	ANTINOMIAN	Literally meaning against the laws of human governance.
243.	COXEY'S ARRNY	A movement founded to help the unemployed during the depression of the 1890s, it demanded that the federal government provide jobs and inflate the currency.
244.	AARON BURR	Thomas Jefferson's first vice president, who killed Alexander Hamilton in a duel in 1804.
245.	AFL	A confederation of labor unions founded in 1886, it was composed mainly of skilled craft unions.
246.	CABINET	This term refers to the heads of the executive departments.
247.	ANTIFEDERALISTS	These were opponents of the Constitution of 1787 who sought to continue the confederation of sovereign states and to keep power as close as possible to the people.

248. **CAPITAL PUNISHMENT** — During the early nineteenth century, a movement arose to end the death penalty.

249. **DARTMOUTH VS WOODWARD** — A landmark 1819 Supreme Court decision protecting contracts.

250. **CONEY ISLAND** — Popular site of New York amusement parks opening in 1890s, attracting working class Americans with rides and games celebrating abandon and instant gratification.

A. D Day
B. Alien and Sedition Acts
C. Capital Punishment
D. Dartmouth vs Woodward
E. AFL
F. Common Sense
G. Camp David Accords
H. American System
I. Denmark Vesey
J. Copperheads
K. Antinomian
L. Birds of Passage
M. David Walker
N. Channing
O. Dorothea Dix
P. Détente
Q. Coney Island
R. City Upon a Hill
S. Aaron Burr
T. Antifederalists
U. Big Stick Diplomacy
V. Bill of Rights
W. Coxey's Arrny
X. Colonization
Y. Cabinet

Provide the word that best matches each clue.

251. **COPPERHEADS** — Not every person living in the North during the Civil War favored making war against the Confederacy. Such persons came to be identified as Copperheads.

252. **BILL OF RIGHTS** — The first ten amendments to the U.S. Constitution, which protect the rights of individuals from the powers of the national government.

253. **D DAY** — June 6, 1944, the day Allied forces landed on the beaches of Normandy, in France, leading to the defeat of Germany.

254. **AARON BURR** — Thomas Jefferson's first vice president, who killed Alexander Hamilton in a duel in 1804.

255. **FINNEY** — The "father of modern revivalism," Finney devised many techniques adopted by later revival preachers. He encouraged many women to participate actively in revival.

256. **COXEY'S ARRNY** — A movement founded to help the unemployed during the depression of the 1890s, it demanded that the federal government provide jobs and inflate the currency.

#	Term	Definition
257.	CHANNING	America's leading exponent of religious liberalism, Channing was one of the founders of American Unitarianism.
258.	AMERICAN SYSTEM OF PRODUCTION	The high cost of labor led to the establishment of a system of mass production through the manufacture of interchangeable parts.
259.	ANTIFEDERALISTS	These were opponents of the Constitution of 1787 who sought to continue the confederation of sovereign states and to keep power as close as possible to the people.
260.	COMMITTEE ON PUBLIC INFORMATION	U.S. propaganda agency of World War I.
261.	BAY OF PIGS	A failed plan to assassinate Cuban leader Fidel Castro and liberate Cuba with a trained military force of political exiles.
262.	CITY UPON A HILL	Phrase from John Winthrop's sermon, "A Model of Christian Charity," in which he challenged his fellow Puritans to build a model, ideal community in America.
263.	AFL	A confederation of labor unions founded in 1886, it was composed mainly of skilled craft unions.
264.	DENMARK VESEY	A former West Indian slave who organized an attempted rebellion against slavery in Charleston, South Carolina, in 1822.
265.	COURT PACKING	President Franklin Delano Roosevelt's controversial plan to appoint Supreme Court justices who were sympathetic to his views, by offering retirement benefits to the sitting justices.
266.	CARPETBAGGERS	People who moved to the South following the Civil War and helped to bring Republican control of southern state governments during Reconstruction.
267.	AMERICAN SYSTEM	Henry Clay's program for the national economy, which included a protective tariff to stimulate industry and a national bank to provide credit.
268.	CONEY ISLAND	Popular site of New York amusement parks opening in 1890s, attracting working class Americans with rides and games celebrating abandon and instant gratification.

269. CARTER — President, 1976. His progressive racial views reflected an emergent South less concerned with racial distinctions and more concerned with economic development and political power.

270. BLACK POWER — A rallying cry for more militant blacks advocated by younger leaders beginning in the mid-1960s.

271. BRAIN TRUST — Close advisors to President Franklin Delano Roosevelt during the early days of his first term whose policy suggestions influenced much New Deal legislation.

272. CALHOUN, JOHN — As vice president, Calhoun anonymously expounded the doctrine of nullification, which held that states could prevent the enforcement of a federal law within their boundaries.

273. CAPITAL PUNISHMENT — During the early nineteenth century, a movement arose to end the death penalty.

274. BEAT GENERATION — A cultural style and artistic movement of the 1950s that rejected traditional American family life and material values and celebrated African-American culture.

275. DAWES ACT — Legislation passed in 1887 to authorize the president to divide tribal land and distribute it to individual Native Americans.

- A. Finney
- B. Beat Generation
- C. American System
- D. Court Packing
- E. Channing
- F. AFL
- G. American System of Production
- H. Brain Trust
- I. D Day
- J. Calhoun, John
- K. Coxey's Arrny
- L. Dawes Act
- M. Antifederalists
- N. Bill of Rights
- O. Capital Punishment
- P. Denmark Vesey
- Q. Carter
- R. Black Power
- S. Bay of Pigs
- T. Coney Island
- U. Copperheads
- V. City Upon a Hill
- W. Aaron Burr
- X. Committee on Public Information
- Y. Carpetbaggers

Provide the word that best matches each clue.

276. COLUMBIAN EXCHANGE — The process of transferring plants, animals, foods, diseases, wealth, and culture between Europe and the Americas.

#	Term	Definition
277.	CABINET	This term refers to the heads of the executive departments.
278.	DARTMOUTH VS WOODWARD	A landmark 1819 Supreme Court decision protecting contracts.
279.	BIRDS OF PASSAGE	Immigrants who never intended to make the United States their home.
280.	DAVID WALKER	The free black author of An Appeal to the Colored Citizens of the World, which threatened violence if slavery was not abolished.
281.	BILL OF RIGHTS	The first ten amendments to the U.S. Constitution, which protect the rights of individuals from the powers of the national government.
282.	CHANNING	America's leading exponent of religious liberalism, Channing was one of the founders of American Unitarianism.
283.	DECLENSION	A term associated with the Massachusetts Bay Colony, referring to the declining zeal of later generations or movement away from the utopian ideals of those Puritan leaders.
284.	ANTINOMIAN	Literally meaning against the laws of human governance.
285.	BLACK POWER	A rallying cry for more militant blacks advocated by younger leaders beginning in the mid-1960s.
286.	CARPETBAGGERS	People who moved to the South following the Civil War and helped to bring Republican control of southern state governments during Reconstruction.
287.	COPPERHEADS	Not every person living in the North during the Civil War favored making war against the Confederacy. Such persons came to be identified as Copperheads.
288.	CALVINISM	Emphasized the power and omnipotence of God and the importance of seeking to earn saving grace and salvation.
289.	DAWES ACT	Legislation passed in 1887 to authorize the president to divide tribal land and distribute it to individual Native Americans.

290. AFL — A confederation of labor unions founded in 1886, it was composed mainly of skilled craft unions.

291. COMMITTEE ON PUBLIC INFORMATION — U.S. propaganda agency of World War I.

292. COXEY'S ARRNY — A movement founded to help the unemployed during the depression of the 1890s, it demanded that the federal government provide jobs and inflate the currency.

293. AARON BURR — Thomas Jefferson's first vice president, who killed Alexander Hamilton in a duel in 1804.

294. CARTER — President, 1976. His progressive racial views reflected an emergent South less concerned with racial distinctions and more concerned with economic development and political power.

295. AMERICAN SYSTEM — Henry Clay's program for the national economy, which included a protective tariff to stimulate industry and a national bank to provide credit.

296. CONEY ISLAND — Popular site of New York amusement parks opening in 1890s, attracting working class Americans with rides and games celebrating abandon and instant gratification.

297. AMERICAN EXCEPTIONALISM — Notion that America houses biologically superior people and can spread democracy to the rest of the world.

298. CENTRAL POWERS — In World War I, Germany and Austria-Hungary and their allies.

299. COURT PACKING — President Franklin Delano Roosevelt's controversial plan to appoint Supreme Court justices who were sympathetic to his views, by offering retirement benefits to the sitting justices.

300. CALHOUN, JOHN — As vice president, Calhoun anonymously expounded the doctrine of nullification, which held that states could prevent the enforcement of a federal law within their boundaries.

A. Central Powers
B. Channing
C. Declension
D. Coxey's Arrny
E. AFL
F. American System
G. Calhoun, John
H. Carpetbaggers
I. Coney Island
J. Aaron Burr

K. Birds of Passage
M. Dawes Act
O. Committee on Public Information
Q. David Walker
S. Dartmouth vs Woodward
U. Carter
W. Columbian Exchange
Y. Antinomian

L. American Exceptionalism
N. Black Power
P. Bill of Rights
R. Cabinet
T. Court Packing
V. Copperheads
X. Calvinism

Word Search

1. Find the hidden words. The words have been placed horizontally, vertically, or diagonally. When you locate a word, draw an ellipse around it.

G	G	G	V	F	Y	I	W	V	J	C	G	N	B	V	L	Q	X	X	P	H	C	V
F	L	B	I	G	S	T	I	C	K	D	I	P	L	O	M	A	C	Y	M	Z	R	U
P	N	U	Y	I	M	E	G	G	R	Y	E	D	E	F	P	W	X	S	S	S	K	F
J	A	L	I	E	N	A	N	D	S	E	D	I	T	I	O	N	A	C	T	S	N	A
E	K	B	K	S	Z	C	A	P	I	T	A	L	P	U	N	I	S	H	M	E	N	T
Q	B	G	V	H	H	A	M	E	R	I	C	A	N	S	Y	S	T	E	M	E	P	R
F	B	E	A	T	G	E	N	E	R	A	T	I	O	N	K	G	Y	L	D	X	Q	A
P	O	P	G	Z	C	E	B	I	L	L	O	F	R	I	G	H	T	S	I	K	L	X
I	H	T	F	W	Y	Y	O	C	Y	J	I	O	S	D	B	N	A	Z	L	C	W	I
G	U	L	V	D	T	R	Z	B	N	W	W	W	I	X	Z	C	N	H	Z	X	B	S
C	A	M	P	D	A	V	I	D	A	C	C	O	R	D	S	A	Z	H	H	Z	W	P
D	B	A	Y	O	F	P	I	G	S	Y	O	E	I	Z	I	B	L	B	Z	T	A	O
U	F	X	C	X	V	B	L	A	C	K	C	O	D	E	S	I	M	S	W	V	D	W
N	M	R	M	F	V	H	N	E	W	H	Q	S	K	W	F	N	W	O	L	G	Y	E
F	N	M	U	A	Y	C	L	U	H	Z	I	U	B	R	Q	E	N	D	P	U	L	R
P	E	N	O	E	S	A	Q	P	D	L	O	F	H	Z	E	T	R	E	X	E	C	S

1. Henry Clay's program for the national economy, which included a protective tariff to stimulate industry and a national bank to provide credit.
2. A failed plan to assassinate Cuban leader Fidel Castro and liberate Cuba with a trained military force of political exiles.
3. An historic 1979 peace agreement negotiated between Egypt and Israel at the U.S. presidential retreat at Camp David, Maryland.
4. During the early nineteenth century, a movement arose to end the death penalty.
5. A cultural style and artistic movement of the 1950s that rejected traditional American family life and material values and celebrated African-American culture.
6. This term refers to the heads of the executive departments.
7. Laws passed by Southern state legislatures during Reconstruction, while Congress was out of session.
8. Passed in 1798 designed to curb criticism of the federal government.
9. In World War II, the alliance of German and Italy, and later Japan.
10. The proclaimed foreign policy of Theodore Roosevelt, it was based on the proverb, "Speak softly and carry a big stick,".
11. The first ten amendments to the U.S. Constitution, which protect the rights of individuals from the powers of the national government.

A. Bay of Pigs
D. Axis Powers
G. Alien and Sedition Acts
J. Black Codes
B. American System
E. Capital Punishment
H. Camp David Accords
K. Cabinet
C. Big Stick Diplomacy
F. Bill of Rights
I. Beat Generation

2. Find the hidden words. The words have been placed horizontally, vertically, or diagonally. When you locate a word, draw an ellipse around it.

J	O	H	I	Y	I	E	O	J	K	V	M	M	Q	I	Z	F	V	F	B	U	B	F
D	O	T	O	T	S	C	L	V	Y	S	P	B	J	F	Q	F	G	G	J	V	I	C
F	T	P	B	T	Q	E	Q	F	M	I	R	L	D	H	D	K	T	O	A	J	L	O
M	C	O	L	A	D	N	X	B	C	L	S	A	T	Y	P	W	G	R	M	A	L	K
C	A	B	I	N	E	T	Y	L	S	V	D	C	C	G	I	P	A	M	E	C	O	B
F	M	R	W	T	U	R	J	A	A	R	H	K	A	M	E	Q	F	X	R	B	F	F
L	N	T	V	I	W	A	P	C	D	A	U	T	A	W	N	L	J	V	I	L	R	I
F	V	C	L	N	A	L	J	K	N	H	H	U	R	T	B	X	R	I	C	A	I	N
C	L	O	E	O	X	P	E	C	U	U	W	E	O	F	P	M	X	F	A	C	G	N
R	V	I	I	M	Z	O	E	O	L	M	K	S	N	S	Q	V	K	E	N	K	H	E
G	Z	T	Z	I	X	W	V	D	Y	I	I	D	B	J	N	E	A	K	S	P	T	Y
Y	W	V	N	A	L	E	I	E	P	L	K	A	U	S	X	N	W	Q	Y	O	S	B
V	O	C	U	N	Q	R	N	S	W	M	Q	Y	R	O	C	H	J	N	S	W	Z	V
U	D	B	N	N	X	S	C	J	B	O	V	P	R	A	B	K	Y	H	T	E	G	N
V	C	A	P	I	T	A	L	P	U	N	I	S	H	M	E	N	T	L	E	R	K	K
C	A	M	P	D	A	V	I	D	A	C	C	O	R	D	S	W	B	K	M	F	Z	I

1. This term refers to the heads of the executive departments.
2. Laws passed by Southern state legislatures during Reconstruction, while Congress was out of session.
3. In World War I, Germany and Austria-Hungary and their allies.
4. Literally meaning against the laws of human governance.
5. The "father of modern revivalism," Finney devised many techniques adopted by later revival preachers. He encouraged many women to participate actively in revival.
6. Henry Clay's program for the national economy, which included a protective tariff to stimulate industry and a national bank to provide credit.
7. October 29, 1929, the day of the stock market crash that initiated the Great Depression.
8. The first ten amendments to the U.S. Constitution, which protect the rights of individuals from the powers of the national government.
9. A rallying cry for more militant blacks advocated by younger leaders beginning in the mid-1960s.
10. Thomas Jefferson's first vice president, who killed Alexander Hamilton in a duel in 1804.
11. During the early nineteenth century, a movement arose to end the death penalty.
12. An historic 1979 peace agreement negotiated between Egypt and Israel at the U.S. presidential retreat at Camp David, Maryland.

A. Black Power
B. Bill of Rights
C. Finney
D. American System
E. Central Powers
F. Black Tuesday
G. Black Codes
H. Antinomian
I. Cabinet
J. Capital Punishment
K. Camp David Accords
L. Aaron Burr

3. Find the hidden words. The words have been placed horizontally, vertically, or diagonally. When you locate a word, draw an ellipse around it.

C	A	L	H	O	U	N	J	O	H	N	B	G	B	Y	L	X	C	K	V	C	O	X
L	S	S	C	S	H	L	O	E	B	C	E	Z	I	C	A	E	J	K	T	E	L	C
R	D	B	A	I	W	E	D	Z	E	A	A	Z	L	C	F	S	P	J	T	R	I	E
U	Z	R	V	E	C	D	Y	G	A	L	F	O	L	S	R	R	R	M	G	I	R	S
T	V	D	I	B	P	E	B	T	T	V	L	K	Y	K	U	P	S	K	A	R	C	A
H	W	Y	F	R	Y	X	O	G	G	I	I	L	Y	N	G	J	B	C	Z	O	I	Q
R	B	R	C	A	I	T	N	M	E	N	Y	Z	A	G	R	A	J	F	A	U	T	O
X	G	T	I	I	V	Q	G	D	N	I	B	S	N	N	T	W	R	A	L	Y	P	C
T	Q	L	K	N	K	Q	H	B	E	S	U	N	K	W	D	A	I	G	A	K	K	A
Y	T	V	M	T	C	P	L	T	R	M	L	G	K	Z	Z	Y	G	K	A	D	C	B
M	V	D	B	R	T	V	S	H	A	Y	S	F	N	V	H	Q	M	F	U	H	O	I
V	Z	Q	E	U	B	I	G	S	T	I	C	K	D	I	P	L	O	M	A	C	Y	N
B	R	V	O	S	X	W	P	H	I	B	O	N	U	S	A	R	M	Y	C	Y	Y	E
O	V	S	B	T	R	K	I	N	O	B	G	S	O	S	J	L	B	Q	T	P	G	T
N	E	Y	A	C	Z	D	J	B	N	C	B	L	A	C	K	T	U	E	S	D	A	Y
X	K	X	C	A	P	I	T	A	L	P	U	N	I	S	H	M	E	N	T	I	C	R

1. Group of unemployed World War I veterans who marched on Washington, D.C., in June 1932 to ask for immediate payment of their war pensions.
2. A confederation of labor unions founded in 1886, it was composed mainly of skilled craft unions.
3. This appellation was used to refer to common soldiers serving in Union armies during the Civil War.
4. A cultural style and artistic movement of the 1950s that rejected traditional American family life and material values and celebrated African-American culture.
5. The proclaimed foreign policy of Theodore Roosevelt, it was based on the proverb, "Speak softly and carry a big stick,".
6. Emphasized the power and omnipotence of God and the importance of seeking to earn saving grace and salvation.
7. This term refers to the heads of the executive departments.
8. October 29,1929, the day of the stock market crash that initiated the Great Depression.
9. Close advisors to President Franklin Delano Roosevelt during the early days of his first term whose policy suggestions influenced much New Deal legislation.
10. During the early nineteenth century, a movement arose to end the death penalty.
11. As vice president, Calhoun anonymously expounded the doctrine of nullification, which held that states could prevent the enforcement of a federal law within their boundaries.

A. Capital Punishment
B. Brain Trust
C. Beat Generation
D. Calvinism
E. Calhoun, John
F. Cabinet
G. AFL
H. Big Stick Diplomacy
I. Bonus Army
J. Billy Yank
K. Black Tuesday

4. Find the hidden words. The words have been placed horizontally, vertically, or diagonally. When you locate a word, draw an ellipse around it.

B	I	G	S	T	I	C	K	D	I	P	L	O	M	A	C	Y	N	S	P	D	N	L
P	Y	I	C	D	F	M	V	Y	N	N	R	K	J	X	S	Z	R	G	Z	M	Y	I
I	R	J	B	H	U	O	Y	D	B	I	R	D	S	O	F	P	A	S	S	A	G	E
L	T	B	L	P	Z	R	C	Z	W	Y	W	F	E	J	W	G	Y	S	U	U	S	Y
X	N	F	A	Z	R	Q	A	Z	L	T	Y	S	G	A	K	C	Y	I	U	X	A	A
U	H	I	C	C	G	U	L	Y	L	L	L	O	Z	T	G	F	N	F	C	X	J	R
N	C	N	K	A	B	E	V	B	L	A	C	K	T	U	E	S	D	A	Y	Z	E	Z
U	H	N	P	P	I	X	I	A	N	T	I	F	E	D	E	R	A	L	I	S	T	S
W	U	E	O	S	L	D	N	Q	L	S	X	R	O	A	I	J	S	N	T	F	O	S
G	W	Y	W	O	L	I	I	M	R	H	X	H	Q	Z	Q	D	V	Q	C	Y	O	B
X	T	J	E	A	Y	S	S	D	N	T	Q	M	B	O	N	U	S	A	R	M	Y	L
K	U	G	R	P	Y	I	M	B	I	L	F	B	A	Y	O	F	P	I	G	S	L	I
O	L	G	R	X	A	W	N	S	P	O	F	D	Q	Y	W	W	W	F	Y	Y	Q	K
V	A	L	I	E	N	A	N	D	S	E	D	I	T	I	O	N	A	C	T	S	G	F
K	O	M	P	U	K	N	I	P	O	F	Y	A	X	I	S	P	O	W	E	R	S	T
A	F	Q	G	Y	W	X	E	Q	P	Q	M	E	M	G	H	N	S	D	P	A	M	N

1. Emphasized the power and omnipotence of God and the importance of seeking to earn saving grace and salvation.
2. Immigrants who never intended to make the United States their home.
3. A failed plan to assassinate Cuban leader Fidel Castro and liberate Cuba with a trained military force of political exiles.
4. A rallying cry for more militant blacks advocated by younger leaders beginning in the mid-1960s.
5. October 29, 1929, the day of the stock market crash that initiated the Great Depression.
6. The proclaimed foreign policy of Theodore Roosevelt, it was based on the proverb, "Speak softly and carry a big stick,".
7. The "father of modern revivalism," Finney devised many techniques adopted by later revival preachers. He encouraged many women to participate actively in revival.
8. This appellation was used to refer to common soldiers serving in Union armies during the Civil War.
9. These were opponents of the Constitution of 1787 who sought to continue the confederation of sovereign states and to keep power as close as possible to the people.
10. Group of unemployed World War I veterans who marched on Washington, D.C., in June 1932 to ask for immediate payment of their war pensions.
11. Passed in 1798 designed to curb criticism of the federal government.
12. In World War II, the alliance of German and Italy, and later Japan.

A. Black Power
B. Alien and Sedition Acts
C. Black Tuesday
D. Axis Powers
E. Billy Yank
F. Bonus Army
G. Big Stick Diplomacy
H. Calvinism
I. Bay of Pigs
J. Antifederalists
K. Finney
L. Birds of Passage

5. Find the hidden words. The words have been placed horizontally, vertically, or diagonally. When you locate a word, draw an ellipse around it.

I	A	M	E	R	I	C	A	N	E	X	C	E	P	T	I	O	N	A	L	I	S	M
A	D	B	V	B	X	O	C	S	Y	C	W	A	A	R	O	N	B	U	R	R	A	H
B	R	E	B	I	G	S	T	I	C	K	D	I	P	L	O	M	A	C	Y	S	N	Y
L	B	A	A	L	I	E	N	A	N	D	S	E	D	I	T	I	O	N	A	C	T	S
A	P	T	V	X	A	K	I	G	B	B	W	C	I	S	N	R	I	F	U	B	V	H
C	B	G	M	X	N	C	Q	G	B	Z	W	A	B	P	Q	Z	X	S	L	A	S	N
K	U	E	V	M	G	Q	P	J	I	A	C	A	L	V	I	N	I	S	M	I	I	Z
P	L	N	X	M	C	U	N	I	L	X	Z	M	A	I	R	A	B	C	F	V	N	R
O	T	E	Q	Z	W	F	C	O	L	I	B	L	C	P	G	H	A	X	S	H	X	Z
W	K	R	C	D	O	E	K	J	Y	S	L	N	K	J	V	T	Y	T	G	K	C	Y
E	P	A	R	I	D	F	U	X	Y	P	B	I	C	X	B	S	O	P	P	J	C	C
R	U	T	T	K	D	O	G	P	A	O	L	S	O	S	T	H	F	R	I	W	F	Z
C	Q	I	P	W	F	I	F	M	N	W	V	M	D	I	T	Y	P	U	L	R	Q	L
R	R	O	U	A	L	S	R	N	K	E	B	E	E	T	R	O	I	E	M	P	M	A
T	N	N	G	P	K	F	Q	S	U	R	H	S	S	U	Y	H	G	Q	B	X	F	F
N	E	C	F	W	E	R	G	A	S	S	E	X	D	G	I	H	S	S	D	K	V	L

1. Thomas Jefferson's first vice president, who killed Alexander Hamilton in a duel in 1804.
2. The proclaimed foreign policy of Theodore Roosevelt, it was based on the proverb, "Speak softly and carry a big stick,".
3. In World War II, the alliance of German and Italy, and later Japan.
4. A cultural style and artistic movement of the 1950s that rejected traditional American family life and material values and celebrated African-American culture.
5. This appellation was used to refer to common soldiers serving in Union armies during the Civil War.
6. Notion that America houses biologically superior people and can spread democracy to the rest of the world.
7. Emphasized the power and omnipotence of God and the importance of seeking to earn saving grace and salvation.
8. Laws passed by Southern state legislatures during Reconstruction, while Congress was out of session.
9. Passed in 1798 designed to curb criticism of the federal government.
10. A failed plan to assassinate Cuban leader Fidel Castro and liberate Cuba with a trained military force of political exiles.
11. A rallying cry for more militant blacks advocated by younger leaders beginning in the mid-1960s.
12. A confederation of labor unions founded in 1886, it was composed mainly of skilled craft unions.

A. AFL
D. American Exceptionalism
G. Axis Powers
J. Calvinism

B. Big Stick Diplomacy
E. Billy Yank
H. Black Codes
K. Black Power

C. Bay of Pigs
F. Beat Generation
I. Aaron Burr
L. Alien and Sedition Acts

6. Find the hidden words. The words have been placed horizontally, vertically, or diagonally. When you locate a word, draw an ellipse around it.

G	B	I	L	L	O	F	R	I	G	H	T	S	M	B	I	L	L	Y	Y	A	N	K
E	I	R	L	Z	T	D	X	D	Q	R	Y	Z	K	K	O	R	B	Y	B	E	E	X
O	W	D	M	L	A	N	T	I	N	O	M	I	A	N	R	P	N	Q	E	B	Z	A
A	U	O	K	F	Y	D	A	A	R	O	N	B	U	R	R	D	P	O	A	G	F	G
X	W	D	L	I	X	B	H	G	T	U	I	M	H	L	H	Q	Z	Q	T	Z	Y	K
Q	A	H	W	Z	B	B	I	Z	Q	Y	F	N	V	L	B	I	D	X	G	T	U	A
T	C	B	I	G	S	T	I	C	K	D	I	P	L	O	M	A	C	Y	E	S	R	R
V	Y	P	Q	F	H	N	F	D	E	M	Y	A	F	Y	U	E	K	H	N	T	Q	W
O	R	M	B	B	L	A	C	K	P	O	W	E	R	F	Q	Q	G	E	E	D	I	J
A	F	L	G	A	N	T	I	F	E	D	E	R	A	L	I	S	T	S	R	J	J	A
S	X	A	P	I	W	V	F	W	N	W	F	O	S	L	X	B	Z	J	A	Y	D	D
C	W	P	W	Z	J	P	R	Z	O	K	E	R	J	T	B	O	R	V	T	G	F	S
A	M	E	R	I	C	A	N	E	X	C	E	P	T	I	O	N	A	L	I	S	M	U
L	S	M	B	A	Y	O	F	P	I	G	S	R	L	I	H	Z	L	W	O	P	V	D
Z	L	X	M	Q	F	N	H	U	J	A	B	E	Z	K	R	C	X	Y	N	J	C	E
A	L	I	E	N	A	N	D	S	E	D	I	T	I	O	N	A	C	T	S	E	M	R

1. Literally meaning against the laws of human governance.
2. Thomas Jefferson's first vice president, who killed Alexander Hamilton in a duel in 1804.
3. A cultural style and artistic movement of the 1950s that rejected traditional American family life and material values and celebrated African-American culture.
4. This appellation was used to refer to common soldiers serving in Union armies during the Civil War.
5. These were opponents of the Constitution of 1787 who sought to continue the confederation of sovereign states and to keep power as close as possible to the people.
6. A rallying cry for more militant blacks advocated by younger leaders beginning in the mid-1960s.
7. Notion that America houses biologically superior people and can spread democracy to the rest of the world.
8. A failed plan to assassinate Cuban leader Fidel Castro and liberate Cuba with a trained military force of political exiles.
9. Passed in 1798 designed to curb criticism of the federal government.
10. The proclaimed foreign policy of Theodore Roosevelt, it was based on the proverb, "Speak softly and carry a big stick,".
11. A confederation of labor unions founded in 1886, it was composed mainly of skilled craft unions.
12. The first ten amendments to the U.S. Constitution, which protect the rights of individuals from the powers of the national government.

A. Black Power
B. Big Stick Diplomacy
C. Aaron Burr
D. Antifederalists
E. Antinomian
F. Bay of Pigs
G. American Exceptionalism
H. AFL
I. Bill of Rights
J. Alien and Sedition Acts
K. Billy Yank
L. Beat Generation

7. Find the hidden words. The words have been placed horizontally, vertically, or diagonally. When you locate a word, draw an ellipse around it.

E	J	S	O	Y	I	C	N	P	B	C	U	J	Q	Z	E	M	Q	I	L	Q	H	I
W	H	J	B	I	R	D	S	O	F	P	A	S	S	A	G	E	Z	Q	M	B	V	H
K	V	L	W	V	S	V	B	C	H	A	N	N	I	N	G	Y	O	O	Y	I	X	T
G	Z	E	P	N	V	B	B	X	A	V	G	P	J	L	B	N	F	V	K	N	E	C
J	T	U	G	N	B	S	J	O	K	Q	S	R	H	L	I	L	J	U	O	V	Z	M
G	S	M	N	B	C	E	N	T	R	A	L	P	O	W	E	R	S	T	M	M	F	C
A	M	E	R	I	C	A	N	E	X	C	E	P	T	I	O	N	A	L	I	S	M	W
V	V	T	P	N	Z	F	R	H	W	Z	R	U	T	B	X	K	B	T	P	G	J	H
N	O	B	O	R	Q	B	X	K	P	V	M	Q	P	V	V	U	J	E	R	P	H	B
R	U	Z	W	C	L	L	M	A	N	T	I	N	O	M	I	A	N	P	L	O	F	A
M	L	N	A	G	A	N	T	I	F	E	D	E	R	A	L	I	S	T	S	Y	O	B
Z	G	L	I	O	F	Z	G	C	R	B	L	A	C	K	C	O	D	E	S	R	G	N
C	A	L	V	I	N	I	S	M	B	E	A	T	G	E	N	E	R	A	T	I	O	N
J	U	S	U	Z	L	Z	C	C	A	R	P	E	T	B	A	G	G	E	R	S	F	B
B	J	V	J	I	V	D	L	R	S	Z	S	N	N	N	N	G	M	G	M	T	W	Y
N	D	R	A	L	I	E	N	A	N	D	S	E	D	I	T	I	O	N	A	C	T	S

1. Notion that America houses biologically superior people and can spread democracy to the rest of the world.
2. In World War I, Germany and Austria-Hungary and their allies.
3. These were opponents of the Constitution of 1787 who sought to continue the confederation of sovereign states and to keep power as close as possible to the people.
4. A cultural style and artistic movement of the 1950s that rejected traditional American family life and material values and celebrated African-American culture.
5. America's leading exponent of religious liberalism, Channing was one of the founders of American Unitarianism.
6. Emphasized the power and omnipotence of God and the importance of seeking to earn saving grace and salvation.
7. Immigrants who never intended to make the United States their home.
8. People who moved to the South following the Civil War and helped to bring Republican control of southern state governments during Reconstruction.
9. Laws passed by Southern state legislatures during Reconstruction, while Congress was out of session.
10. Literally meaning against the laws of human governance.
11. Passed in 1798 designed to curb criticism of the federal government.

A. Black Codes
B. Antifederalists
C. Channing
D. American Exceptionalism
E. Beat Generation
F. Central Powers
G. Antinomian
H. Alien and Sedition Acts
I. Carpetbaggers
J. Calvinism
K. Birds of Passage

8. Find the hidden words. The words have been placed horizontally, vertically, or diagonally. When you locate a word, draw an ellipse around it.

V	G	H	M	C	P	B	L	A	C	K	T	U	E	S	D	A	Y	Y	T	F	K	Y
T	W	Q	C	A	K	Y	G	A	O	N	R	G	F	G	L	F	N	W	S	H	F	L
I	G	R	A	M	Z	W	E	E	D	B	Y	H	D	C	A	L	V	I	N	I	S	M
P	U	K	R	P	B	I	G	S	T	I	C	K	D	I	P	L	O	M	A	C	Y	V
V	O	N	T	D	V	K	Z	M	K	Q	A	V	H	C	B	B	Y	E	N	K	P	Y
L	B	B	E	A	W	K	L	S	Z	C	Q	Q	U	R	A	E	U	K	A	I	T	H
I	W	I	R	V	X	A	Z	X	A	X	I	S	P	O	W	E	R	S	J	Y	C	J
A	M	E	R	I	C	A	N	E	X	C	E	P	T	I	O	N	A	L	I	S	M	U
W	K	M	L	D	Z	Z	O	T	L	O	J	C	A	L	H	O	U	N	J	O	H	N
E	M	K	A	A	W	E	U	M	C	W	R	H	C	F	T	Y	K	L	V	P	D	O
H	A	U	Q	C	S	I	K	A	T	A	W	A	U	N	D	K	P	Y	A	F	E	P
H	B	L	A	C	K	C	O	D	E	S	Y	N	F	I	H	S	A	P	C	X	V	L
U	X	L	Q	O	K	E	V	J	L	I	V	N	V	I	R	P	N	U	M	U	K	Y
Z	Z	B	P	R	H	L	Q	J	L	R	C	I	A	I	S	G	Y	Z	O	W	K	U
D	Y	D	K	D	A	P	D	N	V	C	E	N	T	R	A	L	P	O	W	E	R	S
B	I	R	D	S	O	F	P	A	S	S	A	G	E	P	C	L	M	V	X	K	B	C

1. Laws passed by Southern state legislatures during Reconstruction, while Congress was out of session.
2. An historic 1979 peace agreement negotiated between Egypt and Israel at the U.S. presidential retreat at Camp David, Maryland.
3. In World War II, the alliance of German and Italy, and later Japan.
4. America's leading exponent of religious liberalism, Channing was one of the founders of American Unitarianism.
5. As vice president, Calhoun anonymously expounded the doctrine of nullification, which held that states could prevent the enforcement of a federal law within their boundaries.
6. In World War I, Germany and Austria-Hungary and their allies.
7. The proclaimed foreign policy of Theodore Roosevelt, it was based on the proverb, "Speak softly and carry a big stick,".
8. Immigrants who never intended to make the United States their home.
9. Notion that America houses biologically superior people and can spread democracy to the rest of the world.
10. Emphasized the power and omnipotence of God and the importance of seeking to earn saving grace and salvation.
11. President, 1976. His progressive racial views reflected an emergent South less concerned with racial distinctions and more concerned with economic development and political power.
12. October 29, 1929, the day of the stock market crash that initiated the Great Depression.

A. Central Powers
B. Channing
C. Black Tuesday
D. Calhoun, John
E. Camp David Accords
F. Birds of Passage
G. American Exceptionalism
H. Black Codes
I. Carter
J. Axis Powers
K. Calvinism
L. Big Stick Diplomacy

9. Find the hidden words. The words have been placed horizontally, vertically, or diagonally. When you locate a word, draw an ellipse around it.

S	F	Z	A	R	S	U	Z	Z	J	A	A	R	O	N	B	U	R	R	O	V	C	Y
C	A	B	I	N	E	T	Y	Z	D	V	B	Y	F	H	V	M	W	Q	B	A	A	A
A	O	W	X	I	O	X	L	D	E	V	D	H	K	P	B	Q	U	Y	A	R	M	M
R	E	L	I	Z	W	L	W	V	W	S	D	K	P	S	G	C	B	A	Z	X	P	E
P	N	U	B	I	G	S	T	I	C	K	D	I	P	L	O	M	A	C	Y	V	D	R
E	I	S	T	O	P	G	F	S	Y	P	K	V	D	N	Y	L	D	B	Q	G	A	I
T	B	M	F	S	S	R	S	I	Y	O	T	Y	C	E	J	Q	Z	G	C	W	V	C
B	A	G	I	O	R	Z	E	U	F	W	C	P	D	P	W	V	W	N	I	Q	I	A
A	Y	A	N	C	V	G	I	Q	Z	A	M	G	M	M	O	R	J	G	U	B	D	N
G	O	P	N	M	N	Y	M	W	G	J	L	E	C	H	H	V	H	J	G	A	A	S
G	F	B	E	Z	G	A	Z	E	H	Y	K	P	B	M	G	P	B	U	Y	W	C	Y
E	P	D	Y	B	P	Z	A	Z	F	V	X	F	Y	Q	F	F	K	I	F	V	C	S
R	I	V	P	M	J	Q	C	E	N	T	R	A	L	P	O	W	E	R	S	N	O	T
S	G	L	Q	I	Y	Y	N	G	M	X	L	F	E	L	B	Y	G	U	E	G	R	E
B	S	Z	U	K	V	C	X	B	L	A	C	K	T	U	E	S	D	A	Y	J	D	M
F	A	M	E	R	I	C	A	N	E	X	C	E	P	T	I	O	N	A	L	I	S	M

1. The proclaimed foreign policy of Theodore Roosevelt, it was based on the proverb, "Speak softly and carry a big stick,".
2. An historic 1979 peace agreement negotiated between Egypt and Israel at the U.S. presidential retreat at Camp David, Maryland.
3. Henry Clay's program for the national economy, which included a protective tariff to stimulate industry and a national bank to provide credit.
4. Notion that America houses biologically superior people and can spread democracy to the rest of the world.
5. In World War I, Germany and Austria-Hungary and their allies.
6. This term refers to the heads of the executive departments.
7. The "father of modern revivalism," Finney devised many techniques adopted by later revival preachers. He encouraged many women to participate actively in revival.
8. A failed plan to assassinate Cuban leader Fidel Castro and liberate Cuba with a trained military force of political exiles.
9. October 29,1929, the day of the stock market crash that initiated the Great Depression.
10. Thomas Jefferson's first vice president, who killed Alexander Hamilton in a duel in 1804.
11. People who moved to the South following the Civil War and helped to bring Republican control of southern state governments during Reconstruction.

A. American Exceptionalism
B. Finney
C. Camp David Accords
D. Black Tuesday
E. Big Stick Diplomacy
F. Aaron Burr
G. Bay of Pigs
H. Central Powers
I. Cabinet
J. American System
K. Carpetbaggers

10. Find the hidden words. The words have been placed horizontally, vertically, or diagonally. When you locate a word, draw an ellipse around it.

Y	I	B	C	J	U	L	B	N	K	R	G	X	B	C	K	Z	L	B	S	T	Z	F
X	B	R	I	E	W	P	U	I	C	O	B	O	E	H	R	F	M	O	A	W	A	D
A	L	A	T	O	O	C	L	T	J	N	I	O	A	A	P	N	H	N	N	V	B	N
B	A	I	Y	Q	W	W	A	E	J	J	R	O	T	N	A	R	W	U	T	N	V	E
F	C	N	U	K	W	H	Z	X	D	R	D	N	G	N	M	N	Q	S	I	I	A	G
A	K	T	P	G	N	A	Q	O	P	A	S	A	E	I	Y	R	F	A	F	A	B	U
W	T	R	O	W	R	J	J	D	K	O	O	C	N	N	Q	Y	Z	R	E	J	K	M
O	U	U	N	A	I	H	Z	K	J	N	F	F	E	G	Q	P	J	M	D	W	I	I
S	E	S	A	D	Q	T	P	R	Y	Z	P	Q	R	D	Q	S	K	Y	E	J	S	P
G	S	T	H	P	O	K	Q	W	T	B	A	J	A	N	J	M	T	T	R	T	O	G
U	D	Y	I	U	J	P	V	U	P	B	S	S	T	E	J	S	Y	D	A	N	A	J
U	A	I	L	X	R	W	K	O	K	C	S	I	I	M	G	W	J	B	L	L	Q	L
X	Y	G	L	Q	U	T	U	P	D	P	A	R	O	R	O	F	Y	S	I	K	Z	G
I	A	N	T	I	N	O	M	I	A	N	G	C	N	B	K	U	F	T	S	M	D	V
W	U	I	G	H	R	Q	U	T	Z	O	E	D	C	S	V	W	S	N	T	C	N	N
M	J	V	D	O	J	M	L	L	B	G	C	A	B	I	N	E	T	Q	S	T	H	U

1. Immigrants who never intended to make the United States their home.
2. Group of unemployed World War I veterans who marched on Washington, D.C., in June 1932 to ask for immediate payment of their war pensions.
3. These were opponents of the Constitution of 1787 who sought to continue the confederation of sovereign states and to keep power as close as possible to the people.
4. Phrase from John Winthrop's sermon, "A Model of Christian Charity," in which he challenged his fellow Puritans to build a model, ideal community in America.
5. This term refers to the heads of the executive departments.
6. October 29, 1929, the day of the stock market crash that initiated the Great Depression.
7. America's leading exponent of religious liberalism, Channing was one of the founders of American Unitarianism.
8. Literally meaning against the laws of human governance.
9. A cultural style and artistic movement of the 1950s that rejected traditional American family life and material values and celebrated African-American culture.
10. Close advisors to President Franklin Delano Roosevelt during the early days of his first term whose policy suggestions influenced much New Deal legislation.

A. City Upon a Hill
B. Antinomian
C. Cabinet
D. Antifederalists
E. Birds of Passage
F. Bonus Army
G. Channing
H. Brain Trust
I. Black Tuesday
J. Beat Generation

11. Find the hidden words. The words have been placed horizontally, vertically, or diagonally. When you locate a word, draw an ellipse around it.

J	K	C	A	B	I	N	E	T	G	N	H	X	R	Z	R	F	Z	J	P	Y	M	F
J	P	H	J	K	N	C	T	H	E	J	I	Y	H	M	I	L	A	N	I	H	O	G
Q	V	K	D	Y	O	A	W	N	Y	V	X	B	M	X	J	V	H	N	G	D	O	J
A	A	M	E	R	I	C	A	N	E	X	C	E	P	T	I	O	N	A	L	I	S	M
B	E	A	T	G	E	N	E	R	A	T	I	O	N	J	S	R	Y	P	K	E	Y	U
J	Q	O	A	J	C	E	F	H	H	B	L	A	C	K	C	O	D	E	S	W	J	C
K	L	W	N	R	A	R	A	T	I	C	C	L	J	T	F	X	C	H	C	T	X	C
R	V	I	J	M	L	F	I	N	N	E	Y	C	I	Y	V	R	Z	Y	Z	H	V	K
X	S	E	E	L	V	H	O	C	Q	Q	Z	H	E	A	T	Q	F	H	T	A	C	E
B	I	G	S	T	I	C	K	D	I	P	L	O	M	A	C	Y	H	F	X	L	A	K
G	K	M	L	U	N	X	C	S	J	J	O	S	R	K	G	G	S	V	D	A	R	U
V	Y	J	S	S	I	O	A	M	E	R	I	C	A	N	S	Y	S	T	E	M	T	U
G	Q	N	H	S	S	B	A	E	Q	F	W	C	F	M	Q	J	B	M	Q	J	E	T
Y	P	J	U	L	M	P	L	M	D	S	C	I	H	L	T	W	H	A	P	J	R	C
P	M	Z	A	U	I	C	A	R	P	E	T	B	A	G	G	E	R	S	E	O	I	F
C	F	A	H	A	E	N	C	A	M	P	D	A	V	I	D	A	C	C	O	R	D	S

1. Notion that America houses biologically superior people and can spread democracy to the rest of the world.
2. A cultural style and artistic movement of the 1950s that rejected traditional American family life and material values and celebrated African-American culture.
3. People who moved to the South following the Civil War and helped to bring Republican control of southern state governments during Reconstruction.
4. The "father of modern revivalism," Finney devised many techniques adopted by later revival preachers. He encouraged many women to participate actively in revival.
5. Henry Clay's program for the national economy, which included a protective tariff to stimulate industry and a national bank to provide credit.
6. The proclaimed foreign policy of Theodore Roosevelt, it was based on the proverb, "Speak softly and carry a big stick,".
7. An historic 1979 peace agreement negotiated between Egypt and Israel at the U.S. presidential retreat at Camp David, Maryland.
8. President, 1976. His progressive racial views reflected an emergent South less concerned with racial distinctions and more concerned with economic development and political power.
9. Emphasized the power and omnipotence of God and the importance of seeking to earn saving grace and salvation.
10. Laws passed by Southern state legislatures during Reconstruction, while Congress was out of session.
11. This term refers to the heads of the executive departments.

A. American System
B. Calvinism
C. American Exceptionalism
D. Finney
E. Carpetbaggers
F. Cabinet
G. Camp David Accords
H. Big Stick Diplomacy
I. Beat Generation
J. Black Codes
K. Carter

190

12. Find the hidden words. The words have been placed horizontally, vertically, or diagonally. When you locate a word, draw an ellipse around it.

H	L	P	S	N	M	T	T	Y	A	X	N	T	M	A	Z	Q	I	C	J	T	R	H
G	X	U	M	A	D	G	E	S	S	U	T	D	U	K	C	A	F	G	W	H	H	A
O	T	B	F	J	Y	Y	U	C	T	P	E	I	U	S	Z	T	Q	R	W	F	V	Z
T	A	N	T	I	F	E	D	E	R	A	L	I	S	T	S	C	A	R	T	E	R	W
F	G	G	C	D	N	U	Z	N	Z	W	G	T	Y	X	W	F	T	X	A	D	Z	L
P	J	A	M	B	I	G	S	T	I	C	K	D	I	P	L	O	M	A	C	Y	Q	E
L	C	A	F	P	Z	F	A	R	B	E	A	T	G	E	N	E	R	A	T	I	O	N
D	S	X	C	A	P	I	T	A	L	P	U	N	I	S	H	M	E	N	T	W	Q	G
U	E	I	J	X	M	G	V	L	S	U	R	L	A	A	R	O	N	B	U	R	R	X
Y	Q	S	W	T	Q	X	C	P	R	W	Q	O	W	R	Q	T	S	X	T	N	X	H
U	I	P	V	B	R	X	T	O	Q	Y	J	U	B	I	L	L	Y	Y	A	N	K	Q
H	R	O	J	I	H	N	U	W	T	Y	J	E	P	N	G	V	M	C	U	B	E	N
Q	D	W	I	B	R	Y	Z	E	I	B	Y	G	U	G	J	Z	K	J	Q	F	S	D
I	K	E	D	F	O	L	C	R	H	N	D	H	Q	B	A	Y	O	F	P	I	G	S
C	R	R	N	B	H	P	O	S	V	L	X	L	Y	V	G	X	V	B	T	E	V	L
J	H	S	S	E	W	D	N	X	B	L	A	C	K	C	O	D	E	S	B	N	U	Y

1. These were opponents of the Constitution of 1787 who sought to continue the confederation of sovereign states and to keep power as close as possible to the people.
2. President, 1976. His progressive racial views reflected an emergent South less concerned with racial distinctions and more concerned with economic development and political power.
3. This appellation was used to refer to common soldiers serving in Union armies during the Civil War.
4. In World War I, Germany and Austria-Hungary and their allies.
5. In World War II, the alliance of German and Italy, and later Japan.
6. Laws passed by Southern state legislatures during Reconstruction, while Congress was out of session.
7. The proclaimed foreign policy of Theodore Roosevelt, it was based on the proverb, "Speak softly and carry a big stick,".
8. Thomas Jefferson's first vice president, who killed Alexander Hamilton in a duel in 1804.
9. During the early nineteenth century, a movement arose to end the death penalty.
10. A cultural style and artistic movement of the 1950s that rejected traditional American family life and material values and celebrated African-American culture.
11. A failed plan to assassinate Cuban leader Fidel Castro and liberate Cuba with a trained military force of political exiles.

A. Big Stick Diplomacy   B. Central Powers   C. Carter   D. Beat Generation
E. Capital Punishment   F. Antifederalists   G. Aaron Burr   H. Black Codes
I. Axis Powers   J. Bay of Pigs   K. Billy Yank

13. Find the hidden words. The words have been placed horizontally, vertically, or diagonally. When you locate a word, draw an ellipse around it.

E	D	R	L	C	I	T	Y	U	P	O	N	A	H	I	L	L	J	C	A	R	W	S
K	Z	F	J	H	N	G	F	B	U	Y	L	E	A	S	J	U	W	K	L	B	X	C
K	B	I	L	L	O	F	R	I	G	H	T	S	M	K	Q	Z	R	D	F	J	S	O
Q	D	E	B	P	R	X	T	R	Z	B	M	V	E	Z	Q	V	S	W	M	A	K	L
H	Q	M	O	C	R	P	Q	D	Z	A	I	B	R	A	I	N	T	R	U	S	T	O
Z	I	F	N	A	S	D	H	S	W	Y	M	E	I	U	H	P	B	M	C	B	X	N
Y	P	B	U	L	H	O	R	O	A	O	U	M	C	Q	T	Y	T	G	A	Y	O	I
O	P	J	S	H	X	L	T	F	N	F	U	S	A	R	T	I	O	B	L	F	L	Z
I	V	P	A	O	O	T	Z	P	T	P	O	R	N	T	I	O	T	B	V	K	J	A
D	G	F	R	U	G	S	Z	A	I	I	S	O	S	P	D	E	X	J	I	O	F	T
D	T	G	M	N	F	K	C	S	N	G	D	A	Y	R	F	P	Z	Y	N	P	P	I
W	A	S	Y	J	H	I	P	S	O	S	C	F	S	J	U	N	M	Q	I	G	Z	O
K	P	B	E	O	D	N	E	A	M	V	M	L	T	V	Z	G	A	O	S	A	R	N
S	A	C	Z	H	T	D	L	G	I	P	B	Y	E	C	T	Y	T	T	M	T	V	E
H	Q	N	V	N	V	C	K	E	A	B	O	W	M	I	B	P	O	J	D	U	L	O
H	G	H	D	M	C	E	K	L	N	W	S	C	F	L	V	H	K	D	X	E	A	O

1. Group of unemployed World War I veterans who marched on Washington, D.C., in June 1932 to ask for immediate payment of their war pensions.
2. A failed plan to assassinate Cuban leader Fidel Castro and liberate Cuba with a trained military force of political exiles.
3. Henry Clay's program for the national economy, which included a protective tariff to stimulate industry and a national bank to provide credit.
4. A confederation of labor unions founded in 1886, it was composed mainly of skilled craft unions.
5. Literally meaning against the laws of human governance.
6. Close advisors to President Franklin Delano Roosevelt during the early days of his first term whose policy suggestions influenced much New Deal legislation.
7. The first ten amendments to the U.S. Constitution, which protect the rights of individuals from the powers of the national government.
8. Immigrants who never intended to make the United States their home.
9. Emphasized the power and omnipotence of God and the importance of seeking to earn saving grace and salvation.
10. The effort to encourage masters to voluntarily emancipate their slaves and to resettle free blacks in Africa.
11. As vice president, Calhoun anonymously expounded the doctrine of nullification, which held that states could prevent the enforcement of a federal law within their boundaries.
12. Phrase from John Winthrop's sermon, "A Model of Christian Charity," in which he challenged his fellow Puritans to build a model, ideal community in America.

A. American System
B. Colonization
C. Brain Trust
D. Bay of Pigs
E. Bill of Rights
F. Calvinism
G. Calhoun, John
H. AFL
I. Bonus Army
J. Antinomian
K. City Upon a Hill
L. Birds of Passage

14. Find the hidden words. The words have been placed horizontally, vertically, or diagonally. When you locate a word, draw an ellipse around it.

```
R O O H A J O K U Z H F O X Z M B S R C R Z F
W U C Q T H Z C O N E Y I S L A N D Z A W G O
T A M E R I C A N E X C E P T I O N A L I S M
P S P E C V W A B B L A C K C O D E S V C S U
A B X Y H X C E N I O M S T F K P G L I H V C
A L B R U I G X W Q W V Z D D A C T V N A Z B
A A W R T F E D A V Z R F P O G Q S J I N B C
R C Q C E N T R A L P O W E R S B A F S N O O
O K R N P I P S D R U H K Y L I L P E M I N G
N P B X Y Q F K W A F L N H S Q E Y A Q N U D
B O B R P U K C W A K I E H E K X M L U G S Y
U W I Q A C A M P D A V I D A C C O R D S A I
R E E M B I R D S O F P A S S A G E C L K R A
R R P I J H H G U A K V Y B Y F X G P I W M V
D T E B I M A J K I I R M Z U Z V Z X E C Y M
A Y Z H S U K Y W U O O X W E H Z V G L P C N
```

1. Popular site of New York amusement parks opening in 1890s, attracting working class Americans with rides and games celebrating abandon and instant gratification.
2. Notion that America houses biologically superior people and can spread democracy to the rest of the world.
3. Group of unemployed World War I veterans who marched on Washington, D.C., in June 1932 to ask for immediate payment of their war pensions.
4. An historic 1979 peace agreement negotiated between Egypt and Israel at the U.S. presidential retreat at Camp David, Maryland.
5. Emphasized the power and omnipotence of God and the importance of seeking to earn saving grace and salvation.
6. A rallying cry for more militant blacks advocated by younger leaders beginning in the mid-1960s.
7. America's leading exponent of religious liberalism, Channing was one of the founders of American Unitarianism.
8. In World War I, Germany and Austria-Hungary and their allies.
9. Laws passed by Southern state legislatures during Reconstruction, while Congress was out of session.
10. Thomas Jefferson's first vice president, who killed Alexander Hamilton in a duel in 1804.
11. Immigrants who never intended to make the United States their home.
12. A confederation of labor unions founded in 1886, it was composed mainly of skilled craft unions.

A. Central Powers
B. Aaron Burr
C. Birds of Passage
D. Calvinism
E. Camp David Accords
F. Black Power
G. Bonus Army
H. Coney Island
I. Black Codes
J. AFL
K. American Exceptionalism
L. Channing

193

15. Find the hidden words. The words have been placed horizontally, vertically, or diagonally. When you locate a word, draw an ellipse around it.

H	O	A	L	I	E	N	A	N	D	S	E	D	I	T	I	O	N	A	C	T	S	Y
L	X	L	P	L	S	S	R	S	F	B	B	U	F	Y	M	L	N	D	X	C	Y	V
N	A	B	X	R	X	B	Y	K	C	S	S	T	J	N	N	H	J	V	V	F	D	Y
F	Y	A	A	M	C	E	Q	A	A	C	A	R	P	E	T	B	A	G	G	E	R	S
E	Q	W	M	B	C	A	X	O	L	J	U	B	L	A	C	K	C	O	D	E	S	A
U	U	U	J	O	I	T	B	V	V	L	Z	D	E	H	C	W	V	W	I	B	B	X
F	U	H	K	N	O	G	B	X	I	X	L	P	S	A	A	U	L	J	D	A	W	P
Z	F	B	D	U	N	E	V	W	N	O	Z	R	F	P	N	H	X	V	A	N	M	K
V	G	D	Y	S	A	N	J	L	I	E	H	H	L	L	T	M	L	C	R	T	D	Q
U	O	R	M	A	X	E	G	F	S	A	F	S	C	Z	L	X	T	A	J	I	V	H
B	U	C	R	R	P	R	H	O	M	F	M	D	B	F	G	R	J	R	V	N	D	U
F	R	U	J	M	F	A	L	B	I	L	L	Y	Y	A	N	K	E	H	A	O	O	Z
L	C	G	K	Y	C	T	W	S	W	C	F	J	A	T	W	E	N	W	H	M	B	F
X	X	O	P	P	G	I	B	R	A	I	N	T	R	U	S	T	K	W	G	I	K	Z
O	R	M	S	Y	Y	O	C	A	L	H	O	U	N	J	O	H	N	V	P	A	N	Z
Z	B	O	W	F	I	N	N	E	Y	R	B	A	Y	O	F	P	I	G	S	N	B	M

1. Close advisors to President Franklin Delano Roosevelt during the early days of his first term whose policy suggestions influenced much New Deal legislation.
2. The "father of modern revivalism," Finney devised many techniques adopted by later revival preachers. He encouraged many women to participate actively in revival.
3. Literally meaning against the laws of human governance.
4. Emphasized the power and omnipotence of God and the importance of seeking to earn saving grace and salvation.
5. A failed plan to assassinate Cuban leader Fidel Castro and liberate Cuba with a trained military force of political exiles.
6. A cultural style and artistic movement of the 1950s that rejected traditional American family life and material values and celebrated African-American culture.
7. People who moved to the South following the Civil War and helped to bring Republican control of southern state governments during Reconstruction.
8. Group of unemployed World War I veterans who marched on Washington, D.C., in June 1932 to ask for immediate payment of their war pensions.
9. This appellation was used to refer to common soldiers serving in Union armies during the Civil War.
10. As vice president, Calhoun anonymously expounded the doctrine of nullification, which held that states could prevent the enforcement of a federal law within their boundaries.
11. Passed in 1798 designed to curb criticism of the federal government.
12. Laws passed by Southern state legislatures during Reconstruction, while Congress was out of session.

A. Brain Trust
D. Calhoun, John
G. Black Codes
J. Bonus Army
B. Alien and Sedition Acts
E. Calvinism
H. Bay of Pigs
K. Billy Yank
C. Carpetbaggers
F. Beat Generation
I. Finney
L. Antinomian

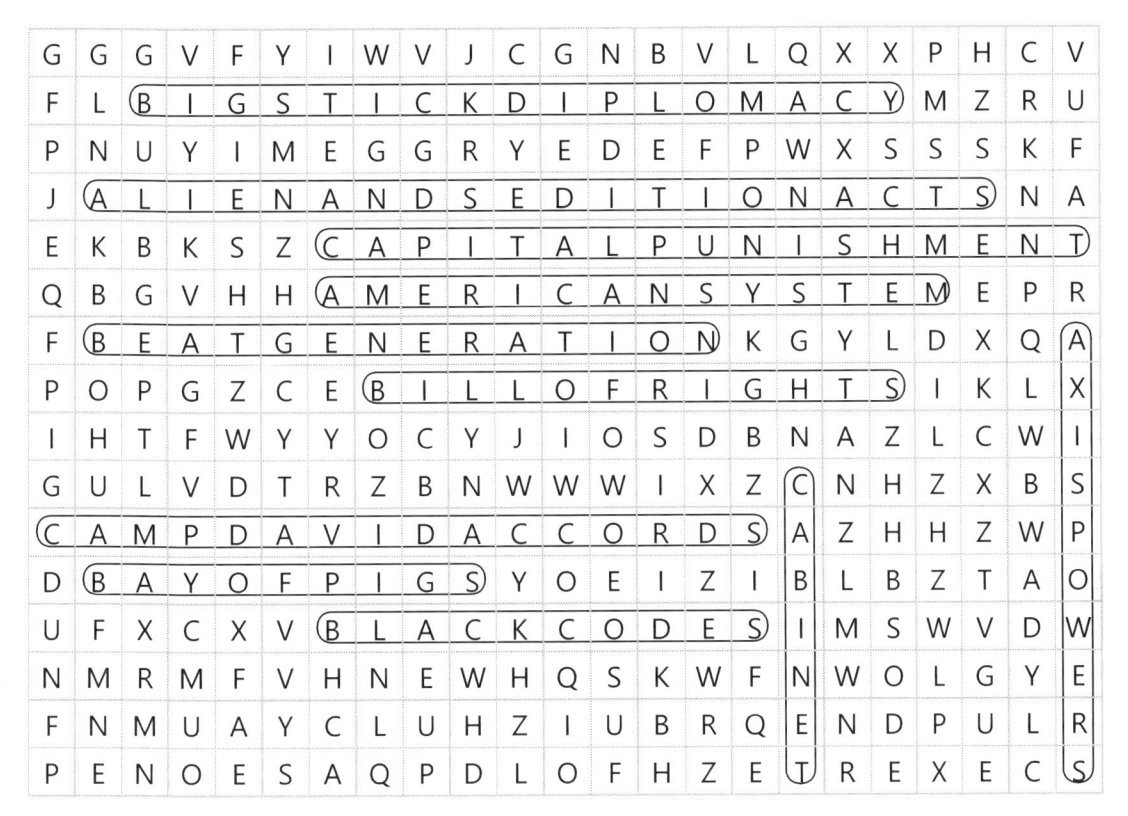

1. Find the hidden words. The words have been placed horizontally, vertically, or diagonally. When you locate a word, draw an ellipse around it.

G	G	V	F	Y	I	W	V	J	C	G	N	B	V	L	Q	X	X	P	H	C	V
F	L	B	I	G	S	T	I	C	K	D	I	P	L	O	M	A	C	Y	M	Z	R	U
P	N	U	Y	I	M	E	G	G	R	Y	E	D	E	F	P	W	X	S	S	S	K	F
J	A	L	I	E	N	A	N	D	S	E	D	I	T	I	O	N	A	C	T	S	N	A
E	K	B	K	S	Z	C	A	P	I	T	A	L	P	U	N	I	S	H	M	E	N	T
Q	B	G	V	H	H	A	M	E	R	I	C	A	N	S	Y	S	T	E	M	E	P	R
F	B	E	A	T	G	E	N	E	R	A	T	I	O	N	K	G	Y	L	D	X	Q	A
P	O	P	G	Z	C	E	B	I	L	L	O	F	R	I	G	H	T	S	I	K	L	X
I	H	T	F	W	Y	Y	O	C	Y	J	I	O	S	D	B	N	A	Z	L	C	W	I
G	U	L	V	D	T	R	Z	B	N	W	W	W	I	X	Z	C	N	H	Z	X	B	S
C	A	M	P	D	A	V	I	D	A	C	C	O	R	D	S	A	Z	H	H	Z	W	P
D	B	A	Y	O	F	P	I	G	S	Y	O	E	I	Z	I	B	L	B	Z	T	A	O
U	F	X	C	X	V	B	L	A	C	K	C	O	D	E	S	I	M	S	W	V	D	W
N	M	R	M	F	V	H	N	E	W	H	Q	S	K	W	F	N	W	O	L	G	Y	E
F	N	M	U	A	Y	C	L	U	H	Z	I	U	B	R	Q	E	N	D	P	U	L	R
P	E	N	O	E	S	A	Q	P	D	L	O	F	H	Z	E	T	R	E	X	E	C	S

1. Henry Clay's program for the national economy, which included a protective tariff to stimulate industry and a national bank to provide credit.
2. A failed plan to assassinate Cuban leader Fidel Castro and liberate Cuba with a trained military force of political exiles.
3. An historic 1979 peace agreement negotiated between Egypt and Israel at the U.S. presidential retreat at Camp David, Maryland.
4. During the early nineteenth century, a movement arose to end the death penalty.
5. A cultural style and artistic movement of the 1950s that rejected traditional American family life and material values and celebrated African-American culture.
6. This term refers to the heads of the executive departments.
7. Laws passed by Southern state legislatures during Reconstruction, while Congress was out of session.
8. Passed in 1798 designed to curb criticism of the federal government.
9. In World War II, the alliance of German and Italy, and later Japan.
10. The proclaimed foreign policy of Theodore Roosevelt, it was based on the proverb, "Speak softly and carry a big stick,".
11. The first ten amendments to the U.S. Constitution, which protect the rights of individuals from the powers of the national government.

A. Bay of Pigs
D. Axis Powers
G. Alien and Sedition Acts
J. Black Codes

B. American System
E. Capital Punishment
H. Camp David Accords
K. Cabinet

C. Big Stick Diplomacy
F. Bill of Rights
I. Beat Generation

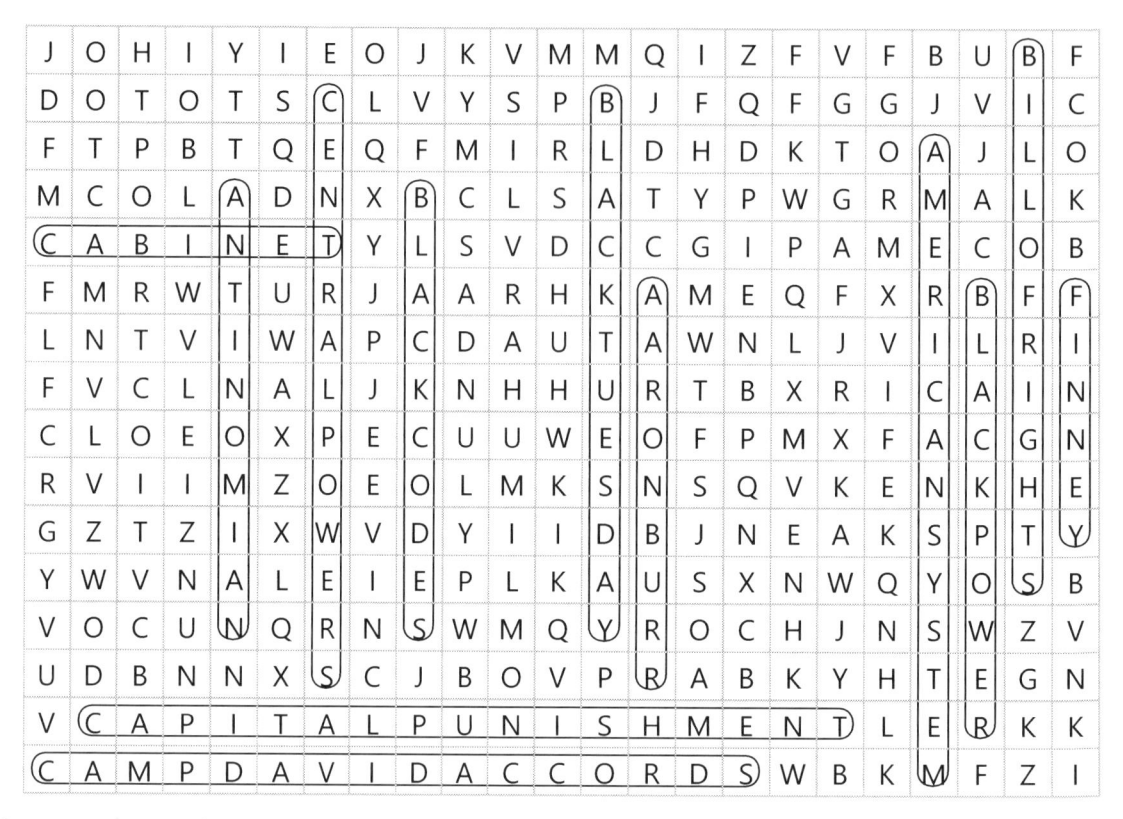

2. Find the hidden words. The words have been placed horizontally, vertically, or diagonally. When you locate a word, draw an ellipse around it.

1. This term refers to the heads of the executive departments.
2. Laws passed by Southern state legislatures during Reconstruction, while Congress was out of session.
3. In World War I, Germany and Austria-Hungary and their allies.
4. Literally meaning against the laws of human governance.
5. The "father of modern revivalism," Finney devised many techniques adopted by later revival preachers. He encouraged many women to participate actively in revival.
6. Henry Clay's program for the national economy, which included a protective tariff to stimulate industry and a national bank to provide credit.
7. October 29, 1929, the day of the stock market crash that initiated the Great Depression.
8. The first ten amendments to the U.S. Constitution, which protect the rights of individuals from the powers of the national government.
9. A rallying cry for more militant blacks advocated by younger leaders beginning in the mid-1960s.
10. Thomas Jefferson's first vice president, who killed Alexander Hamilton in a duel in 1804.
11. During the early nineteenth century, a movement arose to end the death penalty.
12. An historic 1979 peace agreement negotiated between Egypt and Israel at the U.S. presidential retreat at Camp David, Maryland.

A. Black Power
B. Bill of Rights
C. Finney
D. American System
E. Central Powers
F. Black Tuesday
G. Black Codes
H. Antinomian
I. Cabinet
J. Capital Punishment
K. Camp David Accords
L. Aaron Burr

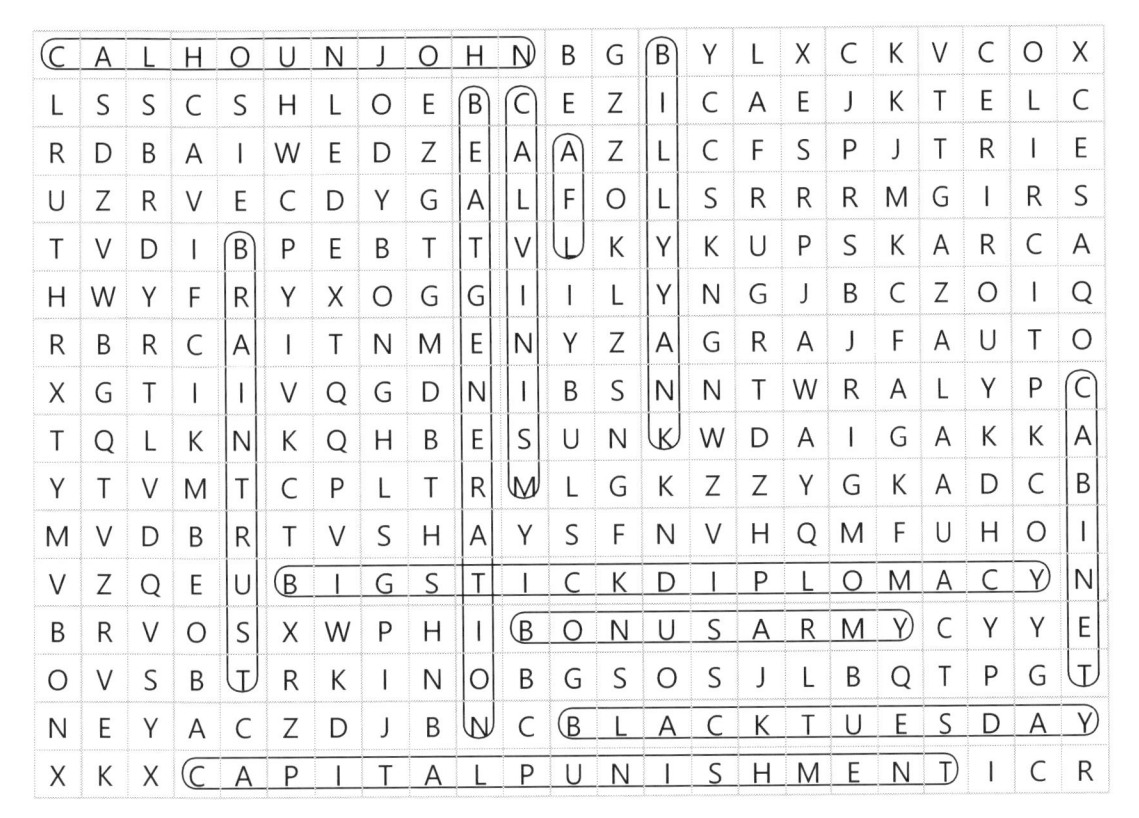

3. Find the hidden words. The words have been placed horizontally, vertically, or diagonally. When you locate a word, draw an ellipse around it.

1. Group of unemployed World War I veterans who marched on Washington, D.C., in June 1932 to ask for immediate payment of their war pensions.
2. A confederation of labor unions founded in 1886, it was composed mainly of skilled craft unions.
3. This appellation was used to refer to common soldiers serving in Union armies during the Civil War.
4. A cultural style and artistic movement of the 1950s that rejected traditional American family life and material values and celebrated African-American culture.
5. The proclaimed foreign policy of Theodore Roosevelt, it was based on the proverb, "Speak softly and carry a big stick,".
6. Emphasized the power and omnipotence of God and the importance of seeking to earn saving grace and salvation.
7. This term refers to the heads of the executive departments.
8. October 29, 1929, the day of the stock market crash that initiated the Great Depression.
9. Close advisors to President Franklin Delano Roosevelt during the early days of his first term whose policy suggestions influenced much New Deal legislation.
10. During the early nineteenth century, a movement arose to end the death penalty.
11. As vice president, Calhoun anonymously expounded the doctrine of nullification, which held that states could prevent the enforcement of a federal law within their boundaries.

A. Capital Punishment
B. Brain Trust
C. Beat Generation
D. Calvinism
E. Calhoun, John
F. Cabinet
G. AFL
H. Big Stick Diplomacy
I. Bonus Army
J. Billy Yank
K. Black Tuesday

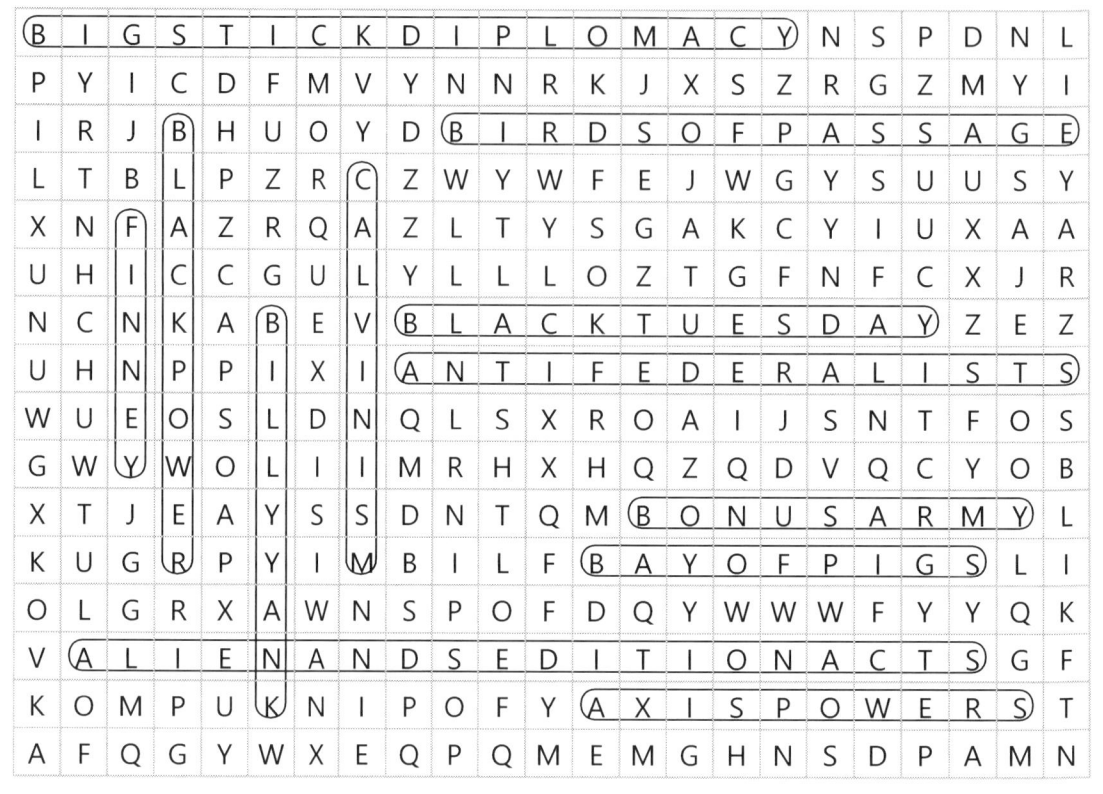

4. Find the hidden words. The words have been placed horizontally, vertically, or diagonally. When you locate a word, draw an ellipse around it.

B	I	G	S	T	I	C	K	D	I	P	L	O	M	A	C	Y	N	S	P	D	N	L
P	Y	I	C	D	F	M	V	Y	N	N	R	K	J	X	S	Z	R	G	Z	M	Y	I
I	R	J	B	H	U	O	Y	D	B	I	R	D	S	O	F	P	A	S	S	A	G	E
L	T	B	L	P	Z	R	C	Z	W	Y	W	F	E	J	W	G	Y	S	U	U	S	Y
X	N	F	A	Z	R	Q	A	Z	L	T	Y	S	G	A	K	C	Y	I	U	X	A	A
U	H	I	C	C	G	U	L	Y	L	L	O	Z	T	G	F	N	F	C	X	J	R	
N	C	N	K	A	B	E	V	B	L	A	C	K	T	U	E	S	D	A	Y	Z	E	Z
U	H	N	P	P	I	X	I	A	N	T	I	F	E	D	E	R	A	L	I	S	T	S
W	U	E	O	S	L	D	N	Q	L	S	X	R	O	A	I	J	S	N	T	F	O	S
G	W	Y	W	O	L	I	I	M	R	H	X	H	Q	Z	Q	D	V	Q	C	Y	O	B
X	T	J	E	A	Y	S	S	D	N	T	Q	M	B	O	N	U	S	A	R	M	Y	L
K	U	G	R	P	Y	I	M	B	I	L	F	B	A	Y	O	F	P	I	G	S	L	I
O	L	G	R	X	A	W	N	S	P	O	F	D	Q	Y	W	W	W	F	Y	Y	Q	K
V	A	L	I	E	N	A	N	D	S	E	D	I	T	I	O	N	A	C	T	S	G	F
K	O	M	P	U	K	N	I	P	O	F	Y	A	X	I	S	P	O	W	E	R	S	T
A	F	Q	G	Y	W	X	E	Q	P	Q	M	E	M	G	H	N	S	D	P	A	M	N

1. Emphasized the power and omnipotence of God and the importance of seeking to earn saving grace and salvation.
2. Immigrants who never intended to make the United States their home.
3. A failed plan to assassinate Cuban leader Fidel Castro and liberate Cuba with a trained military force of political exiles.
4. A rallying cry for more militant blacks advocated by younger leaders beginning in the mid-1960s.
5. October 29,1929, the day of the stock market crash that initiated the Great Depression.
6. The proclaimed foreign policy of Theodore Roosevelt, it was based on the proverb, "Speak softly and carry a big stick,".
7. The "father of modern revivalism," Finney devised many techniques adopted by later revival preachers. He encouraged many women to participate actively in revival.
8. This appellation was used to refer to common soldiers serving in Union armies during the Civil War.
9. These were opponents of the Constitution of 1787 who sought to continue the confederation of sovereign states and to keep power as close as possible to the people.
10. Group of unemployed World War I veterans who marched on Washington, D.C., in June 1932 to ask for immediate payment of their war pensions.
11. Passed in 1798 designed to curb criticism of the federal government.
12. In World War II, the alliance of German and Italy, and later Japan.

A. Black Power
D. Axis Powers
G. Big Stick Diplomacy
J. Antifederalists

B. Alien and Sedition Acts
E. Billy Yank
H. Calvinism
K. Finney

C. Black Tuesday
F. Bonus Army
I. Bay of Pigs
L. Birds of Passage

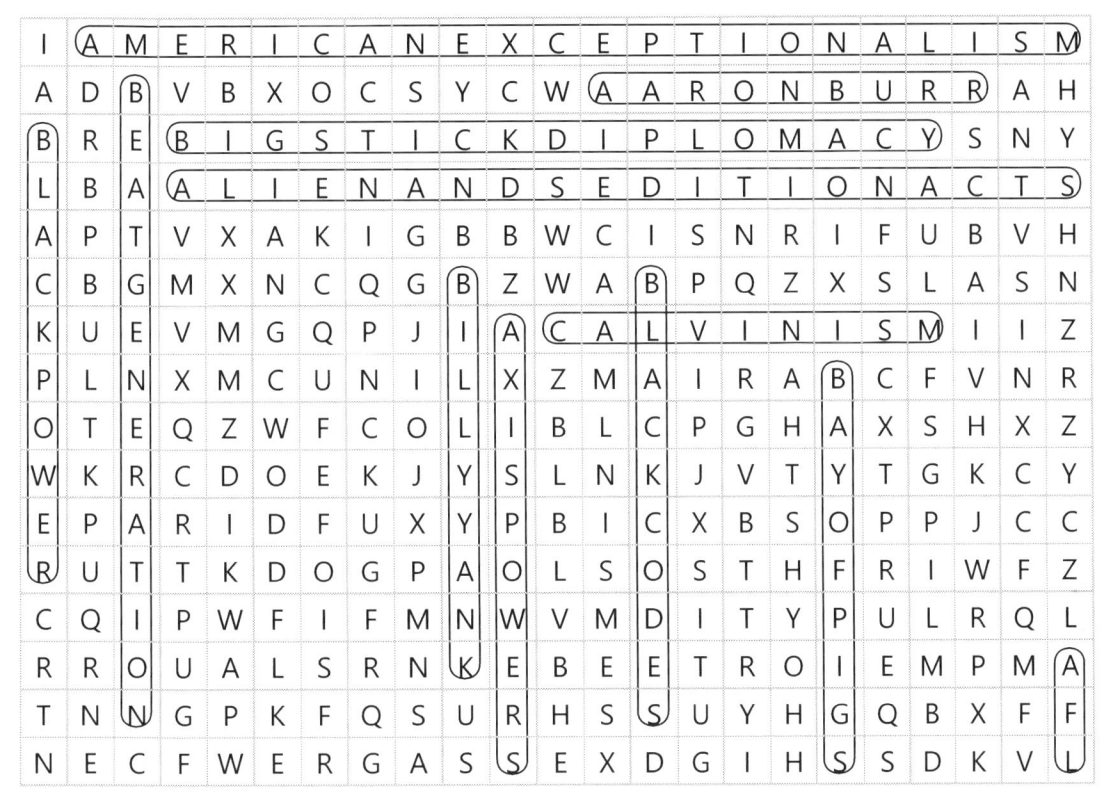

5. Find the hidden words. The words have been placed horizontally, vertically, or diagonally. When you locate a word, draw an ellipse around it.

I	A	M	E	R	I	C	A	N	E	X	C	E	P	T	I	O	N	A	L	I	S	M
A	D	B	V	B	X	O	C	S	Y	C	W	A	A	R	O	N	B	U	R	R	A	H
B	R	E	B	I	G	S	T	I	C	K	D	I	P	L	O	M	A	C	Y	S	N	Y
L	B	A	A	L	I	E	N	A	N	D	S	E	D	I	T	I	O	N	A	C	T	S
A	P	T	V	X	A	K	I	G	B	B	W	C	I	S	N	R	I	F	U	B	V	H
C	B	G	M	X	N	C	Q	G	B	Z	W	A	B	P	Q	Z	X	S	L	A	S	N
K	U	E	V	M	G	Q	P	J	I	A	C	A	L	V	I	N	I	S	M	I	I	Z
P	L	N	X	M	C	U	N	I	L	X	Z	M	A	I	R	A	B	C	F	V	N	R
O	T	E	Q	Z	W	F	C	O	L	I	B	L	C	P	G	H	A	X	S	H	X	Z
W	K	R	C	D	O	E	K	J	Y	S	L	N	K	J	V	T	Y	T	G	K	C	Y
E	P	A	R	I	D	F	U	X	Y	P	B	I	C	X	B	S	O	P	P	J	C	C
R	U	T	T	K	D	O	G	P	A	O	L	S	O	S	T	H	F	R	I	W	F	Z
C	Q	I	P	W	F	I	F	M	N	W	V	M	D	I	T	Y	P	U	L	R	Q	L
R	R	O	U	A	L	S	R	N	K	E	B	E	E	T	R	O	I	E	M	P	M	A
T	N	N	G	P	K	F	Q	S	U	R	H	S	S	U	Y	H	G	Q	B	X	F	F
N	E	C	F	W	E	R	G	A	S	S	E	X	D	G	I	H	S	S	D	K	V	U

1. Thomas Jefferson's first vice president, who killed Alexander Hamilton in a duel in 1804.
2. The proclaimed foreign policy of Theodore Roosevelt, it was based on the proverb, "Speak softly and carry a big stick,".
3. In World War II, the alliance of German and Italy, and later Japan.
4. A cultural style and artistic movement of the 1950s that rejected traditional American family life and material values and celebrated African-American culture.
5. This appellation was used to refer to common soldiers serving in Union armies during the Civil War.
6. Notion that America houses biologically superior people and can spread democracy to the rest of the world.
7. Emphasized the power and omnipotence of God and the importance of seeking to earn saving grace and salvation.
8. Laws passed by Southern state legislatures during Reconstruction, while Congress was out of session.
9. Passed in 1798 designed to curb criticism of the federal government.
10. A failed plan to assassinate Cuban leader Fidel Castro and liberate Cuba with a trained military force of political exiles.
11. A rallying cry for more militant blacks advocated by younger leaders beginning in the mid-1960s.
12. A confederation of labor unions founded in 1886, it was composed mainly of skilled craft unions.

A. AFL
D. American Exceptionalism
G. Axis Powers
J. Calvinism

B. Big Stick Diplomacy
E. Billy Yank
H. Black Codes
K. Black Power

C. Bay of Pigs
F. Beat Generation
I. Aaron Burr
L. Alien and Sedition Acts

6. Find the hidden words. The words have been placed horizontally, vertically, or diagonally. When you locate a word, draw an ellipse around it.

G	B	I	L	L	O	F	R	I	G	H	T	S	M	B	I	L	L	Y	Y	A	N	K
E	I	R	L	Z	T	D	X	D	Q	R	Y	Z	K	K	O	R	B	Y	B	E	E	X
O	W	D	M	L	A	N	T	I	N	O	M	I	A	N	R	P	N	Q	E	B	Z	A
A	U	O	K	F	Y	D	A	A	R	O	N	B	U	R	R	D	P	O	A	G	F	G
X	W	D	L	I	X	B	H	G	T	U	I	M	H	L	H	Q	Z	Q	T	Z	Y	K
Q	A	H	W	Z	B	B	I	Z	Q	Y	F	N	V	L	B	I	D	X	G	T	U	A
T	C	B	I	G	S	T	I	C	K	D	I	P	L	O	M	A	C	Y	E	S	R	R
V	Y	P	Q	F	H	N	F	D	E	M	Y	A	F	Y	U	E	K	H	N	T	Q	W
O	R	M	B	B	L	A	C	K	P	O	W	E	R	F	Q	Q	G	E	E	D	I	J
A	F	L	G	A	N	T	I	F	E	D	E	R	A	L	I	S	T	S	R	J	J	A
S	X	A	P	I	W	V	F	W	N	W	F	O	S	L	X	B	Z	J	A	Y	D	D
C	W	P	W	Z	J	P	R	Z	O	K	E	R	J	T	B	O	R	V	T	G	F	S
A	M	E	R	I	C	A	N	E	X	C	E	P	T	I	O	N	A	L	I	S	M	U
L	S	M	B	A	Y	O	F	P	I	G	S	R	L	I	H	Z	L	W	O	P	V	D
Z	L	X	M	Q	F	N	H	U	J	A	B	E	Z	K	R	C	X	Y	N	J	C	E
A	L	I	E	N	A	N	D	S	E	D	I	T	I	O	N	A	C	T	S	E	M	R

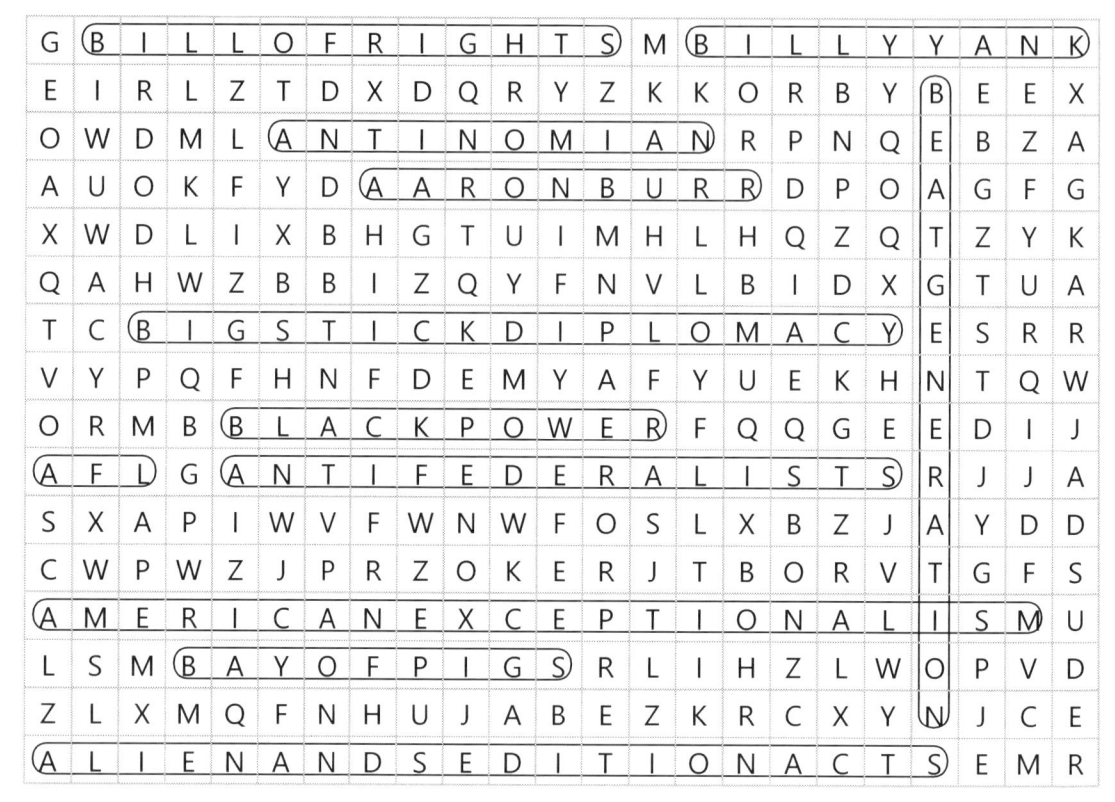

1. Literally meaning against the laws of human governance.
2. Thomas Jefferson's first vice president, who killed Alexander Hamilton in a duel in 1804.
3. A cultural style and artistic movement of the 1950s that rejected traditional American family life and material values and celebrated African-American culture.
4. This appellation was used to refer to common soldiers serving in Union armies during the Civil War.
5. These were opponents of the Constitution of 1787 who sought to continue the confederation of sovereign states and to keep power as close as possible to the people.
6. A rallying cry for more militant blacks advocated by younger leaders beginning in the mid-1960s.
7. Notion that America houses biologically superior people and can spread democracy to the rest of the world.
8. A failed plan to assassinate Cuban leader Fidel Castro and liberate Cuba with a trained military force of political exiles.
9. Passed in 1798 designed to curb criticism of the federal government.
10. The proclaimed foreign policy of Theodore Roosevelt, it was based on the proverb, "Speak softly and carry a big stick,".
11. A confederation of labor unions founded in 1886, it was composed mainly of skilled craft unions.
12. The first ten amendments to the U.S. Constitution, which protect the rights of individuals from the powers of the national government.

A. Black Power
B. Big Stick Diplomacy
C. Aaron Burr
D. Antifederalists
E. Antinomian
F. Bay of Pigs
G. American Exceptionalism
H. AFL
I. Bill of Rights
J. Alien and Sedition Acts
K. Billy Yank
L. Beat Generation

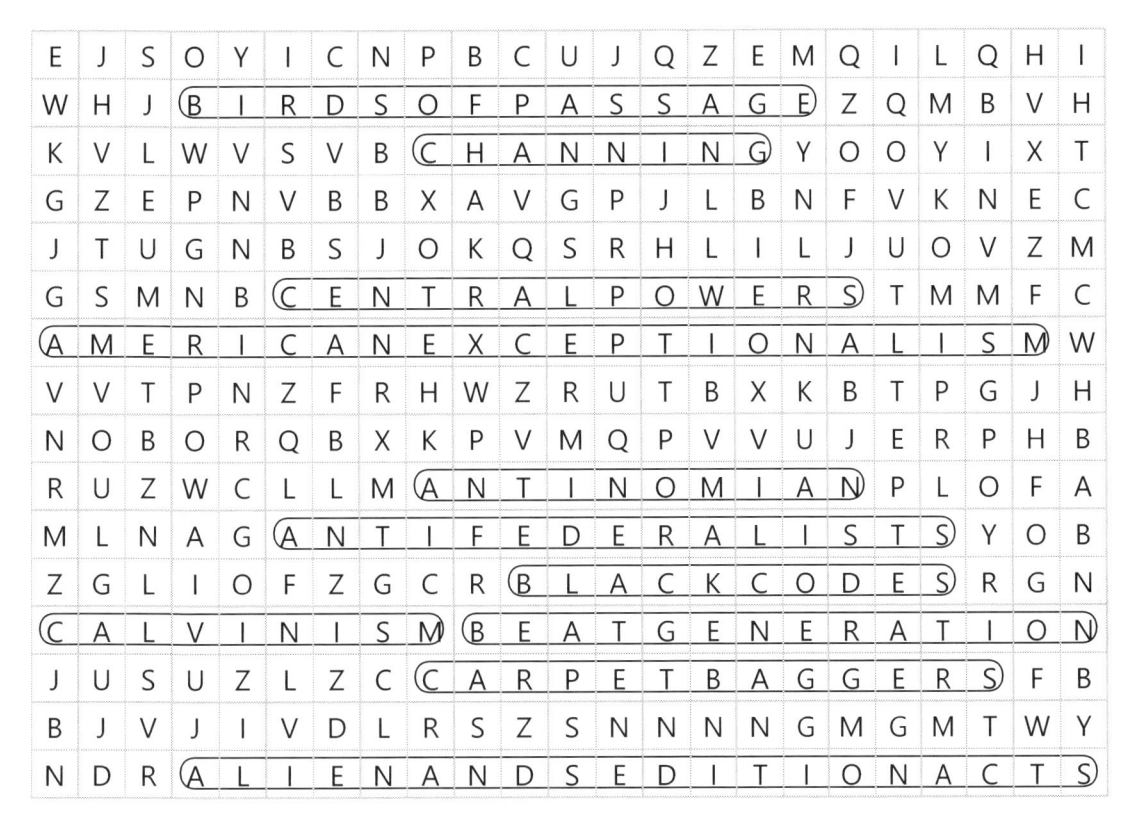

7. Find the hidden words. The words have been placed horizontally, vertically, or diagonally. When you locate a word, draw an ellipse around it.

E	J	S	O	Y	I	C	N	P	B	C	U	J	Q	Z	E	M	Q	I	L	Q	H	I
W	H	J	B	I	R	D	S	O	F	P	A	S	S	A	G	E	Z	Q	M	B	V	H
K	V	L	W	V	S	V	B	C	H	A	N	N	I	N	G	Y	O	O	Y	I	X	T
G	Z	E	P	N	V	B	B	X	A	V	G	P	J	L	B	N	F	V	K	N	E	C
J	T	U	G	N	B	S	J	O	K	Q	S	R	H	L	I	L	J	U	O	V	Z	M
G	S	M	N	B	C	E	N	T	R	A	L	P	O	W	E	R	S	T	M	M	F	C
A	M	E	R	I	C	A	N	E	X	C	E	P	T	I	O	N	A	L	I	S	M	W
V	V	T	P	N	Z	F	R	H	W	Z	R	U	T	B	X	K	B	T	P	G	J	H
N	O	B	O	R	Q	B	X	K	P	V	M	Q	P	V	V	U	J	E	R	P	H	B
R	U	Z	W	C	L	L	M	A	N	T	I	N	O	M	I	A	N	P	L	O	F	A
M	L	N	A	G	A	N	T	I	F	E	D	E	R	A	L	I	S	T	S	Y	O	B
Z	G	L	I	O	F	Z	G	C	R	B	L	A	C	K	C	O	D	E	S	R	G	N
C	A	L	V	I	N	I	S	M	B	E	A	T	G	E	N	E	R	A	T	I	O	N
J	U	S	U	Z	L	Z	C	C	A	R	P	E	T	B	A	G	G	E	R	S	F	B
B	J	V	J	I	V	D	L	R	S	Z	S	N	N	N	G	M	G	M	T	W	Y	
N	D	R	A	L	I	E	N	A	N	D	S	E	D	I	T	I	O	N	A	C	T	S

1. Notion that America houses biologically superior people and can spread democracy to the rest of the world.
2. In World War I, Germany and Austria-Hungary and their allies.
3. These were opponents of the Constitution of 1787 who sought to continue the confederation of sovereign states and to keep power as close as possible to the people.
4. A cultural style and artistic movement of the 1950s that rejected traditional American family life and material values and celebrated African-American culture.
5. America's leading exponent of religious liberalism, Channing was one of the founders of American Unitarianism.
6. Emphasized the power and omnipotence of God and the importance of seeking to earn saving grace and salvation.
7. Immigrants who never intended to make the United States their home.
8. People who moved to the South following the Civil War and helped to bring Republican control of southern state governments during Reconstruction.
9. Laws passed by Southern state legislatures during Reconstruction, while Congress was out of session.
10. Literally meaning against the laws of human governance.
11. Passed in 1798 designed to curb criticism of the federal government.

A. Black Codes
B. Antifederalists
C. Channing
D. American Exceptionalism
E. Beat Generation
F. Central Powers
G. Antinomian
H. Alien and Sedition Acts
I. Carpetbaggers
J. Calvinism
K. Birds of Passage

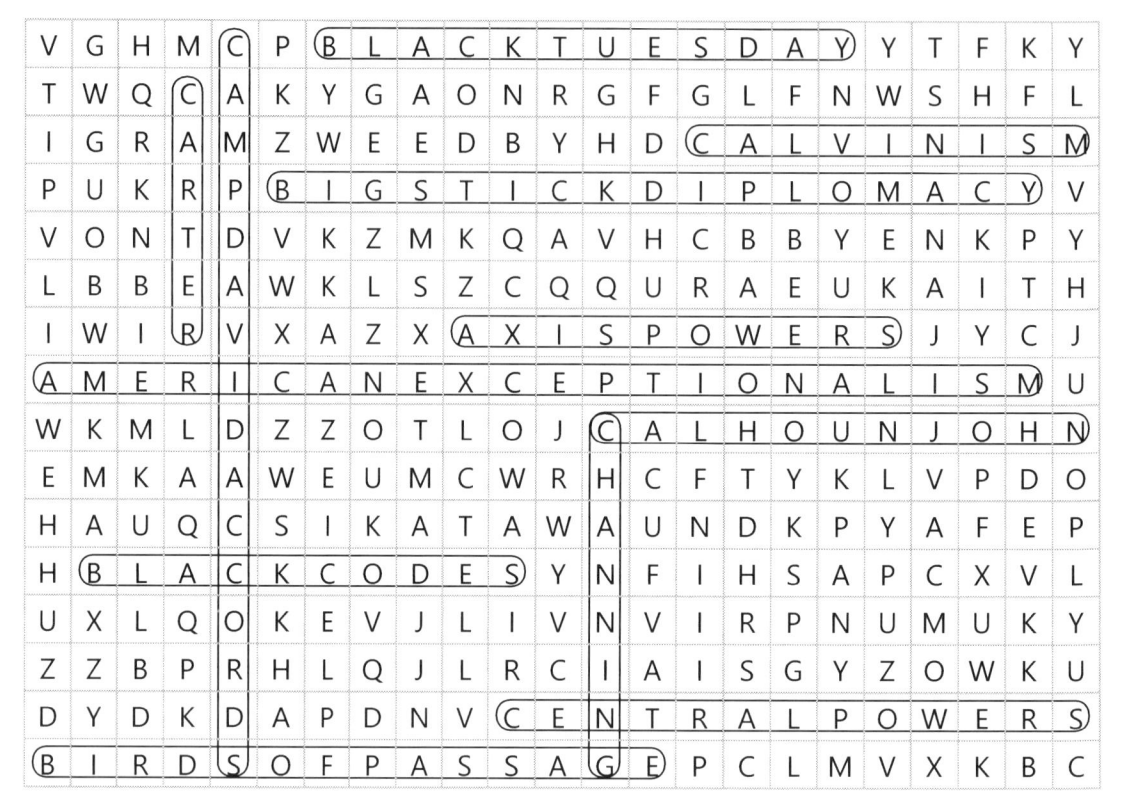

8. Find the hidden words. The words have been placed horizontally, vertically, or diagonally. When you locate a word, draw an ellipse around it.

V	G	H	M	C	P	B	L	A	C	K	T	U	E	S	D	A	Y	Y	T	F	K	Y
T	W	Q	C	A	K	Y	G	A	O	N	R	G	F	G	L	F	N	W	S	H	F	L
I	G	R	A	M	Z	W	E	E	D	B	Y	H	D	C	A	L	V	I	N	I	S	M
P	U	K	R	P	B	I	G	S	T	I	C	K	D	I	P	L	O	M	A	C	Y	V
V	O	N	T	D	V	K	Z	M	K	Q	A	V	H	C	B	B	Y	E	N	K	P	Y
L	B	B	E	A	W	K	L	S	Z	C	Q	Q	U	R	A	E	U	K	A	I	T	H
I	W	I	R	V	X	A	Z	X	A	X	I	S	P	O	W	E	R	S	J	Y	C	J
A	M	E	R	I	C	A	N	E	X	C	E	P	T	I	O	N	A	L	I	S	M	U
W	K	M	L	D	Z	Z	O	T	L	O	J	C	A	L	H	O	U	N	J	O	H	N
E	M	K	A	A	W	E	U	M	C	W	R	H	C	F	T	Y	K	L	V	P	D	O
H	A	U	Q	C	S	I	K	A	T	A	W	A	U	N	D	K	P	Y	A	F	E	P
H	B	L	A	C	K	C	O	D	E	S	Y	N	F	I	H	S	A	P	C	X	V	L
U	X	L	Q	O	K	E	V	J	L	I	V	N	V	I	R	P	N	U	M	U	K	Y
Z	Z	B	P	R	H	L	Q	J	L	R	C	I	A	I	S	G	Y	Z	O	W	K	U
D	Y	D	K	D	A	P	D	N	V	C	E	N	T	R	A	L	P	O	W	E	R	S
B	I	R	D	S	O	F	P	A	S	S	A	G	E	P	C	L	M	V	X	K	B	C

1. Laws passed by Southern state legislatures during Reconstruction, while Congress was out of session.
2. An historic 1979 peace agreement negotiated between Egypt and Israel at the U.S. presidential retreat at Camp David, Maryland.
3. In World War II, the alliance of German and Italy, and later Japan.
4. America's leading exponent of religious liberalism, Channing was one of the founders of American Unitarianism.
5. As vice president, Calhoun anonymously expounded the doctrine of nullification, which held that states could prevent the enforcement of a federal law within their boundaries.
6. In World War I, Germany and Austria-Hungary and their allies.
7. The proclaimed foreign policy of Theodore Roosevelt, it was based on the proverb, "Speak softly and carry a big stick,".
8. Immigrants who never intended to make the United States their home.
9. Notion that America houses biologically superior people and can spread democracy to the rest of the world.
10. Emphasized the power and omnipotence of God and the importance of seeking to earn saving grace and salvation.
11. President, 1976. His progressive racial views reflected an emergent South less concerned with racial distinctions and more concerned with economic development and political power.
12. October 29,1929, the day of the stock market crash that initiated the Great Depression.

A. Central Powers
B. Channing
C. Black Tuesday
D. Calhoun, John
E. Camp David Accords
F. Birds of Passage
G. American Exceptionalism
H. Black Codes
I. Carter
J. Axis Powers
K. Calvinism
L. Big Stick Diplomacy

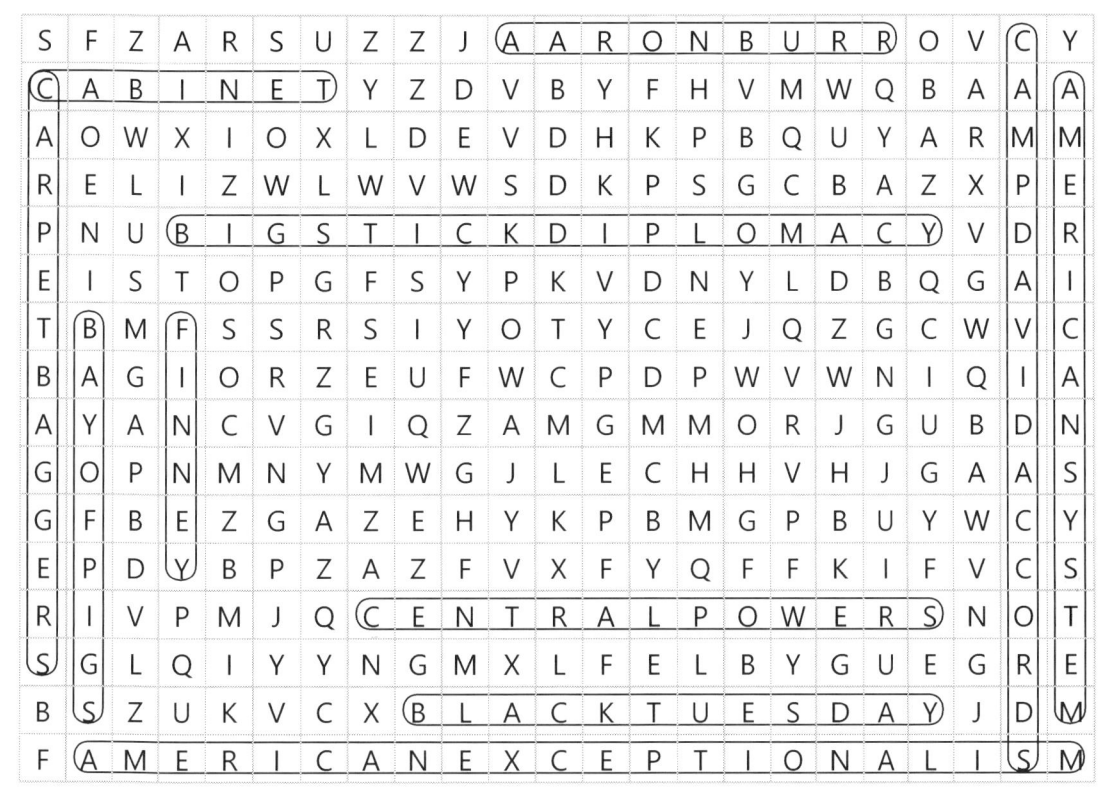

9. Find the hidden words. The words have been placed horizontally, vertically, or diagonally. When you locate a word, draw an ellipse around it.

S	F	Z	A	R	S	U	Z	Z	J	A	A	R	O	N	B	U	R	R	O	V	C	Y
C	A	B	I	N	E	T	Y	Z	D	V	B	Y	F	H	V	M	W	Q	B	A	A	A
A	O	W	X	I	O	X	L	D	E	V	D	H	K	P	B	Q	U	Y	A	R	M	M
R	E	L	I	Z	W	L	W	V	W	S	D	K	P	S	G	C	B	A	Z	X	P	E
P	N	U	B	I	G	S	T	I	C	K	D	I	P	L	O	M	A	C	Y	V	D	R
E	I	S	T	O	P	G	F	S	Y	P	K	V	D	N	Y	L	D	B	Q	G	A	I
T	B	M	F	S	S	R	S	I	Y	O	T	Y	C	E	J	Q	Z	G	C	W	V	C
B	A	G	I	O	R	Z	E	U	F	W	C	P	D	P	W	V	W	N	I	Q	I	A
A	Y	A	N	C	V	G	I	Q	Z	A	M	G	M	M	O	R	J	G	U	B	D	N
G	O	P	N	M	N	Y	M	W	G	J	L	E	C	H	H	V	H	J	G	A	A	S
G	F	B	E	Z	G	A	Z	E	H	Y	K	P	B	M	G	P	B	U	Y	W	C	Y
E	P	D	Y	B	P	Z	A	Z	F	V	X	F	Y	Q	F	F	K	I	F	V	C	S
R	I	V	P	M	J	Q	C	E	N	T	R	A	L	P	O	W	E	R	S	N	O	T
S	G	L	Q	I	Y	Y	N	G	M	X	L	F	E	L	B	Y	G	U	E	G	R	E
B	S	Z	U	K	V	C	X	B	L	A	C	K	T	U	E	S	D	A	Y	J	D	M
F	A	M	E	R	I	C	A	N	E	X	C	E	P	T	I	O	N	A	L	I	S	M

1. The proclaimed foreign policy of Theodore Roosevelt, it was based on the proverb, "Speak softly and carry a big stick,".
2. An historic 1979 peace agreement negotiated between Egypt and Israel at the U.S. presidential retreat at Camp David, Maryland.
3. Henry Clay's program for the national economy, which included a protective tariff to stimulate industry and a national bank to provide credit.
4. Notion that America houses biologically superior people and can spread democracy to the rest of the world.
5. In World War I, Germany and Austria-Hungary and their allies.
6. This term refers to the heads of the executive departments.
7. The "father of modern revivalism," Finney devised many techniques adopted by later revival preachers. He encouraged many women to participate actively in revival.
8. A failed plan to assassinate Cuban leader Fidel Castro and liberate Cuba with a trained military force of political exiles.
9. October 29,1929, the day of the stock market crash that initiated the Great Depression.
10. Thomas Jefferson's first vice president, who killed Alexander Hamilton in a duel in 1804.
11. People who moved to the South following the Civil War and helped to bring Republican control of southern state governments during Reconstruction.

A. American Exceptionalism
B. Finney
C. Camp David Accords
D. Black Tuesday
E. Big Stick Diplomacy
F. Aaron Burr
G. Bay of Pigs
H. Central Powers
I. Cabinet
J. American System
K. Carpetbaggers

10. Find the hidden words. The words have been placed horizontally, vertically, or diagonally. When you locate a word, draw an ellipse around it.

1. Immigrants who never intended to make the United States their home.
2. Group of unemployed World War I veterans who marched on Washington, D.C., in June 1932 to ask for immediate payment of their war pensions.
3. These were opponents of the Constitution of 1787 who sought to continue the confederation of sovereign states and to keep power as close as possible to the people.
4. Phrase from John Winthrop's sermon, "A Model of Christian Charity," in which he challenged his fellow Puritans to build a model, ideal community in America.
5. This term refers to the heads of the executive departments.
6. October 29, 1929, the day of the stock market crash that initiated the Great Depression.
7. America's leading exponent of religious liberalism, Channing was one of the founders of American Unitarianism.
8. Literally meaning against the laws of human governance.
9. A cultural style and artistic movement of the 1950s that rejected traditional American family life and material values and celebrated African-American culture.
10. Close advisors to President Franklin Delano Roosevelt during the early days of his first term whose policy suggestions influenced much New Deal legislation.

A. City Upon a Hill
B. Antinomian
C. Cabinet
D. Antifederalists
E. Birds of Passage
F. Bonus Army
G. Channing
H. Brain Trust
I. Black Tuesday
J. Beat Generation

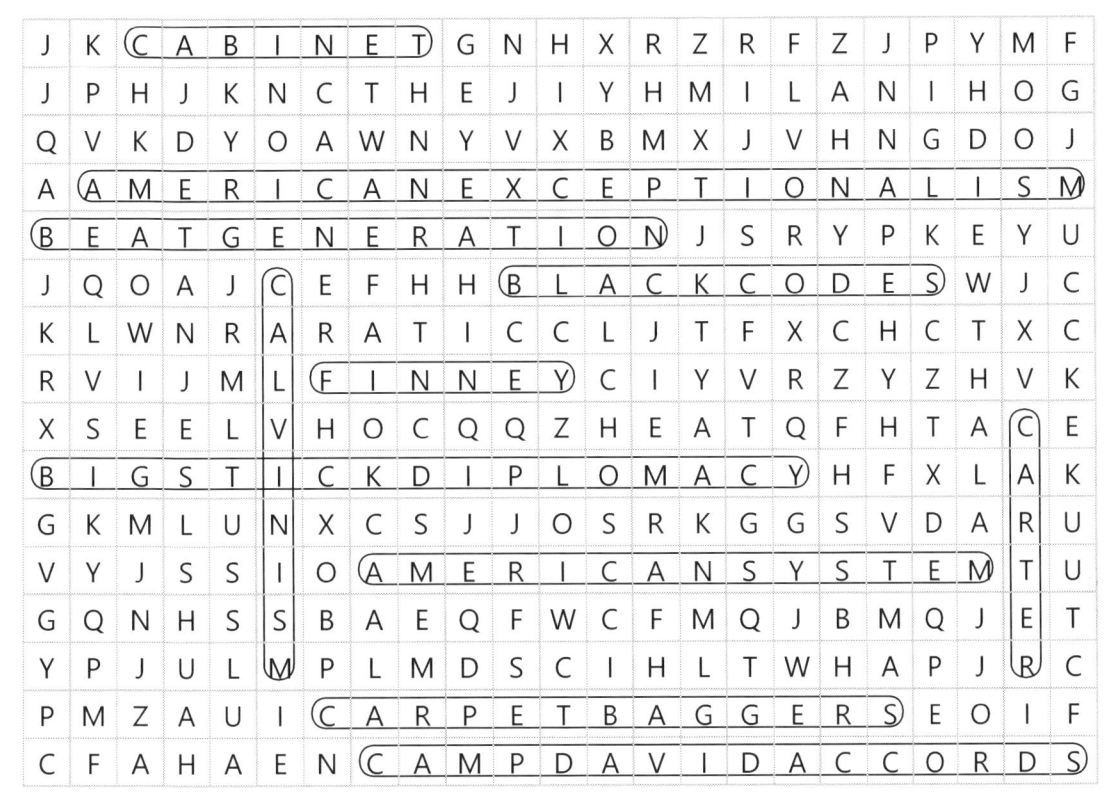

11. Find the hidden words. The words have been placed horizontally, vertically, or diagonally. When you locate a word, draw an ellipse around it.

J	K	C	A	B	I	N	E	T	G	N	H	X	R	Z	R	F	Z	J	P	Y	M	F
J	P	H	J	K	N	C	T	H	E	J	I	Y	H	M	I	L	A	N	I	H	O	G
Q	V	K	D	Y	O	A	W	N	Y	V	X	B	M	X	J	V	H	N	G	D	O	J
A	A	M	E	R	I	C	A	N	E	X	C	E	P	T	I	O	N	A	L	I	S	M
B	E	A	T	G	E	N	E	R	A	T	I	O	N	J	S	R	Y	P	K	E	Y	U
J	Q	O	A	J	C	E	F	H	H	B	L	A	C	K	C	O	D	E	S	W	J	C
K	L	W	N	R	A	R	A	T	I	C	C	L	J	T	F	X	C	H	C	T	X	C
R	V	I	J	M	L	F	I	N	N	E	Y	C	I	Y	V	R	Z	Y	Z	H	V	K
X	S	E	E	L	V	H	O	C	Q	Q	Z	H	E	A	T	Q	F	H	T	A	C	E
B	I	G	S	T	I	C	K	D	I	P	L	O	M	A	C	Y	H	F	X	L	A	K
G	K	M	L	U	N	X	C	S	J	J	O	S	R	K	G	G	S	V	D	A	R	U
V	Y	J	S	S	I	O	A	M	E	R	I	C	A	N	S	Y	S	T	E	M	T	U
G	Q	N	H	S	S	B	A	E	Q	F	W	C	F	M	Q	J	B	M	Q	J	E	T
Y	P	J	U	L	M	P	L	M	D	S	C	I	H	L	T	W	H	A	P	J	R	C
P	M	Z	A	U	I	C	A	R	P	E	T	B	A	G	G	E	R	S	E	O	I	F
C	F	A	H	A	E	N	C	A	M	P	D	A	V	I	D	A	C	C	O	R	D	S

1. Notion that America houses biologically superior people and can spread democracy to the rest of the world.
2. A cultural style and artistic movement of the 1950s that rejected traditional American family life and material values and celebrated African-American culture.
3. People who moved to the South following the Civil War and helped to bring Republican control of southern state governments during Reconstruction.
4. The "father of modern revivalism," Finney devised many techniques adopted by later revival preachers. He encouraged many women to participate actively in revival.
5. Henry Clay's program for the national economy, which included a protective tariff to stimulate industry and a national bank to provide credit.
6. The proclaimed foreign policy of Theodore Roosevelt, it was based on the proverb, "Speak softly and carry a big stick,".
7. An historic 1979 peace agreement negotiated between Egypt and Israel at the U.S. presidential retreat at Camp David, Maryland.
8. President, 1976. His progressive racial views reflected an emergent South less concerned with racial distinctions and more concerned with economic development and political power.
9. Emphasized the power and omnipotence of God and the importance of seeking to earn saving grace and salvation.
10. Laws passed by Southern state legislatures during Reconstruction, while Congress was out of session.
11. This term refers to the heads of the executive departments.

A. American System
B. Calvinism
C. American Exceptionalism
D. Finney
E. Carpetbaggers
F. Cabinet
G. Camp David Accords
H. Big Stick Diplomacy
I. Beat Generation
J. Black Codes
K. Carter

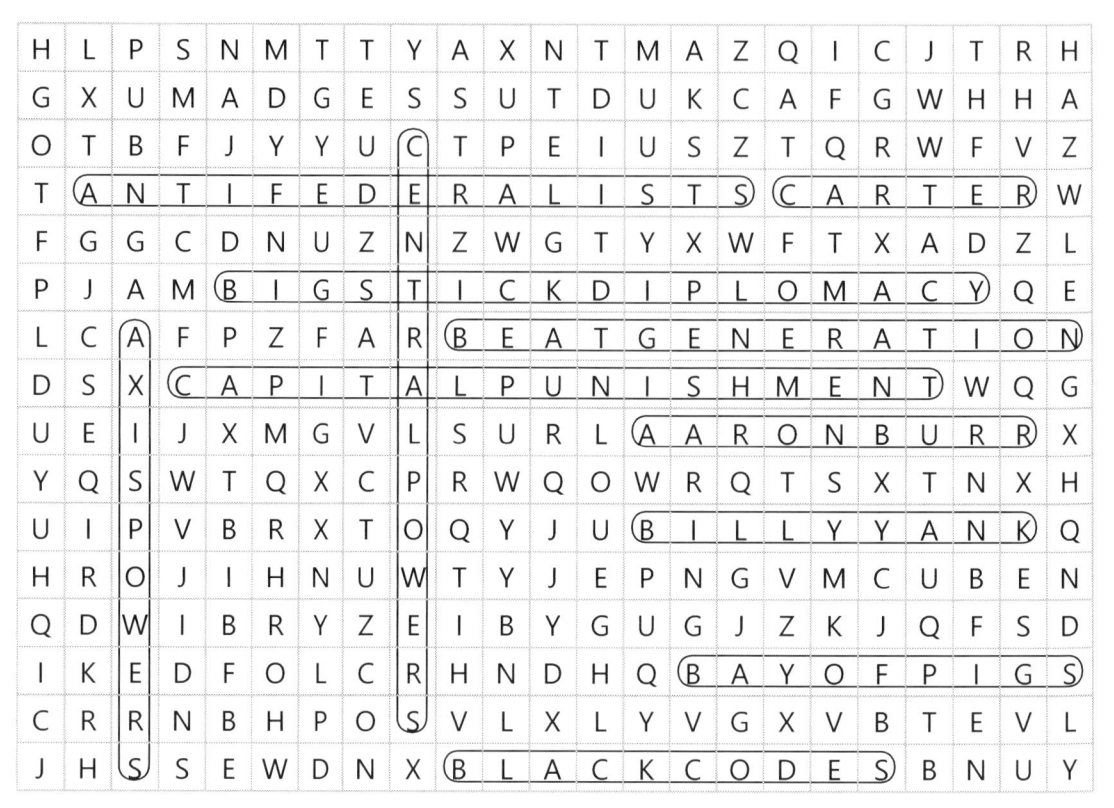

12. Find the hidden words. The words have been placed horizontally, vertically, or diagonally. When you locate a word, draw an ellipse around it.

H	L	P	S	N	M	T	T	Y	A	X	N	T	M	A	Z	Q	I	C	J	T	R	H
G	X	U	M	A	D	G	E	S	S	U	T	D	U	K	C	A	F	G	W	H	H	A
O	T	B	F	J	Y	Y	U	C	T	P	E	I	U	S	Z	T	Q	R	W	F	V	Z
T	A	N	T	I	F	E	D	E	R	A	L	I	S	T	S	C	A	R	T	E	R	W
F	G	G	C	D	N	U	Z	N	Z	W	G	T	Y	X	W	F	T	X	A	D	Z	L
P	J	A	M	B	I	G	S	T	I	C	K	D	I	P	L	O	M	A	C	Y	Q	E
L	C	A	F	P	Z	F	A	R	B	E	A	T	G	E	N	E	R	A	T	I	O	N
D	S	X	C	A	P	I	T	A	L	P	U	N	I	S	H	M	E	N	T	W	Q	G
U	E	I	J	X	M	G	V	L	S	U	R	L	A	A	R	O	N	B	U	R	R	X
Y	Q	S	W	T	Q	X	C	P	R	W	Q	O	W	R	Q	T	S	X	T	N	X	H
U	I	P	V	B	R	X	T	O	Q	Y	J	U	B	I	L	L	Y	Y	A	N	K	Q
H	R	O	J	I	H	N	U	W	T	Y	J	E	P	N	G	V	M	C	U	B	E	N
Q	D	W	I	B	R	Y	Z	E	I	B	Y	G	U	G	J	Z	K	J	Q	F	S	D
I	K	E	D	F	O	L	C	R	H	N	D	H	Q	B	A	Y	O	F	P	I	G	S
C	R	R	N	B	H	P	O	S	V	L	X	L	Y	V	G	X	V	B	T	E	V	L
J	H	S	S	E	W	D	N	X	B	L	A	C	K	C	O	D	E	S	B	N	U	Y

1. These were opponents of the Constitution of 1787 who sought to continue the confederation of sovereign states and to keep power as close as possible to the people.
2. President, 1976. His progressive racial views reflected an emergent South less concerned with racial distinctions and more concerned with economic development and political power.
3. This appellation was used to refer to common soldiers serving in Union armies during the Civil War.
4. In World War I, Germany and Austria-Hungary and their allies.
5. In World War II, the alliance of German and Italy, and later Japan.
6. Laws passed by Southern state legislatures during Reconstruction, while Congress was out of session.
7. The proclaimed foreign policy of Theodore Roosevelt, it was based on the proverb, "Speak softly and carry a big stick,".
8. Thomas Jefferson's first vice president, who killed Alexander Hamilton in a duel in 1804.
9. During the early nineteenth century, a movement arose to end the death penalty.
10. A cultural style and artistic movement of the 1950s that rejected traditional American family life and material values and celebrated African-American culture.
11. A failed plan to assassinate Cuban leader Fidel Castro and liberate Cuba with a trained military force of political exiles.

A. Big Stick Diplomacy
B. Central Powers
C. Carter
D. Beat Generation
E. Capital Punishment
F. Antifederalists
G. Aaron Burr
H. Black Codes
I. Axis Powers
J. Bay of Pigs
K. Billy Yank

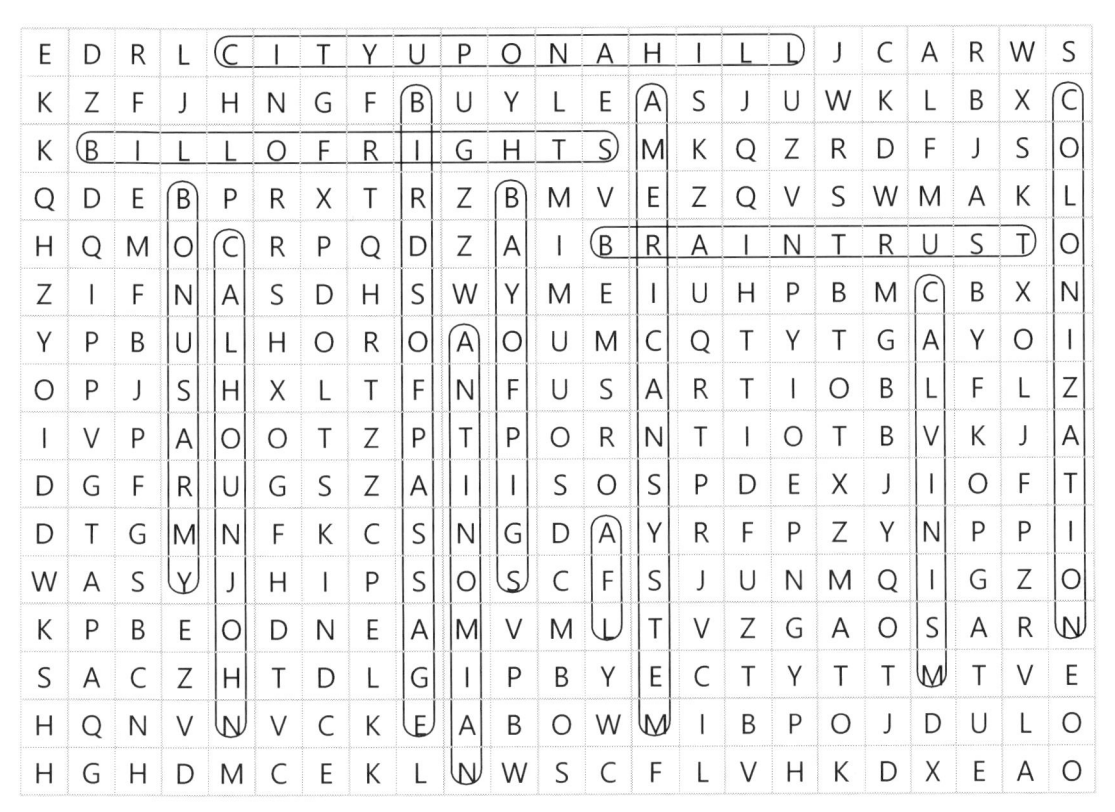

13. Find the hidden words. The words have been placed horizontally, vertically, or diagonally. When you locate a word, draw an ellipse around it.

E	D	R	L	C	I	T	Y	U	P	O	N	A	H	I	L	L	J	C	A	R	W	S
K	Z	F	J	H	N	G	F	B	U	Y	L	E	A	S	J	U	W	K	L	B	X	C
K	B	I	L	L	O	F	R	I	G	H	T	S	M	K	Q	Z	R	D	F	J	S	O
Q	D	E	B	P	R	X	T	R	Z	B	M	V	E	Z	Q	V	S	W	M	A	K	L
H	Q	M	O	C	R	P	Q	D	Z	A	I	B	R	A	I	N	T	R	U	S	T	O
Z	I	F	N	A	S	D	H	S	W	Y	M	E	I	U	H	P	B	M	C	B	X	N
Y	P	B	U	L	H	O	R	O	A	O	U	M	C	Q	T	Y	T	G	A	Y	O	I
O	P	J	S	H	X	L	T	F	N	F	U	S	A	R	T	I	O	B	L	F	L	Z
I	V	P	A	O	O	T	Z	P	T	P	O	R	N	T	I	O	T	B	V	K	J	A
D	G	F	R	U	G	S	Z	A	I	I	S	O	S	P	D	E	X	J	I	O	F	T
D	T	G	M	N	F	K	C	S	N	G	D	A	Y	R	F	P	Z	Y	N	P	P	I
W	A	S	Y	J	H	I	P	S	O	S	C	F	S	J	U	N	M	Q	I	G	Z	O
K	P	B	E	O	D	N	E	A	M	V	M	U	T	V	Z	G	A	O	S	A	R	N
S	A	C	Z	H	T	D	L	G	I	P	B	Y	E	C	T	Y	T	T	M	T	V	E
H	Q	N	V	N	V	C	K	E	A	B	O	W	M	I	B	P	O	J	D	U	L	O
H	G	H	D	M	C	E	K	L	N	W	S	C	F	L	V	H	K	D	X	E	A	O

1. Group of unemployed World War I veterans who marched on Washington, D.C., in June 1932 to ask for immediate payment of their war pensions.
2. A failed plan to assassinate Cuban leader Fidel Castro and liberate Cuba with a trained military force of political exiles.
3. Henry Clay's program for the national economy, which included a protective tariff to stimulate industry and a national bank to provide credit.
4. A confederation of labor unions founded in 1886, it was composed mainly of skilled craft unions.
5. Literally meaning against the laws of human governance.
6. Close advisors to President Franklin Delano Roosevelt during the early days of his first term whose policy suggestions influenced much New Deal legislation.
7. The first ten amendments to the U.S. Constitution, which protect the rights of individuals from the powers of the national government.
8. Immigrants who never intended to make the United States their home.
9. Emphasized the power and omnipotence of God and the importance of seeking to earn saving grace and salvation.
10. The effort to encourage masters to voluntarily emancipate their slaves and to resettle free blacks in Africa.
11. As vice president, Calhoun anonymously expounded the doctrine of nullification, which held that states could prevent the enforcement of a federal law within their boundaries.
12. Phrase from John Winthrop's sermon, "A Model of Christian Charity," in which he challenged his fellow Puritans to build a model, ideal community in America.

A. American System
B. Colonization
C. Brain Trust
D. Bay of Pigs
E. Bill of Rights
F. Calvinism
G. Calhoun, John
H. AFL
I. Bonus Army
J. Antinomian
K. City Upon a Hill
L. Birds of Passage

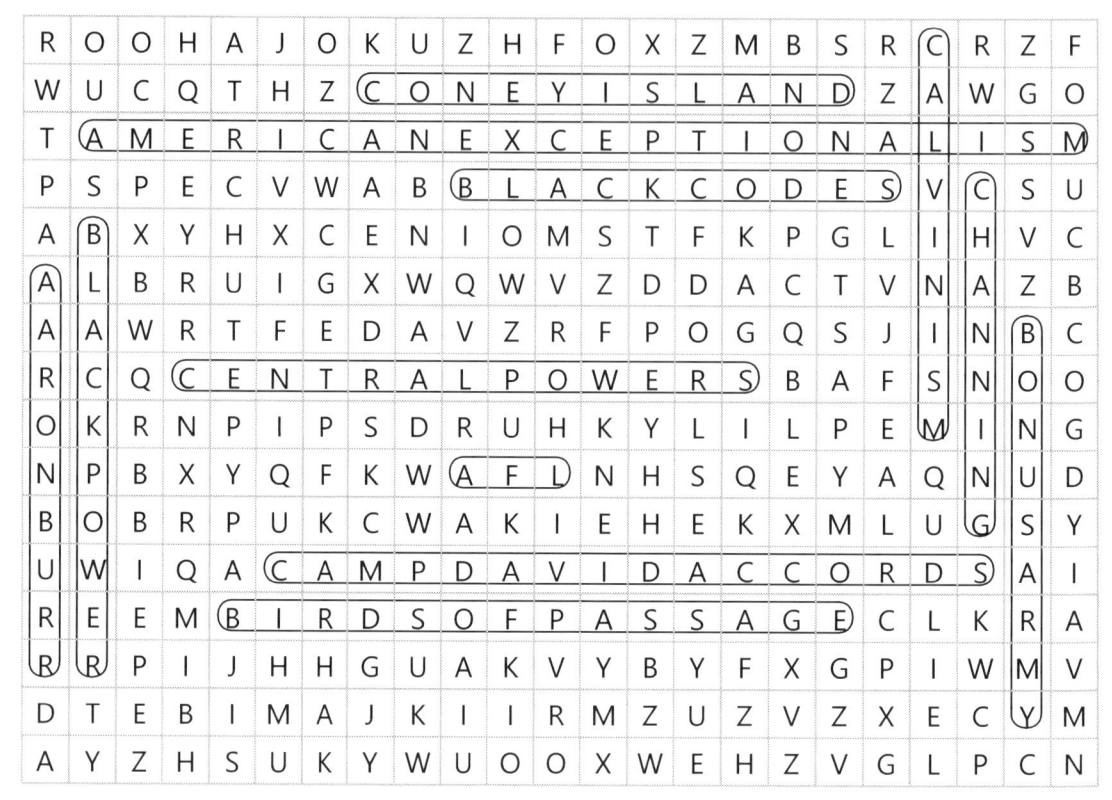

14. Find the hidden words. The words have been placed horizontally, vertically, or diagonally. When you locate a word, draw an ellipse around it.

1. Popular site of New York amusement parks opening in 1890s, attracting working class Americans with rides and games celebrating abandon and instant gratification.
2. Notion that America houses biologically superior people and can spread democracy to the rest of the world.
3. Group of unemployed World War I veterans who marched on Washington, D.C., in June 1932 to ask for immediate payment of their war pensions.
4. An historic 1979 peace agreement negotiated between Egypt and Israel at the U.S. presidential retreat at Camp David, Maryland.
5. Emphasized the power and omnipotence of God and the importance of seeking to earn saving grace and salvation.
6. A rallying cry for more militant blacks advocated by younger leaders beginning in the mid-1960s.
7. America's leading exponent of religious liberalism, Channing was one of the founders of American Unitarianism.
8. In World War I, Germany and Austria-Hungary and their allies.
9. Laws passed by Southern state legislatures during Reconstruction, while Congress was out of session.
10. Thomas Jefferson's first vice president, who killed Alexander Hamilton in a duel in 1804.
11. Immigrants who never intended to make the United States their home.
12. A confederation of labor unions founded in 1886, it was composed mainly of skilled craft unions.

A. Central Powers
D. Calvinism
G. Bonus Army
J. AFL
B. Aaron Burr
E. Camp David Accords
H. Coney Island
K. American Exceptionalism
C. Birds of Passage
F. Black Power
I. Black Codes
L. Channing

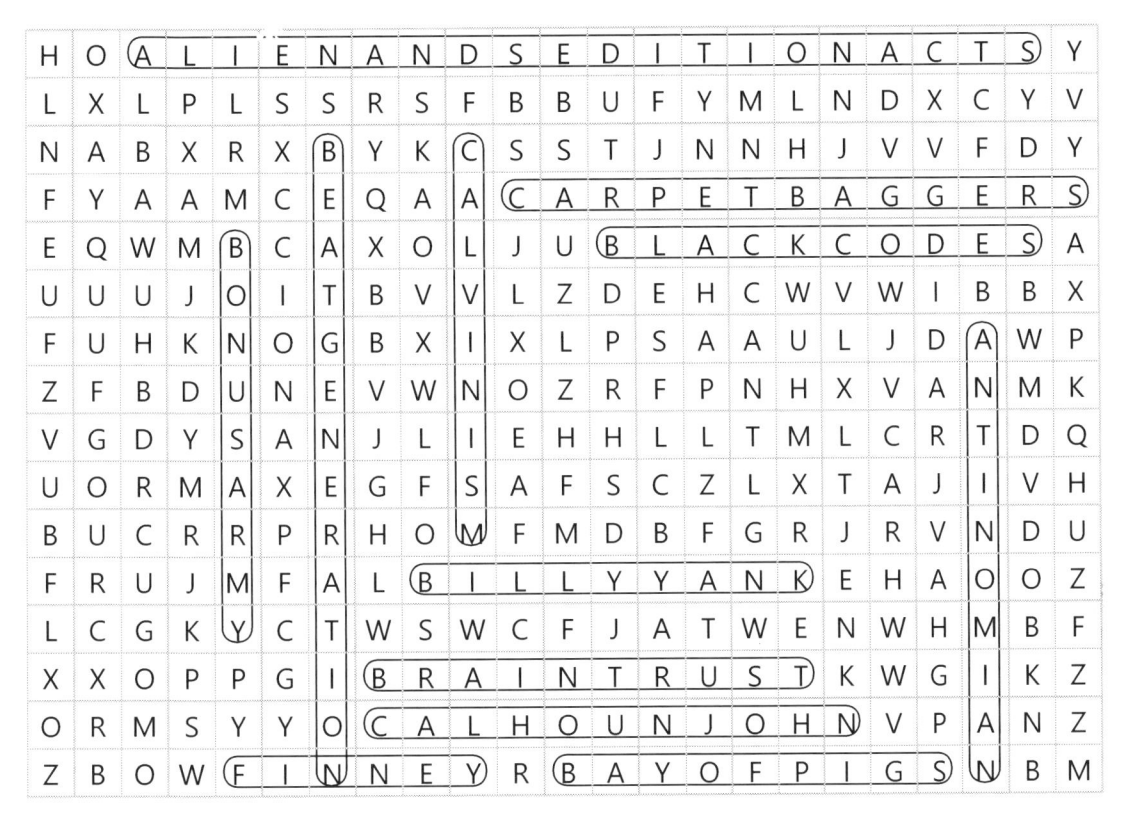

15. Find the hidden words. The words have been placed horizontally, vertically, or diagonally. When you locate a word, draw an ellipse around it.

H	O	A	L	I	E	N	A	N	D	S	E	D	I	T	I	O	N	A	C	T	S	Y
L	X	L	P	L	S	S	R	S	F	B	B	U	F	Y	M	L	N	D	X	C	Y	V
N	A	B	X	R	X	B	Y	K	C	S	S	T	J	N	N	H	J	V	V	F	D	Y
F	Y	A	A	M	C	E	Q	A	A	C	A	R	P	E	T	B	A	G	G	E	R	S
E	Q	W	M	B	C	A	X	O	L	J	U	B	L	A	C	K	C	O	D	E	S	A
U	U	U	J	O	I	T	B	V	V	L	Z	D	E	H	C	W	V	W	I	B	B	X
F	U	H	K	N	O	G	B	X	I	X	L	P	S	A	A	U	L	J	D	A	W	P
Z	F	B	D	U	N	E	V	W	N	O	Z	R	F	P	N	H	X	V	A	N	M	K
V	G	D	Y	S	A	N	J	L	I	E	H	H	L	L	T	M	L	C	R	T	D	Q
U	O	R	M	A	X	E	G	F	S	A	F	S	C	Z	L	X	T	A	J	I	V	H
B	U	C	R	R	P	R	H	O	M	F	M	D	B	F	G	R	J	R	V	N	D	U
F	R	U	J	M	F	A	L	B	I	L	L	Y	Y	A	N	K	E	H	A	O	O	Z
L	C	G	K	Y	C	T	W	S	W	C	F	J	A	T	W	E	N	W	H	M	B	F
X	X	O	P	P	G	I	B	R	A	I	N	T	R	U	S	T	K	W	G	I	K	Z
O	R	M	S	Y	Y	O	C	A	L	H	O	U	N	J	O	H	N	V	P	A	N	Z
Z	B	O	W	F	I	N	N	E	Y	R	B	A	Y	O	F	P	I	G	S	N	B	M

1. Close advisors to President Franklin Delano Roosevelt during the early days of his first term whose policy suggestions influenced much New Deal legislation.
2. The "father of modern revivalism," Finney devised many techniques adopted by later revival preachers. He encouraged many women to participate actively in revival.
3. Literally meaning against the laws of human governance.
4. Emphasized the power and omnipotence of God and the importance of seeking to earn saving grace and salvation.
5. A failed plan to assassinate Cuban leader Fidel Castro and liberate Cuba with a trained military force of political exiles.
6. A cultural style and artistic movement of the 1950s that rejected traditional American family life and material values and celebrated African-American culture.
7. People who moved to the South following the Civil War and helped to bring Republican control of southern state governments during Reconstruction.
8. Group of unemployed World War I veterans who marched on Washington, D.C., in June 1932 to ask for immediate payment of their war pensions.
9. This appellation was used to refer to common soldiers serving in Union armies during the Civil War.
10. As vice president, Calhoun anonymously expounded the doctrine of nullification, which held that states could prevent the enforcement of a federal law within their boundaries.
11. Passed in 1798 designed to curb criticism of the federal government.
12. Laws passed by Southern state legislatures during Reconstruction, while Congress was out of session.

A. Brain Trust
D. Calhoun, John
G. Black Codes
J. Bonus Army
B. Alien and Sedition Acts
E. Calvinism
H. Bay of Pigs
K. Billy Yank
C. Carpetbaggers
F. Beat Generation
I. Finney
L. Antinomian

Made in United States
Orlando, FL
28 July 2024